Prisons and Prayer
Or, a Labor of Love

CW01082937

Elizabeth Ryder Wheaton

Alpha Editions

This edition published in 2024

ISBN 9789362519412

Design and Setting By
Alpha Editions
www.alphaedis.com
Email - info@alphaedis.com

Contents

PREFACE.

DEAR READER: Over twenty years have passed since God called and commissioned me to go to those that were bound. Within five years from the time I entered upon the work, I had been enabled to preach the gospel in every state and territory and had held meetings in nearly every state-prison in the United States and in the prisons in Canada and Mexico. My first trip to Europe was made in 1890. I have not only held meetings in prison, but have endeavored to "preach the gospel to every creature"—to those in authority, governors, prison and railroad officials, and trainmen, as well as to those in churches, missions, prisons, hospitals, alms-houses, dives, brothels, saloons and the slums. In all places God has fulfilled His promise to be with me and has given me evidence that my labor was not in vain in Him.

When I was made to feel that the Lord required me to write of the victories He had wrought and of the work yet waiting to be done I was amazed and am still, though it is more than ten years since God first told me to write for Him. Early left an orphan, my childhood was spent in the country where I had to walk two miles across the fields and through deep snows in order to get to school, and my life-work has been crippled by my lack of education. How then can I write? Yet the command of the Lord has been upon me and the cry of the needy has rung in my ears. Words cannot describe the cruel wrongs, the awful injustice, the scenes of desolation and degradation that have come to my knowledge. Much has been done, much is being done; and yet, O how much still needs to be done, in behalf of those in prison! Wrongs that are indescribable still cry to God for vengeance in this our own land. Cruelties that are beyond the power of language to describe *still exist*, and the cry of the oppressed comes up to the ear of Him who has declared "Vengeance is mine, I will repay."

One reason I have for writing, is to show the great need of Holy Ghost workers—those whose hearts God has touched—to carry the gospel to those whose lives are darkened, blighted and blasted, and tell them of a mighty deliverance from the bondage of sin, and of freedom in Christ.

Reader, if you could see the many inside prison walls going insane, you would not wonder that, by the grace of God, I am determined to prosecute my work as I have never done before, to save these poor prisoners from despair, and to do with my might what my hands find to do.

I have kept no diary or journal and nearly all of ten years' correspondence was destroyed at one time by fire. Hence I have written largely from memory, and without any attempt to give an orderly and connected account of my work. I have endeavored to put before you, dear reader, such glimpses of the work and the field as would fairly illustrate that which has been done and that which needs to be done.

I ask for my imperfect work your kind consideration, and trust that you will overlook my many mistakes and pray God's blessing to rest upon the effort; and if I can only awaken in your hearts a deeper compassion for lost girls and fallen men and the heart-broken friends who mourn the loss of loved ones, I shall not have written in vain.

In the selection, arrangement and preparation of manuscript, I have been assisted by several friends who have been much interested in the work, whose labor and patience can only be rewarded by Him whom we serve. Among these are Brother and Sister Shaw, of Chicago, who have so kindly given the introduction to the work, having full knowledge of its contents and ability to judge of its merits. I will also mention Brother and Sister Kelley, of Tabor, Iowa, who have rendered valuable assistance.

With many prayers and tears I send this work forth, hoping it may find a place on your book-shelf and a corner in your heart, and that you and I, dear reader, may meet where there are no prison walls, iron bars, nor breaking hearts. And may there be gathered there with us at Jesus' feet many of those whom we are striving to comfort and save, while together we crown our Savior Lord of all, and through an endless eternity worship Him who gave His life a ransom for the lost—"because He loved them so."

"MOTHER WHEATON."

INTRODUCTION.

This world is, to a large extent, a great prison house. Nearly all of its inhabitants are prisoners surrounded by walls of sin and darkness. Many are bound down by the curse of rum, others by the besetting sins of lust, unholy temper, envy, revenge, malice, hatred, jealousy, prejudice, pride, covetousness, or selfishness resulting from a carnal mind. Out of the vast multitudes that are led captive by the devil at his will, a few that have violated human law have been sentenced to various prisons and reformatories. This book has much to say about the men and women behind prison walls. It records the sad story of many prisoners in a way that very few can read without being moved to tears and that will awaken sympathy in the hardest hearts. It also tells of the work of God among prisoners both in this and other countries. It records some of the brightest of Christian experiences on record, showing how many prisoners that have been slaves to worse than human law and have lived in greater darkness than in the prison dungeon, have been made free by being translated into the light that outshines the noonday sun, and how they have been enabled to live noble, Christian lives behind the bars.

We are well acquainted with the author, having known her for several years and having had the privilege of entertaining her in our home more or less during that time. This acquaintance has enabled us to know something of the burden that rests upon her soul for prisoners. She has doubtless spent more time in the work, visited more prisons and traveled farther than any other living prison worker. She has visited practically all of the prisons of the United States and Canada and most of them many times, and twice she has crossed the sea. Her mission has been a mission of loving service, with but little financial reward. But the Master who laid this work upon her heart has given her rich reward for all her toil and privation and suffering, for many have been converted through her instrumentality. Some have gone to their reward. Many others, both in and out of prison, are living honest, useful lives.

Had this work been written only for the hasty reader who has but a few hours at the most to give, much that it contains might better have been omitted; but such as these can easily select from its pages that which is most to their liking, while those who are deeply interested in the work of soul-saving, as well as the prisoner whose spare hours drag heavily and slowly, will here find food for study and encouragement that will repay for many days of careful reading.

In many respects, such a work as is here represented has never been done by any other person. For these hundreds of pages give but a few glimpses, as it were, of the work "Mother Wheaton" has done. We have assisted her in gleaning from the many hundreds of letters still in her possession (though much of her correspondence was destroyed by fire) and in arranging and preparing matter for publication. We have listened as with eyes filled with tears she has told us of the needs of the work, and with every day thus spent we have become more deeply interested in the work to which her life has been given. In a memorial service it was said of the late Bishop William Taylor: "He was not an organizer nor an administrator; not a statesman, in the ordinary use of those terms. He was rather a great religious pioneer. He blazed pathways through unknown moral wilds, and left the work of organization mainly to those who might follow after." Such, in her field of labor, has largely been the work of Mother Wheaton.

No place has been far enough away, no stockade hard enough to reach, no day warm enough or cold enough or stormy enough, no prison official or stockade captain sufficiently abusive, to discourage her when she felt that the Master bade her go forward.

With a burning love for all the sinful and all the needy, she has gone from north to south and from east to west, seeking the lost as one seeks for hidden treasure. Through nights of weariness and days of toil she has sought them and loved them and wept over them, man or woman or child, as a mother weeps over and loves her own. She has borne their burdens and shared their sorrows—ever bringing to them the cheering word, the testimony or inspiring song, the faithful warning, the earnest prayer, the plain gospel message, the hearty hand-clasp, the loving "God bless you."

We believe and pray that these pages may be greatly used of God to reach thousands of hearts and stir up many to carry forward the work so dear to her, when "Mother Wheaton" has crossed over to meet those that are waiting to welcome her on the other side.

Yours, in Jesus' love, ETTA E. SHAW.
S. B. SHAW.

Chicago, Ill., 1906.

CHAPTER I.

Biography and Call to the Work.

I was born May 10, 1844, in Wayne County, Ohio. My parents, John and Mary Van Nest Ryder, were honest, hard working people, and were earnest Christians. One year after my birth, my father died, leaving my mother with five little children—three boys and two girls. Mother married again and had two children. The little girl was buried the day before mother died. My half-brother, J. P. Thompson, still lives in Ohio. Five years after my father's death my mother followed him to the better land, and I, with the rest, was left an orphan. Well do I remember the night my mother died. She was so troubled about leaving her children alone in the world, but continued long in earnest prayer until she had the assurance that God would care for them, and then she sang the old-time hymn,

"There is a fountain filled with blood, Drawn from Immanuel's veins,"

and went shouting home to glory. What a lasting impression is made on a child's heart by the life or death of a godly father or mother!

By mother's death I was almost crazed with grief and could not be comforted. At her grave I was separated from my brothers and sister, and went to live with a family to whom mother had given me before her death. Some time after this, the family moving away, I went to live with my grandparents, under whose careful religious training I remained until married. I received little education, as my opportunities were very limited.

From my earliest recollection I was deeply convicted of sin. This conviction followed me until at the age of twelve years I gave my heart to God and received the witness that I was His child. I united with the people called Methodists and tried to walk in the light I had, until God called me into His vineyard.

MARRIAGE.

At the age of eighteen I was married to Mr. J. A. Wheaton. We lived happily together, but in two years I was called to give up not only my dear husband, but also our little baby boy. They were buried in one grave, and I was again left alone in the world. O my breaking heart! I was in despair! I did not know then God's wonderful comforting power as I now do. I was scarcely more than a nominal Christian, a fashionable proud woman, moving in high society, left to face the battle of life alone. To try to drown my sorrow I rushed deeper into society and fashion—only to be plunged into deeper despair. What I suffered during those years is beyond the power of tongue or pen to describe. My anguish of heart and mind were so great that at times reason almost tottered on its throne. And had it not been for the goodness and mercy of God in sending me timely aid through true Christian friends, I should never have been able to have triumphed over it all.

Soon after I was converted, I felt the call of God to His service. I longed to be a missionary. My heart especially went out to the colored people and the Indians, and to the poor unfortunate ones of my own sex. Their sufferings touched my heart, and it was this class with which I did some of my first prison and missionary work in after years. But in those days there was very little encouragement to a woman to do such work. O how those who are called of God now should appreciate their privileges!

Though hindered and discouraged, this call did not leave me. I lived in the church for years, always doing my part in church work. I was proud and vain, but knew no better; yet I longed to be all the Lord's.

SANCTIFICATION.

Several years after my conversion I heard of holiness or entire consecration to God, and the baptism of the Holy Spirit for service. After this, for about ten years, I was under conviction for a clean heart, seeking for a while and then growing careless, receiving little help from the formal professors around me. As I counted the cost, at times it seemed too great. I knew it meant to give up fashionable society, home, friends, reputation and all: and to take the way of the lowly Nazarene. I heard at this time of a holiness meeting about forty miles from home, which I attended. Here I heard the pure gospel preached, and light shone upon my soul. I saw that none but the pure in heart could see God in peace. After wrestling in prayer until about three o'clock in the morning, I seemed held by an invisible power, pure and holy, and was so filled with awe that I feared to speak or move. Soon I heard a wonderful sound, soft, sweet and soothing, like the rustle of angels' wings. Its holy influence pervaded my whole being; a sound not of earth, but distinctly audible to both myself and the sister who was in the same room! I listened enraptured. I feared it was death, and my breath grew shorter and shorter. I did not move nor open my eyes. Presently Jesus stood before me, and O the wonderful look of love—so far above the love of mortals, so humble, meek and pleading! In the tender voice of the Holy Spirit came these words: "Can you give up all and follow me? Lay your weary, aching head upon my breast. I will never leave you nor forsake you. Lo, I am with you alway even unto the end of the world." I was enabled by the Holy Spirit to say, "Yes, Lord Jesus." I knew it was Jesus. When I said "Yes, Lord," the power of God fell upon me, soul and body, and I was bathed in a sea of glory. When I had recovered from my rapture, Jesus had vanished as silently as He came; but the blessing and power remained. The sister whispered and asked, "Did you hear that sound?" And then she told me that this was for my benefit. This occurred November 11, 1883. That day the people looked at me and wondered, seeing the great change God had wrought in me by His power. The night following we had an all-night meeting. Again God spoke to me by His Holy Spirit, saying, "Go and honor my Son's name, and I will go with you." I prayed, "O Lord, if this is Thy voice, speak once more." The same words came again. I obeyed and God did most wonderfully reveal Himself to me. I knew I was called to His service and to work for lost souls.

STATE PRISON, COLUMBUS, OHIO.

MY CALL TO PRISON WORK.

The question is often asked me, "How did you become interested in this work, and learn to understand the needs of the prisoner?" It was through this call from God. None of my relatives or friends were ever convicted of crime. When I was a young woman I attended the state fair at Columbus, Ohio, and with a delegation visited the state-prison at that place. While waiting for a guide to show us through the prison a young man was brought in by an officer. I saw him searched, and later as the heavy iron doors closed behind him with a clang, my sympathies were aroused. While being shown through the prison I saw this young man with his hair close cut, dressed in prisoners' garb, placed by the side of hardened criminals. There my first interest was awakened to try to make the burdens lighter for the prison-bound. As we were leaving the prison I noticed some small articles which had been made by the inmates in their spare moments. Among these I saw and was especially impressed with a miniature statue of a prisoner dressed in stripes, holding in one hand a ball and chain, the other hand shading the eyes. Upon the pedestal of the statue were these words, "What shall the harvest be?" I shall never forget the impression then made upon my mind. It is still fresh in my memory.

Years after this, shortly after my commission to preach the gospel, as I was traveling one night to reach an appointment, stopping at a station in Iowa to change cars, three prisoners in handcuffs, who were being taken to the state-prison, were brought in. My heart was moved with deep compassion for them. Many were curiously inspecting them, as if they thought they had no tender feelings. Approaching these men, I gave them my hand, saying, "I am sorry for you, but God can help you in this hour of trial," and I tried to cheer them, and told them I would sometime visit them in the prison if I could. I did not then know I was so soon to enter upon my mission. But the burden of those in prison kept coming heavier upon me. I told my friends I must go and

PREACH THE GOSPEL TO PRISONERS

but they for a time thought me almost crazy. But as one of old, I felt that "Woe is me if I preach not the Gospel." So I gladly obeyed the divine call and went forward.

But I was not led into this work by any morbid sentimentalism or enthusiasm. These would have worn off when the novelty was gone. No, this work was given me of God, who Himself laid the burden of the convict world upon my heart. Day and night there came up before me the cry of despair from inside prison walls—the wail of woe from those in dungeons whose hearts were breaking and whose minds were shattered and whose souls were lost in despair, and the call came direct from the mouth of the Lord, "Go and stand in the breach! Tell them of a Savior's love—of a way of escape through the blood of Jesus Christ, who is mighty to save and strong to deliver them from the snares of the enemy that has sought to destroy them soul and body. Tell them there is deliverance for the captive. Tell them there is consolation in the gospel of Christ for those who are heart-broken and forsaken and forgotten by all but an omnipotent God. Tell them that God lives and rules and reigns in heaven and is able to save to the uttermost and to comfort in their dying hours with the hope of eternal life beyond this vale of tears."

But how could I go? The Lord Himself showed me how to go and where to go and that I was to leave results to Him and He would give the increase—that He would multiply the bread and fish for the hungry multitudes—He would feed the famished souls to whom He sent me, just as when He walked this sin-cursed earth—that He was the same yesterday, today and forever. I saw that my life must be entirely and forever surrendered to the Lord for His service, and that my future was to be left entirely in the hands of the Master whose I am and whom I serve.

Thus the call came day after day and night after night until I believe I should have gone insane had I not then and there yielded my time and talent, all I had or ever would have, to the service of Christ to go just when and where He would have me go, do as He would have me do, and trust Him for my support. I was shown that I would never come to want. I was made to understand that these poor unfortunates in prison were just as dear to God's heart as I was and that souls would be required at my hands were I to fail to comply with the commission to go and lift up the fallen and comfort the dying and relieve those distressed in body and mind. I was made to know that there was power in prayer and that God could save the very lowest criminal or the worst woman on earth and by the transforming influence of the Holy Spirit and the cleansing blood of Jesus, save, purify and sanctify and lift them up even within the pearly gates of heaven; and that instead of devils in human form, they could be made saints that could take up the glad refrain unto Him that had redeemed them and washed them in his own blood and made them kings and priests unto God.

Yes, God called me. And His name shall be exalted through all eternity for what He has done for me and through me during all these years. His has been the hand that fed, clothed and supported me. Never has God failed me in this pilgrim journey and He has supplied all my needs. My heart goes out in gratitude and thanksgiving while I write, for all He has done for me. O, the heights and depths, lengths and breadths of His boundless love for lost humanity! How wonderfully has He led me! How His guiding hand, His protecting care have been over me! Amid discouragements, disappointments and misunderstandings God has given me victory through the blood of our precious, loving Savior; and I know that He is able to do exceedingly abundantly above all we can ask or think.

When I saw the criminal at the bar of justice, I was reminded that we must all soon appear at the judgment bar of God. Then I saw that the Lord wanted me to tell of a Mighty Deliverer from the sins of intemperance, unbelief, skepticism, infidelity, covetousness, licentiousness and hypocrisy. My eyes were opened to see that thousands of poor helpless souls were drifting to their eternal doom without God and without hope, and that ofttimes in their hours of most desperate need there was no one to help, no one to point them to the blessed Savior and to really snatch them as "brands from the burning."

Then I took courage and said, "Yes, Lord, I will go and do my best to help save them from destruction and an eternity in hell." Since then I have spent more than twenty years of constant toil among the masses and have reason to declare that God has given me success beyond what I could have thought possible.

Multitudes have been saved, representing all ranks and stations of life. Many are today singing the songs of the redeemed with the glorified hosts in the other world, who were counted by many to be beyond redemption, already doomed and lost forever.

For such I have taken courage and have pleaded before the Lord His written Word, asking for their soul's salvation; and now they are forever with the Lord. O faithless one, is there anything too hard for the Lord? And has He not told us "All things are possible to him that believeth" and "Him that cometh unto Me I will in no wise cast out" and that "if we confess our sins He is faithful and just to forgive us our sins and to cleanse us from all unrighteousness"? During these years that I have stepped out on His promises I have proved that His word never fails. It is faith in the living God which brings results in the salvation of immortal souls. Never have I doubted God's power to save the vilest person, and now I want to tell, for His glory, just a little of what God has wrought as well as show something of what needs to be done. Bless the Lord, O my soul, for a faith prompted of the Spirit that will not waver—a confidence in God which takes no denial but cries "It must be done." In answer to such a faith, criminals of the deepest dye have been awakened and saved and women of the worst possible character have been converted and reformed and purified, and some have been set apart for the service of God and have done a mighty work. Others, as we have said, have gone to swell the grand, triumphant strain around the throne of God, where angels and archangels unite to make all heaven resound with the praises of our King—among those of whom it is said, "These are they which came up through great tribulation and have washed their robes and made them white in the blood of the Lamb." After I see the King in His beauty, clothed in majesty and glory and power, I want to look in the faces of those whom God has used me to help, who have come up from inside prison walls and from haunts of sin—yea, from the scaffold itself—those who have died in the triumphs of a living faith, victorious over death, hell and the grave.

Since my call to the work of the Lord He has caused many homes to be opened to me and has given me many very dear friends. Among those of earlier years were dear Brother and Sister H. L. Hastings, of Boston, who kindly gave me a home and cared for me in sickness and special time of need. And in later years are those at the Missionary Training Home at Tabor, Iowa, with whom I have made my headquarters since 1895. I would specially mention Mrs. Hattie Worcester Kelley, who had a call from God to assist me in prison work and traveled some with me until her health failed; also Mrs. Georgia Worcester and her husband, and her father, Elder Weavers, who is president of the Home; with their faithful helpers in charge and assisting in the work, who have given me a hearty welcome among them.

It was here I became more directly interested in foreign missionary work. I have at different times taken with me in my prison and slum mission work several of the missionaries now in foreign lands. Among these are Mr. and Mrs. Wm. Worcester, now in Africa, whom I accompanied on their way as far as London; Grace Yarrett, recently sailed for India, and a number of others.

FAMILY REUNION AFTER A SEPARATION OF FIFTY-TWO YEARS.

The following from a paper published in Elkhart, Ind., December, 1902, under the above heading, will explain itself:

> J. M. Ryder of Indianapolis, Ind.; Emanuel Ryder of Bryan, O.; Elizabeth Ryder Wheaton, prison evangelist, and Lida Ryder Hoffman of this city met in a family reunion Dec. 8, after a separation of fifty-two years, this being the first time in all these years that the brothers and sisters, who were left orphans in early childhood, have been together. * * * The brothers and sisters sat for a group picture as a memento of the day, and left for their different missions and homes, not likely to all meet again this side of the great River.

J. M. RYDER, MRS. E. RYDER WHEATON, EMANUEL RYDER, MRS. LIDA RYDER HOFFMAN.

JOHN RYDER, DECEASED.

I also give the reader a sketch written by my brother and published in his home paper at Bryan, O., some years since.

> Like Moses and the prophets of old; like Jesus and his disciples; like Martin Luther and John Wesley, and a host of other great lights who have been chosen at different times to be teachers and leaders of the children of earth, so in like manner and like purpose was Elizabeth Ryder Wheaton chosen.
>
> Her chief mission has been to the inmates of jails and penitentiaries, reformatories and the lowly outcasts in the houses of perdition, among people who never find room in the pews.

Unconnected with church or other organization, but aided by an angel band, a Christ love, great charity, force of character that knew not fear where duty called, she has worked for the uplifting of the fallen.

For twenty years she has toiled and struggled in her great life work, giving her teachings, her songs and her prayers, shedding tears of love and sympathy for the poor souls in the bondage of sin.

For twenty years she has traveled up and down her home land and several foreign countries.

The world her country, to do good her religion, giving her light, her life, wherever the most needed; never stopping, except from sickness or exhaustion from overwork; often meeting friends on the long and rugged road who gave her sympathy, shelter and food; at other times the floor her couch and but little to eat—but whether good or bad conditions, always thankful.

In her chosen work, in the past twenty years, no person has done more good or has had so much influence in causing people to lead better lives, to quit sinning, to get out of hell and enjoy the happiness that follows from leading conscientious, truer lives.

Her good intentions, her words of warning and sympathy, her sweet soul songs of love, her prayers in angelic power, have moved the people outside of the churches in the different avocations and walks of life as they had never been moved before, the masses perceiving by subtle agency that here was a person deserving love, respect and honor.

She had great influence with the employees of the different railway companies, the good-will of the superintendents of many of the great railway lines of the country, frequently getting passes from New York City to San Francisco and return, a distance of seven thousand miles, for herself and companion.

She has spoken in more reformatories, jails and penitentiaries, and, I believe, done more good, unconnected with any organization, than any other in the twenty years.

HER LIFE HISTORY.

It is too long a story to attempt to go into details—to tell of her trials, hardships and sickness; to tell of her individual successes, as well as her successes when she has swayed great bodies of people, moving the half of them to tears, causing them to have higher thoughts, better motives, and to bless the hour she was among them; or of how she entered the southern stockades alone, even when warned by the Warden that her life might be taken, and in ten minutes had the inmates as tractable as little children, where the officials would not enter, except in a body and thoroughly armed; how she stood her ground when menaced by drunken western desperadoes; or of the times she divided her raiment and her scant purse with the destitute, and the many times she escaped great danger by being forewarned, etc.

Bereft of both parents at the age of five years, and cared for by cold and indifferent strangers, she misses the mother's love, guidance, sympathy and protection.

When she started out on her mission she left a good home with all the substantials and many of the luxuries of life, with but little education, without money or friends, alone to travel unbeaten paths, to do a work that no one had ever tried before; untrained in the great work she was to follow, but impelled by a higher Spirit force she could not resist. "Do this work. I will be with you to the end. When great troubles come, I will be your shield and your helper. I will warn you of great danger. I will protect your life. You will gather many sheaves, and, when you are through with earth, have a high place in the heavenly abode."

Whenever needed, the angel band assists her to say the right words for the time and occasion, according to perceptions and conceptions of the people addressed.

She is gifted with a voice that is always musical, clear and distinct, and of such compass that it can be heard a mile, or down to the minor notes, but always with the pathos that touches the tender chords of the soul.

Now she is old, broken in health and strength. Soon she must lay her weary body down, a willing sacrifice for the lowest children of earth.

And now with this brief outline of the work, the life and the powerful soul magic of Elizabeth Ryder Wheaton, I close.

Respectfully,

EMANUEL RYDER,
Brother of Mrs. E. R. Wheaton.

CHAPTER II.

A Letter to My Prison Children.

You, dear ones, are my especial care and have been for over twenty long years; and your eternal good will continue in a sense to be first in my thoughts while life lasts.

My own childhood was lonely and desolate. As I have already told you, my father died when I was one year old, and mother died when I was only six. I was taken from my mother's grave by an old man who had, with his wife, asked mother for me before she died. My stepfather went to law with my grandfather, who was guardian for myself and sister, for my father's fortune, and the suit was carried from one court to another until all was gone and we little children were penniless.

Sister and I were reared by our grandparents, and were given a very limited education. We were taught to work as rigidly as if we were paupers. The experience was hard but I can now see how good it was for me in after years to know how to do all kinds of work and be able to do with my might what my hands found to do.

All my life I have known much of SORROW AND DISAPPOINTMENT. It has seemed that I have never been allowed to keep long anything that I loved. When I was a child, my pets would sicken and die, and the friends that I loved best would either move away from me or die; and my heart was being continually crushed and broken by these trials.

I loved to learn and was passionately fond of music, but I was not permitted to gratify my desires in either direction. Why all this was true, I know not, unless it was that I might learn deeper lessons of sympathy and compassion for others that are in trouble.

Perhaps, dear ones, because of these very experiences I can feel more deeply and tenderly for you and I want to tell you that amid all the sorrows of earth I have found *one Friend* that has never forgotten or forsaken me and that has promised never to leave me. *And this same Jesus loves you.* If you but give Him your hearts He will never fail you. Though all the world should forsake and despise you, Jesus loves you just the same.

It is He that has put into my heart this love for you and your souls' salvation that I cannot explain; this love that grows deeper and stronger and that can only be made plain in the judgment. He has taught me to feel for you when you are forsaken and forgotten, when even friends turn away because you are doomed to the prison cell, the stripes, and even the scaffold.

Often you are misunderstood and misjudged, and sometimes you grow bitter towards every one, and sometimes you censure your best friends. I plead with you to look on the bright side. Think of all God has done for you and how wonderful it is that He loves you with all your sins, that He loves your precious, immortal souls.

You are my children. For Jesus' sake, and yours, I am a homeless wanderer on earth. I have given up home and friends and have gone into the darkest places of earth, and have endured hardships and faced danger of every kind. I have endured untold sorrow of mind and heart. I have wept and prayed night and day, and for you I have sacrificed all.

But dear ones, notwithstanding all this, I am happy in the love of Jesus. His love is everything to my heart. His love and sympathy is enough for me, and I know that He is able to provide all that I need. He has kept me nearly sixty years, and I am sure that He will not now forsake me.

Let this encourage you, dear prisoners, to know that God loves and cares for you. When the way looks the darkest, when all hope fails, when the last friend has forsaken you, then look up to Jesus and believe His word. I know your trials are hard to bear. I think of you as you leave the jail for the penitentiary with the handcuffs on and the sheriff and the deputy guarding you so closely, and the world against you. I think of you as the prison doors close behind you. I think of you in your loneliness as the days and months and perhaps years go by, and again I say, yes, I know your trials are hard to bear. But look up through the dark clouds and remember that God lives and that He loves you. In your little lonely prison cell He is with you and is waiting to save you. Do not conceal your sins, for God's Word says, "He that covereth his sin shall not prosper; but whoso confesseth and forsaketh them shall find mercy."

Let the past be cleansed by the blood of Jesus. If you trust Him, He has promised to separate your sins as far from you as the east is from the west. Do not rest until His Spirit tells you this is done. Then, "forgetting the things that are behind," press forward to those things that are before.

Obey the rules. Show by your daily life that you intend to do right, the very best you know. If those in authority over you seem to be unkind or unjust, bear what comes as brave soldiers. Even inside of prison walls you can win glorious victories over self and sin.

There is joy in heaven over one sinner that repenteth. I seek to show you the way to the kingdom of heaven, where there is no more temptation, no sin, no sorrow, no pain; to the place where Jesus has gone to prepare a home for those who love Him, follow Him and trust Him.

My heart yearns over you in your sad exile from wife, children, mother, father, husband, brother, sister, friends. Truly the way of the transgressor is hard.

But, my prison children, I beg of you do not go from one prison to another. Flee from sin. I do not and dare not smooth over your sins. Prove yourselves worthy of the confidence of good people. Give God your hearts and be true to Him and He will not forsake you.

Some of you are doomed to the scaffold! How long, O Lord, how long must such things be in a Christian land? O, that I had the power to abolish capital punishment! But I will do all I can to help you prepare for death. Jesus loves you. He was taken from prison and executed as a criminal. He was innocent, yet He suffered death for a guilty world. He was tempted in all points like as we are, yet without sin. "And being tempted, He is able to succor them that are tempted." And though you pass through the valley of the shadow of death, if you but trust Him, He will go with you and you need fear no evil.

GIVING THE BOYS COUNSEL.

CHAPTER III.

A Plea for the Prisoner.

IN THE SHADOW OF THE WALL.
By OLLA F. BEARD.

(The writer of this poem was a personal acquaintance and friend. At the time the poem was written her father was warden of the penitentiary at Fort Madison, Iowa, and she took great interest in his work.—E. R. W.)

Oh, those wond'rous gloomy walls! What a chill their shadow calls To creep and tingle through our veins! Moving all our soul contains Of pity for the woes within— Those who move within this pall, Those who bear a load of sin, In the shadow of that wall.

Yes, you think their lot is hard; So do all you can t'retard Their sad downward course in time, And save them from a greater crime. But pause and come with me to view Various pictures in the hall Of the innocent and true, In the shadow of this wall.

There's a mother, good and true, With a face of palest hue; Eyes are dimmed and faint to-day, With their brightness washed away By the tears she's nightly shed; Yet she does not fail to call Blessings on her dear boy's head, In the shadow of the wall.

There's a father, too, bowed o'er With age, and his head is hoar. Ah! it surely broke his heart With his honored name to part. Now instead of his boy's arm, A cane-stalk keeps him from a fall, As he walks about his farm, In the shadow of the wall.

There's a wife, too, in the gloom, Yet within her heart there's room For the one whose name she bears; She will share e'en now his cares. Vows were said to God above, And, tho' friends forget to call, She will keep her vow of love, In the shadow of the wall.

There are children, bright and gay, Now at school and now at play; Why do playmates push them off, Only at their tears to scoff? Can innocence, then, guilty be? Why are they shunned, each one and all? Ah! these children e'en we see, In the shadow of the wall.

And O, for shame! to scorn some one For the deed another's done; For their road is hard at best; They should never once have guessed, From the things you do and say, That you once those facts recall— How they're living day by day In the shadow of the wall.

But a word we'd say for him Who inhabits those walls dim: Shun him not; help if you can— Let him try to be a man. When he's paid now for his sin, Let not scorn bring other falls, Just because he once has been In the shadow of the walls.

He has yet a heart, tho' scarred; He has yet a soul, tho' marred; And he has to live and try Till his time shall come to die. Sweet Charity, that suffereth long, Let us now as guard install. She will lead him from the wrong— From the shadow of the wall.

We would not pet the sin and crime; Let reproof fall in its time. But reproof should have an end, When the sinner tries to mend! Give him every chance you can— Lend a helping hand to all; Lead the woman or the man From the shadow of the wall.

A LETTER TO PRISON OFFICERS.

DEAR PRISON MANAGERS: You and I are trying to help the prisoners to a better life. We want to elevate, to lift up these men and women to a higher plane of existence. How are you to proceed? What are you to do, is the question. How are you to command the respect of those under you? Just where to draw the line, and how to enforce discipline? What advantage will you give to the men who are striving to obey rules, and do what is right? Something must be done, and done soon. The criminal classes must be reached, reformed, saved and sent out of prison better prepared to face the world and the temptations which will be thrust upon them at every turn. Great responsibility rests upon you. Many of you are doing nobly and accomplishing great good.

There is hope for every prisoner. You can reach them by kindness. Brutality will never accomplish anything in the way of prison reform. By such a course a man is often turned out of prison a demon, a fiend in human form, or an idiotic criminal.

But to make him a good man, a noble creature, as God intended he should be, he must have kindness shown him. Be *firm* and *honorable* in all your dealings with the convict, for he has his rights, and they should be respected if we are ever going to make the prison world better.

Let us ask God for help to know how to reach the manhood, the womanhood, the better nature in the creature God has seen fit in His wise providence to make just a little lower than the angels, in His own likeness and image. He intended all should be free and equal, but the people license the saloon, the gambling den and the brothel to degrade their brothers and sisters. Some say these are necessary evils! I say never, never! Let there be better conditions.

There is hope for the sinner if we only get the Holy Spirit to teach us how to reach him. I never go into the presence of convicts without earnest prayer to God to give me wisdom, and the Holy Spirit to teach and guide me what to say and sing, and how to reach their hearts. God has given me what success I have had in helping the criminal classes, in giving hope to the discouraged and in relieving the minds of some who were partially deranged. Oh, this wholesale slaughter of men's minds! It is horrible. It is heart-rending. And yet some go right on committing the greatest crime against these men, by robbing them of their reason which God intended them to enjoy as their birthright.

Which is the greater crime, the whipping post and the lash with all their attendant horrors and misery, or the iron rule that crushes out all hope in the name of discipline? I believe in law and order, and that men must be in subjection to rules and regulations. I always urge upon them implicit obedience and subjection to the rules of the prison. But these should be reasonable and humane.

What you and I need is to know our man and then we will know how to deal with him. Study human nature as well as the law, and study the law of the all-wise God in the Bible and see if you will not have a clear conscience as well as a clear brain to manage and control those under your direction.

I know prisons that are regulated entirely by kindness, and oh, the blessed, restful, quieting influence there is there, and scarcely any insane. All are satisfied with the treatment they receive and they are willing to die for their officers. I know these things, for I am behind the scenes.

After long years of service as a prison missionary, in nearly all the state prisons in all the states and territories, I find only an ever increasing desire to be a worker together with Christ in reaching the masses of prisoners who are incarcerated in our state, county and city prisons. My success has largely been due to my sincere and intense desire to lead them to a better life here and life eternal in heaven, and to the victory gained over myself to never let anything or anybody prevent my doing all I could for the prisoner, as if he were my own child or brother. Again, my determination has been to give all a fair trial and a liberal amount of confidence. Yes, we must place ourselves in their condition; let our boy or brother, our mother or sister be in prison, let us think how we would exercise every means we had in reaching or relieving them.

All prisoners are human, and yet, how few professors of religion show interest in them. They are doubted at every turn. Daggers are driven to hearts which are longing for a better life, a purer atmosphere, a new creation. Poor souls! God pity them. O the hearts that cry out for better things! the souls that are yearning for the good and true! O the thousands of prisoners who may be diamonds in the rough, jewels for whom Christ died. Souls, immortal souls are at stake. We must soon meet these things at the judgment. O to be clear of the censure, the rebuke, the reproof of God Almighty in the final day of accounts.

O brother, sister, have we had charity that suffereth long and is kind? Have we tried by example and precept to show the criminals that we were really their friends and sincerely cared for their souls? How long has the good Lord borne with us, and shall we not be in earnest to save those who are not Christians, to encourage them to a better life, to cheer up the dying convict, to show them there is a God in Israel who hears and answers prayer, one who said, "Like as a father pitieth his children, so the Lord pitieth them that fear Him"?

WORTH WHILE.

It is easy enough to be pleasantWhen life flows by like a song,But the man worth while is the one who will smileWhen everything goes dead wrong.For the test of the heart is trouble,And it always comes with the years,And the smile that is worth the praise of the earthIs the smile that shines through tears.

It is easy enough to be prudentWhen nothing tempts you to stray;When without or within no voice of sinIs luring your soul away.But it is only a negative virtueUntil it is tried by fire,And the life that is worth the honor of earthIs the one that resisteth desire.

By the cynic, the sad, the fallen,Who had no strength for the strife,The world's highway is cumbered to-day;They make up the item of life.But the virtue that conquers passion,And the sorrow that hides in a smile—It is these that are worth the homage of earth,For we find them but once in a while.

—ELLA WHEELER WILCOX.

PREJUDICE.

I find but little difference between humanity in prison walls and the humanity outside. Prisoners are our brothers and our sisters. We must soon meet them all at the judgment. They are naturally supposed to be guilty of crime of some kind. But they are not all criminals. Wicked men, willing to shield themselves, oftentimes throw suspicion on others, who are placed under arrest and convicted by circumstantial evidence or false testimony. Others, of course, are of the worst types of humanity. Some of them seem unworthy of the name of man or woman, yet even these Christ died to save, and God is able to deliver them and how shall His name be better glorified or His power be more manifest, than in their transformation?

Very many are so prejudiced against all those who are counted as criminals that they believe them to be utterly incapable of any good and are quick to believe that they see in them evidences of the deepest depravity.

A sad yet amusing illustration of this fact comes to my mind. Chaplain H., of the Reformatory for Boys at Kearney, Nebraska, is an honest-faced, true-hearted young man, full of zeal in the service of God. At one time when I stopped at Kearney he called for me at the train. As I looked at him he said, with a smile, "Did you think it was one of the boys whom the superintendent had sent for you?" I replied, "Yes; I did at first; you are so young, Mr. Chaplain;" and then he related to me the following circumstances which I give as nearly as I can in his own words:

> "At one time Prof. Mallalieu and myself had been to Lincoln on business, and were returning together. We were quietly resting, and I was sitting with closed eyes, meditating, when a lady happened along and recognized the Superintendent, and said 'Have you got a boy there, taking him to the Reform Schools?'
>
> "Considerably amused, he replied: 'Yes; this is a very bad fellow; I have had a lot of trouble with him, and have just recaptured him, and now I am watching to see that he doesn't make his escape.' The woman leaned over and, scanning my face and features, said: 'He has an awful bad look on his face; you can see he is a criminal and needs to be under strict discipline.'"

The dear young chaplain said, as he laughingly related this instance, that he learned a lesson in human nature that day. That woman, who imagined that she saw in the face of that young looking, honest, devoted Christian young man evidences of guilt and depravity, was only one among thousands who are led by prejudice when they imagine that they are exercising great discernment.

A LOOK INTO THE CELL.

Reader, could you and I walk together down the cell-house corridor in almost any of our large prisons, at almost any hour of the night and pause and listen to the sighs and smothered sobs and often to the deep groans that might be heard welling up from hearts that are broken and crushed by sorrow and remorse; could we, dear reader, cast one sidelong glance in passing the rounds of the cell-house with the guard, who, with muffled tread wends his ceaseless march throughout the night, your heart, as well as mine, would be deeply moved. On those stone floors, guarded by double locks and iron bars, as well as by the living sentinel, you might see many a mother's boy kneeling in silent prayer to his mother's God, and as he prays and communes with his own thoughts, you might hear again the groans of anguish as the poor unfortunate thinks of home and mother, wife and children, or other loved ones.

Then look with me into that poor man's cell, void of comfort, with nothing that would remind you of home; a close narrow cell, a poor hard cot, a straw pillow, if any, and kept under strict watch day and night; left many times without one ray of hope, without a gleam of sunshine or a kind word. I wonder there are not scores of insane men in our state prisons for every one that we find, and there are many, very many, who are either partially or entirely insane. I am convinced that oftentimes men are crazy when the officers suppose they are only obstinate and rebellious and mean. Often do I note insanity lurking in the eyes and often as the prisoners file past me at the close of a service and I clasp each one by the hand, as is my custom, among the many who are so glad to have a kind word and a hand-clasp at parting I notice those who are not sane by the peculiarity of the clasp of the hand. Some have a clasp like a mad-man, others a limp, lifeless hand-shake, with cold, clammy hands. Oh, what wisdom is needed to know how to deal with these poor, helpless souls! I find many of them with hearts as tender and sensibilities as acute as any I meet outside.

INSANE PRISONERS.

While I was having a service for the criminal insane at Anamosa, Iowa, state prison, a young man was very anxious to see me and tell me something. As I waited to talk with him he said to me in *such a pitiful way*, "Go and tell my dear mother I will try to help her. Won't somebody help my poor mother?" This was the burden of his heart. Poor boy! in his partial derangement his whole concern seemed to be for her. He is only one among many!

WITH INSANE PRISONERS AT ANAMOSA, IOWA.

A TOUCHING INCIDENT.

At one time I was on the train going north from Indianapolis. My brother, J. M. Ryder, was with me. I was singing a hymn, and walking to the end of the car as I sang I saw two men bound together by handcuffs. One of them I supposed to be an officer. He was a fine looking man, well dressed. It was a few days before Christmas, but I noticed some holly-berries pinned to his coat. I remarked, "You have holly-berries before Christmas day!" With tears rolling down his face he answered, "My little girl pinned this on me. She said, 'Papa, you will not be here when Christmas comes, and I will pin it on now before you go.'"

I said, "You are an officer, are you not?"

"Oh, no!" he said, "I am a prisoner," and then he told me his sad story. Money belonging to some one else, a relative, if I remember rightly, had been left in his care. Under pressure of need he used some of it, being confident that he could replace it before it was needed; but the shortage was discovered, he was arrested, found guilty and sentenced. With a broken heart he said, "I never will live to serve out my sentence. This will surely kill me. I am not a thief, but I was so sure I could replace the money before it was needed."

Reader, think you this man was any more a criminal at heart than thousands who move among men honored and respected? Who can question that there are thousands who, perhaps, do not transgress the letter of the law, yet more deliberately and wilfully wrong their fellow men than this poor man? And this case is only one of many; and where shall we draw the line? Oh, let us have fervent charity one for another.

I am not biased in my judgment. I know sentimentalism is not salvation. That can come only through true repentance and faith in God and must be evidenced by restitution and good works; but if you could see, as I have seen, the meetings in the prison guard-room between husband and wife, mother and son, or between father and his wayward boy, if you could see the tears and sobs as they meet and part, and above all at the last parting before execution, I believe you would never feel like criticising or being harsh in your judgment again. Could you have gone with me during these twenty years, could you have had the confidence of these prisoners as I have had it, you would realize that they are, in very many cases, as truly open to conviction and as easily reached as those outside of prison walls, and are they not my children? Do I not know their faults? Do they not confess to me their guilt? But back of all I see Jesus hanging on the cross of Calvary, between two thieves, dying, and in His death agony, while the blood is oozing from the print of the thorns upon His brow, while the eyes are growing glassy in death, with the cold death sweat standing out upon His face, I hear Him say to the penitent thief, "This day shalt thou be with me in Paradise." And again, as He remembers all those who have so cruelly wronged Him, he cries, "Father, forgive them, for they know not what they do." If the Son of God gave Himself for us, if with His dying breath He prayed for His persecutors, if He who knew no sin and understood all hearts could say, "They know not what they do," God help us to be willing to forgive those who have transgressed the law either of God or man.

These prisoners need a helping hand, need a friend with wisdom, tact and judgment, one in whose heart there is the one thought above all others of the need of their immortal souls, their eternal destiny.

You and I, reader, must do our part in reforming a lost world, in saving lost sinners. Then let us remember how good God has been to us by keeping us out of prison, by keeping us out of the evil surroundings and influences that might have brought us there. Let us give the poor prisoners a fair show and fair play. Many of them long for better things, for one more chance to prove themselves worthy of the confidence and sympathy of their fellow men. After twenty years of toil among those who are bound, I do bless God that He ever called me to carry to those in prison the glad message of His love and seek by love and faith and prayer to lift them up to better things.

PREPARED TO DIE.

Once while holding services in a prison, there came to me a prisoner saying, "Mother, I want to tell you I was saved since I saw you." (Only a few days previous.)

Then he told me that he was under sentence of death and that he was so troubled that he cried to God to forgive his sins and pardon his crime, and that God had forgiven him and that he was now prepared to die. He said that when the Lord forgave him he was so happy that the officers put an extra guard over him, thinking that he had suddenly lost his mind.

I exhorted him to maintain his faith in God and never doubt His saving power; to walk softly before God; to keep humble and meek and pray much. Truly there is pardon for every sinner who, in the depths of his soul, repents of his sin. God's love and power are so great that He will save to the uttermost all that come unto Him, not willing that any should perish.

Reader, perhaps you have not the opportunity to know these souls as I know them, and so to help you understand them I give in other chapters many extracts in their own words, taken here and there from the thousands of letters I have received. I believe this will help you to understand that hundreds, shut out from the companionship of their fellow beings, are as easily moved by kindness, as capable of gratitude, as easily won to repentance, as willing to give up sin, as thousands of those outside, who perhaps have never been tempted as they were tempted and have never fallen as they have fallen. In quoting from these letters few changes have been made, except in spelling, capitalization and punctuation.

Some young souls are making, for a stated time,This, their maiden effort, on the sea of crime.Oh, Christians, teach them early what to me is plain;Crime ever *has* and ever *will* result in lasting pain.Do not be *too* lenient, nor *too* soon forgive,Lest all *vice* should flourish and no *virtue* live.Society demands it, the *guilty* should atone—But take care you punish those, and those *alone*!Keep them in your prison till by *virtue* shownThey will know what *is* and what is *not* their own.But let all be careful lest by *word* or *act*Those who should *reform* them from their *good* subtract.Rule them wisely, gently—by some *humane* plan,All their faults to conquer as best becomes a Man.When your work is finished and their habits changed,Give them honest labor, by the State arranged;Show them honest labor *can* a living gain,While the *social outcast* harvests *want* and *shame*!Treat them fairly, kindly; teach them all the trueWill be friendly with them while *the right* they do.Both principle and policy declare this course is wise;Then why longer act the fool and wisdom's voice despise?Crime never *can* nor *will* decrease until in *Wisdom's School*/Men learn the noted lesson, "Right *through* Law should Rule."

—*H. P. McKnight.*

PRISONERS MARCHING.

CHAPTER IV.

A Brief Pen Picture of Prison Life.

For the instruction of children and others who have never visited one of our large penitentiaries I insert the following sketch of such a visit written by Mrs. F. M. Lambert, author of "Holy Maternity," which was written for this work:

> The prisons and buildings connected with them are enclosed by a high stone wall. Of course there is a gate, or gates, opening upon driveways leading into the yard where the shops are located. The gate is securely locked and guarded, the guard having a little room built on the wall over the gate. There is a main entrance to the building through which criminals as well as visitors enter. The officer closes and locks the large door behind you upon entering. On Sabbath mornings many things are seen and heard there. The officers come in and take up the work of the day. The warden or deputy takes a large bunch of keys and opens a side door that leads into the cell room, and the guards follow him into the corridor. Soon is heard the rattling of the keys, and the opening and closing of heavy doors, followed by the tramp, tramp, of many feet. Passing out at a side door with the officer, you may watch the men passing down to their breakfast in the dining-room, which is on the ground floor of the chapel, perhaps one hundred feet from the prison building.

> Each guard marches with his company of men, from twenty to fifty in number. They march in single file, each man with his right hand resting upon the right shoulder of the man in front of him.

> The officers wear dark blue uniforms, while the convicts are dressed in suits made of heavy woolen goods, generally striped, the stripes being black and white, a little over an inch wide, even the caps being striped, and of the same material as the suits.

> You follow the officer across the yard, and notice the large greenhouse with its beautiful plants, flowers and shrubs. But, looking back, you see the great high wall of the

prison, and remember that the little spot in the prison yard and the sky overhead is all the glimpse of the world that these poor men get, and, no doubt, is all that some of them ever will get, for some of them are shut in there for life.

PRISON CHAPEL AND DINING ROOM.

THE CHAPEL SERVICE.

You follow the officer up the steps of stone into the entrance hall, and watch the men pass out of the dining-room up the stairway into the chapel; then you follow and are led to a seat near the pulpit, facing the assemblage. Your eyes wander quickly over that strange lot of from two hundred to five hundred men, and, in some prisons, over a thousand constitute the audience. When all are seated, the guards seat themselves on high stools placed along the sides of the room, facing the rear door, while the prisoners face the pulpit at the farther end of the room.

Then the prison choir sings and the organ peals forth its beautiful strains, the prisoners joining in the singing. You cannot keep back the tears as you look into their faces and think that only for sin they might be free. Verily, "the way of the transgressor is hard." Prayer is offered, and the chaplain, and those who have permission, talk from the written word of eternal life. Invariably your eyes sweep over that strange audience, and here and there you see a man, or perhaps a young boy, in tears, and you know the tender chord in their hearts has been touched. God grant it may be so! Several testify to hope in Christ.

Services over, the prisoners are marched to their cells and locked in. They must all attend the morning service, but are not compelled to attend the Sunday school in the afternoon. Few prisons conduct Sunday schools. In the afternoon, in company with the chaplain and some of the guards, you may visit the cell rooms, and are allowed to distribute papers and tracts, and speak personally with each prisoner.

THE CELL ROOM is a long room with a stone floor and whitewashed walls, the cells running through the middle of its entire length. The cells are narrow, little rooms, perhaps four feet wide and six or seven feet long. They vary somewhat in size. They have doors of strong bars of iron, and no windows. All the air received must enter through this grated door in front. The back of each cell joins with the back of the row of cells on the other side, thus forming a double row facing in opposite directions.

Rows of cells are built in tiers, one row above another, with a narrow platform running along in front, with an iron railing.

Each man's name, and the number of his cell, is placed over his door. A wide corridor runs all around the main room, which admits the circulation of air from the large grated windows. Sabbath is rather a hard day for the men, for they had rather be at work than locked in lonely cells, with only their own thoughts and troubled consciences for company.

Many of the men who are there for long terms have their cells fixed very nicely, and one can usually tell those whose hearts cling to home or friends. But there are some who seem to care for nothing. One boy had his cell ornamented with festoons of newspapers folded and torn into patterns representing lace curtains. Another, a life convict, had his cell festooned with colored tissue paper. This man was a trusty, who had the care of the flowers and plants. In some prisons the cells are not provided with Bibles, and some prisons have no chaplains.

Some of the men are very expert at making beautiful things, such as pin cushions, picture frames, hair-braided watch guards, pen-holders, workboxes, toy chairs and many other things. One man I saw was making designs for embossed rocking-chair backs; another had his tools for repairing watches.

CORRIDOR IN CELL HOUSE.

THE WORKSHOPS.

On Monday morning we may visit the workshops and see the men at work. Here we see all kinds of work; farm implements, such as hoes, rakes, pitchforks and many other things, probably all made of iron. These tools pass through many hands before they are complete. Each process is done by a separate set of men. For instance, the hoes are made by some and sharpened by others. It takes only a few seconds to sharpen a tool. As soon as this is done it is passed on to others who polish it, and the handle is inserted and painted.

Some rooms are so warm from the many furnaces, and the red-hot irons which are being beaten into shape, that a person can scarcely stay long enough to see the work done, and is glad to move on to cooler departments. The men seem to look well, but you cannot help wondering how they ever work and endure the terrible heat. They are not allowed to talk to each other, and are continually under the guard's eye. Here and there one looks up with a nod and a smile.

Each man in the shops is given a certain amount of work to do, and if he does any more than his allotted task, he is paid for it. The amount is kept for him. But very few except long-timers and experts can gain any time to do extra work.

After going through all the shops we pass on to

THE HOSPITAL,

which is in the rear of the chapel, and in the same building. Here are sights that touch hearts. Some are dying with consumption, and some with broken hearts. One poor boy's sunken cheeks and thin, wasted hands especially touched me. Taking him by the hand, I began to talk to him. He said: "No one cares for *me*." "Yes, God cares for you and He loves you." "Why does He let me stay here and die if He loves me?" "Have you a mother?" "Yes, I have a good Christian mother, but she doesn't know I am here." "May I write and tell her you are sick? I am sure she wants to know about you?" "Oh, no; I had rather die all alone than to have mother know I am here."

So it is all through these places. For, though I have briefly described one prison, they are all in a great measure alike, yet vary in different states to some extent. All are not so clean and neat as this one spoken of, and though a prison might be lined with costly gems, it is still a prison, and without Jesus in the heart it is only a living tomb to those confined therein. Let none think that it is a pleasant place to be. One man may want to be a Christian, or at least a moral man and a man of cultured tastes, and such men find it doubly hard when they must work side by side with the most degraded criminals. One may leave the prison worse than when he went in.

In these places children hide their ruined lives and breaking hearts from their dearest earthly friends. No mother to smooth the dying one's pillow, though small it may be! No sister or brother to wipe away the bitter tears that *will* fall; no father to say good-bye. O mothers, let the memory of your boy's innocent childhood fan all your tenderness and love into a flame that would leap over the highest breastwork Satan could erect and take your boy or girl back to your heart. If you have been a true Christian and have done your duty faithfully, trust still in God. What we need is faithful teaching among the unsaved, to warn them against their danger, before they get into such awful places.

NEW FEDERAL PRISON AT FT. LEAVENWORTH, KANSAS.

CHAPTER V.

Letters of Introduction and Kind Words from Governors, Prison Officials, Etc.

From the great number of letters which I have received, of the character indicated by the title of this chapter, I give a few which may be of interest to the reader. These will suffice to show the general interest of those in positions of honor and trust and their willingness to share a part in the work I have tried to perform for humanity, by making it possible for me to prosecute and carry it on. Many letters of like topic have been lost or destroyed, and, space being limited, I hope those who have done a like part may not feel slighted. The true records are kept by the recording angel, and every one shall receive a just reward. "Inasmuch as ye have done it unto one of the least of these, my brethren, ye have done it unto me."

Such letters received in the Southern states will be found in the chapters on work in Stockades and Prison Camps. Also some relating to Street and Rescue work in the chapters on these respective topics. I should like very much to give some personal letters from railway officials, expressing their appreciation and interest in the work, but I have refrained lest by such some might be caused some annoyance. To them much gratitude and credit is due, from all who have received encouragement or spiritual benefit through my feeble efforts made in the name of Jesus.

FROM GOVERNORS.

Executive Department,

Indianapolis, Ind., Dec. 4, 1891.

Hon. J. B. Patten, Warden,

Jeffersonville, Ind.

Dear Sir:

This will be presented to you by Mrs. Elizabeth Ryder Wheaton, an evangelist whose work is especially among prisoners. I hope it will suit your pleasure and convenience to extend to her the privilege of addressing the prisoners of your institution.

Yours truly,

I. J. CHASE, Governor...

Executive Department,

Indianapolis, Ind., Aug. 3, 1893.

Capt. Jas. B. Patten,

Warden Prison South,

Jeffersonville, Ind.

Dear Sir:

This will be presented to you by Mrs. E. R. Wheaton, a prison evangelist of long experience and considerable reputation. She comes with the highest recommendations of her work from prisons heretofore visited. She desires to conduct services in your chapel, and I trust you will afford her every reasonable facility for so doing.

Very respectfully,

CLAUDE MATTHEWS.

Governor's Office.

Topeka, Aug. 5, 1893.

Hon. S. W. Chase,

Lansing, Kans.

Dear Sir:

This will introduce to you Elizabeth Ryder Wheaton, a prison evangelist, who comes to us very highly recommended.

She is desirous of holding service, or taking part, at least, in the prison.

Any favors shown her will be appreciated by

FRED J. CLOSE, Private Sec'y.

Dear Chase:

I have just come in, and take pleasure in endorsing the above letter. I bespeak for this lady a full opportunity to address the prisoners, as I have no doubt but that the service will be productive of good.

Yours,

L. D. LEWELLING, Governor.

Executive Office.
State of Idaho.

Boise City, Dec. 19, 1895.

To Whom It May Concern:

This will introduce Elizabeth Ryder Wheaton, a lady who is devoted to prison work. Any favors shown her will be gratefully appreciated.

Respectfully,

W. J. McCONNELL, Governor.

Executive Chamber.

Lincoln, Nebraska, Oct. 10, 1896.

Warden Leidigh:

My Dear L.:—

This will introduce to you Mrs. Elizabeth Ryder Wheaton, who is interested in prison reform work and in visiting prisons for the purpose of holding suitable services on the Sabbath day. Kindly extend such courtesies as you can, and make the necessary announcements so that she can conduct services in the chapel, and much oblige,

Very truly yours,

SILAS A. HOLCOMB, Governor.

Executive Chamber.

Carson City, Nevada, Dec. 13, 1902.

Mrs. Henderson:

Mrs. E. R. Wheaton, the bearer of this, desires to do some charitable work at the prison and she desires to have services there tomorrow, as Mr. Henderson is not there. She is coming down with Mr. Harris and will explain her mission to you.

Yours truly,

R. SADLER, Governor.

PRISON OFFICIALS.

Sheriff's Office.
Suffolk County.

Boston, Oct. 24, 1885.

Mr. Bradley:

Let the bearer visit the jail and see any person she desires to.

J. B. O'BRIEN, Sheriff.

North Carolina State Penitentiary.

Raleigh, N. C., Nov. 14, 1885.

Mrs. Elizabeth R. Wheaton.

My Dear Friend: Your postal just to hand, and in reply I am glad to say my daughter is much better than when you were in Raleigh, but she is still very far from being well. The general health of the prisoners is very good at this time. I shall be very glad to have you at our prison as you pass on your way south. We have all of the convicts in the prison every Sabbath, and I shall be very much pleased for you to have service for us. We can arrange for the service on any Sabbath morning or evening, as may be most desirable or convenient to you.

I regret that I did not meet you when you were here last. May the good Lord bless you very abundantly in your Christian work.

Your Friend,

W. J. HICKS, Architect and Warden.

Warden's Office,
Nebraska State Penitentiary.

Nobesville, Nebr., April 11, 1886.

R. J. McClaughry,

Warden Penitentiary,

Joliet, Ill.

Dear Sir:

This will introduce to your favorable notice Mrs. E. R. Wheaton, Prison Evangelist. Mrs. Wheaton is highly recommended by some of the most prominent persons, and any favors that you can show her will be in a good cause.

Very respectfully,

C. F. NOBES, Warden.

San Francisco, Aug. 18, 1888.

Mrs. E. R. Wheaton.

Dear Madam: I have just received yours of the 17th inst., and in reply will say that you have always been welcome to visit the jail and enjoy every privilege granted to others of your sex.

Mr. G.'s mother has not been allowed to enter his cell for some time past. The utmost freedom consistent with our rules of order is given to all those employed in the good work in which you are so earnestly engaged. Should you find it convenient to visit the institution again prior to leaving our State, we will be pleased to admit you, and should you prevail on the sheriff to allow the special favor you seek, we will gladly comply with the order.

Respectfully yours,

JOHN ROGERS, Chief Jailer.

Dakota Penitentiary North.

Bismarck, Dak., Oct. 27, 1888.

Hon. D. S. Glidden,

      Warden Penitentiary,

           Sioux Falls, Dak.

Dear Sir:

This will introduce to you Mrs. Elizabeth R. Wheaton and Miss Mary M——, Prison Evangelists.

They paid us a visit several days ago. While they came without introduction, I welcomed them and gave them opportunity to examine the prison; also called officers and prisoners together in the evening and held services. We were well repaid for our time and trouble. They left a lasting and good impression. I think that you will like their singing and prison talk. I bespeak for them a cordial greeting. Fraternally yours,

           DAN WILLIAMS, Warden.

      Warden's Office,
    Penitentiary at Anamosa.

        Anamosa, Iowa, Dec. 2, 1888.

This is to certify that Elizabeth R. Wheaton this day held religious services in the prison chapel at this prison, which were very interesting and instructive, and were highly appreciated by both convicts and officials. I am convinced that much good will result from the meeting. Mrs. Wheaton is very earnest in her remarks, and her singing is charming. I can heartily commend her to all prison officials whom she may choose to visit.

      Very truly,

        MARQUIS BARR, Warden.

    Ohio Penitentiary, Warden's Office.

    Columbus, Ohio, Sept. 10, 1889.

To Prison Officers:

This will introduce Mrs. Wheaton, who has been at our prison and worked among the boys. There is none who will command more respect and no more earnest worker than Mrs. Wheaton. She will do good Christian work wherever she goes.

Respectfully,

W. B. PENNINGTON,
Deputy Warden, Ohio Penitentiary.

Huntsville, Tex., Sept. 20, 1904.

Mother Wheaton,

Tabor Iowa.

My Dear Madam: Your favor of the 4th instant came duly to hand, and we certainly appreciate your kind remembrance.

I made the men a talk last Sunday in the Chapel and told them of your kindly words sent them by you through me, and I know they all appreciated it. May God bless you in your good work, and grant that your days may be long; that you may be able to turn many poor, wayward men and women from their evil ways.

With my very kindest regards, I beg to remain, madam,

Yours most sincerely,

T. H. BROWN, Asst. Superintendent.

Dict. T. H. B.

Sioux Falls, South Dakota, Aug. 31, 1891.

To My Brethren—Wardens:

Gentlemen: Having observed the work of Mrs. Elizabeth R. Wheaton as a prison evangelist, I most cheerfully recommend her to your kind consideration and co-operation. Her presence is a benediction, and her work is in no sense subversive of good discipline, but, on the other hand, is most healthful and helpful.

Fraternally yours,

THEO. D. KANOUSE,
Warden of South Dakota Penitentiary.

Warden's Office.
The Anamosa Penitentiary.

Anamosa, Iowa, Oct. 8, 1894.

To all who entertain an interest in our common humanity:

We deem it only just and proper to express our endorsement of the labors and influence of Mrs. Elizabeth Rider Wheaton among the inmates of prisons.

Her visits to this prison have invariably been attended with good results, and she leaves within these walls a fragrant and wholesome influence.

Most respectfully,

P. W. MADDEN, Warden.
J. M. CROCKER, Chaplain.

Southern Illinois Penitentiary.

Chester, Ill., Menard P. O., Oct. 22, 1893.

Dr. V. S. Benson, Asylum for Criminal Insane,

My Dear Doctor:

This will introduce Mrs. E. R. Wheaton, a prison evangelist who wishes to hold open air services at your place. I am deeply impressed with her earnestness and eloquence, and feel that she has done us good down here.

J. D. BAKER, Warden.

Superintendent's Office.
Virginia Penitentiary.

Richmond Va., June 8, 1893.

To Whom It May Concern:

Mrs. Elizabeth R. Wheaton, evangelist, whose mission is among prisoners, has visited and held meetings at this institution which have made a decided impression upon the convicts, and I heartily recommend her to the favor of prison officials and other good people.

B. W. LYNN, Supt.

Colorado State Penitentiary.

Canon City, Colo., April 11, 1904.

To Whom It May Concern:

I wish to say that Mother Wheaton, who has from time to time visited the Colorado State Penitentiary, has been the means, I believe, of accomplishing much good with the inmates of this institution. Her earnest efforts and kind, motherly advice have instilled in the hearts of the prisoners an apparent desire to be better men. I certainly most earnestly commend her to the kindly care of those whom she may meet.

JOHN CLEGHORN,
Warden Colorado State Penitentiary.

South Dakota Penitentiary.

Sioux Falls, S. D., March 12, 1904.

Mrs. E. R. Wheaton,

612 E St., Elkhart, Ind.

Dear Madam:

I take this opportunity of thanking you for the visit made to this institution some time ago. Your work among the prisoners has had good effect in more ways than one. A number of the inmates have told me that your encouraging and Christian talk to them has helped them and that they are trying to live Christian lives and that by the help of God they expect this to be their last term in prison.

Hoping that you may be able to visit this institution again, I am,

Yours truly,

O. S. SWENSON, Warden.

South Dakota Penitentiary.

Sioux Falls, S. D., June 5, 1905.

To Whom It May Concern:

This is to certify that Mother Wheaton, the bearer of this letter, has visited the South Dakota Penitentiary in the capacity of a missionary. I am glad of the opportunity to say that she is doing much good to those unfortunate enough to be placed in an institution of this kind and I heartily commend her work.

Very respectfully,

H. T. PARMLEY, Warden.

Nebraska State Penitentiary.

Lancaster, Neb., May 22, 1905.

Mother Wheaton's visits to this institution always seem to cheer up the inmates and make most of them look forward to better things. They feel that she has a mother's heart for all.

A. D. BEEMER, Warden.

Office of the Commissioners of the
District of Columbia.

Washington, Aug. 19, 1893.

Mr. W. H. Stoutenburgh,

Intendant Washington Asylum.

Dear Sir:

The commissioners direct me to ask that you will give the bearer, Mrs. Elizabeth Rider Wheaton, a hearing, and such favorable action as you properly may with respect to the object of her visit, which is to arrange for the holding of religious exercises at the asylum.

Very truly,

W. TINDALL, Secretary.

PERSONAL LETTERS.

Kansas State Penitentiary.

Lansing, Kan., Oct. 17, 1894.

Mrs.   E.   R.   Wheaton.

Dear Sister:

I am in receipt of your card and am glad to hear of your good success. I enclose you a money order for eight dollars and seventy-five cents, of which fifty cents comes from the deputy warden, and the balance from prisoners.

You will remember that I gave you one dollar and twenty-five cents, making a total of ten dollars.

Excuse me for being so particular, but money drawn from the prisoners goes on record, so would like your receipt to show for it.

Wife and children are well.

Fraternally,

F. A. BRIGGS, Chaplain.

Kentucky Branch Penitentiary.

Eddyville, Ky., Nov. 13, 1897.

Mrs. Elizabeth Rider Wheaton.

Dear Sister:

I suppose you remember your visit to our prison; the boys often speak of you. We would be glad to have you visit us again whenever it would be convenient. I will soon have to submit my annual report and I write you that I may get a statement from you that I may embody in the report. I herewith enclose statement; if you will sign and return to me I will be very thankful. I have forgotten the lady's name who was with you. If you could get a like statement from her for me I would be glad to embody it also. In my report I will speak of your visit in a way that will introduce you into other parts of the United States.

Hoping to hear from you soon, I am,

Yours most respectfully,

D. F. KERR, Chaplain.

Missouri State Penitentiary.
Office of Warden.

Jefferson City, Nov. 22, 1897.

Dear Mother Wheaton:

Your card duly received and we were all glad to hear from you, D. especially. Enclosed you will find a letter from her which she is very anxious for you to answer. Mrs. Pike and I both ordered books from Mr. McKnight at Columbus and are perfectly delighted with them. Mrs. Spahr has ordered one too. We are all about as usual, some three or four sick. We have fifty-two women at present. Hope you are well and prospering in the Lord's work. Will be pleased to hear from you often. With much love,

I am sincerely yours,

BELLE MAGEE,
Matron State Penitentiary.

Pittsburg, Kan., April 18, 1898.

My Dear Mother Wheaton:

Your kind letter just received. God bless you for your kind, sympathetic heart. I have often thought of and prayed for you. I still feel that God will open the way for me to re-enter the prison work. I am trusting Him. He is my all and in all.

I hear occasionally from the boys at Fort Madison. God has used you marvelously. May you be spared long to tell to those around what a dear Saviour you have found.

Your son in the gospel,

C. S. LASLETT,
Former Chaplain Fort Madison, Iowa.

Eph. 3:18-21.

Anamosa Penitentiary.

Anamosa, Iowa, Oct. 5, 1899.

Dear Mother Wheaton:

At last we have your handkerchiefs finished, and can send to you. The girls did not get those tiny slippers finished in time to have them at the turnkey's office the evening before you went away, so will enclose them now. They are very small, but we know you will appreciate the motive rather than the result.

They are all doing nicely and I feel quite encouraged with the present outlook.

I trust that you are better and that your general health may remain good for years of usefulness yet in life.

With best wishes from myself and my father, the Deputy Warden,

I am sincerely yours,

MRS. ANGIE M. WATERMAN, Matron.

Kansas State Penitentiary.

Lansing, Kan., Oct. 5, 1899.

Dear Mother Wheaton:

Your card of yesterday reached me today, but too late to attend your service at the Home, which I would have been pleased to do. Accompanied by our daughter we went to Kansas City, Mo., Monday evening for a short visit and returned home yesterday noon. I examined eight new prisoners just before starting and upon my return found sixteen more. Then two more today. Twenty-six in all this week! So I have been very busy.

Your handkerchief was found in Chapel and my sexton and night watch want you to know that you have found "two honest boys in the pen." I send it enclosed.

Are you going to remain here over another Sunday, and if so, will you be out again or do you go to the Military Prison?

The little book to Baby Esther, the poem and a tract, came this evening, for which please accept grateful thanks. May the blessed Lord greatly bless you in your noble work. May He comfort, strengthen and keep you.

Sincerely yours in Jesus,

R. A. HOFFMAN, Chaplain.

Iowa Soldiers' Home.

Marshalltown, Iowa, July 18, 1901.

Mrs. Elizabeth R. Wheaton.

Dear Sister. Your card came, after a little delay, duly to hand.

We regret very much your being sick and especially with that dreaded disease, the smallpox. There has not been a case of it at the Home and not any in town that I know of.

Our family is well. Matters at the Home in usual shape. Thirty-four of the boys have died since January 1, and so we are being mustered out, because of service no longer needed. It will be a wonderful relief to us all to be invited to that "house not made with hands, eternal in the heavens."

Your visit here was well received, much enjoyed and very profitable. Your coming again will be hailed with delight.

Very truly, your brother,

JESSE COLE, Chaplain.

Michigan State Prison.

Jackson, Mich., Sept. 9, 1903.

Dear Mother Wheaton:

The work still progresses nicely. Many of the men speak in the highest terms of the services you held here and wish to hear you again and those who pray often remember you in their prayers.

We are very thankful to you for your interest in the inmates of Jackson Prison. God bless you in your mission of love. We send the sincere wish and offer the earnest prayer that God may make your book a strong influence in the upbuilding of Christian life and character.

Rusk, Tex., April 7, 1904.

Mrs. E. R. Wheaton.

Dear Sister: Your kind postal was read to "The Boys" last Sunday and I was requested to answer it. They enjoyed your words of love and sympathy very much. The "old timers" remember you well, and the new men know you through the old ones.

John B. Reagan is Assistant Superintendent, J. H. Meeks, Warden or, as he is called here, Underkeeper; J. H. Walker, Assistant Financial Agent, and I am Chaplain.

We would like so much for you to visit us. If you make arrangements to come let me know and I will meet you at the depot.

Yours in the work,

J. L. DAWSON.

Accompanying the following tribute from Bro. Munro, chaplain of the Mission to the "Tombs" Prison in New York City, we give cuts of the old "Tombs" where I have held services a number of times, and of the "New Tombs" which has not been occupied a great while. Also a short extract taken from the annual report of the chaplain.

THE OLD TOMBS

THE NEW TOMBS

Gospel Mission to the Tombs.
Rev. J. J. Munro, Chaplain.

New York City, June 24, 1904.

Dear Sister Wheaton,

Prison Evangelist,

Chicago, Ill.

I am glad to hear that you are writing a book on prison labors. You certainly have had much experience in that line. I trust your book will have a wide circulation in which the marvels of God's free grace to men and women behind the bars will be fully seen.

I take much pleasure in commending your prison labors for the Master. For when you came to the Tombs it gave me great joy to hear you speak to the prisoners. And your earnest words for lost souls will not be soon forgotten. Success to you and may God's richest blessing be with you.

In the Master's name,

JOHN J. MUNRO.

EXTRACT.

"Crime among boys and young men has increased greatly during the last few years. I cannot account for this except on the ground of a noticeable increase in the social high pressure.

"The temptations today are greater than ever and swamp the young men by the hundreds before they reach their majority. I meet these boys in prison—white and colored—and talk to them. I find out their needs and try to help them.

"Nowhere in the wide world can the power of sin be more clearly seen than in the Tombs Prison. It is a wreckage pool where hulks and derelicts that have been abandoned in the ocean of life come to a standstill. What an army of fallen humanity! They can go no further. When they realize their condition they weep, groan and bitterly lament over their misspent lives. Can these men be transformed by the power of the Gospel? These moral and physical wrecks, with bleared eyes, sunken and emaciated cheeks and many other marks of sin. What a besotted multitude! Yet the Gospel of Jesus can reach them. 'He can save to the uttermost all that come unto God through Him.'"

Nebraska State Penitentiary.
A. D. Beemer, Warden.

Lancaster, Neb., May 22, 1905.

To Whom It May Concern:

I have lately become acquainted with Mrs. Elizabeth Wheaton, familiarly known as "Mother Wheaton," the prison evangelist, and I take pleasure in recommending her and endorsing her work among those who are detained in prisons and jails.

Her manifest Christian spirit, sympathy with the unfortunate and condemned ones, sincere humility, all entitle her to the esteem and confidence of all, and I believe her work productive of much good.

Signed,

P. C. JOHNSON,
Chaplain of Nebraska Penitentiary,
Lancaster, Neb.

Huntsville, Tex., Aug. 8, 1904.

To Whom It May Concern:

This is to certify that Sister Elizabeth R. Wheaton, prison evangelist, has visited our prison and held a profitable service. She is a consecrated woman and has her heart in the work. Would to God that we had more such women. May the Lord raise them up and help these poor unfortunate men who are confined within prison walls. All the prisoners who know her love her and call her mother. May the Lord in his mercy preserve her and give her many souls for her labor.

W. T. McDONALD,
Chaplain Penitentiary.

Charlestown, Mass., Oct. 30, 1885.

Dear Mrs. Wheaton:

I am sorry I had no opportunity to see you before you left. I trust we may see you on your way to the south. Mrs. Chapman informed me last evening of your whereabouts and the Warden wished me to convey his regards to you and say that he should like to see you here again, if convenient or consistent with your plans, on Sunday next (Nov. 1).

Accompanying this please find some notes from different prisoners. The Warden would be glad to have you here some Saturday P.M. in order that you should be in the yard, at liberty with all the men, that you might speak with them at your freedom or pleasure personally. I trust that the divine light is flooding your spirit and I pray it may do so forever.

I hope that Christ is ever a satisfying portion to you and that your comforts in Him are numberless and rich.

May God Almighty fill you with himself.

Respectfully,

J. W. F. BARNES,
Chaplain Mass. State Prison.

P. S. Also find herewith a paper drawn up by one prisoner and signed by thirty-three others.

J. W. F. B.

Charlestown, Mass., June 4, 1887.

Dear Sister Wheaton:

Things here seem to be getting on to the praise of Jehovah. I had a good, long letter from Sister B. this morning. It is most blessed to feel that Jesus abides in the ship and commands the winds and sea as well. Praise his glorious name!

What a blessing it is to be on the altar in God's service, ready to go or stay; ready to labor or to rest; to bear burdens or be free.

I trust that the fullest rays of the Sun Divine may warm your heart and make your life fruitful.

God be with you richly in all things.

With best of wishes,

J. W. F. BARNES, Chaplain.

Massachusetts State Prison.

Charlestown, Feb. 13, 1896.

Dear Mrs. Wheaton:

Your postal to the Warden concerning —— was put into my hands. This is the first moment I have had to devote to an answer. He is in the city working. He has made excellent friends. He stands well in the church he has joined; is connected with a very large Bible class of young men and frequently has to be its teacher. He is active in the church, but closely confined to his work.

We are in fair condition, comparatively, in the prison. We have tonight, 761 prisoners. I send you one of our reports with this.

A. is still keeping a Rescue Mission and doing well.

I presume you are still after the welfare of the prisoners. I have been very ill since I saw you, but am able to be at my work again. Our little prayer meeting on Saturday P. M. still goes on doing good. The Lord is with us in the enlightening and building up of souls.

Such work as you used to do has been left out of the prison life and no one is allowed now to go into the chapel on Sundays. Once each month I take in some people to help us sing in our praise service. The same people every time, however. Pray for us.

Sincerely yours,

J. W. F. BARNES, Chaplain.

Massachusetts State Prison.

Charlestown, June 14, 1899.

Dear Sister Wheaton:

Yours came on Monday last. I was glad to hear from you, and to get the enclosures in your letter. They are good—very good—for my work and my own life. I heartily reciprocate all your good wishes for me and pray that you may be preserved from all evil.

We have had some blessed conversions here and one or two of our men have gone to their reward in great peace and joy.

F. is doing well and much loved in his work for Christ. He is at same address I sent you before.

Truly yours in the work,

J. W. F. BARNES, Chaplain.

PERSONAL WORK.

CHAPTER VI.

Some of My Prison Boys.

The writer of the following letters was one of the most remarkably conscientious persons I ever knew. As a prisoner, he was very highly respected by the officers. His chaplain has ever remained his sincere friend and counselor. Years have passed since he left prison life and he still remains an earnest Christian and an honorable member of society. No one but his pastor, employer and former friends know his past history.

He was converted in prison during services I held in 1884 or 1885. He presented me some years ago with a book of poems of his own writing. Not being able to carry them with me, I have lost trace of them. Otherwise would be glad to furnish some of them to my readers.

To Mrs. Wheaton, My Dear Mother in the Lord:

I call you by this name because I am young and have lost my mother in the flesh, and I am writing this letter because, as you have given up all for Jesus' sake, you only can help me as I wish. You can pray for me as a mother prays for a son. I am twenty-four years old, have an eighteen years' sentence, have served four years of it and expect to serve the whole of it for I have no influential friends to help me.

I had not been here a year until I realized what eighteen years of prison life meant—the deprivation of all earthly pleasures, and the wasting away of youthful hopes and ambitions in vain regret. Grief, misery and despair overwhelmed me every night, and every night I wished that I were dead. A great struggle was going on in my soul. A struggle for either life or death, and, thank God, life had the victory.

I am now a Christian. A night of revelation came to me in which God, as Judge, and Jesus, as Saviour, revealed to me—the one, the power and glory; the other, the love of God.

But my way is not like the peaceful flow of a river, but like a stream of cascades. By leaps I draw nearer to God. In the meantime I do not keep the image of Jesus before me. Pray, dear mother, this special prayer for me, that my faith may be constant; that self shall no more come between it and Jesus; that surroundings shall not weaken it; that youth shall not neglect it. Jesus has stamped my soul with his blood. It can never be effaced, but my soul does not thrill as often as I wish with the joy of right-doing. Belief in Jesus permeates my whole being. Why do I sometimes stray from his love? Repentance is doubly grievous then, and repent I must. My conscience compels me. The prayers of a saintly woman will be heard. You will pray for me for Jesus' sake.

Yours in the Lord,

SIGNED.

Thanksgiving Day, 1885.

Dear Mother in the Lord:

With what mingled emotions of joy, gratitude and love, I read your faith inspiring letter. I did not expect it, for one Sunday in the chapel the Chaplain read one from you addressed to us all in general. He also told us something about your way—what a lonely, weary way. What a sorrow yours has been! Can we poor mortals ever forget our sorrow? Does it not rise to the surface at times and overwhelm us, so that nothing but the soothing presence of Jesus can comfort us? "I will not leave you comfortless; I will come to you."

A common saying here is: "I don't believe in a man coming to prison to reform." Ah! little they know what reform is, for where on earth does one need the Spirit that reforms more than in prison? Our poets tell us that prisons are the types of hell. I bless God for bringing me to this prison. Out of its depths I cried and He heard me, nor do I pray to be free from its thrall. Indeed I do pray for His will to be done in me and beseech Him to keep me here until He calls me to Himself, rather than I should go free again and forget Him. That I never can. Though I fell to the lowest depths, I could never forget Him. Dear Mother, we will meet Him—Jesus—in Heaven. Oh! I do not want the pleasures of this life! I do want to be, like you, His humble follower. How I wish I could be near you always that your faith might ever increase my own. I need, very much I need, the pure and tender influence of a holy praying "mother." My own mother had a loving heart, but neither she nor my father did I ever see praying. My precious Saviour was never revealed to me from the lips of either. What would have become of me had God deferred this discipline? Would I not have gone on in sin until too late, even had I been sent here for a short term of years? My only thought would be for them to end, that I might pursue again the delusive hopes of sin.

I fully realize my position here. I see the providence of God that makes it a blessing.

I would tell you the way Jesus came to me, or rather how I came to Him. When first I came here I did not think of what was in store for me—eighteen years of prison life. I was wild and thoughtless. The strangeness of the place helped to divert my mind, but the solitude of my cell at night forced me to look into the future. At length my fate dawned upon me. Oh! it was terrible! During the day I would try to forget the thoughts of the night by being more wild than ever, but the night brought the ordeal again and it was driving me to despair. I longed to be dead, but one night the thought came: "Suppose you were dead, what then? Would you be at rest?" I say thought, but if ever the Holy Spirit spoke to the soul of man, it spoke to mine that night. In an instant I saw the enormity of my sins and the punishment in store for me. In terror I cried: "O, what shall I do? Oh, I cannot die! I cannot meet this doom!" Need I say that my cry was not in vain? No, the spirit of Jesus taught me of Himself that night, and the Chaplain showed me some words in the gospel of John. I never read the Bible before, but there were Christ's words, and those words I now read often. The Psalms and St. John contain for me the Way of Life.

I do not forget you in my feeble prayers morning and night, and I hope you will be indeed my "Mother" for Jesus' sake. Amen.

June 16, 1890.

My Dear Friend and Spiritual Mother:

I thank you very much for your kind letter, which I received today. I pray that you may die in the harness, leaving your work to just pass over the river into Heaven.

Have you heard that our dear Chaplain's helpmeet has recently taken this journey? The Chaplain takes it just as one would expect he would, calmly, with faith unabated, rather increased, for he said to me the day after the funeral: "The peace of God in my heart passeth understanding." This evidence of real trust in God's mercy, and that He is and heaven is, has been the means of bringing me nearer to God.

I am reading a book by "H. W. S." entitled "Frank: the Record of a Happy Life." It is very inspiring. I have been convinced for some time that the higher Christian life was a reality, and had experienced its blessings. But I lived upon the experience, drawing my strength from it and not God, consequently I soon got back to where I was before. But the Holy Spirit has of late been urging me to seek it again, so that I have consecrated myself anew to the Lord, and he has blessed me wonderfully, taking away the irritable feeling that certain trials were sure to bring me. I forget self and think only of doing good to those who before I felt like shunning. It makes me very humble in my happiness. Dear Mother, I am sure you have enjoyed this blessed experience of living moment by moment to God, being kept by Him from all sin and the power of temptation.

I have read that many Christians do not believe that the blood of Christ cleanseth from all sin. This appears very strange to me. I don't see how they can be so blind. When this blessed thought was shown me I could not help believing it, it seemed so plain, and was really needful for us to have in order to live up to the commands of the gospel.

Tuesday P. M., 17th.

They are celebrating the Battle of Bunker Hill today. We have had our holiday and are now in our rooms for the rest of the day. It is a perfect summer day, mild, with a refreshing breeze floating through the windows. My bird hangs above me chirping, enjoying himself, while the murmur of voices in the guard room, with now and then the joyous shout of a baby, make me feel like shutting my eyes and imagining myself far away from these stones and bars.

I firmly believe that an educated Christian who is wholly consecrated shall be used by the Lord where an uneducated one would not. You know it was to Paul, the highly educated, that was intrusted the greatest work of the Apostles, viz: To convert the heathen world. In Athens, the center of intellectual life, he preached, quoting to them from their own poets and converting certain philosophers of whom was Dionysius, one of the city's judges. Intellectual ability is a talent which the Lord requires us to use for His kingdom. We need never fear for education, "While near the school the church spire stands," as the Quaker poet, Whittier, puts it.

Our prayer meeting is growing both in numbers and in interest. We hold an election of officers today. I resigned the leadership owing to my duties in the library being such that I could not attend regularly. I, however, accepted the place of chairman of the standing committee. The Warden has allowed the teachers of the night school to organize a society for the purpose of general culture. Last Friday the constitution and by-laws were submitted for approval. Next Friday the election of officers will be held. I have been embarrassed by several members asking me to accept the position of president. I know that I am not qualified for the position, but they think otherwise and are persistent. These, and other tokens of regard and respect for me by my fellow prisoners, I am very grateful for.

It makes me feel, too, that my Christian life here has not been without results among them. They respect my scruples—something I hardly think people outside are in the habit of doing. You will understand that I look upon all this as the Lord's doings, and feel no self-praise over it. To Him be all the praise for giving me the courage and strength to let my light shine before the men in this prison. O! it is good to be on the Lord's side, to let Him order my way. I pray that I may never have a will of my own in this respect. I feel so perfectly willing to remain here and serve Him in my feeble way, only praying that if a larger opportunity comes to me I shall not be found wanting, only believing that with the opportunity will come added strength and power from on high. The Holy Spirit has so witnessed to my spirit that God is and that He is a rewarder of them that diligently seek Him, and that Jesus is my Saviour, that the bare thought of being unfaithful brings intense pain to my soul. No, I can never be happy away from my Saviour. With His faith filling my being, His peace shall abide with me.

I pray daily for my spiritual "Mother," that the Lord shall bless her in all heavenly places in Christ Jesus, that the Holy Spirit shall rest upon you, giving you the word of truth to speak to the lost souls in all the places you go to.

With much love, I remain

   Your son and brother in the Lord,

         —— ——.

            Oct. 23, 1894.

My Dear Mother:

I have been waiting to hear from you so I could write and let you know of the good news that has come to me. I am no longer in prison. I have been let out on parole. This means that I am still a prisoner, but am given larger liberty. I shall not be allowed to leave this city nor engage in mission work, that is to give my whole time to it. I have to report to the secretary of the Board of Prison Commissioners every month. When I get a room I am going to devote the most of my spare time to study. I go to a mission at the North End, but have no regular church connections. I have been living with Mr. —— since coming out, but will leave him within a week. He has been a good friend to me. He has been so ill all this year that he has been to the prison only a few times.

I am happy in my new life. The Lord is blessing me wonderfully. There is no other life worth living here below but following in the way of the Lord.

With much love, I remain

   Your son in the Lord,

A TALENTED YOUNG MAN.

Soon after entering upon prison work, I found in one of our eastern prisons the writer of the following letters and articles. He was at that time young, gifted, scholarly and very prepossessing in appearance. His penmanship was beautiful, perhaps the most so I have ever seen, but he had fallen under evil influences and the very gift that should have been used for a better purpose proved a curse and at the time I first saw him he was under sentence for forgery. He seemed to be clearly converted in a meeting I held in the prison and proved faithful during the remainder of his term. But after he went out into the world I lost trace of him. He was only one among thousands who need sympathy and help and encouragement. I trust that, if living, he is still true to himself and to God. Some of his letters follow, also the discourse on the Agony in the Garden in the form of a letter found in the appendix is of his writing.

Oct. 29, 1885.

To Mrs. —— Wheaton.

Madame: Not being able to shake hands, and having thus been deprived of the pleasure of verbally telling you what we had to say, we now have recourse to our pen. Our hearts have heard, understood and treasured your words of last Sunday.

Dear Lady, yours is a special task. In your field of labor are gathered crowds unnumbered, inert, inanimate, forming, as it were, a great desert, a Dead Sea uninhabited by any living thing. There lies a small world to be reconquered; such are the men who are to be reclaimed. How act upon them? How move their hearts? How gain mastery over them? In these questions lies the secret of the future.

Holiness in your heart and the omnipotent hand of Jesus in yours cannot fail to bring about the reformation of a host of criminals. He will save them. Oh! climb the heights, display the brilliancy of those universal truths in whose presence every being gifted with reason and accessible to reflection feels compelled to bend the knee. Deeds, examples, striking evidence and incontestable proofs of abnegation, devotedness, charity and sacrifices are required. These are the sermons that awaken souls from their torpor; these the weapons that triumph over the world, however criminal, careless, frivolous and hardened it may be.

SIGNED.

December 1, 1885.

Mrs. Elizabeth R. Wheaton,

Somewhere in America.

Let me begin this letter by saying something very true concerning

RUM.

Let thy devotees extol thee, And thy wondrous virtues sum; But the worst of names I'll call thee, O, thou hydra monster, Rum!

Pimple-maker, visage-bloater, Health-corrupter, idler's mate; Mischief breeder, vice promoter, Credit spoiler, devil's bait.

Almshouse builder, pauper maker, Trust betrayer, sorrow's source; Pocket emptier, Sabbath breaker, Conscience stifler, guilt's resource.

Nerve enfeebler, system shatterer, Thirst increaser, vagrant thief; Cough producer, treacherous flatterer, Mud bedauber, mock relief.

Business hinderer, spleen instiller, Woe begetter, friendship's bane; Anger heater, Bridewell filler, Debt involver, toper's chain.

Memory drowner, honor wrecker, Judgment warper, blue-faced quack; Feud beginner, rags bedecker, Strife enkindler, fortune's wreck.

Summer's cooler, winter's warmer, Blood polluter, specious snare; Mob collector, man transformer, Bond undoer, gambler's fare.

Speech bewrangler, headlong bringer, Vitals burner, deadly fire; Riot mover, firebrand flinger, Discord kindler, misery's sire.

Sinews robber, worth depriver, Strength subduer, hideous foe; Reason thwarter, fraud contriver, Money waster, nations' woe.

Vile seducer, joy dispeller, Peace disturber, blackguard guest; Sloth implanter, liver sweller, Brain distracter, hateful pest.

Wit destroyer, joy impairer, Scandal dealer, foul-mouthed scourge; Senses blunter, youth ensnarer, Crime inventor, ruin's verge.

Virtue blaster, base deceiver, Spite displayer, sot's delight; Noise exciter, stomach heaver, Falsehood spreader, scorpion's bite.

Quarrel plotter, rage discharger, Giant conqueror, wasteful sway; Chin carbuncler, tongue enlarger, Malice venter, death's broadway.

Household scatterer, high-hope dasher, Death's forerunner, hell's dire brink; Ravenous murderer, windpipe slasher, Drunkard's lodging, meat and drink!

The rum vender's power is something enormous. We do not delude ourselves into thinking that the fight for national prohibition will be easily won. In many respects the liquor dealers will prove an enemy harder to vanquish than the slave dealers were. For slavery was an institution with a local habitation. It was restricted to certain well-defined limits. The whole world knew where it was and what it was doing. But rum is everywhere. Its upholders are woven into the warp and woof of society in every city and hamlet. It has a thousand heads, and it can hide them in times of danger with wonderful facility. Slavery was bold, brazen and defiant. It could be nothing else. But the liquor dealers, with equal bravado and strength, are enabled to resort to the cunning and subtlety of the serpent, when bravado is imprudent.

Then the liquor dealer's influence over his victims does not end with control of the bodies. His slaves are his allies. He owns them, many of them, body and soul for such a cause. They will fight for rum and vote for rum as persistently as the saloonist himself. These facts may as well be appreciated. When it comes to defiant antagonism, when temperance men boldly array themselves in professed opposition to the traffic in alcohol, the struggle will be severe. But it is certain there will come no time in the future when it will be less severe. The liquor power is *a rapidly growing power*. God knows it is strong enough now, but it becomes stronger with each passing day.

Are we willing that such a class of men not only hold such an enormous power, but add to it indefinitely? In the census for 1880 the capital employed in the manufacture of liquor was over one hundred and eighteen million of dollars, and the number of persons employed in the manufactories and in saloons aggregated over one hundred thousand. No nation can afford to leave such power in the hands of such men. It is suicidal.

Having *said my say* about "Old Devil" and his "Clerks" I guess I'll write a *little* letter to

My Dear Sister:

Your good, kind letter was duly received. We sincerely thank you. When meeting with savages who don't treat you respectfully please ever remember that in M—— everybody who knows you or about you loves you. Mrs. D. told me to write to Mrs. Wheaton because "*she is a lovely Christian.*"

"O taste and see that the Lord is good." Psa. 34:8.

That is the right way to find out that He is good. We may think He is good, we may have some idea that He is so— but to know it, and to know how very good the Lord is, we must taste his goodness. He alone is good. He is goodness itself; and because He is this, He wants us to taste, to enjoy Him.

Good men and women, and good children, will one day be like the angels in heaven; and they begin to be such already in this world. If it were not for them, if they were not here to be the bearers of peace and happiness, the ministers of mercy and of love, to wretchedness and woe, to the weary and the bowed down, how wretched would this world be! A thousand blessings upon you, beloved sisters, who, from the goodness of your great big heart, endeavor to do good to others. It is through such holy and devoted daughters of our thrice holy King and Father as Sister Elizabeth that we taste and see how good the Lord is.

"You see how large a letter I have written unto you with mine own hand." Galatians 6:11. "I thank my God, making mention of thee always in my prayers." Philemon, 4.

"Now the God of hope fill you with all joy and peace in believing that you may abound in hope, through the power of the Holy Ghost." Romans 15:13.

"Remember them that are in bonds, as bound with them; and them which suffer adversity, as being yourselves also in the body." Hebrews 13:3.

We salute thee, sister.

Your real brother in Jesus,

L. J.

Charlestown, Mass., Oct. 18, 1886.

Mrs. Elizabeth R. Wheaton.

Dear Sister—John 17:20, 21: "Everyone members one of another." "If one suffer all suffer." I do not know that the relation and consequent influence of member upon member can be better illustrated than by the connection of the body, mind and spirit, and the power that any one of the three has over the other two.

The mind depends upon the body to carry out its desires, and the mind is in constant subjection to the body in health and in sickness. The body is controlled by the mind as the ship is directed in her course by the man at the helm. The spirit looks out through the eyes of the body and is entranced with the scene of beauty, or is crushed with the sorrow with which it is seized, according as we look upon a thing of beauty or the eye rests upon things withered and dead.

The life and experience of every man attest the fact that thought and emotion, and the body in which the organs of thought and feeling are placed, are inter-related in such a way and to such an extent that the mind and body control, to a very great extent, the activity of each other. The wise man, looking at the inner life and the outer manifestation of it, from a little different point of view, expresses it thus: "As a man thinketh in his heart so is he. The spirit of a man will sustain his *infirmity*, but a wounded or broken spirit who can bear?" Says a writer in the Laws of Health: "If a man thinks he is an invalid he is one; if he thinks himself incompetent he is incompetent, and so through the whole list." By faith in Christ, as true and confiding as the trust of a child; by boldness at the throne of grace; by firmness in resisting temptation, and by resolution in the performance of every duty we are able to maintain the connection we have formed with Christ, the head of the body; to bear the fruit of the vine; to suffer with each other; to be honored with the members of the body, and to rejoice with those who rejoice.

As the connection of the body, mind, moral nature and spirit is such as to give one part influence over the other parts and the power to modify their health and action, so the relation which is formed with the household of faith, when we come into Christ, is to be honored by striving for the faith of the gospel and by an effort to keep the unity of the Spirit in the bond of peace.

If one in Christ now, this oneness can be maintained among the brotherhood in but one way, and that is by being one with Christ and God in purpose, plan and effort for the salvation of men and by striving together for *the faith* of the gospel. The unity of God's people cannot be maintained by erecting standards of our own—by making our own opinions bonds of fellowship and tests of soundness—by prescribing this and forbidding that. The unity is to be maintained by striving together for *the faith* of the gospel. The same thing is true with reference to the multitudes who are following Christ as they have learned him. The unity of all these distracted bodies is not to be brought about by any effort to form a union, but by an effort on the part of each one to grow up into Christ, the living Head; by all agreeing to disagree in their opinions; and by all striving together for *the faith* of the gospel. This lesson is to be taught the world by the disciples of Christ, and if we do not teach the lesson aright, we may expect, and we ought to receive the question: What do ye more than others?

When we are growing in favor with God and man; when we are increasing in the knowledge of divine things; when our lives are hid with Christ in God; when we are appropriating the spiritual food which God has furnished; when we are proving to the world that we have passed from death unto life; when we are loving each other with pure hearts fervently; when we are continuing steadfast in the apostles' doctrines and in the fellowship, in the breaking of bread and in prayers, we are giving to the world and to professed Christians everywhere a living demonstration that we are striving together for the faith of the gospel.

"How beautiful upon the mountains are the feet of him that bringeth good tidings, that publisheth peace; that bringeth good tidings of good that publisheth salvation; that saith unto Zion, Thy God reigneth!"

Beloved, I wish above all things that thou mayest prosper and be in health, even as thy soul prospereth. III John 2.

Yours in His love,

L. J.

UNDER DEATH SENTENCE.

In 1887, I found the writer of the following letters, with nine other men, under sentence of death in the prison at Ft. Smith, Arkansas. Before his cell door stood his wife and four little children. They all seemed heart-broken and I was deeply impressed with the sad, touching scene. After talking with them and praying for them, I was led to believe that the man was innocent of the crime for which he and another young man had been condemned. The evidence against them was purely circumstantial. The other man was afterward given his liberty, but this one was held, as many believed, for want of money to hire lawyers to properly plead his case. I still believe him to be an innocent man.

I left the state a short time before the day set for the execution, but prayed the Lord to let his life be spared if he was innocent. Some time after I learned that he, with several others, had been given a life sentence in the Ohio penitentiary. I went to the President and Attorney General in Washington, D. C., several times, trying, if possible, to secure his pardon. They were kind and courteous and after looking up the evidence would have granted him a pardon if the judge who had passed the sentence would request it, but he refused to do so and finally died. Then all hope seemed gone. The wife died of a broken heart. The children all died and the dear old parents, broken-hearted, lingered on, hoping against hope, until now they, too, may have passed away. But the poor man lingered in prison, with health, hope, friends, youth, all gone; forgotten by the world, waiting for death to end his misery. I say hope gone; I mean, hope for freedom here. His hope of heaven proved an anchor to his sorrowing heart. He proved himself a consistent Christian and a good, quiet, obedient prisoner. A letter from Chaplain Starr, Columbus, Ohio, tells me that he had been finally pardoned and was released January 4, 1904.

I find in my possession two papers received from Washington regarding his case of which I give the reader verbatim copies:

Department of Justice.
Washington.

Case of M——, Western District of Arkansas.
Offense—Murder.
Sentence—To be hanged.
Petition for pardon filed March 11, 1899.
Commuted to life imprisonment on June 7, 1899.

JAMES F. REED, ESQ.,
U. S. Dist. Atty., Western Dist. of Ark.,
Fort Smith, Ark.

Department of Justice.

Washington, D. C., March 8, 1895.

Mrs. Elizabeth R. Wheaton,

    902 H. Street, N. E.

Sir: The papers in the above case have been referred, in accordance with Department practice, to the United States Attorney for the Western District of Arkansas for his consideration, and he has reported adversely thereon, being of the opinion that the case is not one in which executive clemency should be exercised, trial judge concurring.

In the absence of a counter showing, the report of the United States Attorney will be considered as disposing of the case.

By direction of the Attorney General.

Very respectfully,

WILLIAM C. ENDICOTT,
Attorney in Charge of Pardons.

Fort Smith, Ark., Feb. 20, 1889.

Dear Sister in Christ:

Yours at hand. It found a small portion of us praying to God for aid. We keep up our prayer meeting. There is but three of us who attend regular. It is myself and Mr. M. and T. We want to do all we can to save our souls. I am one who is to be executed on the 19th and I am ready to go if God says for me to go. I am sure to meet you in Heaven where there is no unjust court. I want you to pray for me in good faith, for the prayers of the righteous are powerful and I want you to remember the day I am to die and pray for my soul to go to God where I can see everlasting enjoyment.

I am sad, sister. It hurts my heart to think I have been a good, affectionate man on earth and now I must die for the wicked world or man's evil. I forgive all and will die an innocent man. "God receive my soul" is my prayer.

Brother and sister B. came and prayed for us last week. Write me again and I will give you all the news.

Yours truly,

M——.

I had to stop writing to get to prayer meeting and I tell you, we had a good time. It does me good to get to say a word for Jesus, in jail or out. I am as happy as anyone could be in prison, I am sure. I am blessed with a sure love of God who can save or destroy. We don't have preaching very often in here. There are ten in here who are found guilty of murder. It is no wonder people think they can't get justice. I am sure it is on account of so many bad people being in the territory and around it.

I am thankful I am even spared to see a few more days and to let me have more time to try for justice. I am doing all I can and so are my friends and relatives. I have a good father and mother to pray for me day and night and am sure there is many a prayer gone to Jesus in my behalf.

Hoping to hear from you soon, I say good-bye. I am,

Yours very truly,

M——.

Fort Smith, Arkansas, March 13, 1889.

Dear Sister in Christ:

Yours at hand. It found me well and still pleading to God to prepare my soul to meet my fate on the 19th of April. It is an awful day for me to think of. I do hope and pray to God I won't be put to death in such a cruel manner. I don't deserve such a death, or any punishment at all for the accused crime. I don't fear death, but I don't want to disgrace so many good people as it will be a disgrace on all my relatives and me as clear of murder as a child, and I don't believe God will allow me to be put to death without a cause, but if God tells me to go on the scaffold I will obey Him.

I had a dear brother come to see me this week, and when he left me it just looked like it was the last sight of the dear brother, although he said, "I will come to see you again before ———," then he choked down and went away. He meant, "Before you are executed." It would do my dear old parents an awful sight of good to get a letter from you, stating what I said in regard to a future home. I do wish you would write them.

We keep up our prayer meeting as regular as the time comes, except we are hindered by a good cause. Seldom we miss our meeting and prayers together. I am sorry to say there is only three of us and I am all the doomed one of the three. I want you when you are visiting prisons in Texas to inquire for a man by the name of John H., as I have heard he was arrested in Texas somewhere and was in jail. This is the same name as the man we are accused of killing, and it may be the same man. I wrote to Paris, Texas, but he was not there. If you find him let me know at once. You can ask him if he ever knew Henry M. and William W. He might deny us, so you can give me a description and I can tell if it is him. Ask him of what nationality he is.

God bless you all and send me relief at the last hour. Amen. I am,

Your true and affectionate brother in Christ,

M——.

Fort Smith, Arkansas, April 11, 1889.

Mrs. Wheaton,

Dear Sister in Christ:

Your kind and welcome letter at hand. I hope you are being blessed by our Almighty God. I am sure you are worthy of great praise in well-doing. I am very sorry to inform you I am not pardoned yet, but I thank God I have been respited till June 29. It was thankful news for me and I am sure it is the power of our God who wants justice done in everything here on earth. Oh, what a great promise Jesus has promised us all if we will humble ourselves and get low down at his feet! I am one that wants to bow as low as I am required. I am a servant for Jesus as long as I remain in this sinful world.

I am so glad my dear old pa wrote you. I don't get any letters from him. I suppose he writes so pitiful to me the jailer won't let me have his letters. I do not know any other cause. I receive letters from my brothers and sisters regular. I thank you for the letter father sent you. My misfortune is an awful burden on their poor, old and feeble hearts, but I pray God to stay them and help them to bear their sorrows and I am sure He will do so.

Mr. W., my partner, is granted a free pardon and the President did not have time to investigate the evidence in my behalf, so he respited me for further investigation. Several of the senators are taking an anxious part for me and it is thought I will get a pardon. I trust in God I will be set free and can be able to help catch sinners for Jesus; I am sure I am willing.

I am sorry to inform you Brother M. was convicted of a brutal murder as the evidence shows. I hope he is not guilty, but we must not say.

It is a sad place here. Brother George B. and Brother T. have gone back in the world. There is nothing done for Brother George yet and his time is short.

The President refused to do anything for M., that one-armed colored man, so he must meet his Jesus on the 19th of this month. There is three more, but the President has not ruled on their cases yet. I don't know whether they will be hung or not. I hope not. God help them all.

I want you to please write me. It does me good to read a letter from you. Write soon.

M——.

Fort Smith, Ark., May 1, 1889.

Dear Sister in Christ:

Yours at hand. It found us all in good health, and for myself, I am looking to Jesus. We still keep up our prayer meeting. It is a great comfort for me to get to tell Jesus how I feel and to hear the other brothers pray and talk for Him. Of course I know it is hard for me and some others to bear this punishment, yet I feel the kindness of our kind Saviour in my poor, sad heart. I only ask God to save my life and I am willing to spend the rest of my days in his service. I can only trust God that all will come out right.

I will tell you of the dear ones who were hung on the 19th. It was J. M. and A. Both were colored men. M. had the Catholic priest pray for him and he said he was going to heaven. He was very moody and pale; but he seemed to know his doom. Poor fellow! God pity us all, for we have souls to save. A. joined the Methodist church and was baptized the same day he was hung. He was the bravest soldier I ever heard of. He smiled and said, "Good-bye, Henry." I had to shed tears to see and feel the nerves quivering when he and I both knew that it was death caused the quivering of his pulse. Poor boys! They are better off than I am, if they had made their peace with God.

Brother M. was convicted and is sentenced to be hung July 17. There is five to be hung on that day. One colored man and one Indian woman and one Indian man and F. C. and Brother M. Myself and George B. got a respite. His is till June 21 and mine till June 29. W. got a free pardon and I am held on the same evidence. It is because I was poor and did not send a man to plead for me at Washington, but people think I will come out all right yet. I leave it all to God, who can do me justice without money.

For the sake of each poor unfortunate soul you may chance to meet, I ask God to be near you and show and tell you a word to say to the poor condemned ones—a comforting word for their souls' sake. Joy and peace be with you. You have my prayers, as weak as they are. Jesus be with us all. Amen.

Write me soon.

M———.

Ft. Smith, Ark., May 20, 1889.

Dear Sister in Christ:

Yours at hand. It found us all well but Mr. T. He has been complaining, but he is better now. We were blessed with Mr. and Mrs. B. to sing and pray for us this morning and it was a great comfort to us all. She was refused at first, but after she came in and told us we sent her to Mr. C. and he told her to "sing and pray for those men as much as she wanted to." It is queer for a living being to not want the distressed to find relief, but it seems as though there was but little mercy shown us here, and, dear sister, I am sure there are some good hearts in here and God surely will not allow them to be put to death. Yet it has been done, and it can be done again, and I am not trusting in a single word or act of man. I am reading my Bible and asking God to open my heart to all faith and charity and reveal all the required secrets to my heart so I can become one of his children in faith and be sanctified in Him. I am so glad you wrote me. It does me good to hear from you. Write soon, as I can only stay here till June 21. Good-bye.

M———.

Columbus, Ohio, March 30, 1890.

Dear Sister in Christ:

Yours found me in some better health than I was when you last saw me. I am so glad you will continue to write me. Like all other persecuted souls, I sometimes think I have no friends. But it cannot be so in my case.

I do not faint or shudder at the idea of dying in prison. It is just as near heaven from this prison as it would be if I was at home in the tender care of dear parents and brothers and sisters. Yet I cannot say I am as happy here as there at home. I am not. I feel sure my time is short in this world. I have a hard time. I am in a sea of tears daily. Oh, it is so hard to be bound and shut out from a free world, but this is all for some purpose, unknown to me at present, but by the help of God, I my burden will bear.

"I'll praise my Maker while I've breath, And when my
voice is lost in death, Praise shall my nobler powers
employ In that Eternal World of joy."

"Lord, remember me for good, Passing through this
mortal veil; Show me the atoning blood When my
strength and spirit fall. Give my sorrowing soul to see
Jesus crucified for me."

"May God be your helper and bless you," is my prayer continually.

I do not aim to impress on your mind that I am punished by the prison laws, for I am not. I haven't had a bit of trouble with any one since I came into this institution. I have to work hard and I do more than I ought to, but I am afraid I won't please my superiors in power over me. I put in many a sleepless night from weariness of my daily labors. But I could not stand any punishment, so I had better over-do myself than to be over-done. My sorrow is now as much as I can bear. I am in need of all good praying people's prayers, so I ask you and your friends to pray for me.

I am honored with all the attire of a first-grade-prison man. I have the red stripes you told me to get and my mustache. The boys you know are well.

M——.

Columbus, Ohio.

Dear Sister in Christ:

Blessed be our God! He has saved us thus far and has given us an ark to carry us over Jordan, safe to Eternity. We, as fallen men, sometimes err in thinking we are not under God's protection, but I say we are. Jesus came, not to bring saints, but sinners to repentance. It is not the righteous that are called, but sinners. There is only one way and that is by Jesus Christ, and that is to humble ourselves to all that is right. Life has yet many opportunities for serving God and his Church. Hitherto the Lord has brought me and still in his loving hands I will cheerfully, hopefully rest and trust till the shadows of earth shall be changed for the sunlight of eternity, when my heavenly home is reached, to be blessed forever with the Lord.

Sister, Brother M. says "God bless you," and you have his prayers. Bro. F. C. says he hopes to see you soon. Bro. B. is all right as far as I know. They all say write to them. Bro. T. has forgotten his pledge. May God soften his heart again to say "Thy will be done."

I close by asking you to write soon. God bless you and all co-workers. Good-bye,

M. ——.

SENTENCED FOR LIFE.

Early in my prison work I found in one of our penitentiaries a man sentenced for life who claimed to have acted only with the motive of self-defense. That man is still confined in prison, though he is one of the best of prisoners and has given evidence of being a good, Christian man, worthy of pardon. I wrote to the governor once in his behalf, but too late to avail anything, as his term of office was just expiring. While that poor man has been held there, pardons have been granted to Chinamen, Spaniards and other foreigners who were wicked and guilty, yet this Christian man has been kept in confinement all these long years, until there is only one other besides himself who is now left of the prisoners who were there on my first visit. The other has gone insane and I have feared that the one of whom I write would lose his mind also. His article on the need of prison reform entitled "Meditations of a Prisoner," found in another chapter, will, I believe, commend itself to every fair-minded reader.

I give a few selections from his letters. I feel sure he should be a free man. O the indifference of those who have the power to free such worthy cases and will not! May God give power to the faint and grace to the afflicted and let us pray God to show the governors of our land to whom to give pardon and freedom and from whom to withhold.

State Prison, December 21, 1902.

Dear Mrs. Wheaton:

Your kind and welcome letter received and I was very glad to hear from you and I do hope you will soon be strong again. The world needs many Mother Wheatons, so it can ill afford to lose you, but if the Lord calls you home we must all submit, for He does all things for the best.

I was much surprised to see by your letter that you had written to Governor S. in my behalf. From my heart I thank you, dear Sister, and may God bless you for your kindly interest in me. But Governor S. will leave the office tomorrow and the newly-elected Governor will take his seat. It is too bad that you have gone to all that trouble for nothing. But the fact that you did so will always be most gratefully remembered by myself and Charles G. He also wants me to send his kind regards and thanks for your good will to him.

When you have your book ready please send me one. Could you say about when it will be ready? I suppose you would like to know how we spent Christmas. It was spent in the dining-room, but we had a nice dinner and were kindly remembered by the Warden and Chaplain and everything was very nice and pleasant.

I will close with kind regards and best wishes, and may God bless you.

Sincerely yours in the Master's service,

E.

State Prison, Aug. 19, 1903.

Dear Mrs. Wheaton:

I have just received your welcome letter and was very glad to hear from you, also to know that you were well. It is a wonder you never get tired of traveling so much. When I think of how you are constantly battling for the right in the interest of lost sinners as we are it brings forth the thought in my mind—does it pay? If one only looks at the general result he can but say—it does not pay that one pure life should be worn out in the cause when so few are made to see the error of their ways and turn to the path of truth and right along the way of righteousness.

But again, if one life is truly brought into the light and a soul saved, then we must admit it pays. And I know that your pilgrimage of mercy brings forth good, for all who know you speak kindly of you. Well, if a little spark of love is kindled in the heart of the most hardened by the kindly deeds of another, who can tell how great that spark may become? So let us not weary of well doing but press on, hoping for the best and accepting the worst in true Christian resignation.

I gave your message of love to all the men here. All were glad to hear from you. O, my dear friend, I am so often troubled in heart by the attitude of some people. Certainly I have been very sinful. I have fully realized all that was wrong in my life. It has been my endeavor to cast it all out of my life and to build on a foundation of righteousness and faith in its place. I have been blessed in my effort by the help of many who I feel have a personal interest in me. At the same time no man has been more inhumanly treated by those who profess to be Christians than I have been and am.

Yes, my friend, we are commanded to pray for such people. This I have done for nine years, but the persecution still goes on. May God forgive them.

Now, a few words about the prison. Everything is changed here. We have all new officers and guards, also another Governor. The Chinese cook you spoke to was pardoned last January. I was denied.

I am, with love, your sincere friend,

E.

Dear Sister:

Your welcome letter duly received and I was glad to hear from you and to know that you were well.

Well, sister, I am again denied a pardon. Guess I must die here. Well, "The Lord is my shepherd, I shall not want." Still the lack of a Christian spirit is felt as rendered to me. You remember the Chinaman who was cook for the Warden? Well, he was pardoned, likewise several Indians and many others who were without faith, but Christians— oh, well, prison is a good place for them it seems.

With kind love and best wishes to you, I remain,

Yours in His service,

E.

State Prison, Feb. 29, 1904.

Mrs. E. R. Wheaton:

Yours received and I was glad to hear from you. I am getting along very nicely, but the heart is often sad. Oh, I was so much disappointed, and while I was almost heart broken over it I have also felt sorry for the friends that stood by me. Why, just think of it—there are five members on the Board of Pardon, and they all voted against me! So you see it is not the Governor alone who is against me, but every one of them.

My dear friend, I don't think you would be able to do anything for me. The Lord is strong certainly, but the ones who have my freedom in their power leave the commands of the Lord out of the question. Read the 18th chapter of Matthew, from the 21st verse to the last of the chapter, and you will see what I mean.

Now, dear sister, may God help, bless and comfort you in this seemingly cold world of ours, is the prayer of your friend,

E.

FAITHFUL INSIDE AND OUTSIDE OF PRISON WALLS.

Another case with which I was very much impressed in the early days of my missionary work was that of a young man of rare ability, gifted and sensible, who was spending a term in one of our United States prisons. He was converted and began working for God among the other prisoners. After faithfully serving his time, he left the prison with good prospects. He was taken into an office and did exceedingly good service for the company, also for God and souls,—his past being known only to his pastor, employers and prison officials. After several years he married a most estimable lady who was doing missionary work. They prospered well. He was promoted from one position to another. For nineteen years he has lived a devoted Christian. All who know him honor and respect him. His wife has recently passed over to the kingdom of heaven. He is still living a true and noble life and he is only one of many who have served time inside of prison walls, who are living for God outside and for Heaven at last. I quote a few extracts from letters received from him during the time of his incarceration.

In Prison, January 12, 1885.

My Dear Friend:

Your kind note was received and I was very much pleased to hear from you, but was pained that you should think for a moment that I was forgetting you. Since you left us we have had several very earnest and interesting meetings—the fruit of your presence and labor among us. Praise God, He can find his way inside prison walls as well as outside. He is no respector of person. Many men, not before confessing Christ or even anxious sinners, have stood up manfully for prayers and may God give them grace to accept and believe. It is very simple, my dear sister, is it not? How I wish that all could see it! It only means total surrender to Him, to give up the old longings and desires and trust Him from day to day. Then comes the "perfect peace" which is vouchsafed to them whose mind is stayed on God. Of course, you will see us again. Our dear Chaplain and Warden are doing everything possible for the spiritual welfare of all the men. The Warden dignified our first meeting by giving us his personal religious experience at the commencement of the service, and he is willing and anxious to encourage in every way possible the religious sentiment now prevailing. As for our Chaplain, I do not believe there is his equal. I who am so closely associated with him can truly testify to his untiring zeal in behalf of all of us. If ever there was a living man, free from any selfish or worldly motives, I believe it is he. The moral tone has been increasing ever since he came among us. I shall not feel at all slighted if you save your strength and time by not writing to me. Just send me some little message by F. or any others (for I see them all daily), and I shall be just as well pleased. It is not because I do not like to have you write me, but I had rather spare you, or help you.

If you will let me know the address of that dear lady at Raleigh whom you stayed with, I will gladly make her something and would like very much to make something for any other of the dear friends who are good to you on your pilgrimage of love and mercy. Shall not forget to make something for your brother. May God bless and keep you and make his face to shine upon you for many years yet to come, and may we finally meet in heaven where there shall be no more parting and sorrow.

Your loving brother in Christ,

C. W.

August 8, 1886.

My Dear Friend:

Do you think we have forgotten you? Why, no indeed! We think and speak of you almost daily, but you are moving so that we hardly know where to locate you. A day or two ago L., who is my friend, got a postal card from you, and as he cannot write, by permission just now and I have the privilege to do so, I drop these few lines for him as well as for myself.

How glad we are to know the Lord has prospered your work. How literally is the promise of Christ fulfilled, "Lo, I am with you alway, even unto the end of the world." It seems so wonderful that all people are opening their doors to Christian workers, the doors which a few years ago were closed and to be opened only through the power of God, who, as Daniel said, would "set up a kingdom which shall never be destroyed," but it shall break in pieces and consume all these kingdoms and shall stand forever. Our Sabbath School is not in session this month but will renew its course the first of September. We like our new Warden very well. Our dear Chaplain is still with us and is quite well and engaged as ever in his life work. His place would be very hard to fill here. I have been reading this morning the 34th Psalm—"all my fears," "all his troubles," "all his afflictions"—a deliverance from all. "There is no want to them that fear Him." This Psalm is full of comfort. Praise His name! We can find help and comfort in any part of His holy Word. We all pray for God's blessing upon you and your work and for the conversion and salvation of all whom you minister unto. It does not seem too great a thing to ask of the Lord. Both L. and F. send their love to you and L. will write you soon. Also Mr. A. and Mr. R. and many more send love and best wishes. I shall always consider you my friend, and if in the Providence of God we shall never meet in this world I hope to meet you with recognition in our eternal and glorious home above.

Truly your friend,

C.

January 29, 1890.

My Dear Friend and Mother:

Your letter received yesterday made me very happy. It was so good of you to write so soon and send such a nice long letter, too. I trust I am getting to value a letter from you as I ought, as I realize more and more how your time is so zealously occupied and needed. I have ever valued your letters for the help they gave me, but I value them now for their scarcity. In the future, when perhaps you may be no more, I shall esteem them among my most valued treasures. Yet I may be called first! We know not the hour, whether in youth, or old age, or in our prime when the angel of death shall come to summon us to eternity. "Watch therefore, be ye also ready," are words that I try to keep ever in mind, or rather to keep my mind so stayed on Christ that moment by moment He shall keep me saved so that I shall never need to whip myself into keeping watch for my Lord. I am glad you believe in and have the blood cleansing freedom from all sin. It is an experience that meets with much opposition from worldly Christians and from some whose good works follow them. These latter really enjoy the experience, but are prejudiced at the name given to it by others. I know that it meets with much opposition. The "Christian Witness" comes to the prison every week. It is an exponent of holiness and very interesting, as well as spiritual. I have a magazine which contains a story of an ex-convict which would do some good to those who think there is no hope or reform for such an individual. I shall mail you the magazine, and if you can read it do so and give it to others to read.

After a silence of several years my father has written me again. You know he is living in C. and was formerly an instructor in the State Prison at S. He is now old and broken in health, making him incapable for steady work, so he is residing at a soldiers' home. He expresses great anxiety in regard to my future, thinking me friendless, etc. I have written him a long letter reviewing the principal incidents of my prison life. How good God has been to me and how my mind is at rest as regards the future because I have left it in His hands. To find favor with my God is all I desire. Having that, whatever my condition I shall be like St. Paul, content. That is my view of a successful future or life. Wealth, power, ability, all things that men aspire to in this life, do not make or lead to success in my mind. Nothing but the favor of God brings it to man, and that favor comes through the "washing of regeneration and the renewing of the Holy Ghost." Oh, I am so glad that I know this—even me! How can man doubt the wondrous love of God when He is so patient to all who will but look and see. Well, said someone, that they do not want to look and see lest they should be healed and be saved. My poor old father is a church-member, but I fear he knows nothing about Holy Ghost religion, Jesus Christ's religion, pure and undefiled. I want to do just right all of the time. I know my heart is right because I hate sin and love righteousness. If the Lord has no other work for me when I leave here, I would like to labor under your guidance. When are you coming this way again? I would love to greet you once more before I die.

C.

From every nodding flower, from every whispering breeze From mountain's lofty height, from towering trees, From softly twinkling star, from lightning's giddy flash, From the softest twitter of a bird and thunder's awful crash, From hills the ants may call their own, From crested elders 'round their throne, From babbling brook, from storm-lashed wave, From nature smiling, nature grave, From earth and air, from sky and sea, There comes the self same voice to me, Like softest note of cooing dove, And sweetly whispers, "GOD IS LOVE."

—A Prisoner.

ADMINISTRATION BUILDING, MITCHELVILLE, IOWA.

CAMPUS AND PLAYGROUND, GIRLS' INDUSTRIAL SCHOOL,
MITCHELVILLE, IOWA.

CHAPTER VII.

Letters from Co-workers, and Some of My Prison Girls.

In speaking of prisoners or of those within prison walls many think only of men being found there. This is due doubtless to the few women compared to the number of men found in these places. In my efforts to do good to all, I have been especially mindful of those of my own sex, and have ever endeavored to encourage and lift up my sisters who have fallen victims to sin and misfortune. I give in this chapter a few letters from sisters who are directly interested in the care and work for the prison bound; also extracts from letters from a number of my prison girls. The co-operation in my work and the kindness and hospitality ever shown me by the sisters, matrons, wives of officers, etc., are especially appreciated, and all these dear ones are often remembered at the throne of divine grace. These too shall all share in the fruit of the toil and labor in the final reckoning. Neither will my girls whom I have tried to help, that have shown their appreciation and have tried to serve the Lord, be forgotten.

Women who are the victims of sin and are condemned by society and the law, have as much right to be restored and encouraged when they amend their ways, as have men. The following letters are, I believe, sufficiently explanatory in themselves, and may be read with interest.

Huntsville, Texas, Aug. 19, 1904.

Dear Mother Wheaton:

Mr. Baker, Superintendent of Prison, said he would like for you to visit our prison once a year; they all were pleased with you. Dear Mother, please pray for little George, that he may be truly converted to God and take an interest in his studies. It seems that he has no desire for them. My greatest aspiration is to live to see him saved and have an education. How my heart goes out for him! I feel that I won't be with him long. I sometimes think that I had rather see him put away before I go, then I would know where he was. When you go to the Faith Home pray for us that if it be God's will that I may be relieved of afflictions and that my husband may be able to do a great and lasting work for the poor unfortunate men. Dear mother, I write you because I have confidence in you. May God bless you.

MRS. MARY MCDONALD.

(Wife of Chaplain at Huntsville, Tex., a great sufferer.—E. R. W.)

CHAPLAIN'S RESIDENCE, HUNTSVILLE, TEXAS.

My Dear Mrs. Wheaton:

Your letter to one of our boys was handed to me by him today. I enjoyed reading it, and want to write you at once. I think V. was very seriously impressed by your service here, although I have not yet had an opportunity to talk with him as I have wanted to. He was sick yesterday and not in school. Tomorrow I hope to see him again. I am so glad that you had the opportunity of seeing his parents. I know they will be greatly benefited spiritually by your visit. I am sure our blessed Lord leads you, as you carry peace and comfort wherever you go. Dear Mother, you comforted me. I was impressed, as I have never been before, by the *power of prayer*, and I know your prayers are heard and answered. This text came to me *over and over* while you were here, "The effectual, fervent prayer of a righteous man availeth much." I felt instinctively that your prayers could help me. Oh, my friends! I *appeal* to you to pray for me. I may be here only until April, but if God has work here which He wishes *me* to do, I know He will order it that I shall stay longer. But I do want to be *filled* with His Holy Spirit, that while I stay I may do *everything* that is possible to warn and encourage these poor fallen brothers to seek a Savior's love and forgiveness. I *want* a power which I feel *might* be mine, but it has not yet come. I want to reach the boys and tell them of Christ's love, but I have not the power of speech. I cannot convince them that *my* Savior is their Savior too. So often they say to me, "Well, I guess that kind of a life is the best kind to lead after all, but I never will make a start in a place of this kind."

The next day after you left one boy said to me that he had never before heard a talk that had impressed him as he was impressed Tuesday. I believe he is seriously awakened. I think *three* others are, also, beside the one of whom I told you the day you left. I think V. is one.

There is a boy here who says he heard you in Kansas City eight or nine years ago. He was not at service, but saw and recognized you. He thought you would know him if you saw him.

Yours in Christian love,

FANNIE A. HOYT,
(Teacher and wife of Officer.)

Buena Vista, Colo., Oct. 24, 1896.

Atlanta, Ga., Nov. 12, 1893.

Dear Mrs. Gore:

This will introduce to you Mrs. Wheaton and Mrs. ——, Prison Evangelists. You will be so glad to meet them and they to meet you and talk about our dear boys "shut in."

God bless you.

MRS. CHARLTON EDHOLM.

Mrs. A. B. Gore, Oakland, Cal.

Anamosa, Ia., Nov. 20, 1893.

Dear Mrs. Wheaton:

Anna H. has written you about the death of Emma S. She had a hard cold, not so bad as some of the girls, however, when she left here. We tried to persuade her to remain here over Sunday, where it was warm, as it was very cold and stormy. She, however, insisted upon going. We of course could not compel her to stay, although we felt it was for the best. When she reached Algona she was too sick to go into the country five miles where she was going to stay. Tuesday morning she was taken out, and Thursday afternoon died with La Grippe or Pneumonia. Several of the women here have had La Grippe. All seem to be improving, as I insist upon their taking excellent care of themselves.

Now, Mrs. Wheaton, I hope you will write to Anna, also a letter to all the girls that I can read to them. They will be glad to think you have not forgotten them. Trusting that you are in good health and that you see good results from your labors, I remain your friend,

JENNIE A. POWERS.

Jefferson City, Mo., Jan. 25, 1900.

Dear Sister:

Your card was received in due time. All glad to hear from you. The quarantine is still on at the prison. No news there. No visitors allowed. No baskets sent in, only money. Mr. Cook has not missed a day at work since last winter. He was off twelve days to visit his dear mother. She will soon pass to the other side. Your card was filled with sadness. Be cheerful and rejoice, for soon you will go to glory to praise Him forevermore. I will write some to Sister Kelley. Write me a long letter. Chaplain P. has been on the sick list. Everything going on nicely. Never had a better warden than now in the last eighteen years that I have known this prison. Hoping to hear of your good health, I am ever,

CLARA COOK.

WOMEN'S PRISON, ALLEGHENY CITY, PA.

Western Penitentiary, Allegheny, Pa., June 7, 1904.

Mrs. Wheaton:

I am glad to learn that you are about to embody your experiences as a missionary to the inmates of the prisons and penitentiaries of the various states in which you have labored in the name of the Master. It has been no easy work. It has demanded much faith, hope and charity on your part. You have gone with untiring zeal to those who are despised and forsaken on account of their criminal acts.

In the spirit of our blessed Lord and in obedience to His command you have gone year after year to the habitations of disgrace and sorrow and carried the cheering and helpful promises and the forgiving mercy of our dear Savior.

You will have a rich reward from our Heavenly Father. I am sure your words of gospel truth and your songs of praise have often touched the hearts of the female prisoners under my care. The most rebellious and hardened have felt and testified to the gracious power of the gospel of love as you have uttered it here. My hope and my prayer is that the Almighty Shepherd may guide, keep and sustain you in this noble work of your life.

Allegheny, Pa.

Allegheny City, Pa., Dec. 31, 1893.

Dear Mrs. Wheaton:

I will try and answer your kind and welcome letter which came to hand a few days ago. We were all very glad to hear from you. Our dear sister, Mrs. Jones, is dead. The dear old lady who was up to the workhouse with you when you were here. She was a dear friend to all the girls here, but she has gone home. She can come to us no more, but we can go to her. The last words she said when she was here was good-bye, and that she would meet us all in heaven. We have very nice meetings now and would like to have you with us. We pray for you every day and we want you to pray for us that we may see the right way and that we may go out of here with light hearts and go about doing good.

We had a nice Christmas. Our Warden treated us with turkey, and we were all so glad that he was so kind to us.

Well, we will begin a new year tomorrow, and I hope we will lead a different life, a better life, for if we believe in Jesus He will save us; yes, He will keep us through the dark valley. He will go with us to the end, as He has promised, if we will put our trust in Him. I have gained a great victory since you were here. I have forgiven an enemy that I thought I never could forgive.

Well, I will close by sending you my love, and as I have only one sheet of paper my friend will send this on to you. I remain,

Your sincere friend,

Lucy F.

Allegheny City, Pa., Feb. 16, 1896.

My Dear Mrs. Wheaton:

I am so glad to hear from you once more. I had been thinking of you so much of late and I asked God to let me hear from you or send you to us, and so you see He answered my prayer. I cannot express how glad we all were to receive your kind and loving letter. It was read to all and I do wish you could have peeked in to see how quiet all were to listen to it, and our two matrons, too, for they do love you.

I was very sorry to hear of your being so sick, but God has raised you up for He has work for you to do yet. I pray for you every night and morning that He may strengthen you and keep you, for you are to us like the rain is and the sunshine to the flowers, for we know that you do love us poor unfortunate ones.

Will you please send us the hymns called "Tell of the Unclouded Day" and the one called "When the Pearly Gates Unfold"? Dear Mother, pray for us all, but pray for me especially, for I am in great sorrow and trials. Pray that God may raise me up friends and that He may keep me.

Good-bye, hoping to hear from you soon, I remain, yours in Christ,

LAURA M.

Allegheny City, Pa., Feb. 16, 1896.

My Dear Mother:

I wish I could tell you how much joy and happiness your letter gave me. It came just at the time when I needed it most. I am sick and feeble, suffering with spine and lung trouble, have not been able to work for the last three weeks. Can go to my meals and wait upon myself, and I have my Jesus with me. Oh, how He comforts and helps make the rough places smooth, and in the lonely hours of the night when the pain is almost beyond endurance, I think of my Savior and what He suffered without sin, and of what a weak coward I am to complain.

Mother, we are some of us so impatient when we have pain, and I am afraid I am one of those. Please pray for me that I may bear mine with Christian fortitude.

I hope it may please God to let me live to get out of this place and have a home for myself and baby, and if my dear Mother Wheaton would come and see me and rest herself for a few weeks, would it not be nice? Mother, I am a widow with one child and some means, but not much. Still I intend to use some of my money, when I have control of it, to do good to others. I have suffered, God has opened my eyes and showed me my sins and selfishness of former years, and I thank Him for sparing me to see it in this light.

Many of the girls that were here when you last visited us have gone out and a good many are going out this year. Pray for them. I pray for you every night. God bless and keep you is the prayer of your friend,

L. R. T. No. 9722.

Allegheny City, Pa., Feb. 16, 1896.

My Dear Mother Wheaton:

Your very welcome and unexpected letter received. It is impossible to tell you with what joy and heartfelt gladness we all gathered together to hear it read. You do not know how often your children speak together of you, of where you are and what you are doing and what keeps you so long away from your Western flock. It was so long since last we heard from you that we are beginning to think our Heavenly Father had need of you and had taken you home, but all praise to His name. He has spared you to send us another loving, encouraging message, which we promptly answer in love and sympathy, each one giving a word, although only three different handwritings will be seen. Remember when reading the words that twenty-five of your lone children are here represented in your letter.

You speak of wishing for your prison children when you were sick. O, how gladly many of us would minister to your wants, to be under the influence of your kind and loving advice, following in your footsteps of love and life as it is in Christ Jesus our Lord and Master. But though we are separated by so many miles, thanks be to the Almighty we can feel the influence of your continued prayers, and many of us are greatly encouraged to keep on striving, knowing that the crowning day will come by and by.

Each one says: "Ask Mother Wheaton when she is coming." Do not be too long in coming, for some of your dear ones are leaving every month during the spring, and we are anxious to receive your blessing before entering the cold, heartless world of sin and sorrow. Yet some of us will take Jesus with us, and in His name begin life again. Pray for us all that our hearts may be fully and entirely given over to God, with our hands in His hand, be led to the mercy-seat. Yes, dear Mother, we shall, with God's help, "strive to enter in at the straight gate."

These are the names of those who send you special love and requests for prayer: Emma M., Emma W., Pearl S. (who is very sick), Laura M., Anna M., Ella A.

With love and best wishes from our matrons, we close, hoping soon to see you.

Good-bye, God bless and keep you always and send you to us again. All join in best wishes to you.

Allegheny City, Pa., Feb. 14, 1897.

My Dear Mrs. E. R. Wheaton:

Perhaps you will be surprised to get this letter, but I have heard so much about you that I feel as though I was personally acquainted with you, so I hope you are well, dear Mother, and that you are doing work for the Master and that He will give you a great many souls for your hire.

O, I do want to see you. Indeed I would like to hear you sing and pray. The girls all want to see and hear you. Pray for them. One woman in here said that you were the only person that ever did pray a prayer that touched her heart and brought tears to her eyes. The old girls talk about you so much to the new ones that they all love you, although they have not seen you. They tell over and over of your love and sympathy and that you know how to reach poor unfortunate souls. You know that they need kind words and a loving smile to cheer up their broken hearts.

Dear Mother, you know that a smile goes where a dollar cannot go, for it goes to the heart and makes it so very happy.

Good-bye, hoping to hear from you soon, I remain,

Yours truly,

LINA S.

Allegheny City, Feb. 14, 1897.

My Dear Mrs. Wheaton—Dear Mother:

I will say dear, for you are dear to me. O, you do not know how I have been longing to see you and once more hear you sing some of your beautiful hymns. O! just to hear you pray once more in this world. There are only eighteen women of us now, and when you were here last time there were thirty-three.

O, dear Mother, do make me a special subject of prayer that God may keep me and guide me in the right way. I have been trying to lead a Christian life for six years now. When all earthly friends have forsaken me Jesus comes and speaks to me, and He alone comforts me, and I thank God for a full and free salvation. O bless His holy name! Hallelujah in the highest to God!

Our matron, Miss S. J. Arner, sends you her best regards. I am very sorry to tell you that Miss Osborn was called home by the death of her sister; pray for her and for me, Laura M., No. 9351, that God may spare my life that I may work for the Master when I am a free woman. The two Morgan sisters send you their love. All of the girls send love to you. Come on a week day and perhaps you can get the widow's mite.

Good-bye, I remain, yours in Christ,

LAURA M.

Allegheny City, Pa., March 21, 1897.

Dear Friend:

I received your very kind and welcome letter and was very glad to hear from you, and dear Mother Wheaton, your letter did me good as I sit and hear it read to me. I shall try to keep it, and get it read often to me, as it does comfort my broken heart. I am a poor orphan girl. My mother died when I was about twelve years old, and I have wandered on in sin and I have fallen by the wayside. Will you pray for me that I may come to live just as you do, my true, strong friend. I do wish I could see you today, to hear you pray and sing. All of the girls wish to see you and hope that you will come on some day through the week so that we can write out a money order for you. Perhaps it may be only a couple of dollars or three, but it will be like the widow's mite.

I remain, yours truly,

LINA S.

Allegheny, Pa., March 21, 1897.

Mrs. E. R. Wheaton.

Dear Mother: We received your very kind and welcome letter. O, we are so glad that you sent us a letter and some tracts. Mrs. S. J. Arner, our matron, read the letter in the dining-room to all of us and we did enjoy it so much. Indeed I feel that I had a visit from a dear friend. I hope you are well and I pray for you that God may strengthen you in your labors. You have done a great work, but God has more for you to do yet before you shall pass through the pearly gates of Heaven, for you have cheered so many broken hearts. God sent you to cheer those in prisons. I was just thinking today, O, how happy you will be in the end when Jesus shall say unto you: "Come, ye blessed of my Father, inherit the Kingdom prepared for you." And O, dear Mother, He will say to you: "I was in prison and ye visited me." I am still looking unto Jesus. He has been my only friend for these years in prison. He keeps me day by day and makes me feel happy in prison. He causes me to hear "songs in the night." Pray for me that God may keep me and my children.

I dreamed that I was sent to preach the gospel to some poor soul and I have dreamed it three times over the same.

First time I said, "No, I cannot do it," and the Lord laid me on a bed of sickness, and then I said, "Lord, I will go." I had no rest by night or by day until I consented to go.

All of the girls join me in love to you. We hope that these few lines may find you well and happy, for you are always so happy and bright. One of the old girls said that your face has such a happy smile on it and a light shines over you while you talk to them. Write soon.

LAURA M.

This is an extract from a letter by an orphan girl, a type of many other poor girls whose fates are equally as sad:

Spokane Falls, ——, 1889.

O if I was only free, the greatest pleasure of my life would be to go with you and work for God. Your kindness has won my heart. I have never had any one to be kind to me; I have known nothing but sorrow all my life. My past is almost a blank. Dear, kind sister, look on me with pity—a friendless, motherless girl. I am alone in the world. I was drawn into this place through cruel treatment. I have no money, and I am helpless. If God does not have mercy on me, I do not know what will become of me. If I had only a good, kind friend like you to guide me through life, I would have been a far better woman than I am. If God will save me I shall live in the future a life of honor and work for God.

Pray for me. Tell me in what way I am going to help myself. O sister, I am so troubled; sometimes I think I will end my miserable existence. But I know if I should take my own life that it would be a terrible sin; but how can I help thinking such things in a place like this? No friends, no home, and no money; sick at heart, sick in body, sick in mind.

Lancaster, Neb., Jan. 27, 1895.

Mrs. E. R. Wheaton, Washington, D. C.

Our Dear Friend: We received your kind letter of the 7th inst. We were glad to hear from you and to know that you were enjoying good health. Dear Mother, if we may address you thus, we were very glad to hear our friend, Mrs. Beemer, spoken of so well, for she is a friend never to be forgotten. And Mr. Beemer is just a splendid warden, kind to everybody; and we ask you to pray that they may be retained here for another time. Dear Mother, indeed we will know how to appreciate our freedom in the future. Of course you do not know our names, but I will give them in the following words that each sends to you. Hattie and Edna send their regards to you. Nannie says to pray for her. Annie sends her best regards to you and wishes you well. Hattie R. sends love and best wishes. Annie H. is the one who was sick when you were here and sends love to you, and knows that God answered your prayers that she might be restored to health. Effie joins in sending love, and my prayer is that God may bless you and help you in all your good work. So we close for this time, asking you to pray for us poor unfortunate girls.

We remain, your loving children,

H., E., A., N., H., A. and EFFIE.

Canon City, March 27, 1899.

Dear Friend and Mother:

I know you are my friend and everybody's friend. I heard your kind letter and cannot help writing to you. I cannot write very good, so please excuse mistakes. Your letter found all the girls well. I have often thought of you and wished that I could be a Christian like you; but I am a poor sinner and have been all my life. I never heard one word out of the Bible in my life till I got in jail. I never had any Christian parents, and therefore I am a deep sinner, but I want to do better. My conscience tells me that I must try to be a better woman. I have been a very bad girl, but I think my Savior will forgive me, if I repent in time. Sometimes I nearly go crazy just thinking what a life I have led. O if I would die now what would become of me? I want you to pray for me, mother, for I do believe you can help me by praying for me.

I have not long in here now. My time expires on the 25th day of December, 1899; pray that I will be a better girl. I want to go home to my brother if I can when I leave here. I am tired of this life. My soul is tired. O, I am so wicked! I have tried to pray the best I knew and I got scared. Something seemed to bother me, and I was afraid to go to sleep. Mother, why do I get scared? Is it because I have sinned so much? But I will try again and again. I am willing to do right and live an honest life, and I will or die in the attempt. I have had a lot of trouble in my life and it drove me to all my downfalls, but I can see that I am sending my soul to everlasting torment, so I want to turn now and seek for the Lord. Tell me how I can, mother.

Mother, this is the best I can do; may God bless you in all your undertakings. The matron was glad to hear from you and also the girls. Pray for me.

ANNA 4309.

Waupun, Wis., March 6, 1899.

Dear Sister Wheaton:

Thank God I received your kind and Christian letter last week. We are getting along nicely with our meetings and I know and feel that God is with us every day and especially the eleven that have given their hearts to God and let His dear hand guide their every footstep.

Our dear Matron gave me your letter. I am as contented as can be. I believe it God's will that I should be here, and His will be done. I love our dear Heavenly Father with all my heart and soul and I love all my sisters and brothers and I love my enemies and I pray for them and ask God to bless them.

I have ten months more and I hope you can come here again before I go. Our Matron is with us in our meetings every Saturday. I read my Bible and pray three times a day, and I have more strength to perform my daily work, and I know our dear Savior will not forsake me or leave me alone because I know Jesus loves me now, and I know He will answer my prayers.

I told you before it is my second term, but when I sit in my little room reading my Bible I thank God for it, for I know it was God's will that I should be here a second time, for there is work for me to do here as well as when I am free, and He put me here to show me He wanted me for one of His own dear humble children and I know and feel it now.

"Happy day, happy day, When Jesus washed my sins away; He taught me how to watch and pray, And live rejoicing every day."

And I want you to pray for us all that we may have more of God's grace given to us day by day and help us to be humble and meek and willing to be led by His loving hand and pray for us that God will keep us from all temptation and sin and may we ever prove faithful. "Have mercy upon me, O God, according unto the multitude of Thy tender mercies. Blot out my transgressions." Every word here is just as I feel in my heart.

"I may not do much with all my care, But I surely may bless a few; The loving Jesus will give to me Some work of love to do.

"I may wipe the tears from some weeping eyes, I may make the smile come again, To a face that is weary and worn with care, To a heart that is full of pain."

Mrs. J. G.

Anamosa, Iowa, Aug. 11, 1901.

Elizabeth R. Wheaton,

     Tabor, Iowa.

Dear Mother:

We received your kind and loving letter yesterday. Was more than glad to hear from you, but sorry that you have been so sick; but I praise God for His healing divine. We did not have the smallpox in the prison. There were cases of them in town, but the warden quarantined the prison and vaccinated every prisoner. Dear mother, I am trying to get a parole. My petition is now before the Governor with a thousand signers, besides several letters from friends. I have had three good homes offered to me if the Governor will only parole me. I desire so much to be where I can live a better life and take care of my little boy and help my parents, who are in very poor health. I do pray so much for a better place and better companions, where I can do something for my own and others. Dear Mother, will you pray for me? I always remember what I promised you when you bid me good-bye; that was, to pray for you every day. I am so glad we have a Savior who will hear our prayers though we are behind prison walls and our prayers are weak.

With love and prayers,

FROM D. F. TO MOTHER WHEATON.

Anamosa, Iowa, Oct. 6, 1903.

Dear Mother Wheaton:

I thought I would write you a few lines. We are all well at present. We cannot express how thankful we were for your visit to us. We only wish you could have staid longer. Mrs. Waterman has prayer and song service every morning. It is something wonderful. We all wish so much to hear your voice. Mrs. Waterman spoke to us about writing to you and I was only too glad to write and ask you to pray for us all. I believe and know it will do good. I am trying very hard to pray and be a good Christian. I will ask you to pray for me.

Respectfully yours,

G. Mc.

GROUP OF GIRLS IN AN INDUSTRIAL SCHOOL.

SOUTHERN ILLINOIS STATE PRISON AT CHESTER.

CHAPTER VIII.

Incidents in My Prison Work.

LETTER FROM THE PRISONERS AT CHESTER, ILL.

Southern Illinois Penitentiary,
Menard, Ill., Nov. 27, 1902.

Dear Mother:

We are writing you from within these dark grim walls. Although we are condemned as the outcasts of society and separated from friends and loved ones and continually laboring under great mental strain and worry, still there is no pain or sorrow great enough to destroy our happiness in our thoughts of you. Your love and thoughtfulness for us and our spiritual welfare is a priceless jewel that all the wealth of the world cannot buy nor sorrow rob us of. No, never. Although the world has condemned and despised us, but we know that there is one—if only one—that loves even the outcasts.

Several of your boys have gone from here since you were among us. Some have crossed to the beyond; others to blessed freedom. Still a greater number are left here with fondest recollections of all you have done for us, which is one of the greatest among our causes for thanksgiving. It is hardly necessary to say, Remember us. We all remain your sons until death.

YOUR BOYS OF CHESTER, ILLINOIS.

An extract from a report of the Chaplain of the Southern Illinois Penitentiary will be of interest:

Chester, Ill.

To the Honorable Board of Commissioners,

Chester, Ill.

Gentlemen:

I take pleasure in making a report of my first year's work as Chaplain.

The regular chapel services have been held every Sunday at 9:40 a. m. The chapel has been well filled at all regular services and crowded on special occasions. The attendance at religious services is voluntary, but most prisoners consider it a privilege to attend.

The words of encouragement I have received from prisoners in conversation and by letter make me feel that good is being accomplished. More than one hundred men have given me their names as Christians or seekers of religion.

I attend all calls made by the prisoners during the week and visit one cell house each Sunday evening.

My visits are so planned that I see each prisoner in his cell at least twice a month and give him a chance to make his requests known.

The men have been urged to study the Bible and have been furnished tracts and other helps in Bible study. I have been astonished in making my rounds to find so many men reading the Bible. One hundred and fifty new Bibles have been purchased during the year. Six hundred Sunday-school quarterlies have been furnished the prisoners each quarter during the year and they have been urged to keep in touch with the outside world by studying these lessons. The Sunday-school lesson is read every Sunday as a scripture lesson and comments are made upon it.

The sick in the hospital and the shut-in prisoners in the cell houses are visited daily and are supplied with books and papers. Some of them read a book each day.

The Murphy Temperance Pledge has been furnished and more than five hundred prisoners have signed the pledge. If the saloons could be closed out poor-houses, jails and prisons would soon be almost empty.

Respectfully submitted,

W. N. RUTLEDGE, Chaplain.

SUICIDE OF A PRISONER.

While on my way to the State Prison at Chester, Illinois, in the year 1888 (if I remember rightly) I was especially impressed by the sad appearance of a fellow-passenger, a mother, accompanied by three children. I was sure that she was in deep trouble. I said to my helper, "Mary, that woman is going to the Penitentiary." She said, "How do you know?" I answered. "I feel sure of it and I will convince you that I am right."

Having entered into conversation with the woman, I assisted her as I found opportunity in caring for her children. When I asked her where she was going, she said, "I am going to Chester." I said, "I, too, am going to Chester and will gladly assist you in getting off with the children."

At the station we parted, but the next morning, which was the Sabbath, as I passed through the guard-room of the State Prison I saw this woman talking to her husband, who was a prisoner. She sat beside him and he was holding one of the children and she had another in her arms. The third was playing near by. All were too young to know of the sorrow that had come to their home, or the shame that had fallen upon them. They were with papa and mamma and felt safe and happy. Alas! how little they knew how soon they were to be left fatherless!

I passed on and was busy during the entire day for I had the liberty of the prison and the privilege of working among the prisoners. So busy was I that for the time being I had lost sight of that poor wife and mother, but only the next morning the Chaplain called for me and said, "Sister Wheaton, I have oh, such a sad task before me this morning! I wish you would do it for me." I said, "Chaplain, I will try. I am willing to do anything that I can to help you." And then he said, "Do you remember the man and woman you saw yesterday in the guard-room talking?" I said, "Yes; I remember them well; I met the woman on the train on my way here." He replied, "Well, that man was so heart-broken at the thought of parting with his wife and children that he asked her to promise him that if he should die in the prison she would have him brought home for burial. She promised him she would do so and last night that poor man committed suicide in his cell and now someone must go and tell that woman of her husband's death." I said, "Chaplain, that is a hard thing to do, but I will try." He said, "I wish you would,—being a woman you can comfort her better than I could." Well, I went along the hall until I came to the door of the room she occupied, for, she too, as well as myself, was a guest of the kind warden's wife. I opened the door softly and looked in. In memory I can see her yet as she sat with one child in her lap while the other two little ones were playing around her knee. She was softly singing some old country tune. As I looked my heart failed me. I turned away in sorrow and returned to the Chaplain and said, "Chaplain, I cannot do it. I cannot break that poor woman's heart. I just can't tell her," and he said, "Then I will have to do it. Someone must tell her," and so he broke the message as best he could. Never will I forget the anguish of that poor woman's heart as she wept out her grief and suffering!

I tried to comfort her as best I could. I took the same train with her as she started for home with her husband's body in the baggage coach ahead. As best I could I ministered to her and those poor helpless children as long as our journey carried us over the same road and when I changed cars I tried to utter some words of comfort, but oh, friends, what could I say, what could I do? Only the sympathy of the loving Savior could reach her case and I left her, never to meet her again on this side, but oh, may we not hope that in some way God found a way to have mercy upon that poor, misjudged man and that those loved ones may meet again where no mistakes will be made by judge or jury? For many believed that poor man to be innocent of the crime with which he was charged. If I remember rightly a barn had been burned and he had been accused of setting it on fire and had been convicted through purely circumstantial evidence. Brokenhearted over his disgrace and the thought of again being separated from wife and children, the poor man made a rope of the bed-clothing in his cell and used it to take his own life.

"I HAVE NO FRIENDS."

On the 4th of July, 1903, I was in the Ohio Penitentiary at Columbus. Officers and chaplain were kind, as usual. After holding services in the hospital, I held service with the men under death sentence; then went to the prison-yard where all the others were having a holiday. There the Chaplain assisted Sister Taylor and myself to hold services in the open air. Many seemed glad to get the message of love in song and prayer and preaching and many came to shake hands with us, while singing the closing hymn.

One poor old man, a foreigner, handed me a little package about as large as a walnut. The paper was soiled from contact with his hand that warm day. The poor man in tears said, "Good-bye," and I forgot all about the little package till on the train that night going east, where I found it in my pocket and found inside a silk handkerchief and a 25 cent silver piece. On the paper was written his name and number and these words, "I have no friends." I wept over that small token of love as I do not often weep over a gift. I have that little handkerchief safe. It seems sacred to me. How I felt repaid for my hard day's toil.

That night while I was holding services on the train the conductor said, "Mother, I don't see how you stand so much hardship;" I said, "Conductor, I had even forgotten that I had had neither dinner or supper today."

I think I know something of what Jesus meant when He said to His disciples after ministering to a needy soul, "I have meat to eat that ye know not of."

Chaplain Starr in one of the following letters refers to the open air service on July 4th; also to some of the men under death sentence with whom I had labored. The Indian woman to whose death and burial he refers is the same one who is mentioned in the letters of W. H. M. in another place.

Columbus, Ohio, July 11, 1903.

Mrs. Elizabeth R. Wheaton.

My Dear Sister: Your letter received this morning was a very pleasant surprise. We have now an additional man in the Annex. There are three men sentenced to electrocution in September and October. What change may come we do not know. I gave them your letter; they will read it over by themselves, and the tracts also. They still say that your visit with them on the Fourth of July did them much good. I have also delivered your letter to D., and with it a letter from myself, giving him encouragement and offering to render him any friendly assistance. The old Indian woman, Elsie J., whom I think you have several times seen in the female prison, died on the 9th, and we gave her a Christian burial yesterday. She was converted and baptized some time ago. I am glad that you are preserved and sustained in your great work as prison evangelist. If D., and N., and W. write to you I will forward the letters to your address. With kind wishes and regards, I am,

Your brother,

D. J. STARR, Chaplain, O. P.

Your talk in the yard on the Fourth of July did good.

Columbus, Ohio, Sept. 26, 1903.

Dear Sister: Your recent postal came duly to hand. I received your letter in July from the South and wrote you a reply, but have kept it until the present time, not knowing where to mail it so it would reach you. I will now send it in this letter, so that you will see that I have not forgotten you and answered your letter at the time. You inquire concerning the men in the Annex; we have now six men in the Annex. One of them has been granted a new trial and some others are expecting to get new trials. They do not take any great interest in religion, but yet they read the

Bible some and talk about it. I will tell them of your interest in them and assure them that they are not forgotten in your prayers.

Sincerely yours,

D. J. STARR, Chaplain, O. P.

Ohio Penitentiary, Feb. 22, 1904.

Mrs. Elizabeth R. Wheaton.

Dear Sister: I have just received your letter from Washington, D. C., inquiring about the men in our prison death cell.

There are ten there now and two have been taken out for new trials. If these are sent back we shall have twelve. The largest number, until this list, ever in the Annex was nine.

Murders, as well as other crimes of violence to person and property, are on the increase and society is trying to protect its life—without much security, so far.

Perhaps three of the men are Scripturally penitent, three others interested and four indifferent to religion—so far as we can see. The men have Bibles, religious song books and papers, library books and religious letters from relatives. They are not allowed to correspond without especially good reasons for permits to do so. I hold a little meeting and Bible study with those who care for it almost daily at 2 p. m., at which time you might help us with your prayers.

Sentiment is not salvation. The trouble, both in the prison and out of it, is, men will not seek after God. Yes, I am busy and ought to be busy about my Master's business, and so are you.

With best wishes, I am,

Respectfully yours,

D. J. STARR, Chaplain.

WAY OPENED IN ANSWER TO PRAYER.

I had for many years prayed for an opportunity to preach in one of the largest state prisons. Again and again I had been refused by both the warden and chaplain. But at last through a new governor of the state I was permitted to enter this prison for religious services.

Calling at the office of the governor and asking permission to go to the prison and assist in the services, he said, "Certainly, we shall be glad to have you. There will be no difficulty, as we have new officers. You can preach in the prison." Before I had left the Governor's private office the warden of the prison being present spoke and said, "Certainly, they would be very glad to have you take part with them." I asked if I should not see the chaplain, but the warden said he would be all right, and be pleased. But I insisted that it was only courtesy to see the chaplain. And asking the governor to please write a note to him, he did so and remarked that the state carriage was waiting at the door and I should be driven to the chaplain's house.

Arriving at his home I was met by his little daughter who carried my card to her father and he soon came into the room asking what I wanted. "I should like, if you please, to take part with you in the services at the prison chapel tomorrow (Sunday) as I have been some years in prison work," I replied. "No indeed," he answered, "I cannot allow a woman to speak in my meetings. I will never permit any woman to take my pulpit." I made no reply, but that the state carriage was waiting for me and I must go, but said to him, "Here is a letter from the governor. Will you kindly look at it before I leave?" He took the message and noting its contents he changed color and seemed confused; saying, "I never did allow a woman to speak in my meetings. But seeing the governor's request and your years of experience, I will allow you to come in the morning and conduct the women's meetings." The governor's letter read as follows:

Executive Department, Oct. 24, 1891.

Dr. O. W. G.,

Chaplain of Penitentiary.

Dear Sir:

The bearer, Mrs. E. R. Wheaton, is a prison evangelist of national reputation and experience, who brings letters of strong recommendation from wardens of the prisons she has visited, and I commend her to your kind consideration. She has expressed a willingness, if not a desire, to participate in your services tomorrow afternoon in the chapel and I trust you will afford her every facility for so doing.

Respectfully,

DAVID R. FRANCES.

A WOMAN CONVERTED AND HEALED.

I went praying for an outpouring of the Holy Spirit. While I was speaking I was impressed to step down the aisle and lay my hand upon the head of a vicious looking colored woman. I afterward learned that she was a life time prisoner and a very dangerous woman. Instantly the power of God fell upon her and she was wonderfully converted then and there, and to the best of my knowledge is still true to God. The other women seeing this, their leader in sin (for so she was) so changed, were subdued and convicted of their sins. The meeting closed with victory for God. The chaplain was convinced and said, "You have won the worst woman in the prison. You have the hearts of all the prisoners now, for her influence is great. You come and preach to the men this afternoon. I am convinced." Years have come and gone. Governors, wardens and chaplains have been changed; but God does not change, and the doors of that prison are still open to me, and God always blesses every service.

Some years later upon visiting this prison again we found this poor colored woman much afflicted and walking on crutches. The sister with me and I prayed for her, and she was instantly healed, throwing her crutches aside at once. The matron then gave her the key to go down and unlock the outside door for us, having so much confidence in her. She received a pardon from the governor later.

Another woman in the same prison was also prayed for and was instantly healed by the Lord, of a large tumor, and ran and praised God for what He had done for her.

A CHANGE WROUGHT.

For some years another prison was closed to me. Why, I never knew. I prayed that the doors of that prison might be opened to me. When the Lord sent me back there I found such a change as I had never before witnessed in the same length of time. There was a good Christian chaplain, one of the best of wardens, and good deputies. Every prisoner was in an improved state of mind and morals, and all in harmony and glad to obey the rules of the prison. I was treated with courtesy and kindness, and was given all the time in the services, and was entertained. When I left I was conveyed to the depot with ladies as escorts, and a "trusty" as driver. Such are the wonderful workings of God through faith and prayer. The meetings in this state prison were owned and blessed of the Lord. The Holy Spirit led and all seemed to enjoy and appreciate them. The chaplain said, "How much good was accomplished!" All were united in harmony and God was glorified.

A CHAPLAIN IN MY AUDIENCE.

At another time, arriving at a certain city where there was a state's prison, I met in the depot a young lady wearing a Salvation Army bonnet. She was crying at not being met by friends as she had expected, and I asked her to go with me. She gladly did so and I proceeded to the prison to ask permission to hold services for the prisoners on the next day which would be the Sabbath. Obtaining the consent of the chaplain I waited till the time for the service on Sabbath morning and returned. The guard refusing to admit me, I sent for the chaplain. When he came he also refused me, saying he could not permit me to hold the service, as he thought I belonged to the Salvation Army. A friend suggested that I should go to the Governor at his residence, saying that he was a kind man. I did so, and was very kindly received. Having listened to my request he said, "Yes, you may have your meeting in the prison,"—he having heard of my work before. He wrote a card for me to carry with me, and I took it and returned to the prison. The preacher and the Sisters of Charity had all gone to the women's department. The men were out in the large yard. I called, "Boys, come on, we are going to have a meeting." How they hurried pell mell to the chapel! And such a meeting! The power of God fell. Just then the chaplain entered, much surprised of course, and I said, "Chaplain, I am permitted through the kindness of the Governor to hold this service. Will you please be seated?" Had a most glorious meeting, closing with results altogether satisfactory to the chaplain.

IMPRESSED TO TARRY.

While holding a meeting in a certain city, I was impressed day after day to tarry. I did not know why. I wanted to go, but still the Lord impressed me to wait. One evening a cry was heard, "A man is shot." Immediately the Spirit impressed me, "That is what I detained you here for." I rushed out into the night, and inquired where the man had been carried. They told me to the hotel. I went immediately, got admittance to his room and found him in a dying condition, with no one that knew God to pray for him. And there by the bedside of the dying man, some mother's boy,—dying without God and without hope in the world,—I tried to point him to the Lamb of God that taketh away the sin of the world, hoping that the Lord would give him a chance at the eleventh hour to seek salvation, and I believe God heard my prayer for this soul.

ENCOURAGEMENT BY THE WAY.

In the Pacific Garden Mission in Chicago one night, after addressing the audience and singing the Gospel to the people, I gave an invitation to all who desired to lead a new life and serve the Lord to come forward and publicly confess Christ and repent of their sins. Instantly a fine looking young man rose in the rear of the hall, hurried to the front and grasped my hand, saying that he saw me three weeks before in the Deer Lodge, Montana, State Prison. He said that three days before, he was released and had come to Chicago, and passing along the street he heard me singing a favorite hymn at the open air meeting before services in the hall, and was attracted in. With hand raised, he promised to be a Christian and live for God and meet me in Heaven. He said he had my Bible that I gave to the matron of the prison, who, when he was leaving, gave it to him. "Cast thy bread upon the waters, for thou shalt find it after many days." Many others gave themselves to the Lord that night but this was one of my prison boys, and I was his mother, in that sense, as my life has been consecrated to God for that special line of work.

The day following, on my way east, I was compelled to stay over night at a way station where we were to change cars. As I left the train I heard, as usual, the call of cab-men but passed on into the waiting room. Several followed me, but one took me by the hand and addressing me familiarly said, "Get into my cab, mother, it is all right; I'll take you where you wish to go." Mother Prindle, who was with me said, "Do you know Mother Wheaton?" He replied, "I have read about her," but the look in his kind eyes told me it was one of my boys from prison. He was now settled in life, a good man, with a wife and two children. He escorted us to the jail where I desired to hold services, then to the home of a minister, and from there to our lodging house.

I bless God, and will through all eternity, that the dear Lord ever called me to work in the prisons as well as in other lines of Christian work. There are many all over this land now serving God, leading good, honest lives, a blessing to their country and an honor to God's cause, who were found in prisons and slums, discouraged and having given up all hope of ever being anything but miserable and wretched. They are now serving the blessed Christ who came to seek and to save that which was lost, and destroy the works of the devil, not willing that any should perish, but rather that all should be saved. O reader, many are the lives we might rescue from the ranks of the enemy if we were more in earnest and lived in close touch with God, and more under the power and inspiration of the Holy Spirit.

Once in a meeting I was attending, the minister in charge took another young preacher by the hand, and said: "I want you to preach for us." The one addressed came to the front of the platform and said: "Yes, I will; but first I want to say I was once in an insane prison, an awful place. No one will ever know all we had to suffer there. I was insane through drink—no one could help me. I was sin-hardened and hard-hearted, but this Mother (pointing to myself) came to our criminal prison and sang and prayed and talked to us, and was kind to us, and my heart was melted, and I wept—

something I could not, would not do until then. Her kindness won me, and I was saved, truly sanctified, and I have been preaching the Gospel for four years."

A CASE OF CRUEL NEGLECT.

At the best, life in prison is hard. How much worse when cruelty and neglect are added to the necessary restrictions that are placed upon those in confinement. I knew of one young colored man in prison in the south who was compelled to endure the winter weather without proper clothing or covering. His one blanket was so short that his feet were so badly frozen they had to be amputated. Think you that such things as these do not cry to God for vengeance?

ANOTHER SUICIDE.

Well do I remember a promising young man, who, when I was preaching in a prison in a southern state, began trembling and ran back into his cell and called for an officer to bring me to him. I found that he was quite weak from a bullet wound he had received in a drunken row in a saloon, he having killed a man in the fight. He was a young man with bright prospects before him, but bad company and a love for strong drink had wrought his ruin. He told me of his uncle who was a minister, a prominent evangelist. I was much surprised that a nephew of so popular a minister should be in state's prison for such an awful crime, crushed with shame and remorse. Could it be possible? His mother was a rich lady.

This young man either because of his wealth and position, or because of his good conduct in prison, or both, was given privileges and often sent outside the prison grounds. Often I plead with him to come to Christ. But one day the old demon of drink had overcome him and having secretly obtained some liquor, while at a game of cards he shot himself. Let us throw the mantle of charity over that blighted life, and leave him in the hands of a just God. Who will be willing to answer at the bar of God for that soul? "Woe unto him that giveth his neighbor drink, that puttest thy bottle to him and makest him drunken also."—Hab. 2:15. "Vengeance is mine, I will repay, saith the Lord."

JUST OUT OF PRISON.

"O the wrongs that we may righten, O the skies that we may brighten, O the hearts that we may lighten— Helping just a little!"

While traveling on the train one day, the brakeman said to me: "There is an ex-convict in the smoking-car." "All right, I will go in and see him," I said. I went and took him by the hand as he sat alone in the rear seat of the car, sad and dejected, with no money, no friends, no home. His mother had died while he was incarcerated in prison; home broken up, nowhere to go. How glad I was to take this poor soul upon my heart, and intercede for him in silent prayer; and then have him come into the other coach and share my lunch. At parting he promised me he would live a temperate life, and serve God the best he knew. I believe the dear Lord had me travel on that train to meet that poor unfortunate and help and strengthen his faith in Christianity, by showing him attention outside as well as inside the prison walls. How often a soul is saved from a downfall by a word in season; a kind hand-clasp, a "God bless you; cheer up, look up, better days are coming," etc. When hope is well-nigh gone, and friends have forsaken, and all has failed; yet we can always tell such that "God never fails."

DYING IN PRISON.

One day as I was alone in a gloomy prison a poor boy called to me and said, "Write to my mother, but don't tell her where you found me. Please don't tell her, for it would kill her. She never could live and know her boy was in prison." On the dirty floor, lying on a pile of still dirtier straw I found this poor prison boy dying. I fell on my knees and poured out my heart to God in his behalf.

"That head had been pillowed on tenderest breast, That form had been wept o'er, those lips had been pressed, That soul had been prayed for in tones sweet and mild; For her sake deal gently with some mother's child."

Do not tell me that it does not pay to labor and pray with these dear lost ones. For if I can be the means of rescuing but one soul from eternal punishment, thank God, it pays me.

WILL IT PAY?

Some gentlemen were once looking at a large building erected for newsboys, that they might be brought under religious and refining influences. One of the spectators asked a large contributor to the benevolent institution this question: "Now you are erecting this building at a cost of many thousands of dollars, and I admire your motives, but suppose that after all this great expense only one boy was saved here— would you still think it paid for time, labor and money expended?" The man answered quickly and earnestly, "Yes, sir; if it was my boy." The most precious thing in the sight of God is a soul. For the redemption of every soul on earth was paid the precious blood of the Lamb of God. Count it not then a light thing in His sight for one to be saved or lost. For "There is joy in the presence of the angels of God over one sinner that repenteth— more than over ninety and nine just persons who need no repentance." Hundreds have been saved under my observation and instrumentality both inside and outside of prison walls, and my motto has been, "Throw out the lifeline across the dark wave."

SAVED AND PREACHING THE GOSPEL.

Upon a warm July day, starting to walk out from Bismarck, N. D., to what I took to be the state's prison, but which proved to be a large water reservoir, being overcome by the heat I fell, and crawling to a shade I lay down with my Bible under my head. After a time I saw some distance away some persons driving in an open hack and signaled to them till they saw me and came to me. They drove me to the home of the warden of the prison where I was kindly received by the warden's wife and made comfortable. Late that night I held service in the prison corridors. This was in 1885, and in 1901 I was leading a meeting in a mission in Portland, Oregon, and asked all who had something special for which to praise the Lord to speak. A brother arose and said:

> "I want to thank the Lord tonight for the privilege of hearing 'Mother' Wheaton preach outside of prison walls. I have heard her in many a prison. Years ago, one night at 9 o'clock, when all the prisoners had been locked in their cells, the officers unlocked the doors to let this sister sing some hymns and hold services in the corridors. One hymn that especially touched my heart was 'Throw out the life line.' I was an opium fiend, a morphine fiend, a whisky fiend, and an all around bad man, and was ready to despair. But God touched my heart and saved me and called me to the ministry. At this time I was with my other sins a deserter from the United States army. When my time expired I went and gave myself up and was sentenced to five years more in prison. But God had mercy on me and in seven months I was pardoned out. Since that time I have lived an honest life, and for eight years have preached the gospel."

This man was married to a Christian woman and has done much to rescue men from the pit from which he had been taken, and is still preaching.

IN SOLITARY CONFINEMENT.

One Sunday I sang perhaps thirty hymns and preached seven times to prisoners in solitary confinement, where I dare not see them or clasp their hands as I do in other prisons. There are hundreds there, and as I sang in all the prison wards or corridors many different hymns, the dear souls cheered and responded with their clear voices as best they could to show their sincere appreciation of my efforts to brighten their lonely prison life.

Each was "some mother's boy." Reader, is there not a sympathetic chord in your heart for these poor unfortunates?

CRAPE ON THE DOOR.

I once felt impressed to go to a certain prison and hold services. Arriving at the place early in the morning, I thought I would go to the prison first before I would telephone for a cousin who often helped me in the singing. When I arrived at the prison, the chaplain said, "Mother Wheaton, the Lord sent you to help me. To-day I have a funeral service of a prisoner, something we have never had at this prison." I did not telephone then for my cousin, as the services were arranged. I worked all day in the prison, holding services with both men and women prisoners, visited the hospital, and went to the city jail at 5 p. m. and held services, and then went to my relative's home and was greatly shocked to find crape hanging on the door. I found my cousin cold in death. Relatives asked me, "Who told you?" I said, "God impressed me to come at this time." And I went with them to the grave of my dear cousin, and kneeling beside the open grave, I promised to faithfully do God's holy will, and meet the departed one in Heaven.

IN A POLICE STATION.

In 1903, while I was in San Francisco, I was impressed to go to the police station about nine o'clock one night. I found, on arriving, an ambulance bringing in prisoners, among them a woman who was arrested for drunkenness. I talked and prayed with her. Hearing a noise like one in distress, I walked on through the corridors and I found a young soldier who was badly wounded in one eye and the head. He was standing alone in his cell in great pain. The bandage had been torn off, and the blood was running down his face, though his wounds had evidently been dressed by a physician before coming there. He was crying from the pain, and was under the influence of drink. I wiped the blood off his face, and put the bandage on his eye again. Then I knelt in prayer with him. I left the city on an early train, and never saw him again, but I believe God heard and answered my prayer for his salvation.

BURNED IN HIS CELL.

I went into one of our western cities to hold services at the jail. On the way from the depot I stopped at a store, where a young clerk told me of a horrible crime that had been committed in the jail. That the prisoners had been trying to make their escape, and one young prisoner had revealed the plot to the jailer, and thus saved his life. The prison wall had been "worked" in a cunning manner, and the prisoners were about to escape, when this poor boy informed the jailer of what was being done. The other three prisoners were so enraged that they threw coal oil over the boy, set fire to his clothing, and he was burned alive in the cell. I was grieved at hearing this, and felt that I could see them punished severely. They were in an underground prison for safe-keeping until the wall could be repaired. The officers were afraid to let me go in, but I told them I was not afraid, and went down the stairs ahead of the officers. I saw only one dim candle burning, and called for a light. A lamp was brought, and I went boldly into the presence of those criminals. I sat down and thought of the awfulness of it all. So, as I wept, I sang "Some Mother's Boy," and they cried like their hearts were breaking. I went over to them, where they were sitting together on an old bunk, and we cried together. They were humble and convicted, and it was love that did it all—God's love which showed them that though their sins were as scarlet, they shall be white as snow, though red like crimson they shall be as wool. God heard prayer for them and I trust they were forgiven.

THE INNOCENT IN BONDS.

In a certain state prison the officer called my attention to a man and said, "That man is innocent of the crime he was sentenced for." "Then why do you keep him here?" I asked. "Because he serves for his friend, willingly allowing the guilt to be placed upon himself rather than see this friend who was really guilty suffer." On leaving the prison I came upon this man with an officer on the train, and had the pleasure of talking to the man and hearing his story. I referred him to Psalms 15:1, 2, 4. "Lord, who shall abide in thy tabernacle? Who shall dwell in thy holy hill? He that walketh uprightly and worketh righteousness, and speaketh the truth in his heart. He that sweareth to his own hurt, and changeth not." He was being taken to another court for trial.

CONFESSED HER GUILT.

A woman in a prison was convicted of sin under my preaching, and sent for me to come to her cell, where she gave me such an account of her crimes that I was shocked, and yet was powerless to liberate an innocent man that she said was in —— state's prison for a crime she committed. She asked me to go and tell him for her that she was the guilty one, and try to have him freed, but wanted the matter kept secret. Now that she was under conviction of her sins, she could not rest. I went to the state prison she named, found the man, and told him her story. His agony was pitiful to behold. He said, "O how I loved my wife and baby. I am an innocent man. How can I live my sentence out in this way? Nothing to live for." Such bitterness as he held toward that wicked woman, for her crime and duplicity! I left him in an agony of grief. And yet there are so many who are serving as unjustly for others' crimes! This woman had killed the wife thinking she herself would then get the husband.

UNDER SENTENCE OF DEATH.

Going into the presence of two condemned men on our national holiday, the chaplain remarked, "I wish you could reach these men's hearts. You have often helped others in this prison who were under death sentence." I prayed in silence for wisdom, and as I walked into their presence, I said, "I have come to sing to you and have a little visit with you, but if you prefer to be alone, I will go away." They said they would be glad to have me stay. I sang several songs, and before I had spoken of religion, I was made glad to see tears in their eyes, and then we knelt in prayer, and I prayed God to pardon their sins and make them pure in His sight.

I do not believe in capital punishment. Lord hasten the day when the crime of putting men to death legally shall be done away with. It does not stop crime. I thank God that one noble warden gave up his honorable position and salary, rather than take the lives of any more men. I wish God would raise up men all over our land who in like manner would be brave enough to refuse to sacrifice human lives because the law licenses them to do so. When I see wicked men so anxious to see poor, helpless men executed, I think of that authoritative utterance, "Vengeance is mine, I will repay, saith the Lord." Jesus said, "He that hateth his brother is a murderer." There is a day of reckoning coming.

THE RELIGION MOTHER HAD.

Many times prisoners have said to me when speaking to them, "That's the kind of religion mother had. You remind me of my own dear old mother;" and many, even statesmen, and the attendants in the capitol, and in the President's mansion, have said to me with uncovered heads, and tears in their eyes, "That is the kind of religion mother had. I wish I was as good as she was." I find the crying need to-day in all stations of life; from the palace to the dungeon, is real, genuine, heartfelt, common-sense salvation, not to be cranks and fanatics, not to be one-sided or half-way professors of religion; but to have the Holy Ghost in our hearts and lives, and a burning desire to help every one into the Kingdom of Heaven. Being "all things to all men" that we might win some wandering souls to Christ.

O the joy of knowing that you are doing just what God wants you to do— winning souls for His Kingdom, from all walks of life; often in houses of ill-fame souls are truly saved and reformed. Often in saloons men and women are impressed by the straightforward message of love brought them. You say, "No use to try." O thou of little faith, wherefore did'st thou doubt? I have much encouragement among the criminal classes, for they are despised and rejected by earthly friends.

I might give many more instances, but this is probably sufficient. Let no one think for a moment that these poor unfortunates have no tender feeling, no remorse because of sin. They see their shame and feel the separation from home and loved ones. There must be places to confine criminals and protect the lives and property of other people, but we must remember that behind all the guilt there are precious souls that live through all eternity.

Sin is treacherous, the human heart deceitful above all things and desperately wicked; perhaps under unfavorable conditions the heart of the most moral man or woman may generate the evil of the human nature and cause it to show its corruption in crime. All that saves some people now from the felon's cell, or gambler's hell, is that they hold the propensity of their corrupt hearts in with bit and bridle. And thousands tread the earth in freedom, who, if justice could find them out and fasten their guilt upon them, would be in the prison stripes and iron cells. So be not so ready to cry "Crucify him!" "Stone her!" until you can look into your own heart and see that it is pure and clean.

CAPITAL PUNISHMENT.

Thank God! that I have lived to see the time When the great truth begins at last to find An utterance from the deep heart of mankind, Earnest and clear, that ALL REVENGE IS CRIME! That man is holier than a creed—that all Restraint upon him must consult his good, Hope's sunshine linger on his prison wall, And Love look in upon his solitude. The beautiful lesson which our Saviour taught Through long, dark centuries its way hath wrought Into the common mind and popular thought; And words, to which by Galilee's lake shore, The humble fishers listened with hushed oar, Have found an echo in the general heart, And of the public faith become a living part.   *   *   *   *   *   *   *

No more the ghastly sacrifices smoke Through the green arches of the Druid's oak; And ye of milder faith, with your high claim Of prophet-utterance in the Holiest name, Will ye become the Druids of *our* time! Set up your scaffold-altars in our land, And, consecrators of Law's darkest crime, Urge to its loathsome work the hangman's hand? Beware—lest human nature, roused at last, From its peeled shoulder your encumbrance cast, And, sick to loathing of your cry for blood, Rank ye with those who led their victims round The Celt's red altar and the Indian's mound, Abhorred of Earth and Heaven—a pagan brotherhood!

—JOHN GREENLEAF
WHITTIER.

INTERIOR OF CHAPEL-DINING APARTMENT AND ROW OF
CELLS, CHESTER, ILL.

CHAPTER IX.

Conversion of Desperate Prisoners Prevents a Terrible Mutiny.

During the fall of 1888, I was deeply impressed that I should visit the state prison at Waupun, Wis. Following the guidance of the Spirit, I reached the place, after a long journey, on the evening of November third. A dear Christian girl was with me. It was a lovely moonlight night and as we came to the prison, the yard was plainly visible through the heavy iron grating. My companion called my attention to its beauty but my heart was heavy and I could only reply, "Sister, pray! O do pray! There is something awfully wrong here—some danger pending—something terrible!"

The officers of the prison welcomed me heartily and the chaplain said: "I am glad you have come and shall be pleased to have you take the service tomorrow morning." (It was Saturday.) His wife entertained us during our stay and after taking us to their own rooms he said: "There's a man here who is a terror to both the officers and prisoners. All are afraid of him. Neither kindness or punishment seems to affect him. I wish you could do something to help him." My reply was: "I cannot do anything, but God can." And earnestly did I look to God for help.

The next morning a heavy burden still rested upon my heart and I prayed God to go before me to that prison chapel and lead the meeting Himself and give me the right message. Nor did I plead in vain, for many souls were that day deeply convicted of sin and some were blessedly saved as was clearly manifested a little later.

After the sermon my friend and myself sang a hymn and this was greatly used by the Spirit in connection with the sermon in reaching the very depths of hearts. It was the custom to hold an after meeting for thirty minutes, but those who wished to remain were expected to secure cards or tickets, granting permission, on the previous day. That Sunday the chaplain said: "All who wish to remain to this service can do so without a card, as these ladies are here."

A hardened looking criminal (whom I afterward learned to be the one to whom the chaplain had referred the night before) arose to retire with a few others. I went to him at once and took him by the hand and urged him to stay, but he said: "No, they don't want me here. This meeting is for good people and I am too bad to stay." But I pleaded: "No, you stay—we want you to stay. I want you to stay." And then he said: "Well, I'll stay for your sake," and sat down. The meeting progressed under the power of the Lord and many arose to say that they had been very wicked but were sorry; and if God could and would forgive them they would lead a different life and be good men. Some told how their dear old mothers were good and had prayed for them and that they wanted us to pray for them and they would serve the Lord.

I noticed that many of the men as they arose glanced furtively at the man to whom I have referred and that he sat looking at each one as he spoke and evidently had great influence over the other prisoners. At last he arose and said, "Men, don't be afraid of me. If there is any good in this religion you are talking about, go ahead and get it. I'll stand by you and nobody shall say before me, 'There's your praying man' or 'There's your hypocrite.' I can't be good—I'm too far gone—but I'll stand by the men who are going to do right." All were evidently deeply impressed by his words. As he sat down I went to him and taking him by the hand, I said, "God loves you and He wants to save you and to help you to live for a better world than this." Again he insisted, "I'm too far gone! It's too late for me to try to do right! There's no hope for me," but still I pleaded with him to return unto the Lord—that there was still mercy and pardon for even him—and that he would yield to the Holy Spirit's pleading and become a Christian. He was evidently very deeply convicted of sin and soon arose and with deep feeling he said, "Men, you know what I have been—watch me from today and see what I will be;" and as he sat down, the prisoners cheered.

Fearful as to what the outcome might be and somewhat doubting his sincerity, the chaplain quickly closed the service and ordered the men to their cells. They obediently left the chapel, but truly God had wondrously wrought that day in the hearts of many of the most noted and hardened criminals. In the afternoon we went, in company with the chaplain, from cell to cell singing, talking, and praying with the men. The chaplain took me to the cell of the man who had given so much trouble—a man who had taken several lives, and there he gave his heart to God and was converted.

PLAN OF THE MUTINY.

After all the prisoners had been locked in the cells and the officers had gone to their homes or rooms, only a few guards remaining on duty, he sent for the warden to come to his cell and requested to be taken out into the prison yard. At first the warden refused to do so because of his being known to be such a dangerous character. Still he insisted, saying that he had something to show him. The warden, who had been an army officer and was a very brave man, was only partially convinced but finally consented saying: "I'm not afraid of you—one wrong move and you're a dead man. I have had enough trouble with you. I will take you into the yard, but beware!"

Well armed, he marched the man into the yard. There the prisoner led him to the extreme end, and taking away some dry leaves and boards he said to the warden, "Look in." The warden did so and, O, what a sight met his eyes! There, in a hole, were knives, guns, and other weapons! Staggering back he exclaimed, "My ——, where did you get those things?" "It don't matter where I got them," replied the prisoner, "but take me back to my cell and then take away these weapons. I intended to liberate the prison tomorrow morning and would have done so if that woman had not come and preached here today. I am a changed man now."

How he got those weapons was a mystery, but he had been long years planning an escape, and had chosen some of the most daring of his fellow prisoners (both those inside and others who had gone out) to aid him! Whether he could have succeeded or not, doubtless many lives either of officers or prisoners or of both would have been lost had the attempt been made. But God wrought so mightily that instead of lives being lost precious souls were saved. Several were converted that day who are still living noble Christian lives. Others may be,—I leave that with God. I do not know whether the leader is still living or not, but have heard that he was dead. At any rate he served his long sentence and claimed to be still a Christian when he left the prison.

HAVOC OF SIN.

Among the many who were converted during that Sunday morning service in 1888, was a very amiable, intelligent, refined-appearing young man, still in his teens, who was serving under life sentence. He was a real "mother's boy," so young and so small that after his conversion I used to call him my little son. He belonged to one of the best families of the state. His father was a physician and a classmate and friend of the governor. For the sake of his broken-hearted parents, as well as his own, and being satisfied that he was really innocent of the crime of which he had been convicted, I began to pray earnestly for his release. But the case dragged on and though he was pardoned some years later, it was not until after his father died broken-hearted and the mother's health had failed under her weight of sorrow and an aunt had gone insane.

During his imprisonment I at one time visited his poor mother in her home. Oh! what havoc sin had wrought! What sorrow! For though I believe him entirely innocent of the crime for which he was condemned, his conviction was the result of his being led astray by evil influences and associates.

Oh, that I could warn young men of the dangers of bad company, and that I could warn parents of the dangers of discouraging their children in waiting upon and serving God.

When this boy was quite young, he wanted to become a Christian and engage in work for souls, but his parents thought it would be a disgrace, as they were aristocratic, but alas! what snares had the enemy set for him, from which he might have entirely escaped, if they had encouraged him to be true to God.

I received many letters from him while he was in prison and quote from two of them. We have not heard from him for years but trust that if alive he is still living for God and Heaven.

Waupun, Wis., July 7, 1895.

Dear Mother, "In His Name":

Since my last letter to you several things of interest have transpired. My attorney went to see the governor and then came to see me. We went over some evidence, and at last I convinced them that I alone can untangle the skein of false evidence.

I located a Mrs. N. and she gave an affidavit which would have cleared me at my trial. She said she felt that she had been the cause of all my suffering, but that she went to LaCrosse at the time of my trial and was met at the train by a detective, who told her if she wanted to keep out of serious trouble to take the first train out of the city, and she did so. I expect to soon have another witness to corroborate her statement. Then if I can locate the sister of the deceased and get her evidence I will have a sure case against those who perjured themselves to send me here.

Yes, I have placed all my life in God's hands and have begun my work here; but, being a convict, I am much hindered. Therefore, in order to do a more abundant and faithful service, I desire my freedom. If I get it, I will try and enter the Moody Institute and take a course of training for the work. Mrs. K. is anxious to have me do so.

Our chaplain will preside over our Christian Endeavor Society. I recently sent out my report to be read at the Boston convention in session the 10th inst., and I ventured, in the light of all events, to place the following motto over our penitentiary: "Wisconsin Prison for Christ" for the coming year, and by the time of the next convention, I hope to be out to represent the Christian Endeavor boys.

Brother H. told me of a song you sing. "Some Mother's Child" is the song. Will says it is simply sublime and I ought to have it. Such songs turn the mind back to home and to the memory of fond parents and loved ones. Such pieces are always very sacred to me.

God bless you and spare you for many years to come, that you may continue to be a Mother to the prisoners of earth. Write me when you can.

I am your loving little son, "In His Name,"

ALBERT.

————————————

Waupun, Wis., Nov. 27, 1895.

My Dear Mother:

Your excellent letter duly at hand. Both Brother Colgrove and I were surprised, for we had concluded that God in His infinite love and wisdom had carried you home.

I am at work here in the official building, in the office of our dear chaplain. Brother Colgrove is in the hospital across the hall from our office. I have talked with the chaplain about your coming, and he says to tell you to come and stay two weeks. He would like to have you spend two Sundays, and in the meantime we will no doubt, under the present warden, be able to secure the evenings during the week for a series of revival meetings.

Lovingly your son in the work,

ALBERT.

————————————

Guilt comes not, thundering on the wings of time,With vice-distorted feature and the leer of crime,But like enchanting vision from a pagan dream,Or softly echoed cadence of a whispering stream,She steals upon us gently, with ever-changing art,And usurps an empire—the waiting human heart!Her outward form is beauty, her voice with Passion tense,She only craves the privilege to gratify each sense;All apparent pleasures 'round her path are spread,But, alas! you seize the flower to find its fragrance fled;But still pursuing, row with bated breath,You clasp her to your bosom and—embrace a death!Then, conscience stricken, you the wreck survey,And with shuddering horror—humbly kneel to pray;While the pitying angels on their pinions bearThe ever sacred burden of repentant prayer,And almighty love descending reasserts control,And mercy in the guise of grace has won a human *soul*.

—*A Prisoner.*

CHAPTER X.

Remarkable Conversion and Experience of George H. Colgrove.

Among the others who were saved that fourth day of November, 1888, at Waupun, Wis., was the very remarkable case of Geo. H. Colgrove. Years afterwards the chaplain said of him, "I regard him as an ideal—one of whom you would expect this report: 'If ever there was a good Christian man on earth he is one.'" At one time he had three Bible classes in prison each week—one in English and two in German—and was the means of the accomplishment of much good in the conversion of prisoners.

GEO. H. COLGROVE.

HIS OWN STORY.

The story of his life and conversion is given, as nearly as possible, in his own words, but as found in two different statements—some particulars being given in one that were not in the other—in order to make the account as complete as I can.

It is very difficult for one in prison, especially, to write of themselves without giving to strangers the impression of either vanity and conceit on the one hand or of craft and deception on the other. Therefore, it is with considerable hesitation that I write. Yet my greet indebtedness to "Mother" Wheaton, who was chosen of God as the agent through whom His wondrous work should be made manifest to the world in my salvation, as also of many others, has at last led me to make the following statement:

Just on the verge of manhood, at the age of nineteen, I obtained some *infidel literature* of the mild stamp, yet scholarly and persuasive withal, containing no harsh criticism of Christian people and principles. This aroused my interest and admiration and led to my obtaining more of a like nature, until under their combined influence my youthful mind was entirely surrendered to such doubts and disbelief as they advocated.

This was the pivotal point in my early life from which I started down the deceitful road that leads from peace, happiness and honor into the depths of sorrow, infamy and despair. Having thus imbibed the subtle poison of infidelity, I soon became blinded and indifferent to the rights of my fellowmen and to the enormity of violating divine law.

BURGLARY AND MURDER.

From this low plane of morality it was easy to enter the path of crime; and this I did, following the precarious calling of burglary for five years. This dark way ended in the midnight gloom of a murderer. Detection, arrest and conviction followed in rapid succession, soon bringing down upon me the crushing weight of a "life sentence." So that on a cold wintry night the officers of the law delivered me within the portals of a living tomb.

Four dark, hopeless, weary years succeeded. Yet the Lord in His great mercy had not forgotten me; and when all the world deserted me, then He in His loving kindness took me up and His favor was manifested through the instrumentality of "Mother" Wheaton.

During the early years of my incarceration no words could portray my intense and bitter hatred of Christianity and anything pertaining thereto. Feeling that I had sold my soul to the prince of darkness, it enraged me to be reminded of a better life, or a possible Heaven.

Burning with the fires of hatred and revenge toward those whom I knew had unjustly deceived and wronged me, my only desire was to escape from here even long enough to rush upon my enemies and hurl their souls into eternity, and then follow them immediately if need be. I continually planned and schemed for the accomplishment of this purpose, and had a plan of escape well defined and was making arrangements to put it into execution, when one bright and beautiful Sunday morning it was announced that a lady preacher was going to hold services in the chapel that day.

Though I did not often attend church, yet on this occasion I swore some big round oaths that I would go up and hear the lady talk.

That was the morning of November 4, 1888. The beautiful sun that shines alike on mansion and cottage, palace and prison, shone as though a special degree of radiance had been granted to light a benighted soul on its way out of darkness into light. But I entered the chapel with cold indifference, drawn only by curiosity—at least so far as I knew; but results proved that God was leading. I awaited developments; *and they came.* Our prison chaplain introduced "Mother" Wheaton, whom I had never seen before, and announced the services as "entirely in her hands." She gave us a short, earnest, impressive address; then she and the sister who came with her sang "Meet me there."

During the singing I heard an accompanying strain, low and inexpressibly sweet, the like of which I had never heard nor imagined.

The two sounds harmonized, yet were distinct, but oh, how lovely! Words fail to convey the most distant idea of their soothing and attractive power.

The thought flashed through my mind, "That is delicious music to fall upon ears that have listened to the sound of murderous guns."

Suddenly and with all the vividness of continuous lightning dispelling dense darkness, revealing all surrounding objects distinctly, the awful depth and blackness of my iniquitous career blazed up before my mental view, like a clear and definite painting of each act in my wicked life—portrayed on canvas by a master hand and set in clearest rays of the noonday sun. And at the same time there was given an assurance of forgiveness, if accepted then.

Surprise, consternation and intense fear came with this revelation of myself to myself, as my depraved spiritual condition was, for the first time, fully realized. Also as distinctly and positively it was granted me to know that *my last opportunity* for divine favor was before me. Accept and be saved or reject and be *eternally lost*! Such was the alternative.

Although every nerve thrilled in rebellion against Christianity and a thousand obstacles seemed to intervene, rendering a change in my course of life impossible, yet I dared not refuse that stern, terrific ultimatum, "*Your last opportunity*," and before its mighty mandate my proud, headstrong, sin-burdened soul *surrendered unto Jesus of Nazareth*.

I wished to fly from the room, but could not. I felt frightened at the power which was mastering me, and thought in a confused way of the ridicule which would be heaped upon me, of my intended escape, and of revenge upon my foes. Ah! what? Revenge? No, no revenge now. No, no. That was all gone. The evil desire had thus suddenly been removed without my knowledge, and in its stead there reigned in my heart and in the depths of my soul a feeling of forgiveness and peace, both between them and myself and between myself and my God.

I said, "Surely the Lord has visited me this day; for I came in here a devil in human form, and now my dark sins are forgiven and I am free. Glory to God!"

The chaplain and warden were nearly thunderstruck to learn that the low, miserable, worthless wretch, the hopeless vagabond, Colgrove, had been brought to the foot of the cross; still they must have entertained but little hope of my remaining in the straight and narrow path that leadeth unto life. How could they? They had not heard that strange music which had floated in on my soul. They could not feel the awakening which was permeating and ringing through the corridors of my heart, nor could they perceive the realizing sense of divine favor which was so clear to my own consciousness.

That very week it was impressed on my mind that I must at once commence the study of the Holy Scriptures for work in the cause of God and devote the remainder of my life to leading my fellowmen, and especially prisoners, into the light of Calvary. I said, "What will it all amount to—I a friendless prisoner, doomed for life?" An answering whisper came, "Friendless, with Jesus for your friend? Study the Word." So in blindness, with fear and trembling, doubts and misgivings, I took from my shelf in the prison cell the neglected, despised and dust-covered Bible and commenced studying the Word to the best of my ability, with none but God to direct or assist me except a hasty explanation now and then from the chaplain as he passed on his hurried rounds through the cell rooms.

I immediately destroyed the implements of destruction and escape which I had made during two years previous to my conversion. Instead of dirks and saws, my hands now grasped the Bible and the cross; and thanks be unto Jesus of Nazareth, they still retain their hold, and I believe with ever increasing strength.

The way thus far has been rendered more pleasant by the hand of the Lord than I then thought possible amid such dark surroundings. With an ever realizing sense of my unworthiness I have been kindly led in the way of life and am eleven years nearer my eternal Home; while in my soul there is the "peace of God which passeth all understanding" which is an additional evidence of the faithful care and guidance of Jehovah. During the last decade the motto of my life has been, as through future years it shall ever be (Isaiah 26:4): "Trust ye in the Lord forever, for in the Lord Jehovah is everlasting strength."

I know not whether earthly freedom will ever be mine, but I do know that, if it is His holy and righteous will, it will be given me; and I know that it matters little, for earthly joys must soon fade away, and down at the close of the earthly journey Jesus is waiting for me. And with my weak and faltering hand laid in His strong and mighty one I shall walk through the dark waters of the Jordan of death, and with Him kindly leading His rescued child we shall enter with joy and eternal thanksgiving the beautiful "city whose maker and builder is God."

The following extracts from letters written me at different times after his conversion will, I believe, interest the reader:

Waupun, Wis., Sept. 5, 1891.

Mrs. E. Wheaton:

Dear Christian Friend: No news received since you were here has afforded me so much pleasure as the announcement of your return.

It was through your earnest work that I was converted. When you came here before there was, I presume, no more sinful, hopeless, hardened, miserable wretch inside these walls than myself. When I entered the prison chapel that Sabbath morning, November 4, 1888, I for one came to observe, sneer and laugh. But while you were singing that glorious anthem, "Meet Me There," power from above opened my spiritual vision to see the horrible condition of my soul, and so enabled me to realize my great need of divine favor. I thank God and will bless His holy name forever that in His infinite wisdom and kindness He brought me inside these walls and sent you, His chosen instrument, to lead my wandering sin-darkened soul into the path that leadeth unto life eternal.

Amid the trials, cares and vexations of the passing days I often look up to the blue vault of heaven's dome and rejoice at the thought that the flying moments and hastening hours are bringing me nearer, ever nearer to the blessed hour when I shall meet Jesus face to face and clasp His rescuing hand, never from Him to part. Ah, never to part! Thanks unto God most high.

May the Lord ever bless you, my dear spiritual Mother. Good-bye.

G. H. C.

Waupun, Wis., Oct. 29, 1891.

My Dear Spiritual Mother:

Your kind letter most gladly received. I am surprised that our boys do not write more frequently to you. They often inquire as to your whereabouts and health and ever have a good word for you and your work. Even many who do not care for their soul's salvation speak favorably of Mrs. Wheaton.

God knows how much your letters cheer me and brighten the prison gloom. After twenty years of infidelity, with all its direful train of evils, leading on from bad to worse, the prison gate threw its protective barrier between society and one who had become almost a devil in human form, thus showing that a just God had taken account of my iniquitous course and had said, "Thus far and no farther." Then followed four years of hopeless misery, borne with the sullen stolidity of despair, while in thought, intent and purpose I sank lower and lower into the horrible cesspool of criminality, and farther and farther away from God. Then, in His infinite mercy, He sent you with the message of salvation, which He crowned with His invincible power of conviction and a realization of my lost and hopeless condition.

My prayers shall ever be with you, dear sister, and if I might send a message by you to all the prisoners from the pine-shadowed shores of Maine to the far Alaskan mountains it would be this: "Ye captives, look aloft to the Star of Bethlehem, and whatever betide, do not fail to grasp the hand stretched out to you from Calvary." Hoping to hear from you soon and praying God to ever bless you I remain,

Yours for God and humanity,

G. H. COLGROVE.

Waupun, Wis., Sept. 4, 1892.

My Dear Mother:

How many, many times I have thanked our kind Father above and praised His Holy Name for sending you to our prison gate on that November night in 1888. Three years and ten months ago today the radiant light of Calvary, fresh from the throne of the Infinite, came, through your ministrations, down into the dark recesses of my sin-burdened heart and crime-laden soul, while mingled with the music of the sweet hymn you and your companion were singing the heavenly strains of an angelic accompaniment so entrancingly and irresistibly soothing and lovely that my hardened heart melted like frost before the noonday sun.

Can you believe that I stayed to that after-meeting when every nerve in my body thrilled to get up and run out of the chapel? Yes, I desired to flee; yet an irresistible power restrained me. I know now it was Satan urging me to flee away from there; for he, of course, readily understood that he was in danger of losing an active member from his minions of evil. But thanks be unto Jehovah, who ruleth over all, Satan failed. God and His servant held the field and a soul was redeemed from death. Glory to God forever and ever. Amen.

The years from that time have been so pleasant and bright, though spent where sorrow, misery and gloom were on every hand, as I journey on to our beautiful home everlasting, which Jesus has gone to prepare.

"Filled with delight, my raptured soul Would here no longer stay, Though Jordan's waves around me roll Fearless I launch away."

"When peace like a river attends on my way Where sorrows like sea billows roll, Whatever my lot, thou halt taught me to say It is well, it is well, with my soul."

"When we've been there ten thousand years, Bright shining as the sun, We've no less days to sing his praise Than when we first begun."

Yes, since your first visit here my bark of life has been "standing away" on her new course over the sea of life, and she is now nearly four years nearer the heavenly harbor, where destructive gales of temptation will never sweep the white sails of purity from the "masts of purpose," nor break the "yard arms" of effort, nor rolling breakers of iniquity dash her upon the rocky shore of eternal ruin.

Mother, please give my kindest wishes to all who are helping you in the great work which Jesus established while on earth and which He left for us to continue until the resounding trump and advancing angel hosts proclaim His return to our earth to claim His own and crown the redeemed. When the sullen and long silent graves shall release their victims and the long absent fleet of the lower ocean shall again whiten the seas with their snowy sails and bring their passengers and crews to join the vast congregation assembled before the judgment seat of Christ.

Ever yours,

G. H. C.

Waupun, Wis., Jan. 14, 1895.

Dear Mother:

Your kind and most welcome letter very gladly received. It is ever one of my chief pleasures to hear from you.

There was a man here by the name of William L., who led a very godless life, being extremely profane. During the past summer he was transferred to the prison hospital. On September 4 I was placed in charge of the sick ward as assistant steward, and I found this man L. in here when I took charge of this department. He had been a bitter enemy of mine for several years, as he was utterly opposed to Christianity, and he tried to utterly disregard me. I continued to treat him kindly, which was, of course, a Christian duty which we owe to our Heavenly Father, and in a short time he grew into the habit of calling on me for favors, and as he sank lower I spent the night with him. One evening he spoke of you and said: "Oh! I wish I could hear 'Mother' Wheaton sing one of her sweet hymns."

During three days and nights he continued to speak of you. The last day on which he mentioned you was in the morning about 8 o'clock. While sitting in his chair beside the bed he said very earnestly and emphatically: "I would give a dollar to hear 'Mother' Wheaton sing one of her sweet hymns just now—right here and now."

About midnight that night he sat in his bed looking upward for some time in silence and then dropped his head in a most dejected manner and in mournful tone exclaimed, "No, no, no." The intense sadness of his manner made my heart ache for him. After that hour he appeared to have given up all hope. The death chill came on while he was in the rocking chair, and he asked me to assist him into bed and send for the prison physician. He expressed himself well satisfied with the treatment he had had while sick, and then, seeing it was too hard work for him to talk, he relapsed into silence, while I offered a silent prayer for the departing soul.

I write this explanation because of the intense desire he had to see you and hear you sing once more.

The Christian Endeavor still exists by the power and blessing of God, and my Bible class is continuing and some good has been accomplished through its instrumentality.

Rev. B. has left us. Our new spiritual guide and counselor is Rev. Simerville, an earnest Christian, whose influence bids fair to lead many hitherto careless ones to turn their footsteps in the straight and narrow path that leads to life. The beacon light to Calvary cheers us on every day to our eternal home. Meet me there. Good-bye, Mother. God bless you now and ever.

G. H. COLGROVE.

Waupun, Wis., Nov. 28, 1895.

Dearest Mother:

Your kind and welcome letter gladly received. Brother Albert wrote you yesterday and I sincerely hope the invitation extended to you by the chaplain and contained in Albert's letter, will be promptly acted upon and that we shall soon behold your face among us once more and again hear the songs of Zion fall from your lips.

Albert is librarian and the chaplain's assistant, while this child is assistant steward at the hospital; thus we shall be able to meet you frequently if you will spend a couple of weeks with us, and a forty-day month can be used to good advantage in Waupun and visiting among the bad boys like us, and your many good friends in this locality.

The Lord has given us a Christian man for warden and I can tell you, dear Mother, we find that the warden, the chaplain and the Lord God Almighty make a strong combination. If "Mother Wheaton" will come and join them the quartette will be complete and this prison can receive such a baptism of grace that his satanic majesty will hate the very name of Waupun.

God's blessing ever be yours and hoping to meet you once more this side the golden gate,

I am your spiritual son,

G. H. COLGROVE.

The following short extract is from a letter to a brother who had become interested in Brother Colgrove and had written him:

Waupun, Wis., April 30, 1897.

Mr. H——, Dear Christian Brother.

Your kind letter received, and I most sincerely hope it may be preliminary to a long continued and beneficial correspondence. It will ever be a pleasure to hear from you, so please write when convenient, and I will do as well as my adverse surroundings will permit.

I am pleased to learn of the continued successful work of dear "Mother Wheaton," and it is a source of great encouragement to me to meet and converse with Sister Kelley. We shall undoubtedly have her for a spiritual leader when our toil-worn "Mother" has been summoned to her rest and reward by the great Master.

Please write soon and often to

Your friend,

G. H. COLGROVE.

Dear Mother:

Your kind and most welcome letter gladly received and the unexpected photo was a very delightful surprise. A thousand thanks. I have many, many times wished I had a picture of the one whom God selected as my helper to lead me from the dark valley of despair in which I was then dwelling up into the radiant light of Calvary.

November 4th next will complete nine years of the homeward journey since Jesus set my face Zionward, so we are nine years nearer the heavenly shore and from the watch tower of the golden city the beacon light beams bright and fair, welcoming us into the port of peace. Our duties are pressing, time is flying, the whistle and signal bells are sounding, and I must close for this time.

Kindly and sincerely yours,

G. H. COLGROVE.

In 1897, as indicated in the two following letters especial effort was made to secure Brother Colgrove's pardon, which I believe would have been successful but for lack of wisdom on the part of some of his friends. As it was Brother C. was doomed to spend the remainder of his life in bondage.

Waupun, Wis., Oct. 10, 1897.

Dear Mother:

When you were here you offered to call on the Governor of Wisconsin in my behalf. I thank you a thousand times for that kindness.

Since you were here I have been promoted to the position of prison librarian. That places me in the Chaplain's office, and it is the position occupied by the Washburn banker when you were here.

I have received a letter from Mrs. Worcester in Natal, South Africa, lately. It was just thirty-five days in coming through. It was intensely interesting. One of our boys died last night and two life members have died since you were here. One was a Christian.

Dear Mother, the enclosed card shows date, locality and offense. I have been here over twelve years, and have a clear prison record. My Christian work you are well versed in, as you were God's chosen instrument for my conversion. Nine years of Christian life on Nov. 4th next.

If possible please inform me when you will be in Madison, and may our Heavenly Father bless you, and crown your effort with success. My papers are all in the executive chambers at Madison. I have recommendations from many parties, and from my trial judge, Hon. A. Scott Sloan. My jury did not support my application, but the judge did. He is now dead, but he gave me a splendid letter, and it should be just as effective. I shall have to ask you to wait for your reward, until freedom comes to me, and then you will not be forgotten. I hope Sister Kelley can accompany you on your Madison trip.

I received a letter from your friend Miss Josephine Cowgill, Jerusalem, with several cards of Palestine flowers; those that grew in Mount Olivet I have framed and they are hanging in our office.

I am on duty from 5 a. m. to 9 p. m.

Sincerely and kindly yours,

G. H. COLGROVE.

Waupun, Wis., Nov. 7, 1897.

Dear Mother:

Inclosed please find copy of letter just received from Executive Clerk. It will be useful perhaps as a reference when you reach Madison. The entire recommendation from my judge is there as is stated herein. My judge is now deceased. A letter received today from ex-Chaplain T. J. Brown, now of Lancaster, Wisconsin, informs me that he will gladly meet you at Madison, and assist you in any way possible. One of our officers is also making arrangements with a Madison party to join you at that time. So we seem well favored and I regard it as indicative of divine favor, for all the present participants are Christians and we may therefore hope for especial favor from our heavenly Father.

The Lord be with you in all your ways. As ever,

Sincerely yours,

G. H. COLGROVE.

The enclosed letter read as follows:

Executive Chamber, Madison, Wis., Nov. 4, 1897.

Mr. G. H. Colgrove, State Prison, Waupun.

My Dear Sir: I have looked up the matter about which you wrote me on Oct. 21st, and find there is a letter from Judge Sloan among your papers. This letter says, among other things: "If it be true that Mr. Colgrove has behaved himself well during his imprisonment and has thoroughly reformed, I think he ought to be pardoned."

Yours truly,

WM. J. ANDERSON, Private Secretary.

Waupun, Wis., May 1, 1901.

Dear Mother and Sister:

Your kind letters of 24th ult, duly at hand, and as you wrote in unison, I hope this companion letter will be acceptable. I am pleased to learn that your book work is progressing and will soon be launched upon the restless sea of activity, and accomplishing good work under the divine blessing, leading souls into the light that never shall fade while Eternity rolls its unending years. Sorry that so much sickness and suffering has fallen to the lot of each of you, but rejoice that it is passed and can not assail you again in this world, and in the world to come "There shall be no more pain; for the former things are passed away." There, the cheeks which we here beheld pale with suffering and tear-stained by sorrow, will be mantling with the rich glow of everlasting health and radiant in the matchless loveliness of deathless bloom. A refreshing rain has broken a long drouth here, and the world looks lovely and sparkling in the golden sunlight this beautiful May morning. As we behold the face of the earth beautified by the hand of God, it is a source of regret that all this harmony of nature, this smiling peace and bloom, is marred and clouded by the dark stain which iniquity has brought into this fair world; and the sad, stern fact confronts us, that "The dark places of the earth are full of the habitations of cruelty." But it is true. Peace in its entirety, and purity in divine perfection, are fled from this world, and we cannot possess them in full until we have passed beyond Jordan's cold wave and through the dark portals which intervene between this sin-darkened land and the glory crowned hills of Immanuel's Land. But it is a soul-cheering fact that we are daily and hourly nearing that blest clime where sin and sorrow can no more cast the cloud of estrangement between us and the Divine Master who arose triumphant over sin and death and in His eternal majesty and power has gone to prepare for our home coming.

Though our barque of life may be tossed by violent seas of strife, and meet with disaster in various forms, so long as we know that Jesus is awaiting us in the Harbor of Peace we are not dismayed by the howling blast nor raging billows of earthly storm, but relying on His unfailing promise we keep in mind the coming greeting of the great Master and remember

"By cool Siloam's shady rill How fair the lily grows; How sweet the breath beneath the hill Of Sharon's dewy rose."

Yes, Mother, I too am glad and thankful that the Lord sent you to Waupun and into our chapel on that glorious autumn morning, Nov. 4, 1888. Surely the good work then accomplished has not been extinguished, although Satan has exerted himself to cast dark clouds of misunderstanding, strife and contention over it all. But the light of Calvary shines amid the gloom, the heavenly sheen of the cross of Christ sheds a halo of undying and imperishable glory over all, that like the pillar of fire that led the hosts of Israel through the wilderness, will lead and sustain each weary heart, until we arrive on Jordan's banks, and raise the song of everlasting triumph, as we view our eternal home.

With kind regards to each, and best wishes for your happiness and welfare, I remain,

Sincerely and kindly yours,
G. H. COLGROVE.

The following letter from a dear sister who is deeply interested in prison work is inserted here because of its reference to Brother Colgrove:

Minneapolis, Minn., Dec. 19, 1900.

My Dear Mother Wheaton:

I cannot tell you how very glad I was to hear from you; and to know that you have been blest all along the way, is indeed good news. Some one asked the question, "What is the best thing that can be said of a friend?" Many answers were given, one good one being "He rests me," but the best answer was "He inspires me." This can be truly said of you. No one more than yourself inspires me to live a true Christian life. I do want to be ready at all times to serve Christ.

"Just ready to do His bidding, If only I do His will. Then I will be ready to meet him When shadows flee away Ready to serve Him perfectly When dawns eternal day."

Last week we had another meeting at the Soldiers' Home. You cannot imagine how we missed you. So many of the sick men inquired for you. One said if you would only come back he would shout for joy. Of course it made me very happy to know that they had received such a blessing from your talk. This same man said he had prayed for you every night.

The young man that called for you to come out to see him in the jail was sent to St. Cloud for two and a half years. The poor colored man was sent to State's Prison at Stillwater for five years.

The strangest thing has happened since the last time Mrs. —— was at Waupun. Mr. Colgrove's wife, whom he had not heard from for twelve years, has been to see him. His young lady daughter, whom he thought dead, is living. Is not that precious news? I am sure Mr. Colgrove must be the happiest man inside of these walls just now. Had a good letter from S. yesterday.

I have Christmas cards for all of the women and some for the men in the prison. Must say good bye.

Your sincere friend and sister in Christ,
GERTRUDE M.

From an editorial written by Brother Colgrove while editor of the Christian Endeavor Department of the prison paper published at Waupun, we clip the following:

> Perhaps our uninformed friends may infer that we advocate the abolition of all punishment in penal institutions. Not at all, brother; nothing so absurd. But we do claim and will maintain to our dying hour that punishment should be judicious, and only when the culprit will not heed any humane treatment nor be influenced by admonition.
>
> When punishment and imposition are used at the mere caprice of some low down scoundrel, instead of discretionary treatment, at the behest of a man of sense, reason and upright principle, the effect has ever been, and will ever be, to develop the worst traits inherent in the nature of the individual whom the laws have already pronounced unsafe, and when released, the consequences of that development, are going to fall on some innocent and unoffending member of the law-abiding class. When we consider the vast amount of mischief which one criminal can accomplish in an incredibly short space of time, have we not cause to be thankful that all over our land are self-sacrificing souls, brave men and women, who are determined in the face of all opposition, ridicule and every evil, to use every possible means within their power, to elevate and reform all of the criminal class, who may by any means be led from the old path of sorrow and misery to themselves and danger to the peace and well-being of their brother men?
>
> Men and women who will place in the hand of the prisoner the Bible, in exchange for the revolver, dagger and bottle? The citizen in his quiet home, who is unacquainted with the prison systems of the various forms which are being used in different states, depends entirely upon the laws of the land to secure him in the peaceful possession of his accumulated earnings. But experience proves that human law alone and unassisted by higher power *is not sufficient to guard the home from intrusion and desecration by those who have no regard for right principles.* The man who has criminal tendencies, and is not striving to restrain them in conformity to divine law, will laugh the human power to scorn, and trample the law of man under

his feet whenever there seems an opportunity of financial gain thereby. *The man who has been led to observe and rightly regard the divine law will have no occasion for inducement for infringing on the laws of the land.* Therefore these reformers, both clergy and laity, *are striking at the very root of crime, when they lift the fallen out of the slough of vice and iniquity,* and *turn his face toward the higher life and the city "whose maker and builder is God."*

During the fall of 1903 I received several letters telling me that Brother George Colgrove could live but a short time. In December, 1903, I visited again the prison at Waupun. I found Brother Colgrove in the Prison Hospital, very weak in body, but peaceful and resting in the Saviour's love. Once more he related to the young sister who was with me the wonderful story of his conversion; and how for over fifteen years he had been kept by the power of God, saved and filled with love for God and souls. We knelt and prayed with him and sang his favorite hymns and as I bade him farewell he said, "Sister, if we never meet on earth again I will meet you in Heaven."

That was our final parting. Brief notes from the chaplain and warden informed me that Brother Colgrove died February 19, 1904, and that funeral services (an unusual thing) were held in the prison chapel February 21. The warden's letter contains this testimony. "He died a Christian."

Bless God for his sustaining grace that is sufficient even amid the trials of a prison life and enabled this one of his children to prove true to God for so many years, inside of prison walls!

O how wonderful is the power of God to seek and to save that which was lost!

SMELTER AND WORK-SHOPS, CHESTER, ILL.

CHAPTER XI.

Work in Stockades and Prison Camps in Southern States.

During the first years of my missionary work I was led to stay much of the time in the South. I was learning lessons in patience, faith and humility before God. The cross was very heavy. In many places I was not allowed to stay with white people if I preached to the negroes. THE RACE QUESTION ran high and the color line was very closely drawn. In those days I could not understand why this should be. I was taught in the word of God that all nations were made of one blood and that God was the Father of us all. I was ignorant and the views of the southern people were new to me. In many cases, perhaps, I offended them when I might have avoided it. I knew no better and they often thought me obstinate. But I was only obeying God the very best I knew in trying to keep immortal souls out of hell, and I knew that I must obey God though all the people should misunderstand and misjudge me. I found nearly all of the prisoners of the South confined in Stockades and Prison Camps. In many cases the prisons themselves were almost empty.

The following are from among the many letters of introduction and recommendation, received while laboring in the southern states:

Montgomery, Ala., Dec. 30, 1884.

Col. J. T. Milner, Superintendent.

Dear Sir: This will be handed you by Mrs. Wheaton, who is a prison missionary. She has been having religious exercises at the various prisons in the state, and I respectfully request that you will permit her to do so at New Castle.

Yours truly,
R. H. DAWSON,
President Board of Inspectors of Prisons.

Raleigh, N. C., June 10, 1893.

Gulf, N. C., C. F. & Y. V. Railroad, Halifax farm (near Weldon); Captain Bradshaw (near Weldon); Captain McMurray (near Weldon, on canal); Captain McIver (near Tillery); Captain Hamlet (near Tillery); Captain Lashley (near Castle Hayne).

The superintendent desires that every courtesy be shown Mrs. Wheaton and Mrs. ——, and that they be given opportunities to talk to the prisoners.

JNO. M. FLEMING, Warden.

———

Rusk, Texas, Jan. 9, 1888.

Mr. George Egbart, Coling Camp.

Dear Sir: This will introduce to you Mrs. Elizabeth R. Wheaton, prison missionary, who is making a tour through southern prisons. She passed the day with me yesterday in the prison. I was pleased with her manner and with her talk to the men. She wants the privilege of talking with your men today at the dinner hour. I think you will be pleased with her. Please give her the necessary attention and may God bless you, bless her effort, and bless the men.

J. C. WOOLAM, Chaplain.

———

EXECUTIVE DEPARTMENT OF ALABAMA.

Convict Bureau.

Pratt Mines, Ala., Nov. 30, 1889.

Mr. Thomas C. Dawson, Warden of State Prison, Wetumptka, Ala.

Dear Tom: This letter will introduce to you Mrs. Elizabeth R. Wheaton and Mrs. ——, two ladies who are devoting their lives to the benefit of convicts all over the United States.

These good ladies have done much good, and they should be treated with every consideration. Give them rooms and access to your convicts at both prisons. I hope a visit from them will result in much good.

Your Father,
R. H. DAWSON,
President Board of Inspectors.

Huntsville Penitentiary, Huntsville, Texas, Jan. 13, 1892.

Capt. Abercrombie, Wynne Farm.

Dear Sir: This will introduce to you Mrs. Wheaton, who wishes to talk to your men in a body. Any courtesies shown her will be appreciated by me.

> Yours truly,
>
> J. G. SMITHER, Asst. Supt.

STATE OF NORTH CAROLINA.

> Executive Department, Raleigh, June 9, 1893.

Hon. A. Deazer, Supt. State's Prison.

Dear Sir: This introduces Mrs. Elizabeth Rider Wheaton, prison evangelist. I have assured her that you will grant any request she may make not in conflict with prison rules.

> Very respectfully yours,
> ELIAS CARR, Governor.

STATE OF NORTH CAROLINA.

> Executive Department, Raleigh, June 15, 1893.

His Excellency, B. R. Tillman, Governor of South Carolina,

> Columbia, S. C.

Dear Sir: I have the honor and it gives me pleasure to state that Mrs. Elizabeth R. Wheaton and Mrs. ——, prison evangelists, have held religious services at the penitentiary farm and at the penitentiary and have given satisfaction to the authorities in both places, and it is thought that their services were productive of great good. With highest esteem, I am,

> Very truly yours,
> ELIAS CARR, Governor.

STATE OF ALABAMA.

Executive Department, Montgomery, April 3, 1896.

To all Wardens of Prisons within the State:

Elizabeth Rider Wheaton, the bearer hereof, is a prison evangelist, and well recommended as a good lady. She is desirous of holding services in the prisons. Any courtesy shown her will be proper and commendable.

WILLIAM C. OAKES, Governor.

STATE OF GEORGIA.

Penitentiary Department, Atlanta, Georgia, June 30, 1893.

To the Captains in Charge of Convict Camps in Georgia:

I desire that each of you extend to these ladies, Mrs. Wheaton and Mrs. —— any courtesies possible during their stay with you, that they may be given opportunities to talk to the men and women in your charge. I will particularly appreciate any kindness shown them. The governor requests that they be shown courtesies.

GEORGE H. JONES, Principal Keeper.

Penitentiary, Columbia, S. C., August 11, 1893.

Mother Wheaton.

Dear Madam: It affords me much pleasure to say that we were glad to have you come down to the prison and visit other camps connected therewith, and we believe that you have done lasting good among the prisoners.

Yours truly,

W. A. NEAL, Superintendent.

Accompanying the above was a list of the convict camps connected with the prison with the following order:

The sergeant in charge of the above camps will please admit Mrs. E. R. Wheaton and Mrs. —— and allow them to hold religious service at the camp with the convicts.

W. A. NEAL.

STATE OF FLORIDA.

Executive Department, Tallahassee, April 21, 1894.

Messrs. West Bros., West Farm, Fla.

Gentlemen: This will be presented by Mrs. Elizabeth Rider Wheaton, prison evangelist, who is visiting the convict camps of the state. Any courtesies and kindness extended to her will be duly appreciated and reciprocated by,

Yours very respectfully,
D. LANG, Private Secretary.

STATE OF GEORGIA.

Penitentiary Department, Atlanta, Ga., March 21, 1896.

To the Captains in Charge of Convict Camps in Georgia:

I desire that each of you extend to Mrs. Wheaton and Mrs. —— any courtesies possible during their stay with you, that they may have an opportunity to talk with the prisoners. Any kindness shown them will be appreciated by this office.

JAKE C. MOORE, Assistant Keeper Penitentiary.

Executive Department, Governor's Office, Jackson, Miss.

Mr. J. J. Evans, Jr., Penitentiary.

Dear Sir: Mrs. Elizabeth Wheaton, who is interested in reform work, desires to talk to the convicts. Any courtesy shown her will be highly appreciated.

Very truly yours,

J. J. COMAN, Governor's Sec.

A STOCKADE.

Many inquire of me what a stockade or prison camp is. I will here explain. A man, or party of men, lease or hire from the state the labor of a certain number of prisoners for a certain length of time. They are "doing time," as the prisoners say, for the state. Both men and women are thus leased out. Their labor is used in clearing up land, working in cotton and sugar cane fields, in mines, in turpentine camps, in building railroads, on brick-yards, in phosphate works or in any place where a company can work together. Their food consists mostly of swine's flesh and corn bread made with meal, water and salt.

The stockades are large rough wooden buildings, erected by the lessee, in which the prisoners are confined at night. The men are generally chained by one ankle to a heavy chain which reaches through the center of the building from one end to the other, being securely fastened to strong posts. They usually sleep on the floor in the same clothing worn through the day—which is generally very scant and poor; but sometimes they may have a bunk and a rough dirty blanket. The stockade is guarded by men with loaded guns, and besides this every camp is abundantly supplied with great, strong bloodhounds. And woe to the unfortunate criminal that must be tracked and caught by them!

Each prison camp has its mode of punishment for those who break the rules or fail to do as much as is allotted to them. The keepers of past years were often very cruel in their treatment, and seemed to enjoy the punishment which they inflicted upon those under their control. These poor souls had no way of redress. If they should speak of the cruelty, they would be treated far worse; the penalty for such a complaint being a severe whipping. Oh, God, how long shall the cry of the prisoner be heard? Lord Jesus, come quickly!

Each camp has its officers, guards, etc., among whom is the whipping boss. And God pity the man or woman who falls into his cruel hands. There is a board of prison inspectors, the president of which travels from place to place looking after the interests of all. The conditions of the stockades are much improved since I first went among them years ago. I have gone to the governors of different states and pleaded for the betterment of conditions in the prisons. Especially have I asked that the women might have better treatment and not be whipped so brutally for slight offenses or violation of the rules which the lessee is allowed to make. Upon one occasion I wrote the governor of a certain state as follows:

Washington, D. C., May 10, 18—.

To His Excellency the Governer of ——.

Dear Brother: I write in behalf of the prisoners in your state prison at B. M. I find them greatly in need of food and clothing. The sick prisoners are suffering with hunger. I held services there one week ago today, and went into the kitchen myself to see what there was for sixteen sick men and those who are supposed to wait on them, and I found only one half gallon of milk a day for all, one chicken, very poor bread, no vegetables, no fruits, and no seasoning but salt. Who is to blame for this? I find you feed those prisoners (miners and farmers) on seven cents a day.

It is an outrage, a sin, a curse on this nation, the suffering you men, you governors or officers, at least allow to exist in prison walls. You permit those men in B. M. prison to be whipped for not furnishing daily from three to five small car loads of coal each, and feed them on food not sufficient to give them strength to perform that amount of labor. God help you, my friend! As you are the first officer of the state you should see that this inhuman treatment is stopped.

Forty men were whipped in one day on two occasions, and on an average there are from six to eight every day. These men are not murmuring, I gave them no chance to tell me of this. But the officers and their wives told me. I saw with my own eyes. The water in those mountains is very impure and many of the men have died from mere neglect. Many more will die soon unless something is done for their relief. Governor, for God's sake, please look after the temporal interests of your prisoners. I would have come to you face to face and talked these things over if possible. Recently I have been to see governors of several of the different states. They are not aware of the treatment of convicts in their own states, but I have seen it all these years of my pilgrimage. The awful suffering I see is just breaking my heart. Poor lost men and women! Who is responsible for the sin and crime and suffering? Largely the saloon. Men and women are born in sin and conceived in iniquity; shut in for years and years for some little crime, and subjected to the hardest labor, serving out sentence in prison under whip and lash. It is inhuman and unjust. What will God Almighty require of you and me in the day of judgment, For surely we must meet it and answer for our stewardship here on earth. May God help me to deal faithfully and do my duty by all classes—to those in authority as well as those in bondage. Now, understand me, I have no personal grievances to bring to you. It is simply mismanagement and the desire to run these prisons on as cheap a scale as possible, to save money for the State and hold position; and something must be done soon.

I told the men to be obedient and faithfully discharge their duty as prisoners. In all my work in every state and territory, Europe, Mexico and Canada, I have never had any trouble; and can go again to all these prisons where I have held services. What object have I? None, but the good of the souls and bodies of those in bonds. They are my children, given me by the Lord, and I feel as much compassion for them as you would for your child. All the officers and people were kind to me and treated me with the utmost respect. All I desire is that you obey God and cause this starving and brutal treatment to cease. Please say nothing of this letter but investigate for yourself and see if these things are not so. Two meals a day (and very little then) for a sick man is not enough.

Yours for humanity,

MRS. E. R. WHEATON, Prison Evangelist.

The following is an extract from the letter I received in reply to the above, from the general manager of the prison mines referred to:

———, ———., ——— 22, 18—.

Mrs. Elizabeth R. Wheaton.

Dear Madam: Your letter of recent date addressed to Gov. ——— was referred to me. I regret exceedingly that you did not call at my office on the occasion of your visit. While there is a great deal of truth in your letter there is much that indicates that you were innocently misled by statements of convicts. I know that you must be a good woman, that your heart is in your work, and from your wide experience, amply capable of advising and instructing one like me. In undertaking the task of uniting to bring our prison systems in this state to a humane basis, we have done more than you can understand. Had you been familiar with the conditions during the past thirty years under the lease system you would realize that much has been accomplished even in the short time we have been at work. I realize that more is yet to be done. But "Rome was not built in a day." The public has got to be educated as well as individuals in immediate charge. I hope therefore you will be patient, and will be only too glad to see and confer with you should you again visit us here. In the meantime I beseech your earnest sympathy and prayers for proper guidance in our work, for I assure you that it is one that requires such moral support as only such as you can fully understand and appreciate. With great respect, I am,

Yours, etc., ———.

PLEA FOR WOMEN CONVICTS.

In some instances women are made to do the farm work, work in brick yards, and to do other kinds of hard work. At one place in the south the women cultivated a thousand acres of cotton, doing other farming and caring for the stockade, horses, mules, cows and hogs and having only men to guard them. They were not allowed a woman matron to care for them when they were sick or dying. I found them in rags and tatters and looking almost like wild beasts. I went to the governor of that state and pleaded with him for my own sex. I begged him to protect the poor women from such cruel treatment and brutal punishment. I asked him to have them taken in from the farm, where they were clearing up the land and compelled to carry logs, to the state prison at the Capitol which was nearly empty, and given proper work and humane treatment.

WOMAN CONVICT AT WORK.

Once upon my knees before a governor I begged him to take the women from the stockades to the prison walls at the capital, and place them under the care of a good matron and give them such work as women should do. Also that they be properly clothed and fed and taught morals and religion. I said, "For the sake of young men which you now employ to control and guard these women, won't you do this?" (I had found several young babes, born in this place.) He promised that he would see that this was done.

But a year later I found these women still in the fields laboring and suffering as before. I again went to the governor. He was now so changed I hardly knew him. I said to him, "Well, governor, I see the affairs of state wear heavily upon you. You look ten years older than you did a year ago when I was here. Why did you not fulfill your promise to me about transferring those women from the stockades to the prison here at the capital? I promised that I would not make public the condition in which I found them if you would look after them. You promised to have them treated better, but it is just the same now." He was surprised at my knowledge of affairs and my firmness and tried to excuse himself, and said that he had brought some of them away to the prison.

Upon one occasion in later years, in a place I had visited for some years, I found that an old colored woman had been tied to a log and severely whipped on the bare flesh. The other women could not bear to see her so cruelly treated, and silently cried unto God to take the cruel captain who had ordered her so punished out of the way. He did so; for when I arrived there in a few days he was struck with death and soon died. God did not allow him to compel the whipping of any more women.

I think that upon only one occasion was I ever treated other than kindly and with respect by any governor. In this case I insisted that the women prisoners, especially, should be more humanely treated. The governor refused to take any action regarding the cruelties practiced but said, "Go to the Principal Keeper." I replied, "I have just come from the Principal Keeper and he sent me to you, Governor. These captains are not permitted to strike one blow without a license from you. It is by your permission that they whip and punish them." He was evidently annoyed to think that I so well understood the condition of the prisons and their management. It was now election time and he was running for office for another term, and he dismissed me without further ado. Many like him are saying: "Am I my brother's keeper?" Yes, you and I dear reader, and those in authority will surely have to answer in the great day of reckoning, if we neglect to alleviate the sufferings of our fellowmen, when it is in our power to do so. There are many kind men in office who really desire better conditions of affairs, but are only servants of those who are higher in authority. Truly the penalty for crime must be paid, but give all a chance to reform and do right before God and man. Can we not let poor fallen human beings see that we do care for them? And that there is hope in Christ for them if they will repent and confess their sin to Him? Did He not come "to seek and to save that which was lost?"

BLOOD HOUNDS.

I never will forget my feelings when first the howls of the bloodhounds sounded in my ears. I was in a stockade and there was a noise such as I never heard before. I was on my knees praying and the wife of the captain came in saying, "There has been an escape and the guards and dogs are after the convict." I just lifted my heart to the Lord in prayer for the poor unfortunate, hunted man. I never stopped to think whether white or black; old or young; innocent or guilty; my one cry was for the life and safety of my boy.

Mothers you know how you would feel were it your boy. Well, I got initiated in that part of prison management that day. I have one thought above all others and that is to do God's will and obey Him and help all in anyway I can into a good life here and a home in Heaven at last; poor heart-sick, home-sick and sin-sick souls. The very thought of the convict being helpless should appeal to our sympathy and God, the Judge of all the universe, is going to call us to give an account for our stewardship. Men and women must be governed but not by brute force. We may overpower them, but do we conquer them? Have we won them to a better life and to good citizenship?

CONVICTS GETTING OUT COAL.

COAL MINES.

The prison stockades vary in number. Sometimes there may be thirty or forty in one state, sometimes probably not half that many. It depends upon the number of prisoners in the penitentiary and into how many sections they are divided. When I was at Coal City, Ga., a number of years ago, it was one of the most weird and desolate-looking places in which I had ever found a stockade located. There were three stockades on the summit of the mountain, and one at its base. At the last place the men were mining coal. When I first went there they used a small car that would hold eight passengers. Then this was abandoned and we were obliged to ride on the engine, as they carried only coal cars for shipping the coal that was mined by the prisoners. I was often in great danger of my clothes taking fire as the fire blazed out of the engine when the men were shoveling in the coal. The railroad zig-zagged up the mountain, and once, a sister and myself were obliged to ride on the coal-box, as the engine was packed with men and one woman before we had arrived from the other train. I had to kneel down and hold onto the side of the coal box with both hands, and as the engine twisted and turned, I was in danger of falling, and it was hundreds of feet down to the foot of the precipices in places where our train crept along. All the way up the mountain I prayed God to protect us. The train was run by prisoners, yet I always felt safe with them.

A TOUCHING INCIDENT.

"Lady, is you a preacher? Coz, if you is, I want you to come over to my house 'long wid me and make a prayer, coz my mother is dead, and my father is in prison over the stockade wall, and they are goin' to bury my mother, and there ain't nobody to make a prayer, 'cept a colored woman who was kind to my mother and loved her coz she was good. We children ain't got nobody to care for us."

It was just as I was leaving the railroad station near the Pratt Mine prison stockade in Alabama that I was accosted as above. The speaker was a small white boy with hands and face so black with coal dust that one could hardly tell that he was white. The sadness of that child's voice touched my heart, and I said, "Yes, surely I will be glad to go with you, my child."

Through the mountain forest the little boy had come in search of some one to make a prayer over the dead mother who, while she was living, had taught her children about Jesus. I found the cabin by his guiding me along the mountain path through the underbrush. Such a sight as met my eyes! A body covered with a ragged sheet, lying on a board held up by a couple of rickety stools. Nothing was in the hut to make it look like home. Two old crones sat by the stump fire in the large fireplace, making free use of snuff and tobacco. It was a dirty little one-roomed cabin. The funeral was to be at once, but the man who was making the rough box which was to serve as a coffin was so slow that we finally waited for the funeral till the next day.

I went to the prison camp and found the husband and father of the little boy, and obtained permission of the officials for him to attend the funeral of his wife, providing that I should be responsible for his return. Well, God understood it all and helped me there in that wild country; for that was when the prison stockades were not what they are today. Conditions are much changed since I first went with a gospel message to those lonely prisoners and sin-bound souls.

MY FIRST MEETING IN A PRISON CAMP.

That night I held my first service in a prison camp. The captain was loth to allow me the privilege, but the Lord touched his heart and he said that I might try. I had come a long distance on the train and had taken little to eat for several days for those were days of much fasting and prayer. The call of God was upon me. I must preach the Gospel to these men. So now, I had but one thing to do, to wait alone upon the Lord. I knelt before God in the little old wooden hut used as an office, and cried to the Lord, "O Lord, help me! O Lord, help me! Show me how to hold a meeting here!" Just after dark a guard came and said, "We are ready for the meeting to begin. Come on." Imagine how I felt when there alone before hundreds of men in rags and tatters, with hands and faces so black and grimy with coal dust (this being in a prison mining camp) that I could scarcely tell the white men from the colored! The building was low and dirty, the men were seated on rude benches, the guards standing with their guns in hand and many great strong bloodhounds by their sides. The room was dimly lighted by three smoky old lanterns hanging on the walls. I had conducted prayer meetings in the church, led in temperance meetings, and labored with church people in the cities, and had been a Sabbath school teacher for years; but I had never before faced a congregation such as I now saw before me. I knelt in silent prayer before stepping upon the rough old box upon which I was to stand while I spoke. I arose and sang an old-time hymn, and again knelt and offered prayer. I told God all about why I was there. I sang another hymn, but could go no farther. All eyes were fixed upon me, and I asked, "Is there one Christian here? If so please raise your hand." I stood trembling and thought, "Must I stand all alone here with no one to pray for me, or encourage me in my labor for the Master?" At last one old colored man timidly raised his hand, followed by another, and then another. How I thank God even now for this—after all these years of toil as a prison worker. Then, I was soon lost in the theme of Jesus and His love. I seemed to see those rough prison miners as dear children once more in the old home at mother's knee at night-fall listening to her "Now I lay me down to sleep." As I closed, seeing that the Lord had spoken to many hearts by His

Holy Spirit, I asked who would kneel with me in prayer and begin a new life. I think every prisoner bowed there before God with the heavy prisoners' chains clanking as only such can do. The sound is inexpressibly sad to me even now after so many years of labor in prisons and the rattling of the great keys in the hand of the guard and the sound of the heavy iron doors as they open and close, receiving "some mother's boy," are still as affecting to me as in those early days of my prison work.

Many of these men on that night in humility and meekness sought and confessed Christ as their Savior. I know not how many who knelt with me there, I shall meet in heaven; but I know that God has said His Word shall not return unto Him void. "He that goeth forth and weepeth, bearing precious seed, shall doubtless come again with rejoicing, bringing his sheaves with him."

At the close of the service an officer informed me that his wife had prepared to entertain me. I gladly accepted of the kind offer and went to their humble home, greatly enjoying their hospitality, for I was much exhausted and very weary with the long journey, the anxiety and the labor of the day. These remained my faithful friends while I knew them. I thank God for those who open their homes to the children of the Lord.

The next morning the lady said, "I will let my little girl go with you to the funeral and to show you the way through the mountains to visit the sick." So I went again to the miserable home of the poor little ones who were left worse than orphans. How my heart was filled with sorrow, seeing the lonely helpless children, two boys and a beautiful little girl, with mother dead, and father in prison! I wondered what their future might be. A few mountaineers' wives had assembled, but there were not enough men present to lift the box that contained the corpse into the old coal wagon. After the short, sad services, with my assistance as a pall bearer the crude coffin was lifted into the wagon, and I helped to steady it as we traveled over the rough mountain road to the cemetery. I had double duty caring for this and making sure that the husband and father did not attempt to escape; for you know liberty is sweet. The Lord of hosts must have kept him true to his promise, and I must say that I can always trust the poor prisoners not to betray the confidence I place in them. At the grave I sang the old hymn. "I would not live always" and we laid the faithful wife and mother away to rest until the trumpet shall call the dead to rise.

What was the cause of the sad plight of this family? Sin. The saloon! There had been a saloon fight, and some one was killed. Some one did the deed. Oh, God! What a reckoning there will be in the end for those who vote to license the saloon, as well as they who dispense the rum, God will open the books and all shall be judged out of the things that are written therein.

"Vengeance is mine, I will repay, saith the Lord of hosts." This faithful wife and mother had spent all her living in an attempt to secure the liberty of her husband. But failing in this, she had come with her children to live in that dreary place, hoping to be able to lead him to a better life, finally dying in want, and of a broken heart. After the funeral I pleaded with the little girl to go with me. But she true to her trust, true to her dead mother's loyalty, said, "Never will I leave my poor father with no one to care for him. Mother never would, I never will. I will go to see him and tell him of Jesus."

Wearied with toil and the journeying from place to place to visit the sick to whom the little girl from the camp had guided me, I returned in the evening with her to her home and then to the camp. Thinking to lie down and take some rest, and kneeling to pray, I was impressed that I must visit the other stockade some two or three miles away. I knew it was the voice of God and said, "Yes." The lady strongly pleading that I must not go, that it was dangerous, said I could not go alone, that I would lose my way, etc. The husband also said one's life was in danger, that several men were found dead in those mountains and no one knew who killed them, etc., and pleaded with me not to go. But I said, "If God sends me, He will see that I am not harmed. He will not forsake me." Soon I started on my way, and presently met the two little boys whose mother had just been buried. I asked if one of them would not show me the way to the other camp, and the older one kindly did so. With my little guide we hurried down that rough mountain side, we being compelled to carry stones to build a bridge across a stream of water, and finally came within sight of the camp. Upon insisting that God had sent me, and that I had held services in the other camp, the captain (overseer) invited me into his home. I had not expected such kindness, but thanking the Lord I accepted it as from Him. They kindly brought us food, but I would not eat, and gave it all to the little boy who was so hungry, and praying for him he started homeward. Here also we had a wonderful meeting. Men with broken hearts wept with longing for a mother's sympathy and a Savior's love. Some came to Christ and were saved, and I believe that I shall meet some of them in the great home gathering bye and bye in heaven.

Early the following morning, I was told that the engine which was to take me on my way was ready to start with its train of coal cars for the station some ten miles distant; but that I would have time to visit the hospital department where many were lying sick. I hurried through the prison yard, filled with hogs and bloodhounds, to the hospital, where I sang a song and prayed. I was turning to go when a guard came running and said, "The whole train is waiting for you, hurry up." As I was hurrying out a door opened and a woman called, "Do come and see my son, he is dying. Do come and pray for him." I ran in saying, "The train may go; I dare not refuse the request." I grasped the dying boy's hand firmly and said, "Take hold on God as I take hold of your hand. He will not forsake you. He will save you; look and live." I offered a short prayer and ran down to the engine, which still waited. There was something seeming so dismal in its sound in those lonely regions. I had to ride on the engine, as there was nothing but coal flats on this train. I was helped on and we were off. The sun was just rising over the mountain and the heavy fog was beginning to rise, and oh, such a blessing I received as we sped along the winding way! I shall never forget the gloomy sight I left behind me there. The poor prison-bound men marching out to the mines with their lanterns on their caps and with their picks and shovels. They never seemed so dear to me, and I began to see more clearly than ever that God had a special work for me to do. I saw the value of a soul bought with the precious blood of Christ. I saw, too, the need of fully consecrated Christian workers. As we wound around the mountain side I knew I had been obedient to my God, and His Spirit bore witness with my spirit that He accepted my weak efforts.

DIFFICULTIES OVERCOME.

I was not always kindly received as mentioned in some instances. We are not carried to heaven upon flowery beds of ease. I have many times been refused the privilege even of singing a hymn in a prison. My singing has often been blessed as a means of touching hearts, and through it souls have been converted and are still true to God. I went to visit another prison mining camp or stockade, in a very lonely region where few people lived. I arrived upon a dark, gloomy night; there was no depot and not a house near. There I was alone, yet not alone, for God was with me. A young mulatto man who proved to be an ex-convict, had come to the train with a lantern, and I asked him to kindly show me the way to the home of the captain of the camp. I found the officer had gone in search of a prisoner who had made his escape, and his wife refused to take any one in in her husband's absence. She said I should go to another officer some distance away. Ascending the steps to the large house my heart sank within me, for I felt that I should be turned away again in the night. The officer himself came to the door to answer my call. Telling him my mission, I asked to stay with them till morning. His wife would not consent to entertain me, and I answered, "Where shall I go? I am alone, and a Christian woman sent of God to help people in prison to a better life." He replied, "There's a boarding house a mile away down the mountain," and the door was shut. I asked my guide, "Is there not one Christian here in these mountains?" He said, "Only one, a poor old colored man, that's been in prison, and he lives up the mountain with his daughter, a young woman." Crying as I went along holding to the brush with one hand, we finally reached the hut at the top of the mountain. I told the young woman my story and asked if I might stay with her for the night. She answered, "No, my father is away and I cannot take in a stranger without his consent." "Then I must stay out on the mountain alone all night." She seemed sorry for me, and said I should wait till her father came. I had not to wait long till he came, and kindly consented for me to stay. I was weary and hungry from my long journey. I saw the old colored man open the basket he had brought home with him. It contained some cold food given him where he was employed. He asked me to share his lunch, but I refused, as I believed he needed all he had.

How thankful I was for shelter in that poor hut that night, though sleeping by my side was that poor unfortunate colored girl with a babe in her arms that cried all the night. There were cracks in the hut through which you could see the stars. What a change the Lord had wrought in the once proud woman that I had been! I remembered that Jesus said, "Foxes have holes, and birds of the air have nests; but the Son of man hath not where to lay his head." And "The disciple is not above his master." I spent the night in prayer and God heard my cries for the poor convicts who were cruelly starved and beaten by the drunken guards and captain who seemed to bitterly hate all who were so helplessly bound under them. This is a strong statement but I will meet it at the Judgment.

In the morning one woman who had turned me from her door sent to find out what had become of me. She said she would give the young woman who had sheltered me a present for not leaving me out on the mountain alone. I had prayed earnestly that God would convict her for her lack of hospitality. Upon going to the officer to learn when I could have a meeting with the prisoners, he unkindly turned me away saying that I should *never* have a meeting there, and that I might as well go.

Well, I did go; traveling eighty miles back to the capital, Montgomery, Alabama, to see the Governor. I knew the Lord had sent me, and how could I meet Him at the Judgment and tell Him I had failed? I knew, too, that Satan had hindered. I asked for the Governor but was told that the President of the Board of Prison Inspectors was the proper person for me to see about the matter. He was sent for and soon came. He was a very kind old gentleman and sat down and asked me what I wished. When I had related the facts he said, "Who dare refuse you holding meetings in that prison camp? You go back there and hold your meeting. I'll write him a letter and let him hear from me." I said, "But he will say he did not receive your letter." He then said he would write a letter for me to present to him. But, how should I get back to the camp? After selling my trunk and such articles of clothing as I could spare, I yet did not have enough money to pay railway fare.

MY FIRST FREE PASS.

Trusting the Lord to in some way provide means for me to get back to the camp, I went to the janitress of the depot, an intelligent mulatto, and told her of my need, as she had previously assisted me in securing half-fare rates on the railroad, she having known the officials since their childhood. She insisted that I should go to the office of the general manager of the L. & N. R. R. and ask for a half-fare rate to the prison camp at New Castle, Ala. Oh, how I dreaded to go to that office! But tremblingly and prayerfully I went, and presenting to him the letter which I was to carry with me to the camp, I told him my desires. Upon reading this letter he handed me what I supposed was a half-fare permit. I humbly thanked him and returned to my lodging. After making preparation to start early in the morning on my journey, before retiring for the night I knelt by my bedside to thank God for the permit. Thinking I would see just how it read before I prayed, I took it up and began reading, "Pass Mrs. *Elizabeth R. Wheaton* From *Montgomery* to *Birmingham, Ala., Prison, Missionary.*" What! Did my eyes deceive me, or was it a mistake. No. It was a free pass, and the following note was enclosed to the Superintendent at the other end of the route regarding a return pass if I should ask for it:

Louisville & Nashville Railroad Co.,
Montgomery, Ala., Jan. 15, 1885.

L. Hage, Esq., Supt., Birmingham, Ala.

Dear Sir: This lady, Mrs. Elizabeth Wheaton, bears credentials showing her to be a prison missionary. Any courtesy you may extend to her, in the way of pass, will be properly applied.

Yours truly,

M. S. BELKNAP, Supt.

Oh, how I did thank God for this manifestation of His goodness to me— doing above that which I could ask or think! Mr. Belknap, that kind R. R. officer, has been dead many years, and perhaps is forgotten by some who knew him better than I, but I shall never forget his unexpected kindness to me. Since then, through the goodness of God and the favor and confidence of the railroad officials, I have received transportation throughout the country, to carry the Gospel of Jesus to men and women of every class.

Upon my return to the prison camp I asked for the officer and told him I had come to hold meeting for the prisoners. I suppose he had received word from the Governor's office, as he so readily consented, asking at what hour I would like to have the service. I thought best to wait till the following day (Sunday) for the services, that I might have sufficient time for my work. The Lord came in mighty power that Sabbath day as I sang the old time hymns, and asked God to forgive and help those precious souls. The Spirit gave me utterance and carried the truth to the hearts of the hearers. Sobs and groans were heard from men in tears who sought forgiveness and gave God their hearts. At the close I took each one by the hand and exhorted them to be faithful to God. I afterwards visited the sick and talked and prayed with them, exhorting them to seek a home in heaven where sin can never come, and where God wipes away all tears. How true the words,

"Down in the human heart, crushed by the tempter, Feelings lie buried that grace can restore; Touched by a loving heart, wakened by kindness, Chords that were broken will vibrate once more."

One Sunday morning I was going to a prison camp to hold meeting. There was no way to get there excepting to walk through the deep mud. There were a couple of boys going towards the stockade leading an old mule. I said, "O, boys, CAN'T I RIDE THAT MULE?" "Certainly," they said. It was with difficulty that I mounted the novel conveyance, and that I remained on the mule's back. For some reason, I was filled with apprehension. I had an impression that there was danger. I asked the boys if they would not lead the animal, but they kept a good distance from it, saying that they wanted to keep out of the mud.

When we reached the camp and the officers came out and helped me to dismount, they looked at me in great astonishment, and one of them said, "What a narrow escape you have made! I only wonder that you got here alive. It is a wonder that old mule didn't kill you. I wonder that the boys let you take it!" I learned that the animal was so utterly uncontrollable and vicious that they could only use him on a dump cart to carry the prisoners' dinner or something of the sort and then he would sometimes kick the cart all to pieces.

I raised my heart in thanksgiving to God, knowing that He who stopped the lion's mouth and held the flames of the fiery furnace had in some way kept this ugly creature from doing me any harm and saved my life.

CHAPTER XII.

Work in Stockades and Prison Camps—Continued.

I once had a novel experience in a prison lumber camp. I was being entertained at the home of the superintendent of the camp and was to hold service with the prisoners at twilight. The superintendent came to the parlor and asked if I was ready for the service. We had not far to go, but I was unable to walk the distance; so a carriage, drawn by some of the prisoners, had been brought to the gate for me. I answered that I was ready, but as I was waiting he again asked if I was ready and why I was waiting. I replied that I was waiting for the horses. He answered, "You come on, the horses will be all right." I had learned to obey the officers, so followed on down through the beautiful yard of flowers and reluctantly stepped into the carriage. Instantly four prisoners took hold of the carriage and we were off. The men seemed glad to assist me and I was so thankful to them. God bless them! I do not think a queen with all her body-guard could have felt more secure or have been more appreciated, than I, there surrounded by my dear prison boys. After the service I was conveyed in the same manner back to the home of the superintendent.

At another time, desiring to visit a certain prison camp, I found there was no way to reach it but to ride on a flat car with the men going from their work. I was glad to go with them and have a chance to speak a word of kindness and sing some hymns that might cheer them on the way.

In the pineries of Florida the stockade prisoners are engaged in taking the sap from the pine trees. The camps are located some miles apart, and in going from one to another the forests are so dense that we were compelled to go in a two-wheeled donkey-cart. We encountered great dangers, there being many poisonous reptiles and alligators in the lakes and rivers which we had to pass.

ASSISTING A COLORED MINISTER.

I arrived one Sunday morning at a stockade where hundreds of men and some women were kept. I went to the keeper, or captain, as he was called, and asked for the privilege of holding a gospel service with the prisoners under his charge. He not only refused me, but was abusive, cursing me and ordering me away. Of course I was much grieved, as I felt the Lord had sent me there to preach the gospel. I was greatly surprised that an official should use such language to a lady, and without provocation. Weeping, I asked if I might sing for the women prisoners. Again, with oaths, he refused me. But Brother Frank Joseph, a colored preacher who knew me, was there to hold religious services by permission of the governor, and he came and invited me to assist him. Of course the captain could say nothing against it and I went with him. But when he asked me to conduct the service I could not at the first sing, preach or pray for weeping, but I told him I would pray God to give them a kinder officer for I knew the one they had was a cruel man. God used even my weakness and my tears to touch their hearts and we had a blessed meeting.

After service I had a chance to talk to the women prisoners. We wept together and oh how thankful they were that there was one woman who would try to help them and make their burdens lighter. They told me how terribly they were treated and said they would be beaten if the captain knew of their telling me of it. How glad I was to carry the message of Jesus' love to them in their distress. Before I left they said they wished they had something to give me, and some gave small tokens of their regards. It was all they had to give and when they urged me I accepted them as from the Lord, feeling that He would in some way reward them and bless their offering as He did the widow's mite.

THROUGH DANGER ALONE.

Desiring to reach another stockade some miles distant I asked the captain if he could not supply me with conveyance and a guide, but he refused. I determined, however, to find the other prison and started on foot alone. The prison women told me that it was very dangerous because of fierce dogs and cross cattle in the mountains; but feeling that God wanted me to go I knew no such thing as fail. After walking some distance I sank down with exhaustion under a big tree and wept out my heart to God for guidance, protection and success. I arose feeling strengthened and comforted and soon came to a farm house and asked a young man who stood in the garden if he could direct me to the prison camp. "Yes, come in, lady, you look so tired and faint and my mother will give you something to eat and we will show you the way," was the kind reply I received. I stopped and rested a while but would neither eat nor drink as I had given myself to fasting and prayer that my way might be opened for services in the camp to which I was going. After a long walk we found the stockade and knowing the young man who was with me, the officers gave their consent for me to hold a service. After I had been singing and talking to the prisoners a while suddenly my strength failed me. I had only time to say, "Will you sing?" Then I saw and heard nothing more. I HAD FALLEN PROSTRATE among those chained prisoners. When I came to myself I heard singing from inside the walls, such singing as could only come from truly broken-hearted, repentant souls. I had been carried outside and the poor prison women were caring for me. A good old colored sister was holding me close to her and pleading with God to restore me. I heard her say, "She's a woman like we is—and she's given her life for us." They were doing all they knew and were crying around me. I said, "Please carry me back into the prison." When they had done so I asked, "How many of you prisoners will kneel with me in prayer and give your hearts to God, take Him as your Savior and start today for heaven? God loves you, Jesus died for you! And if you will come to Him and confess your sins He will save you." Every one knelt before God, and many with prayers and broken sobs cried out their hearts to Him who is not willing that any should perish, but that all should have eternal life. I expect to meet many of them in heaven; for He is able to save to the uttermost all that will come unto God by Him—and able also to keep them from falling.

The following day, traveling from this prison to another stockade, sitting near me in the car was an aged gentleman who on seeing my Bible asked me where I was going. When I had told him, he asked me the nature of my work and how the prisoners were treated in these places; also how I was received by the officials of the prisons generally. Thinking to only entertain a kind old country gentleman, I told him many things which I probably should not have been so free to mention had I known who he was. He asked me many questions about the stockades. I told him that I had never been so cruelly treated as at a camp on the previous day. "Where," he inquired, "Who did such a thing?" In answer to his inquiry I told him who it was. Little did I know that this was God's way of revealing sin.

A MEETING AT DAY DAWN.

Reaching the small station at the foot of the mountain; we had to take a box car only large enough for six persons. The old gentleman was one of the passengers also. Going to the house of the captain at the top of the mountain (such a lonely place), he thought it impossible to have a meeting with the men, as he said they were so wicked and unruly, etc., but finally said I might do so at day-break the next morning. He was very careful, saying, "These men are so wicked and cruel that never could a woman stand before them." I wept and prayed most of the night and cried, "Oh God, can you let me fail now?" In those early years of my labor I traveled much alone but later I usually had a sister accompany me, or sometimes a sister and her husband.

Out in the prison yard at break of day I found hundreds of men all ready to go down into the coal mines. I wondered how to gain their attention and make them all hear my voice. I asked to have the men drawn closer together, as they stood in the prison yard. This being done, I sang a hymn. Oh how I do praise God for the gift of song! I forgot my weird surroundings and the rough appearance of the men and their dangerous looks. I saw them as little boys in the old home far away and then as human souls, hurrying into the presence of God and I felt that I stood between them and the Judgment. Conceive, if you can, how this company must have looked to me, bound in companies of perhaps fifty in a "gang," to a long strong chain to which was fastened a number of shorter chains; these short chains being fastened to the men's ankles.

God enabled me to deliver His message and eternity alone will reveal the results of the seed scattered there that morning. After shaking hands with the men I was introduced to the old gentleman whom I had met on the train the day before. To my surprise he proved to be the President of the Board of Prison Inspectors of the state. I saw him no more after that time, but a year later I visited the prison of which I had told him. I saw at the depot a young colored man nicely dressed, but I knew by his clothes that he was one of the prison boys. He had come to get the morning paper for the warden. I walked with him to the prison, and on the way asked him how they all were at the camp. "All so nicely, thank you," he replied. "Who is your captain now?" I asked. "Has there been any change since I was here last year?" "O yes, ma'am, soon after you was here ma'am, just as soon as Massa (meaning the President of the Board) could find a good man to take de place ob de ole captun what treated de men so bad and 'bused you so, he sent him away." "Oh, is that so?" I said. "Yes, an' we's got a good time now to what we had befo' God sent you heah ma'am. He certainly did send you heah ma'am dat time." So I had only suffered these indignities that these abused ones might have better officers and treatment. The new captain received me very kindly and giving me a seat said my breakfast would be ready as soon as the prison women could prepare it for me. Well, surely the Lord had been at work. Such a change all around! We had a grand meeting and much good was accomplished, the captain furnished a buggy to take me to the next camp and bring me back to the depot.

HELPING TO BURY A PRISONER.

After visiting the hospital department of a stockade where I had never been before, I saw the guards nailing up a long, apparently heavy, box. I said to them, "What have you in that box?" One replied, "A man—a dead man." Soon after I heard an officer say to a guard, "Send five prisoners to go with me to bury that box." I arose from where I had been praying, and hurried out and asked permission to accompany the men with the box, but was refused—the officer saying they had no guard to spare to assist me up the mountain side. "Oh, just please let me go," I said. "I do not need any one to help me to climb the mountain. Please, won't you let me go?" He then consented, and I did not wait for either bonnet or help; but with my shawl over my head I hurried out after the men bearing the corpse. On we went up the mountain side, until we came to a very steep place, and the poor weak prisoners began to tremble under the heavy burden, along in front of the guard who had his gun in hand. I knew if one should fall, the guard might suppose he was trying to escape from him, and fire at him and kill him.

I took up a stick in my left hand to steady myself and placing my right arm under the end of the box added my strength to that of the tired men. When we reached the summit of the mountain we found the grave already dug, but it was much too short for the box. I was almost exhausted and came near falling. The grave being too short, they were going to leave the corpse until morning and then return and bury it. But I said, "Boys, you dig the grave longer and I will sing for you while you work." I sang an old time hymn, and they lowered the box, by pounding and jumping upon it and then hurriedly shoveled in the dirt. Then I said, "Let us pray." And there in that dreary place I prayed for the poor men who had performed this sad rite and for the guard. I forgot my surroundings. I thought only of "SOME MOTHER'S BOY," who perhaps died with a broken heart without a mother's care, now lying in an unknown grave far away from home. Perhaps she had prayed for him and God had sent me to pray over the lonely grave. There we left him where all his mistakes should be forgotten. He may have sought and found pardon in God. Who can tell? The stars were now shining and the stillness filled me with awe. The men hurried down the mountain side to the prison, leaving me behind in the dim starlight. I found my way to the stockade, but found the door locked and with great difficulty I made them hear me and was admitted. At about nine o'clock the prisoners were brought together to have a meeting. The guard ridiculed. The prisoners wondered at seeing a woman preaching. How I trembled! Oh, for some one to share my burden! I asked, "Is there one Christian here among you prisoners?" as I shook hands with them and some of them pointing out an old colored woman, said, "She's a Christian." I clasped her hand, hardened by work, and said, "Will you pray for me, sister?" "Yes," she said, "Yes, I will, honey."

God was there to touch and tender those hearts. They were unused to meetings of this character, and perhaps had never heard of a woman preaching. I well knew that unless God undertook for me the meeting would be a failure. There seemed to be no way to reach these hard hearts. The men and women stared at me. Suddenly I thought of the great danger I was in, and the risk I had to run in getting back to the village that night. I saw the head of a young prison boy droop over on a man's shoulder, too sleepy to listen longer. Then I heard and saw no more, but fell unconscious to the floor. The weariness from the day's labor proved too much for my strength. But God used my weakness to reach these hearts and when I regained consciousness, men and women with tears, sobs and prayers, were crying to God for mercy and forgiveness—pleading for help to be better men and women. I hope I shall meet many of them in heaven "when the roll is called up yonder" for they truly seemed to bring forth fruit meet for repentance.

The following day was spent among the sick and dying in the village. I had asked the privilege in the morning to go with the train men to the prison pest house where the sick prisoners were, but was refused by the train crew, some of them ridiculing me and my work. I had only kindly asked them the privilege, and then exhorted them to come to Christ. I then told them I feared the next message would be judgment from God. God bless the railroad men if some of them do make mistakes! My heart goes out for them as they are always in much danger. I make it a rule of my life to always pray for every train on which I travel with its crew and passengers. And hitherto God has been my help. Bless His holy name!

WRECK OF A COAL TRAIN.

When I had returned to the boarding house in the evening I lay down to rest. Many striking things occurred in this place. As I lay resting, dishes were rattling and children were crying in adjoining rooms, my room door leading into the open hall was standing open, and in came a drove of little pigs. I looked up to see what it was, and one had walked up to the fireplace where was burning a low fire, and stood warming its nose. But they soon grew tired of indoor life and all quickly scampered out as they had come in. They had seemed as much at home there as myself. Amid this confusion I fell asleep. How long I slept I do not know. I was awakened by heart-rending cries from men and women. I sprang up and throwing a shawl over my head, I ran out in the rain to see what I could do to help, for I knew some one was in great agony. What I saw I shall never forget. The coal train and its crew that had gone out in the morning had come in. THE ENGINE WAS DITCHED in a terrible manner and men were crushed in the wreck. Women were screaming as they ran to see if their loved ones were among the victims. I met the same men I had warned in the morning carrying on a board the fireman badly cut and bruised. I said, "Men, I gave you the warning this morning. You rejected my counsel and I thought judgment would come, but I little thought it would come so soon." They carried the wounded man to an old baggage car. People were so excited they did not know what to do. Here I was to learn a lesson in surgery. I found an old pail and brought some water. Some bystanders gave me their handkerchiefs and I proceeded to wash the blood from the poor wounded head and limb, which was much crushed, and helped the doctor to bind up the wounds. Soon there came a call for help from the scene of the disaster. A messenger came running, saying, "Come quick! there is a man dying whom we found under the engine." It was very dark, but I hurried along through the mud and rain after the doctor to the scene of suffering. They had carried him into the nearest hut, and he was lying upon the floor unconscious. Kneeling beside him I raised his head upon my hand. Consciousness returned. I cried, "Jesus can save you even now; He loves you. He will forgive you now, only believe on Him." He replied, "I do believe He does save me just now." Glory to God! He is a present help in time of need; a friend that sticketh closer than a brother. Dear reader, it is better to be saved before the crash comes. The man was suffering terribly. The women, thinking they must do something, had poured turpentine into the wounds thinking it was camphor. We washed the wounds and I assisted the physician in setting the broken limbs. God wonderfully helped me there to practice what I preached, and I found what it means to love my neighbor as myself. These railroad men were my neighbors, and they were suffering and in a dying condition. One of the poor men cried piteously for his mother. I traveled on the train on which one of the wounded men was taken to the city where his mother lived and helped to care for him on the way. We were delayed at that camp for two days. I will never forget those days of service and suffering.

THE SUGAR CAMPS.

At one time, I went into the Sugar Refining Stockades in Texas. Leaving the train, we had to walk a long distance to the first camp. The superintendent was angry at us for coming, and ordered us to go to the next camp. He said there were women at the other stockade and that he would not let us have any meeting, any way, with his men. We asked him if he would please send a boy to carry our luggage, and he refused, so we started on alone, to walk a long way. When we arrived at the second camp we found only one guard and a couple of prisoners working, and no women within miles. When the guard saw the situation, he seemed sorry for us, and we were allowed to rest and wait until the return of the prisoners, who were at work at a distance on railroad repairs. In the meantime he sent a man to another stockade some miles away, and the captain's wife there agreed to entertain us, for which we were thankful. We had a meeting after the men came to camp, and the guards came to us and said that the women at the camp mentioned before had sent word that they would not keep us over night. What *could* we do? Finally I said, "Can you take us to the depot?" They answered that they had no conveyance but AN OLD MULE AND A CART. I said, "That is all right." So they got the mule and cart and helped us in, and handed us our luggage. Then they sent a colored boy to go before the mule with a lantern, and another followed after. In this way we went on until we reached the little country depot, which was all dark. One of the prisoners, who went with us, lighted the lantern inside, and we called to the ticket agent, who had retired, asking him

- 174 -

to please check our luggage to San Antonio. This he refused to do, so I said, "We are Christian women and will give you almost any price, if your wife will allow us to stay with her until morning." He was angry, still refusing to get up to check our luggage. He said he was not paid for night work. We could not have gotten on the car had it not been for a gentleman, going on the same train, who had his servant help us. We went to San Antonio before we could get a place to rest and it was then morning, but God blessed us in holding services in the prison there that day. I never reported the agent who was so rude to us, as I was sorry for him, for I was told he was a cripple, and I thought he needed his work to provide for his family.

IN A GAMBLING SALOON.

From Knoxville, Tenn., I went one night to the coal mine region. I asked the landlord at the hotel for some one to show me a way to the stockade some distance, and he sent his chore boy with me. We had a long walk, and returned after meeting at night. It was late and as we came down the mountain side I saw a light at a little distance, and I said, "Where is that light?" He said, "That is the wickedest place; they kill people there." Without waiting to consider the danger I might be in, I said, "Wait here for me," and I hastened up the valley and into the place, which I found to be a gambling saloon. Then, without waiting, I poured out to them the Gospel message which burned in my heart, I fell on my knees and prayed to God to save them from the destruction to which they were going. Then I rushed out into the darkness again, and found the boy waiting with the lantern and we went on our way. I was thoroughly alarmed next day when I realized the risk I had taken in going into such a place, but God has wrought mightily for me all these years and preserved me from harm. As I write I feel near home and heaven. Jesus is there. Soon I shall be with Him.

CONDITION OF CONVICTS.

I wish that some who whine so much in church about taking up the cross could see the inside of those stockades as I saw them—see the suffering that existed, the sorrowful, heart-broken prisoners with no ray of hope, no one to care about them; everything poor, scarcely enough to keep them alive; the poorest of places to sleep; men fastened to a large post in the middle of the stockade by a heavy chain, compelled to wear their clothing till it would decay on them, often so ragged that they could not hide their nakedness, and guarded by bloodhounds and armed men. It was not proper under other circumstances for a woman to see men in such conditions, but they had souls to be saved or lost, and the Lord had commissioned me to go to these men and tell them that Jesus loved them and wanted to save and deliver them from the power of the devil who got them into such places.

UNJUSTLY CONDEMNED.

Judges often sentence men and women to years of hard labor in prison for the slightest offenses. An old colored man employed in a store took a box of cigars, but regretting the act, returned them confessing his wrong, and asked forgiveness. He was arrested and sentenced to twenty-five years in the stockade; one year for each cigar. Another colored man was found on the street at night carrying five ears of corn. He was sentenced to prison for five years. He with others was working where the earth caved in and killed him. Who will answer in the day of Judgment for that man's life and death? Yes, and his soul? Were I to here relate some things I know to be true, awful in the extreme, they would not be believed. Let us have the laws of God enforced. Let those who may be anxious to punish wrong and have men condemned upon circumstantial evidence, look into their own hearts and lives and see if they have been free from condemnation. I do not want to condemn judges nor jurymen, for they are not all to blame. A man or woman should never be condemned until known to be guilty. People are often prejudiced, and without proper investigation many are condemned to punishment for crimes of which they are innocent. The cries of such are come up before the Lord and He will hear and answer prayer. At one time there were forty stockades in one state and about four thousand prisoners in one state. Let us help those that are down.

In many stockades I found men and women living together promiscuously and children being born in the camp. The poor creatures were subjected to all kinds of abuse and suffering, the women in great need of better quarters, better food, and care. Ofttimes they were afraid for their very lives. Many were killed outright; in one place where they were far out in the coal mines many were brutally whipped and ill-treated. I went to the Lord in prayer, and then to the state authorities and the Governor went out with men and opened the graves of many, who had died in camps. One of the officers was imprisoned for ten years; another made his escape; others were dealt with more or less severely. I had been out there myself, getting on the engine to ride out to the stockade, and requested to see the prisoners after their day's work was done, and as they came up from the mines they were so ragged that I was compelled to turn my back as they passed. I got permission to hold a Gospel meeting. After it was over, I requested the captain to let one of his men take us to the next house, a distance of a mile or more from the camp. When we knocked asking permission to stay for the night, and telling who we were, the woman of the house said, "You had better go and preach to those prison guards, who are killing off the poor prisoners." She said she could not stand it to hear such awful cries as reached her ears even at that distance from the stockade. She told the guard just what she thought of the brutality shown the prisoners and convicts. He said he was not to blame. He seemed to be a kind young man.

In one place I found one old colored man who was condemned to death. He was filthy and dirty and had nothing to lie on but a heap of straw; he was hungry and his cell was dark and damp. My heart ached to see him so shamefully abused. Even condemned men have rights and they should be respected; it is enough for them to know that they are to die a horrible death, without having all kinds of abuse heaped upon them; yet I have seen this in many prisons. How is it that friends are so often denied the privilege of seeing those that are under death sentence or those who are sick and dying? Let the truth be told and let there be some one to investigate these things. I believe that those who are most against prisoners, are those who are not familiar with the conditions. Let good discipline be maintained, but let prisoners never be brutally treated, simply because they are powerless to help themselves. I find many things going on that are not right, but I have never made complaint to the governors of the states, unless compelled to do so, because of cases of extreme cruelty.

NEED OF REFORM.

There is great need of reformation in the management of prisons, and especially in the prison lease system and management of women prisoners in the south. Oh, the shocking sights that have greeted me on almost every hand! There is nothing more heart-rending to me than the terrible, brutal treatment of helpless humanity. These prisoners are entirely at the mercy of officers who are oftentimes void of feeling, coarse and vulgar in the extreme. To get positions and make money is the aim of many of today. The poor unfortunates shut up in prisons and asylums are in many cases most shamefully mistreated. They are supposed to be there for the purpose of reformation or treatment, but were it not for the grace of God in my soul, I never could endure the torture and anguish resulting from the sufferings I find among these poor helpless men and women. I am not supposed to know the conditions in these places, but twenty years of experience going inside these walls have opened my eyes and I get behind the scenes. There is a time of settling up of accounts and there will be a final reckoning day at the judgment bar of God, for what was done in this life, and how many will be weighed in the balance and found wanting!

The following paper by Clarissa Olds Keeler was written to Brother S. B. Shaw and read at the meeting of the National Convocation for Prayer at St. Louis, Mo., May, 1903, and will serve to convey some idea of conditions as they have existed in some parts of our land; though we are glad to say that they are somewhat improved, in many places at least.

"LET THE SIGHING OF THE PRISONER COME BEFORE THEE."

"Now mine eyes shall be open, and mine ears attent unto the prayer that is made in this place."—2 Chron. 7:15.

When attending the Christian Workers' Convention in New York in 1887 a man from Tennessee also attending the convention, said to me, "I wonder the Christian people do not take up the work of alleviating the sufferings of prisoners in the Southern States." For years he had been an eye witness to treatment which he described as "most atrocious," and the condition of the convicts, especially those hired to contractors to work in coal mines, as one of "starvation, fear and disgusting filth." Since these words were spoken to me I have spared no pains to inform myself about this new and most revolting form of slavery, and I can find no words more applicable than these: "This is a people robbed and spoiled; they are all of them snared in holes, and they are hid in prison houses; they are for a prey, and none delivereth; for a spoil and none saith, Restore. Who among you will give ear to this? Who will hearken and hear for the time to come?" (Isaiah 42:22, 23.)

Each one of the twelve convict leasing states has had its own bloody record which has been written down in God's book. Influential politicians, United States Senators from both north and south, members of state legislatures, private citizens, heartless corporations, have all shared in the money coined out of the bodies and blood of convicts in our southern states.

But it is not my purpose now to go over the past. Wherever the convict lease system has been introduced "Its presence has," as a Georgian once said, "been marked by a trail of blood." The accounts of this ghastly institution are too revolting to present.

But I want to call the attention of the Christian people to the present condition of convicts, most of whom are colored, and many of whom are guilty of but trifling offences and some of them none at all.

A man in Buncome County, North Carolina, wrote to the *Asheville Gazette*, under date of March 15, 1903: "Where are we at and where is the society for the prevention of cruelty to animals that they or the Christian world have never heard the cries from the poor unfortunate prisoners in the buck and the ringing of the cruel blood stained lash? I have seen white men beaten until their persons were blue and blood oozing from the lash from the captain's hands in the Buncome chain-gang. And negroes—there is no use talking." These prisoners, the writer says, have been guilty of some misdemeanor and being poor and unable to pay a fine are "sent to the road prison and there the lash is administered on the naked back contrary to the spirit of the constitution in abolishing imprisonment for debt and the lash at the whipping-post."

Now I would suggest that a society be formed for the prevention of cruelty to prisoners. While the good people are praying for the outpouring of the Holy Spirit on other lands may they not forget that we need a baptism of fire right here in our own land.

Our Saviour's last act of mercy and forgiving love was shown toward a prisoner and shall we imitate His example, or shall we not? His last command was: "Go ye into all the world and preach the gospel to *every creature*." How many inmates of our prisons have the gospel presented to them? When we all meet at the judgment, as meet we must, how many will be there from the mining pits and prison pens who can say truthfully, "No man cared for my soul!" Neither do we care for the bodies of these unfortunates; and as proof of this I will give you a few extracts from papers of recent date.

When the National Conference of Charities and Corrections was holding its session in Atlanta the first of the present month, some of the delegates were invited to visit the city prison stockade where misdemeanor convicts are housed at night. This was done "just for the amusement of the delegates." Hear what Mr. Timothy Nicholson of Indiana, a delegate, said about his visit to this "school of crime." He says: "I found in one room one hundred and sixty prisoners, white men and women, black men and women and even children, both black and white, male and female, all mixed together indiscriminately. I was surprised and shocked to find such a condition of affairs in a civilized country. It is simply a shame and disgrace to civilization." The delegates declared the place "inhuman and degrading." Yet this does not fully represent the awful pen picture that might be given of this class of prisoners in the county chain gangs all over the state.

The following extracts are taken from an account given by an Atlanta correspondent of the *Washington Post* written under date of May 5, 1903. "Revelations made to the Ware County grand jury in regard to the horrors of the Georgia convict camps reached Governor Terrell today. Hon. E—— M———, one of the leading members of the Georgia House of Representatives, is involved in the findings of the grand jury.

"According to the report M——— and his brother operate an extensive camp in Lowndes County. Witnesses before the grand jury testified that in the M——— camp the brutalities are such that it is revolting to describe them. For the slightest offence, it is alleged, prisoners are stripped and chained and unmercifully lashed by the whipping bosses. It is also alleged that the M——— brothers go into counties adjoining Lowndes, pay the fines of misdemeanor convicts, carry such convicts to their Ware County (convict) camp and there keep them in serviture long after the term for which the criminals were sentenced have expired.

"The grand jury claims that at least twenty citizens of Ware County are held as slaves in M———'s camp although their terms expired over a year ago. There men are kept in stockade about which armed guards march in order to prevent an escape, and men thus illegally detained who escaped have been chased by bloodhounds and recaptured."

Official reports show that this class of convicts are guilty of but trifling offences and some are vagrants. (For further particulars see *Atlanta Journal* May 5 and 11, 1903.)

The penitentiary convicts of Georgia are worked in coal mines and are subject to the same treatment. An experienced penologist said recently concerning convicts worked in the mines: "In the rooms of the mines are perpetrated practices too horrible to mention. They become the nesting places of a bestiality that in many cases lead the liberated convict into that crime to punish which the mob, the rope and the stake are ever ready." (See Atlanta Constitution, May 14, 1903.)

Under the heading "Convict Camp Horrors," the editor of the Memphis, Tennessee, *Commercial Appeal* says in his paper, dated April 11, 1903, concerning the facts recently brought out by the legislative investigating committee: "The stories coming from Brushy Mountain mines, with side lights from the state's convict system, generally, furnish painful reading to the people of Tennessee. When human beings who through fault or fortune's untowardness are condemned to helpless and unresisting servitude and who are subjected to torments and tortures, floggings and flaggellations which are merciful only where they terminated in speedy death, humanity is outraged and a sort of savagery in the public cries out for speedy vengeance." Continuing the editor says:

"Convicts have been whipped to death. Convicts have been whipped into physical helplessness. Convicts have been whipped sufficiently to keep them in bed for months and injure them permanently. Torturing them in the prison or in the mine recesses is a sin against high heaven." These are some of the facts brought to light by the prison investigating committee.

The average number of prisoners worked in the Brushy Mountain mines is about seven hundred and fifty. These convicts, which form but a part of the number of the state's convicts, and who were so inhumanly treated, earned last year for the state, clear of all expenses, the sum of one hundred and ninety-five thousand, seven hundred dollars. (See Nashville American, March 30, 1903.)

Recent developments also show that many innocent men are kidnapped and worked and treated as convicts; especially is this done in Alabama. Women and children share the same fate. During the recent investigation into the enforced slavery of negroes in Alabama by the United States Secret Service, among the abuses which were unearthed was the whipping to death of a negro woman. "This woman accused of being rebellious was laid across a log and given one hundred lashes. Still showing a rebellious spirit her hands were tied, and the rope was thrown over the limb of a tree and pulled up so as to make it barely possible for her feet to reach the ground. The woman, it is said, died two days later." (See Washington Times, May 29, 1903.)

The system of peonage slavery has been practiced for years in Alabama and Georgia. One of the most successful plans practiced is to bring a negro before a magistrate on a flimsy charge. As the matter has been arranged beforehand, the negro is convicted, and having no money to pay his fine, a white man offers to advance him money provided the negro will make a labor contract with him for the money and trouble he has taken to keep the negro out of jail. He is taken away and begins what is usually a long term of cruel servitude, frequently whipped unmercifully, and every moment watched by armed guards ready to shoot him down at any attempt to escape.

Among the evils which have grown out of the prison contract system, the number of which is legion, is that of turning out men and women, boys and girls, thoroughly educated in these schools of crime. They are thrown upon the world homeless and friendless to poison and destroy those with whom they come in contact. Many soon find their way back into prison, and some end their lives upon the gallows.

We sometimes on a Sabbath morning hear the President of the United States prayed for, but what minister ever prays for the poor parish behind prison bars?

When the book is opened and we hear the words: "I was sick and in prison, and ye visited me not," what are we going to answer?

1415 A. St., S. E., Washington, D. C.

CLARISSA OLDS KEELER.

For about four years at times Mrs. M. A. Perry, of Washington, D C., traveled with me. In answer to my request for a brief report of the work during that time I received a lengthy letter, from which I extract the following:

Dear Sister Wheaton:

I praise God for the privilege of adding a few words for your book. May the blessing of God rest upon it. To the readers I will say: I first met Mrs. Wheaton in Boston, in February, 1893, in the home of H. L. Hastings, the well-known publisher, where she was a guest. She had then spent ten years in prison and other evangelistic work. I had visited a jail and stationhouses, but never a penitentiary. We first went to the Boston and Maine Railway office. Sister Wheaton said: "You pray while I go and ask for a pass to go to the Thomaston, Maine, prison." In about ten minutes she returned with the desired transportation. By the kindness of the railroad officials from ocean to ocean they have helped to forward the work of God. Many earnest prayers are offered by Mrs. Wheaton for these men. We never boarded a train without asking our Heavenly Father to bless the train men from the engineer to the flagman. Many times we have spoken to conductors who have said, "No one ever talks to railroad men about their souls."

At Thomaston we had to wait until Sunday morning to enter the prison. If ever the Lord Jesus Christ revealed Himself in a prison chapel He was in the midst that Sabbath day. While "Mother Wheaton" preached, I prayed for her and the presence of the Holy Spirit was so manifest that every man expressed a desire to serve God. The result of that day's work for the Master will not be known until we meet when Jesus will reward his servants.

We next went to the jail in Bangor, Maine, and God blessed the work there in the salvation of souls. Then we went to the prison in Wethersfield, Connecticut, and from there to the Vermont State Prison at Windsor. But I cannot tell about them all! But wherever we went I saw that the prisoners, both men and women, greeted "Mother Wheaton" with a heartfelt welcome.

We went to the prisons of New York state—to Auburn, Sing Sing, the Troy jail and on to Buffalo. We visited the penitentiaries in Philadelphia and Baltimore, and the workhouses of Maryland and the District of Columbia. We met in these places many precious souls whom the Lord gave his life to redeem and many of them were Christians. The blood of Jesus is all powerful to reach any man or woman who will repent and forsake sin and believe in Him. We have great reason to praise God for the power of the Holy Spirit to reach the hardest hearts. But O, there are behind the bars and "in the shadow of the walls" loving and tender hearts. O, that professors of religion would wake up to the fact that when Jesus, the King of Glory, shall come He will say, "Inasmuch as ye have done it unto the least of these my brethren ye have done it unto me."

May God by his presence and power reveal to the managers of penal institutions in every land and nation that Jesus Christ is the friend of sinners in every condition. I believe the dear Lord Himself has put such love for prisoners in the heart of our sister Wheaton that she is willing to take a mother's place—no matter when she sees them. In riding along on the trains sometimes we came to prisoners (leased out to hard labor) in the most unexpected places. We were soon off the train to look after these men who were marched from the camp or stockade.

I must speak of some of the experiences we had in the prisons, stockades and prison farms of the southern states. We were, in most cases, courteously received and entertained by the wardens and their families. God bless the men who have done what they could! But O, how I have been shocked at things we saw in these places, many of which I cannot write. I wish I could give some idea of how glad the poor manacled prisoners were to see their white-haired "mother" come again. I believe the seed sown shall not be lost.

The women on the farms are required to roll logs, clear land and do all kinds of drudgery.

We went to the camps, the phosphate mines, saw-mills, coal mines, and the turpentine camps. Sometimes we rode for miles in wagons. I think Mother Wheaton never felt that any place was too dangerous or too out of the way for her to go in order to say a word of comfort and to encourage hearts. We sometimes rode on the engine up the mountains to camps where hundreds of prisoners were working. We saw men with iron rings around their necks and a chain and ball attached, some with chains around their waists and running down to their ankles with a ring attached.

I want to speak especially of a visit to one of the state farms where all the prisoners, with two exceptions, were colored women.

When we arrived at the station there was no vehicle in sight but a buggy and mule which a little boy was driving. She asked him to take us to the women's prison, which he kindly did. When we got there between seventy and eighty women were at dinner, sitting on the ground under the trees with their little tin pails which held boiled bacon and cowpeas, with a piece of corn bread in their hands. They had worked from sunrise. How they welcomed "Mother Wheaton"! Many of them were in tears as she began to sing. She asked how many of them had seen her before. Many hands went up and they told where and when they had seen her in the past. How they shook her hand and said, "O, 'deed I is glad to see you once more, honey." But soon they had to go back to the field till dark. After all had their supper we went to the stockade where they were to sleep, to hold a service. Such singing I never heard. Then "Mother Wheaton" preached, prayed and sang. If ever God answered prayer He surely did for those poor women and in place of that stockade there is now a new prison house with things reasonably comfortable.

We went to other farms, stockades and prisons. I do thank God for the privilege of going into these places where "Mother Wheaton" was the first white woman to visit or to pray and sing. Regardless of danger in approaching these out-of-the-way places, her love for God and for those who were despised and downtrodden, carried her through untold hardships. We were at times in danger of bloodhounds, alligators and venomous reptiles.

I am sure that through her intercession with governors and wardens and superintendents "Mother Wheaton's" work has proved a blessing to thousands of prisoners. I have seen the results of her work in many of the states. Her preaching and singing have been used of God, but above all I knew that the hours of prevailing prayer have been a still greater power for good. In answer to prayer God has opened doors and done many wonderful things whereof we are glad.

Again we went to the South to visit prisons and stockades where we had been in former years. Great changes had been made. There was much improvement in their condition. I hope the time may soon come when only the law of love and kindness shall prevail.

We held street meetings in many places. One night after holding one of these open-air services we boarded a train. A man and wife came on the train. She told us that her husband had attended the street meeting and was under such conviction for sin that he could not rest. There on the train, while we knelt in the aisle of the car, he was converted to God and went on his way rejoicing, while we went to visit a penitentiary where hundreds of men and women needed the same work of grace wrought in their hearts.

Often we saw answers to prayer in the healing of prisoners who were sick. God's Word is true. He says He is no respecter of persons, and He is able to do more than we can ask or think. May God bless every soul for whom we have prayed.

Sister Wheaton and myself have spent many long hours at a time together pleading for the men and women behind the bars. It means much to be divinely called to this work.

Oh! how many with broken hearts lie in the lonely cells every night! May God help everyone who reads these pages to remember that there is one MOTHER of all the prisoners who weeps and prays in sympathy with them. I wish every mother and wife, or sister, who has a precious one "in the shadow of the walls," would pray for "Mother Wheaton," that she may be helped of God in preaching the Word, and that God's blessing may rest upon her for her kind loving words and the hand-clasp that reaches so many hearts. Pray that health and strength may be given her as she comes in and goes out among these erring ones.

I know she has been through deep waters and great sorrows. Her life has been one of self-sacrifice in behalf of the unfortunate. May God bless and help her and give her the crown of righteousness that is laid up for the faithful.

One night after worship at the home of the warden with whom we were stopping, Sister Wheaton was singing a hymn, when suddenly the warden asked, "Sister Wheaton, will you come over into the prison-yard and finish that hymn?" She replied she would gladly do so if he thought it would do good. So we hastened to the prison-yard, some little distance away, and quietly entered the enclosure, and she began singing. Her clear, strong voice awakened the sleeping prisoners. The incident was so unusual that some of them (as we were told afterward), negroes especially, awaking suddenly, thought that the Judgment Day had come, and tumbling out of bed, fell upon their knees and began praying for God to have mercy upon them and save their souls; so God evidently used the song to bring conviction to hearts. After the singing we returned as quietly as we had come, trusting the results with God.

NEW MEXICO PRISON, SANTA FE, N. M.

CHAPTER XIII.

Work in Fort Madison, Iowa, and Santa Fe, New Mexico

Soon after starting out in my work, when changing cars in an Iowa town I saw a crowd of people who were curiously gazing upon three young men who were handcuffed, and bound together being taken to the state's prison at Fort Madison. I went up to them, shook hands, and said, "I am sorry for you. Don't be discouraged. Cheer up. Give God your hearts. Obey the rules. Do the best you can and God will do the rest." They seemed cheered and relieved seeing I neither feared nor shunned them. I inquired their names and told them I would try to see them in prison, but did not know how soon.

A few weeks later I went to Fort Madison and obtained permission of the Chaplain, W. C. Gunn, to hold a meeting the following Sunday. This was my first effort to hold divine service in a prison. Then I inquired for the three young men I had seen when on their way there, but could find no record of them. I assured the Chaplain they were there and observing the prisoners closely I saw one of them at work. As our eyes met, I saw a look of distress on his face. He recognized me and was afraid I would tell who he was. He had given a ficticious name—as had also the others.

But before Sunday came I began to think: "What if I should make a mistake and could think of nothing to say when I come before all those hundreds of prisoners?" And then there were the officers in their suits of blue with brass buttons! It all seemed too much for me, and, like Jonah, I took ship and ran away.

That night I started by steamer for Mobile, Alabama—but God knew I did not mean to disobey and He let me work among the stockades in the south until I got boldness to enter other prisons. After a year or more I returned to Fort Madison and was granted the privilege offered me before and from that time to this I have always been made welcome there and have had many blessed seasons within these walls. There is no place where I have been more kindly received by both officers and prisoners than at Fort Madison. Chaplain Gunn and wife were always true and loyal friends. 'Tis now several years since he crossed over to the better shore. I shall ever remember with deep gratitude the kindness of himself and family. Chaplain Jessup and wife, and Warden Jones and wife, as well as other officials, have been especially kind and courteous. To the prisoners at Fort Madison, also, I must give the credit of contributing freely from their small savings to my necessities. While I would gladly mention all who have especially befriended me I feel that this tribute is due to the officers and men of Fort Madison. That it is deserved may be easily seen by the following communications and selections from letters which I find among my papers:

The bearer, Mrs. Elizabeth R. Wheaton, a devoted Christian woman, has for years been visiting the prisons and jails of this country seeking to do good to their inmates. I think she should be kindly received and encouraged by prison authorities. I do not think any one has ever spoken to the convicts in this prison with better effect and I am sure that no one who has ever addressed them will be longer or more kindly remembered by them than Mrs. Wheaton. I heartily commend her and her good work to those engaged in prison management and to good people everywhere as most deserving of their aid and encouragement. It affords me all the more pleasure to give Mrs. Wheaton this testimonial because it was unsolicited and because of the unobtrusive way in which she goes about doing good.

G. W. GROSLEY, Warden.

Ft. Madison, Iowa, Oct. 5, 1893.

Rev. J. M. Croker, Chaplain State Prison, Anamosa, Ia.

My Dear Brother: This will introduce to you our dear sister, Mrs. Wheaton, the prison missionary, who would like to address the prisoners. Any favors shown her will be duly appreciated.

Yours truly,

W. C. GUNN, Chaplain.

Fort Madison, Iowa, June 4, 1897.

Mrs. E. R. Wheaton, Tabor, Iowa.

My Dear Mother: I will first ask your pardon for not answering your letter sooner. But I am always so busy the last days of the month, also the first days, as I have all the time of the contract men to make up to send to the contractors, also have my monthly report to the governor, and as we give the boys a holiday Monday I think you would readily see I have had my hands full.

I sometimes think it is more than I can stand. I want to do right by the men but it is so hard at times to tell just what is right. I sincerely thank you for your kind interest in me. And may our great and good God always be with you is the wish of your true friend.

J. R. JONES, Deputy Warden.

Fort Madison, Iowa, Sept. 6, 1899.

Mrs. Wheaton: Enclosed please find draft for ——, the poor boys' free-will offering in appreciation of your kindness in visiting them. You are thought more of by them than any one else living—even their relatives. Please sign the enclosed receipt, and send it back to me, that I may have something to show what became of the money. Thanking you for your visit.

Yours truly,

W. C. GUNN, Chaplain.

Fort Madison, Iowa, Feb. 13, 1901.

Mrs. E. R. Wheaton, Tabor, Ia.

My Dear Sister: Enclosed find draft for —— from prisoners—entirely a free will offering, given without other solicitation than what you heard me say when you were here. Please excuse delay in forwarding, partly due to uncertainty as to your whereabouts. Perhaps you will write me a short message for the men, who will be glad to hear from you. With best wishes and prayers for your welfare and success in your work, I am, Very sincerely yours,

A. H. JESSUP, Chaplain.

My acquaintance with Mrs. Wheaton began four years ago, at the first Sunday service I held as chaplain of this prison. Standing by my office window before the men had come into the chapel, I saw a motherly-appearing lady enter the prison, escorted by the assistant deputy. A few moments later we met on the chapel platform, and I was introduced to "Mother Wheaton," the woman who for many years had, in prisons and jails, all over the country, sought to quicken in the prisoners' bosom a new life, and lead to the Savior those who all their lives have been rejecting Him. It was my first service with the men, as I have said, and I felt constrained to preach as I had come prepared to do, although on subsequent visits I have gladly granted all the time to Mother Wheaton. After I had preached, Mrs. Wheaton talked, and sang, and prayed, and many of the men were visibly affected, some to tears, by her earnest pleading. Later she went to my office and met a boy who was soon going out, and prayed and talked with him in a manner that must have made him determine to strive for a better manhood. Our prison has received several visits from Mother Wheaton since then, and always, I believe, with lasting good to the men, over many of whom she has exerted an influence for good. Earnest, apt and ready in speech, always seeming to live close to God, and to hold instant communion with Him, and consecrated soul and body, time and means, to her work—these perhaps account for her useful service. That she has a ready sense of humor, too, is perhaps one reason the "boys" listen to her so well. I recall one incident. She had come down from Burlington, where she was obliged to secure a pass on the railroad. The proper officer not being at hand, she went from one to another, until at last one was found with authority to issue a pass, but who did not know her or her mission. "On what ground do you want a pass?" said the railroad man. "I am working for God, and He owns the railroads," was the unexpected reply. "But, madam, where are you going?" gasped the official. Quick as a flash came the answer, "To heaven!" But by this time the railroad man had recovered from his surprise, and seemed equal to the emergency, and proved himself to be a gentleman as well, for he said quietly: "If that is your destination, madam, I am unable to accommodate you, for I regret to say the place is not on our line; but if you want a pass to any place on our road you can have it." In relating the incident in the prison chapel Mother Wheaton added that she secured her pass to Fort Madison, and that when she reached here she thought she was next to heaven, for here she had first attempted her work for souls, in State's Prisons, and here she believed many precious trophies for the Master had been given her.

I noticed on her last visit that while she seemed in usual health, her hair was whiter, betokening the gathering years. I could wish that now she who for so many years has not known the blessing of home, might find a place in which to spend in rest and communion with God, and helpful but gentle ministrations, the balance of her life, until He whom she has followed in her efforts to do good, may say: "Come up higher, thou blessed of my Father. Inasmuch as ye did it unto the least of these my brethren ye did it unto me."

A. H. JESSUP,
Chaplain Iowa State Penitentiary.

Fort Madison, Iowa, April 18, 1904.

WORK IN SANTA FE, NEW MEXICO.

Several interesting experiences have occurred in connection with my visits to the prison at Santa Fe, New Mexico. At one time I found there a good old Christian man, "a trusty," who had charge of the Superintendent's horses, driving the family to town, etc., and had much liberty given him. One day he sat in front of me, driving to town, and I said to him, "I am going to pray to God to remove the 'stripes' from you." He said, "Pray for my release—I know God hears prayer." I did so, as did also my good co-workers, returned missionaries home from Africa on a visit. In three or four days the warden gave him citizens' clothes; and soon after the governor gave him his pardon.

We were led to pray for a pardon for brother T. of the same prison, and in three months he was a free man. At the time I had a sister with me from Japan. On my return from the Pacific coast we again held services in the prison at Santa Fe, and during the meeting I said, "What do you want me to sing, boys?" One said, "Sing, 'Some Mother's Boy.'" I did so, and in the morning, before I left the prison, the officer said to me, "Here is two dollars a man sent in from the prison for you." Upon inquiring the name of the prisoner I found it was J. L. As they told me he was a good man, a Christian, and a good prisoner, I took his case also to the Lord in prayer. Within three weeks he was given a pardon by the governor. The three men mentioned were all Christians.

In none of these cases did I go to the governor, but just left all in God's hands, and prayed if God was pleased to set these men free, that He would impress the governor to give them their release. These cases occurred at different times. I am sure that the hope of pardon has in many cases saved the lives of prisoners, and also saved them from insanity.

I give below a letter received from Brother T., also quote from a sketch of his life, as published by McAuley Water Street Mission, N. Y., and sent me by himself; also letters from the Secretary of the Christian Endeavor Society of the Santa Fe Prison, and very kind letters from Governor Thornton, Superintendent H. O. Bursom, and Brother S. H. Hadley, of Water Street Mission.

May 26, 1903.

Dear Mother Wheaton:

I suppose you will be surprised to hear from me. The last time I saw you was in the Santa Fe Territorial Prison. You had a meeting in the cell house. I was the trusty who went with you to the depot. If you remember, you prayed for the removal of the number from the back of No. 917 and that he would be freed; you also told me you would pray that I would get out of prison. Your prayers have been answered. I was pardoned last Christmas, and am here working among the criminal classes as a missionary. You remember of my having been converted before your visit to the prison. It is a great blessing to me to spend the balance of my life thus, who had been sent to prison for forty years, under conviction and sentence for a crime of which I was perfectly innocent, although I was a great sinner in other respects.

Yours in the grand work,

E. U. T.

SENTENCED TO FORTY YEARS IN PRISON.

On the night of July 6, 18———, I was playing the banjo in a notorious gambling house in Albuquerque, New Mexico. It had been my business for years and I liked the surroundings; they suited me exactly; in fact, I have traveled from my home in the East, from city to city, through all the slumdum of the western cities playing my banjo; I thoroughly enjoyed it and the company which it brought me. * * * I was arrested on suspicion and locked in jail. I had no money, no friends and no character, and I began to realize for the first time what my life was bringing me. I was finally brought to trial and convicted on circumstantial evidence, and sentenced to forty years in prison for a crime that I knew nothing more about than the judge who sat upon the bench.

Dear reader, can you enter into this story with me; can you form an idea of my despair as I received practically a life sentence for something which I did not do? My heart was hard and bitter against myself and everybody else as I was taken to the Territorial penitentiary at Santa Fe, New Mexico. I was in the prime of life, only 28 years old, but, oh, what steps I had already taken in the downward path that leadeth unto death. Every evil habit had fastened itself upon me, and after I had taken my place in the prison I almost went wild with terror and despair when I realized what was before me. I was soon set to work with pick and shovel digging out trenches on the grounds, and I tried to do the work the best I could and be a good prisoner. I presume I was, for a little time afterward I was placed in the library, and had charge of the greenhouse as well.

One Sunday afternoon in the chapel the speaker took for his text, St. John, 3, 14th and 15th verses: "As Moses lifted up the serpent in the wilderness, even so must the Son of Man be lifted up;"

"That whosoever believeth in Him should not perish, but have everlasting life."

The speaker dwelt at length on this actual occurrence and also how God commanded Moses to erect a pole with the brass serpent, and although there were there people dying by the thousands, those that looked on that brazen serpent were healed. He brought the application home to us prisoners—how the serpent of sin had stung us so deeply and our only remedy was to look to Jesus Christ, who was lifted up on the cross, and my hard heart began to melt and a desire came to me to be healed of this terrible serpent's bite. The speaker instructed us when we got back to our cells to read this whole chapter, and when I got back to my cell I took up the book and read, and I prayed to God to open my heart so that I could understand what He wanted of me, and as I read the blessed Holy Spirit came to my poor soul and showed me what a sinful man I was, and I then and there became a child of God. Great peace came to my soul, which at first I could scarcely understand, but although still a prisoner and wearing the stripes, I was a free man in Christ Jesus, and I rejoiced in my new found life. After this, prison life was not so dreary as it was before.

Among the many different workers who came to the prison was Mr. and Mrs. J. E. Wood, of Santa Fe; he is Mail Agent on the road. He is a blessed man, and one who loves the prisoners. Another person I would like to mention is the person known as "Mother Wheaton." I think I should speak of a little circumstance that happened to one prisoner who went by the number 917, and who wore this number in great big cloth figures on his back; he drove "Mother Wheaton" to town, as he was a "trusty," and she said that she was going to pray that the Lord would take that number off his back, and in a few days after that the Warden came in with a new suit of clothes for him without the stripes or number—citizen's clothes. She once said to me: "I am going to pray to the Lord to get you out of here," reminding me of the prayer she made for No. 917. "Mother Wheaton" prayed for my release. On Christmas day, 1902, three months after the above conversation took place, I was in the chapel of the prison in the entertainment that was going on. Governor Otero sat in the balcony.

The custom is that someone shall receive a pardon on Christmas day, and no one has any intimation who it is excepting the Governor. I had not the slightest idea that I would be the lucky man, and after the Assistant Superintendent asked that I play a certain composition of my own, he requested me to step out and he read the pardon; to my surprise my name was in the pardon, and, oh, the joy that came to me when I began to realize that I was a free man, but, dear reader, this pardon, great as it was, did not compare with the joy that came in my soul as I realized that I had received the pardon from my Redeemer, and that all my sins were forgiven and all my past crimes blotted out.

While in the prison I read an account in a paper of the experience of S. H. Hadley, who was then in New York connected with the Jerry McAuley Mission, and I was desirous of going to New York to meet this man. I did so, and before I had been ten minutes in his office he told me what already was filling my soul, that I should be a worker for Christ and try to save those who had fallen, and the down-trodden. I stepped out on the Lord's promises with but very little knowledge, except the knowledge of sins forgiven, and a big hope in my soul of eternal life, and a love that I cannot express, without one dollar in my pocket, but with the simple faith in Jesus. I am working every night and day at every door that is open, and every one that I can open, where I can tell the wonderful story of Jesus' love to sinners. Dear reader, pray for me that God may wonderfully use me.

"The dying thief rejoiced to see The Fountain in his day,
And there I do, though vile as he, Wash all my sins away."

New York, —— 18, 1904.

Dear Mother:

It gives me much pleasure when I think of your going from prison to prison telling the poor boys and girls behind the bars of Jesus. It always gave me great joy when I heard that our dear mother was going to speak to her boys at —— Prison; because I knew you were our friend. I wish to again thank you for the day that you prayed that God would open the prison doors for me. God answered your prayer, and after serving about seven years of a forty years' sentence the prison doors were opened for me, and God sent me to New York to labor for souls. He sent me to Mr. S. H. Hadley, the present superintendent of the old McAuley Mission, and he has been indeed a father to me.

I am so thankful that God sent me to such a good man— one who loves the lost sinner; and one who is willing to do anything in his power to help the helpless. May God's richest blessings be your portion is the prayer of your son in the Gospel.

E. U. T.

McAuley Water Street Mission,
New York, Sept. 11, 1903.

"Mother Wheaton," as the boys behind the prison-bars, yes, and those who have by her prayers gone out from behind the prison-bars, affectionately call her, is one of the unique, missionary characters in this country. She travels all over this land with but one object in view and that is to tell sinners of the powerful, deathless love of Jesus and how no one can be too bad for Him to save. She brings sunshine to many sorrowing hearts and hope to thousands who never knew what hope was until they met her. An ex-convict, who is one of my helpers now, was prayed out of practically a life sentence by Mother Wheaton.

I have seen her curled up in some seat in a day coach at three o'clock in the morning on a Southern railroad because she had not money enough to take a "sleeper" and had to travel all night or lose an appointment to speak at some stockade or prison.

God bless her book and speed it on.

S. H. HADLEY.

Santa Fe, N. M., May 26, 1903.

Elizabeth Wheaton, Prison Evangelist,

Los Angeles, Cal.

Dear Friend in Christ: Yours of 23d received, and am happy to say that Mr. Trout (No. 99) has been pardoned, and is now engaged in bringing souls to Christ down on Water street in the McAuley Mission, New York City, using his musical talents to further the cause in which he is now devoting the rest of his life. I am sure he would be more than pleased to hear from you. All the boys are as well as could be expected, and a visit from you would be much appreciated.

The C. E. S. has increased by seventy, making a total of one hundred and five. God bless you in all your efforts in the cause of Christ is the wish of all.

Respectfully,

P. M., sec. Prison C. E. S.

Santa Fe, N. M., July 28, 1903.

Dear Mother: ... Your letter to Mr. J. W. L. came to hand in due time. I wrote you at Tabor, Iowa, in regard to the God-given gift, sweet liberty, which came to him on the twelfth of July. God has answered your prayer sooner than he had expected. He left the prison gates with full trust and confidence in the mercies of the omnipotent power of God. He is now in W—— with his brother. May God's benign countenance look down upon you and increase the manifold blessing and grace that He has so richly endowed you with. I will distribute the tracts and learn the song. All your boys send their respects and wish to be remembered in your prayers.

Yours in Christ Jesus,

P. M., Sec. C. E. S.

New Mexico Penitentiary, Santa Fe, N. M., Sept. 19, 1903.

Dear Mother Wheaton:

I was pleased to hear from you, and was exceedingly happy to know that you are going to put your experiences and noble work of the past amongst the unfortunates in prison into book form. Certainly, dear mother, no one knows the heartaches and sorrows of this class better than yourself. God has blest you in preparing you for this work and sending you from prison to prison to gather in the wavering souls from eternal destruction.

God grant you many years more of service in the field where souls are perishing and when your earthly career shall have closed, the shining crown of eternal bliss in the presence of the King of Heaven and Earth, will forever be your beacon light to make you think of the ones below. Many, yea many unfortunates not yet born will read from these same prison cells of the work of "Mother Wheaton" in the prisons of our country. My every breath and prayerful utterance is "God be with you till we meet again."

As ever, one of your boys in Christ Jesus,

PHILIP M., Sec. C. E. S.

TERRITORY OF NEW MEXICO.

Office of the Executive, Santa Fe, N. M., Oct., 1895.

Judge E. V. Long, Las Vegas.

Dear Sir: This will introduce to you Mrs. Wheaton, traveling in the interests of the prisons and asylums. She may want to hold a service at the asylum. If so please see that the opportunity is afforded her.

Yours respectfully,

W. T. THORNTON, Governor.

New Mexico Penitentiary, Sante Fe, N. M., Sept. 19, 1903.

Mrs. E. R. Wheaton has been paying our institution visits on various occasions for some years past, and during these visits has done very much valuable work towards furthering the discipline of the institution. Her words of comfort and wholesome advice together with her teachings of Christianity has cheered many a poor, unfortunate soul up to believing and hoping for a better future; to realize that justice demands that some punishment be meted out to wrong doers and violators of the laws of the land; that such punishment is not eternal; that they can receive consolation and comfort their conscience even inside of the prison walls by resolving to be better men, by a closer observance of the moral laws as dictated by their conscience, a faithful compliance of their duties as men or women, and a strict obedience to their overseers acting under the law and, above all, an abiding faith in the Almighty God.

Mrs. Wheaton has taught them to understand that they must not only resolve but must demonstrate by their actions in every day life a sincerity of purpose.

The management feels very grateful indeed for the splendid work so generously devoted in the interest of humanity, which I consider also a most valuable assistance to the prison management in maintaining discipline and turning out discharged prisoners as better men and women, better equipped morally, physically and spiritually to meet and solve the problem of living an honest and upright life, earn and care for those who may be dependent upon them.

H. O. BURSOM, Superintendent.

CHAPTER XIV.

Gone Home from the Scaffold.

"Let the sighing of the prisoner come before thee; according to the greatness of thy power, preserve thou those that are appointed to die."—Psalms 79:11.

"Whosoever hateth his brother is a murderer."

One of the most touching things, and to me the most important of all this God-appointed work, has been my special mission to those who are doomed to execution.

If there ever is a time in our lives when we need a friend, it is when we are sick, in trouble, or about to die. The last words of our loved ones are very dear to us all. Nearly every home has at some time had a call from the death angel. And looking through the bureau drawer, you might see the little garments, shoes and playthings that used to be our darlings' before they went away. Turn the leaves of the old Family Bible and you will see hidden between its pages a lock of hair, perhaps father's or mother's. We look up to Heaven through our blinding tears, and cry out between our sobs: "Oh, God, help me to say 'Thy will be done.'"

In looking over my packages of old letters from the departed ones who have paid the penalty of a violated law, dying either in the electric chair or on the scaffold, I find them coming to pieces, some so badly worn I can scarcely read them. And I know the hands that penned them are now returning back to dust.

In order to show how God saves when they are truly penitent, even men of this class, who are counted the worst of criminals, I will give an account of a few instances which have come under my own observation, and extracts from some of the letters I have received—written before execution. And let us remember that our Savior declared that every sin shall be forgiven to men, except the sin against the Holy Ghost.

INDIFFERENT BUT FINALLY CONVERTED.

The first one who was converted under my ministry, before going to the scaffold, was executed in August, 1885, in the state of Kentucky. On going to jail I found this young man there with the sentence of death upon him. The burden of his lost condition came upon my soul in great power. I felt I should die unless he was saved, and cried mightily to God for his conviction and conversion. I held several meetings there and was entertained a part of the time by the sheriff's wife, who was a Christian lady. She, too, was very anxious for this young man's salvation. As I took the train to leave the place, his mother accompanied me to the depot— crying and pleading, "Oh, pray for my poor boy. It will surely kill me." The bitter wail of that mother's heart seems to still ring in my ears. Letters from the sheriff's wife came often, telling me of the boy's still seeming indifferent. But she said that he often inquired about me and wanted to see me.

I prayed for this soul almost incessantly for forty-five days, being scarcely able to sleep at night; and he was finally converted. After his conversion I received from him the following letters:

——, KY., August 5, 1885.

My Dear Friend:

I received your card this morning and was very glad to hear from you indeed. Mrs. Wheaton, I feel my Savior in my heart. I know that He will save my soul. I am praying to my God every hour in the day. I am praying for God to place something in my heart to tell the people when I go to the scaffold. I want to tell them what my Savior has placed in my heart—the man that suffered and died that I should have everlasting life. I wish you could be with me once more on earth to sing and pray with me, but if not, I will meet you on that other shore. My friend Charley is praying and singing with me every day and night and says he will meet us in the kingdom. They are all well here but Mrs. N. (the sheriff's wife). She has been sick, but is better now. I would like to be with you once more before I die, and if not, look out for me when you reach that happy land. Good-by, good-by. Remember me in your prayers. I have yet nine days to live.

From your friend,

H—— F——.

——, KY., August 12, 1885.

My Dear Friend:

I received your card tonight at my cell door. I seem to see you now at the door of my cell, praying for me. The sheriff came in this morning and put shackles on me. But I thank God that after two days more I will be at rest. I have been praying to my Father to teach me something to tell the world at my last hour. I would like to tell everybody what my dear Savior has done for me. He has given me what I asked Him for and He will go with me to the scaffold. I will see you again, "In the fair and happy land, just across on the evergreen shore." I am ready to go home to rest. I have suffered enough in this world, so I will bid the world good-by. I will have to bid you good-by for the present. I will see you again. I will watch for you. Excuse me for not answering you sooner. I am in my cell and it is very dark for me to write, but I do my best. I fast and pray most all the time. Good-by once more for a while.

From your true friend,

H. F.

Below is an extract from a letter written by the sheriff's wife to me shortly after the execution took place:

Dear Sister:

I fulfill the promise I made to poor Henry the day he was executed, to write you a letter and tell you all about him after he was gone to that bright glory land. It would have done you good to have seen him the last three days he lived. He was as happy as he could be. He had a smile on his countenance all the time and never broke down, no difference who of his friends came to see him. He talked to his mother and brothers so nice and gave them such good advice. He told his mother to not grieve after him, but to rejoice, for he would be so much better off after he was gone, for he knew that he would be at rest. And if they would live and do right they could come to him. The people that were here that day (and there were between four and five thousand) were surprised to see the beautiful countenance he left the prison with. He helped to sing that beautiful hymn,

"And must I be to judgment brought, And answer in that day For every vain and idle thought And every word I say?"

with the chorus,

"We are passing away,"

and he was heard distinctly by all. He clapped his hands
while he was singing; then he stepped on to the trap and
was soon gone. He had a prayer on his lips when the black
cap was drawn over his face, and said, "Good-by" to all his
friends, and repeated, "Good-by." He told me to tell you
he expected to meet you in heaven. His mother and
brothers send their kindest regards to you. May God bless
you.

Your sister in Christ,

S. N.

MOTHER'S PRAYERS.

The case of C—— was one of most intense interest to the public as well as
his immediate friends. For long months I wept and prayed for this young
man. He was hoping for a new trial. He was always glad to see me and to
have me sing for him. He was refined, educated, a member of "one of the
F. F. V.'s," as they say, yet doomed to die on the scaffold. How my heart
longed to see him saved—for Jesus, too, was longing for his salvation.

I was called to other fields of labor before the fatal day and was not sure of
his acceptance with God, but can but hope that his poor mother's prayers
and mine were heard in heaven and that that poor, misguided youth whose
every wish had before been gratified was forgiven. We can but cast the
mantle of charity over the case and leave it with Him who wills not that any
should perish but that all should turn to Him and live. He wrote me the
following:

Mrs. E. R. Wheaton, Prison Missionary:

I appreciate very highly your kindness and sympathy and
more so your prayers. I trust we may all meet in a better
land. Return my thanks to Mrs. Gen T——. Respectfully,

T. J. C.

Aug. 24, 1885.

CLAIMED TO BE INNOCENT.

The following letter is from one who was executed in 1887. He declared to
the very last that he was innocent of the crime for which he was convicted.
He always maintained to me that the person he was supposed to have
murdered committed suicide under circumstances which threw suspicion
upon him. For myself, I do not believe in capital punishment and certainly

- 203 -

if it is ever justifiable it is not in any case that leaves a possibility of doubt regarding the guilt of the accused.

In spite of great hindrances, being in the place, I was led to visit the jail. After having sung for some of the other prisoners an officer came to me asking if I would go down below to visit a condemned man who had heard me sing and requested that I would come to him. Of course I went—though the opening to his cell was so small that I had to stoop very low to get in. If I remember rightly he claimed to be converted that day. I was obliged to leave the city soon after, but heard from him several times before his execution.

Petersburg, Va., April, 1887.

> My Dear Friend: I received your postal and will answer it at once. I was very glad to hear from you, especially as you remind me so much of my dear old mother—not exactly now, but as she was about fifteen years ago. * * *
>
> Mrs. R. sang the same hymn for me that I heard you sing to those in the room above me. She said she would, if she had the chance before she left the city, write it for me and bring it to me, but as she has not been here yet I fear she has left, so I will be very glad if you will be so kind as to write it for me. It is beautiful.
>
> I was very sorry you left so soon. I would have been so glad for you to have been in town longer so you could have called at least once more! But if I never see you on this earth it is comforting to know we may meet in heaven. But, O God! had I received justice, today I would be as free as the birds of the field. There is a blessed hope in knowing while we are persecuted by men, it is only the body they can persecute on this earth, the soul is out of their reach. And before the flesh is cold in death my soul will be soaring above in the realms of bliss to be forever blessed! O forever! Forevermore! It is one of the most consoling of all consolations for me to know that it is only the condemnation of man and the so-called law of the land by which I was convicted—not by—no, not by—the great Judge of all hearts and not by justice at all. Only condemned by man—not by my God and justice. But it is all in God's hands and He will repay, for "Vengeance is mine," saith the Lord. Vengeance is not mine nor do I wish to revenge any one. * * * "Revenge is sweet," is an old adage, but not to me to get revenge and by so doing

lose my own soul, for what is the whole world to gain and lose your own soul? I am charged with that of which I am not guilty, but my protestation is in no way believed. Neither was the only pure one who ever trod the soil of this earth. He was caught and charged, accused, condemned—yes, more than that, was crucified. Was he guilty? No—emphatically no. But his innocence could not save him. Nor did mine do me any good in my trial at all. But, thank God, it will do me good in the world to come, where I will receive justice and I will not be in danger of prejudice as lies and prejudice are the cause of my being in this lonely cell today. * * *

All the boys in the room over me request me to be remembered in my letter to you kindly. Many thanks to you for those tracts you sent me. I hope to be remembered in your daily appeals to our Maker, in whose care I prayerfully submit myself and you to his keeping in the future. God grant it and may we meet in heaven. Hoping this will in no way offend you and that it may be answered soon to one in solitude—yet not alone; condemned—yet not guilty. Your brother in Christ,

W. R. P.

HARDENED IN CRIME.

The case of the writer of the following communications (which were written on postal cards) was one of note. He was supposed to be so hardened in crime and so void of feeling that there was no hope for him— that nothing could reach or save him. But I believed that God loved him just as the Word teaches us, and I laid hold on the promises of the Bible for his soul's salvation. I am sure that God never turns a penitent soul away empty who comes to Him in faith, feeling that He is a rewarder of those who diligently seek Him. "O ye of little faith, wherefore didst thou doubt?"

After the light of God broke in upon this poor man's soul he saw that he was a wretched sinner, but that there was pardon and peace for all who truly repent of their sins and who confess and forsake them. To such God has given the promise of eternal life and that the blood of Jesus Christ his Son shall cleanse their hearts from all sin. This man was convinced of his need of a Savior and deeply convicted of sin and we believe was made ready to meet God. He seemed very deeply thankful to me for my untiring efforts in his behalf and surprised at my faith and confidence in God for him, and through these He was brought by the power of the Spirit unto repentance toward God and faith in our Lord Jesus Christ.

June 18, 1887.

My Dear, Kind Friend:

I received your welcome postal and it makes me happy to read it. I am now ready to go to my fate. I pray every night and day for God to forgive me. I put my whole trust in Him. Pray for me that God will wash my sins away and receive me in heaven. As I expect God to forgive me I forgive and love everybody. Think of me when I am gone. I wish you could pray with me before I go on my long journey, for I love to hear you pray. Good-bye. From your penitent brother in Christ.

A. T.

Jail, June 23, 1887.

Dear Sister in Christ:

My time on this earth is now very short (but seven days) and I am now ready to go to my Father, whom I trust and pray will forgive me my crime and receive me in his heavenly home. I pray every hour in the day and, my dear sister, do the same for me that my sins may be washed away in His blood. Pray that He may give me everlasting life. O, if I could but live my life over again, how I would pray and put all my trust in Him. Dear sister, this may be the last time you may hear from me on this earth, but I hope we may meet in heaven. Good-bye, God bless you and your noble work.

Yours waiting to go to his Savior,

A. T.

May God forgive me.

L., Ky., June 25, 1887.

Dear Sister in Christ:

If you only knew how much a poor sinner like me needs the prayers of such Christians and lovers of God and His Word as you are, you would pray both night and day that He will receive me in his heavenly home, where there is no sin or sorrow, but where all is love and peace. I have now but five short days until all that is of the world will be consigned to the tomb and I do so pray night and day that Jesus will cleanse me of my sins. I think this will be the last time you will hear from me on this earth and when I go to eternity I do so praising God, forgiving my enemies, firm in faith and the belief that my sins are washed away in the blood of Jesus. Good-bye. May we meet in heaven.

A. T.

In 1888 I visited a county jail so crowded with prisoners that I wondered how they could live in that poorly ventilated, filthy prison. They had little to eat and evidently no one to care for them. There were Indians, Mexicans, white and colored all together. There I found TEN MEN UNDER DEATH SENTENCE; and I was convinced that several were innocent of the charges laid against them—being condemned by circumstantial evidence. Those ten condemned men were made the subject of constant, earnest prayer. O, if judges and jurymen could only know what eternal destinies hang upon their decisions, surely they would be less ready to condemn on less than positive evidence. Several of the ten were executed—among them the writer of the following letter:

——, April 2, 1888.

My Dear Sister:

We received your postal. I was so glad to receive it from those who love my soul. I have not forgotten one word you left with me. Jesus Christ is the subject of my day talk and night dreams. I remember you when I get down on my knees to pray. I pray for the Lord's will to be done with me as it is done in heaven. I have forsaken the world for Jesus' sake. His love is shed abroad in my heart. Myself and Brothers W. and A. (whose sentences have been changed) are still serving God—also Brother S. I could not tell you how it is with the other boys, but I talk to them every day. Brothers W., A., and S. join with me in sending their love to you. God bless you. I am your brother in Christ.

———— ————

April 26, A. D. 1888.

Sister Elizabeth R. Wheaton. My Dear Sister in Jesus Christ:

My days have been numbered here on earth by man, but there is no end to the number of days that my God has promised me in heaven—no more a prisoner here on earth, but to live with our Lord forevermore. Let not your heart be troubled about me, for all is well! Yes, indeed, all is well. The love of Christ will bear me home. Jesus Christ is in me and I am in Him. In God I trust, in Him I die. I could not tell you how the case is with the other boys, but I do know for myself I am ready at any time. My dear sister, I have sent the lovely handkerchief you gave me home to my old mother. I told mother who gave it to me and for her to place it in my Bible and put it in her trunk and then I said: "Here is a picture of mine and a lock of hair for my poor, old mother and sisters and brothers." I leave a mother, four sisters and two brothers. If you wish sometime to write to my mother her address is —— ——. Farewell until we meet again.

I am your brother in Jesus Christ,

———— ————

CONVERSION OF A JEWISH BOY.

In the same year, I found in one of the prisons of California, a young Jew under sentence of death. While under the influence of drink, he shot the girl he truly loved. He never realized it till he became sober and found himself in prison. Naturally he was surprised and greatly shocked. Wondering why he was there, and being told of his crime, he was overwhelmed with grief, and remorse of conscience. Poor boy! His was a sad ending. He was so grief-stricken! And yet the courts were against him, and the world at large, for the sin was pronounced murder in the first degree and he must die—*a boy in his teens.*

As I looked through the grating at the poor doomed boy, an old gentleman spoke to me and said something very unkind about him. The boy said, "That man is a *hypocrite.* But I like those hymns you sang. *Won't you sing for me?*" So I sang for him, and he requested me not to talk to him then. So I said, "Can I come and see you again?" "*Oh, yes, come again, do.*" This poor boy was one of the lost ones, and Jesus touched his heart while I sang, "Meet me there." This was from that time on his favorite hymn, and I sang it for him just before he went to the scaffold.

I went back and forth from San Francisco to other places for six weeks, but his case lay very heavy upon my heart. I knew that on the 14th of September he was to go, and that worse still, he was in danger of eternal death. I pleaded and wept for him day and night, that he might be brought to see his lost condition and his need of Christ and yield to God. How I bless God that He hears and answers prayer! "If any man see his brother sin a sin which is not unto death, he shall ask, and he shall give him life for them that sin not unto death."—1 John 5:16.

Before his conversion I received from him the following letters, beautifully and correctly written:

San Francisco, Aug. 9, 1888.

Mrs. Elizabeth Wheaton:

As to religion I do not profess any creed. I do not mean by the above that I hate them—on the contrary, I love religion and hate hypocrisy. I am not an atheist and must admit that I believe in a true, just and most merciful God. I appreciate your visits very much and hope you will call to see me as often as opportunity and convenience will allow, so I now close this brief epistle by sending kindest regards and best wishes. I am

Respectfully,

_____ _____.

"Condemned   Cell."

P. S.—Kind thanks for singing.

San Francisco, Sept. 7, 1888.

Mrs. Wheaton:

I am pleased that you called to see me and hope you will repeat your visits. It grieves me to see you shed tears, and although I say nothing, remember that "still water runs deep." I have faith and believe in prayer, so I believe that the cause of a condemned boy will be heard in heaven and will come to pass. I am not allowed to shake hands, much less give my mother a comforting kiss. I now end by thanking you very kindly for your kindness and consideration to me.

I am, respectfully,

—— ——.

I went, the day before the execution, to see him. No one was allowed to go inside the doomed boy's cell, so I was compelled to submit to the law. The sheriff said positively, "No, you cannot go inside." But the chief jailer said, "I promised that this lady should go inside the boy's cell before the execution, and I must keep my word. I will go in with her." He opened the door and we went in. He was a grand man. Myself and the sister who was with me prayed for the prisoner's salvation. We sang and read and prayed, and at last the presence of the Holy Spirit seemed to fill the gloomy little cell, and to touch the poor boy kneeling there with the shackles on his limbs. (They frequently put shackles on some days before the execution, and place them in the "doomed cell.") We kept on praying and singing and at last the light came into his heart, and God owned him as His child.

On the morning of the execution, I went early to the prison; and as I hurried along there met me a young Catholic priest, who was our mutual friend, and very kind. He said, "*Come quickly, the boy wants you.* He has called for you all night, and they could not find you, so they came for me. I have been waiting for you." This priest had labored with me to convince the poor boy that Jesus was the Christ and that He alone could save him. I hurried on into the prison for my last greeting on earth with the poor condemned boy. There was no loud demonstration—he was going to die, and knew it; but he felt that he was ready. He said to me: "I can hardly wait the hour to go home. I am willing and ready to die. O sing for me my favorite songs. I wish you could go with me to the scaffold, but that is against the law for women to go to the execution in this state." Mothers could not endure such things, but I feel, when permitted, as if I must stay till all is over.

I took a white silk handkerchief and gently folded it around the boy's neck, and said, "I think the rope won't hurt so bad, and the pain won't be so severe with this around your neck." I shall never forget the grateful look on his face, as he smilingly thanked me. He was a very refined young man, and only for whiskey he might be living yet. As I bade him good-bye he said, "Please sing for me *once more* before I go." I sang and passed out among the crowds of people. I seemed to be lifted above the things of earth—I was so thankful for his salvation. Reader, do you know what it is to travail for a soul and then count the hours and moments till you see them go over the river of death, and by-and-by with the eye of faith see them enter the pearly gates into the presence of Him who was crucified for them?

After the execution I received the following kind letter from the young priest to whom I have referred:

San Francisco, Oct. 13, 1888.

Dear Madam:

It was with great pleasure I read your kind and welcome note. I thank you very much for your pleasant remembrance and hope that God will bless your efforts and sacrifices on behalf of the poor prisoners.

In regard to A., I can say that he was resigned to the last and died well prepared, in my opinion. I was with him almost constantly during the last twelve hours. I think his family placed the silk handkerchief in the coffin with him.

Please give my regards to your kind companion and say sometimes a little prayer for me. I hope to see you soon in San Francisco and have the pleasure of renewing my acquaintance. I have the honor of remaining,

Yours truly in Jesus Christ,

Rev. N—— F——.

MYSTERIOUSLY GUIDED.

In April, 1891, I was in Kansas City, Mo. After waiting upon the Lord for some days asking Him where He would have me go next I was impressed to go to the depot and that there it would be shown me what I must do. I did so, but even then was left for several hours in uncertainty as to what train to take, as I had passes on four different lines. I spent the time in earnest prayer. At last, toward evening, I was led to take the Rock Island train for Chicago and impressed that the Lord would show me when and where to stop. I had two sisters and a little boy with me and they could not understand my indecision.

As our train hurried on during the night, I kept asking the Lord where I should stop, and He made it very plain to me that I was to stop at Ottawa, Ill. I knew no one there, and there was no state-prison there, but the Lord showed me to go to the county jail and when I did so found there were several men there soon to be executed. I was told that no one was permitted to see them; but we went praying and the Lord touched the hearts of the officers and we were permitted to hold a service. We were much helped of the Holy Spirit and I believe some of these condemned men were saved—at least they seemed to give evidence of it. One of them afterwards wrote me two letters. These I give to my readers. It is well to remember, however, that not many such prisoners are accustomed to expressing their thoughts in writing and hence their letters fail to express the depth of feeling clearly shown in their words and manner when I am with them. Again all their letters are to be read before they leave the prison, so they do not open their hearts as freely when writing as when speaking with me alone.

La Salle County Jail,
Ottawa, Ill., April 28, 1891.

Elizabeth R. Wheaton.

Dear Sister: We are doing very well. As for Mr. C. and myself, we will do the best we can to reach that Beautiful home in the New Jerusalem, for the Lord saith: "He that believeth and abideth in Me shall have everlasting life." As you must have seen, our belief is a little different from yours in some respects, but, nevertheless, we are all working for that one place and that is heaven. He that leaveth his sins behind him shall be saved. The example of those who died for Christ, for the faith and for virtue's sake are also continually placed before us that we may learn to endure sufferings and even death rather than be unfaithful to God and stain our conscience with sin. The Christian's motto is, "Death before dishonor." Hoping that you will continue to pray for us that we may be cleansed from sin and be saved, we send you our sincere and hearty wishes for your welfare. God bless you and keep you ever for your sincere effort in our behalf. Hoping that we may meet in that beautiful place where the penitent shall find rest, I remain yours in respect,

CHARLIE ——.

La Salle County Jail, Ottawa, Ill., May 6, 1891.

Dear Sister:

I was glad to receive your letter and to hear that you are still praying for us. Mr. F. has gone out, so there are just two of us—me and Mr. C., who, I think, will get a new trial. He sends his kind regards and is doing well.

As for me, I am very close to the grave as I have only four more days to live, but hope that it will be all for the best. I am preparing myself for death as much as possible for so short a time. My thoughts are not of the outside world, but of a higher world, where there is no sin or trouble or care, but everlasting life and happiness. I also hope that we may meet in that haven of rest. I will do as you say, put my trust in God and believe in Him. Life is very short at best, but we all have our cares and troubles and must bear with them the best we can, as we are helpless without the grace of God. Thanking you sincerely for your kind efforts in our behalf, I remain your brother in all sincerity. Farewell.

Yours in respect,

CHARLIE ——.

IN LONG EXPECTATION.

I first saw E. B—— in the jail in Wichita, Kansas. There were many prisoners there at that time and especially in the Oklahoma ward. It was soon after the opening up of Oklahoma territory and the rush for claims. There was great excitement and many lost their lives. Some were thrown from their horses and killed. Others died from exhaustion, running as for life to get the property they so much coveted. There were many things done that were wrong. Some are still lingering inside prison walls for "defending their rights" as they thought. I do not remember just what E.'s trouble was, but he was sentenced to death and the day and the hour were set. I went often to the prison and sang and prayed for the prisoners. They were my friends. I knew and loved them as a mother would, and especially this young boy—the youngest of them all.

I went away to Europe and on my return I again visited the jail in Wichita to hold a service. While singing the first hymn the jailer came into the apartment where I was and said, "The Oklahoma boys have heard you singing and want you to come at once to their ward. They did not know you had returned from Scotland and are so anxious to see you." And such a welcome as those dear boys and men gave me I had received no where else since my return. Some were under death sentences. O how my heart aches even now as I think of the tears they shed and of their warm handclasp. Then I could only fall on my knees and sob out my sorrow for them and my heartfelt thanks to God for the warm welcome and as I wept and prayed I believe good was accomplished and souls saved. Some are dead and gone. Others are in the asylum for the criminal insane. A few were pardoned out. Eddie's case lingered. While hoping for a commutation of sentence he wrote the following letter:

Wichita, May 3, 1891.

Dear Friend:

I received your kind letter. Was glad to hear you were well and still at your post, working for others. I am still in my little cell awaiting what comes and have not heard much yet regarding commitment, but hope it may come in time. I am feeling as though I have a heavy load on my shoulders for a boy, but I hope and pray for the best to come. I want to see the light, if there is any for me. I sometimes think that I am forgotten; and then again I know better, for there is One who never forgets us. I have read those nice tracts you sent me and they are all true. The boys are all well and send their best respects to you and hope to meet you again; and you know I do, for I feel the need of your kindness and appreciate it highly. I know what a kind mother is. I have a good Christian mother and father. Oh, if I were only free again, so I could enjoy life with my dear mother! No one knows how lonely I am. You are only one hundred miles from my home in ———, Illinois. If you go there you could find them by enquiring for them. They would be glad to see you, as I have told them about your being here. I hope some day that you can come and see me on the outside. What a happy boy I would be! If not, I hope we may meet in that brighter home. I have been reading my Bible and find relief. What a book it is, and the good that can be gotten from it! I wish you success through life and that you may save many a poor lost sinner. No one knows the good they can do until they try.

May God bless you, is my prayer.

EDDIE ———.

SENTENCE COMMUTED.

Many of those acquainted with the case were anxious for his release but met with little encouragement. I continued to pray earnestly that at least his life might be spared. When the day appointed for his execution came I was in a distant state some miles from a telegraph office, but I sent a little boy to the office with a message telling him that the Lord might even yet deliver him and if not would sustain him in his dying moments. The same day a wire came for him from the governor changing his sentence to imprisonment for life. He was transferred to a northern prison, but only lived a few years. So far as I could learn he lived and died a Christian, and I hope to see him again by and by in heaven.

A MAN DECEIVED.

At one time I held a service with the prisoners in the county jail in Sedalia, Missouri. Among them was a poor old man awaiting execution. He seemed unmoved, stolid, indifferent. I talked and prayed with him and asked him about his soul's salvation. He said it was all right with his soul and that he was saved. I knew the Lord showed me that he was a deceived man and that the devil had deluded him into thinking he was all right. I was faithful to my convictions, to my God and to his soul. I said to him: "You are not prepared to face the scaffold and death." He seemed indignant that I should doubt his word, but I left him with the warning, "Prepare to meet thy God."

I went to the wife of the sheriff, who was an excellent woman, and found she too was very anxious about his soul. I told her of my burden for him and asked for a room where I could wait on God in prayer and she kindly furnished it. In an hour the old man sent word to the sheriff to send for me to come and pray for him as he was not fit to die. In company with others I went to him and the poor deceived old man repented of his sins and confessed them to God and to us and was blessedly saved and died in the full assurance of faith. His last words were of his hope in Christ and of his acceptance with God. I fully believe that the blood of Jesus—who died on the cross for sinners and was the friend of sinners always—did cleanse his soul. The sheriff's wife told me of his last words and that all was well. We give a clipping from a Sedalia paper concerning the case.

VISITORS EXCLUDED.

WILLIAMSON WILL RECEIVE NO MORE VISITS— PREPARATION FOR THE EXECUTION.

Sheriff Ellis R. Smith has commenced to make his arrangements for the execution of Thomas A. Williamson, and everything will be in readiness before Saturday morning. The rope with which John Oscar Turlington and Bill Price were hanged will be used, the sheriff having received a telegram yesterday from Sheriff Mat S. Ayers, of Saline county, stating that it had been forwarded to him by express. On the day of execution the police force will assist the county authorities in preserving order in the vicinity of the jail building.

No more visitors will be permitted to see and talk with Williamson, except his spiritual advisers. This is in compliance with the condemned man's wishes, which are contained in the following note which he sent to Sheriff Smith yesterday:

"Sheriff Smith: I would like a cell by myself the rest of my time. You can put me any place. I will give you no trouble. My mind is on God. I would like to be upstairs; it is lighter up there. I will go where you put me.

T. A. W."

I received from him the following letters written after his conversion. One of them reached me after his execution:

Sedalia, Mo.

Sister Elizabeth R. Wheaton:

I am well this morning. I thank God for it. I hope this will find you well. I prayed to God to watch over me through the night, and He did. I feel happy. I will meet you across the river. We will have a good time. May God keep you. I am going to heaven. I will meet you in that bright land. I am glad to hear from you.

THOS. A.

Sedalia, Mo., October 29, 1891.

My True Mother:

I got your letter right now. I read it and got on my knees and prayed to God to have mercy on me. My sister, I have my mind on Jesus all the time. I feel happy this morning. Mother, I will meet you on the other shore. Mother S. (the sheriff's wife) is so kind to me! My mind is on God so I can hardly write. I will pray for you.

THOS. A.

INTERCEDED FOR THE LIFE OF A BOY.

I went to a city in 1898, where there were four under sentence of death, and when I went into the jail found many waiting trial. Some were going to state's prison. Others were to die on the scaffold. I was especially impressed with the case of one boy who was under death sentence. I held a service with the prisoners and talked personally to those condemned to die. One man was wonderfully saved and I believe went to heaven from the scaffold. I then went away to other states. But I was so troubled I made inquiries and found that the young boy to whom I referred *was not charged with being a murderer*, and was not deserving of death. I plead to God if there was nothing the law could find in him worthy of death, that his sentence might be commuted, and the poor boy might live. Upon my return I went to the capital to see the Governor, and asked him to grant the boy a life sentence in prison. My request was granted, it was soon all settled and the boy's life was spared. Yet the Deputy Sheriff was very angry at the Governor for granting the commutation!

WENT TO THE SCAFFOLD SINGING.

In May, 1899, another poor prisoner ended his life on the scaffold. The Friday before, two died on the same gallows. I visited them the day before the execution, talked and sang hymns (their favorites), and then we three kneeled together in prayer in the little "condemned cell." Kneeling between my boys, clasping each by the hand, we gave ourselves to the blessed Savior, who said just before he expired on the cross, "Father, forgive them, for they know not what they do." I shall never forget that last prayer meeting with those unfortunate men who had been led astray by evil surroundings and associations, forming habits which finally sent them to early graves, by fearful deaths. Yet, as we knelt there together, just we three and the blessed Holy Spirit witnessing, we promised to meet in Heaven. Jesus met us there and forgave them their sins, and joy filled our souls with love for Him who gave Himself a ransom for us, not willing that any should perish, but rather that all should have eternal life. How my heart rejoiced to hear them say they were prepared to go, and the parting was very sweet. A solemn hush filled the little cell—sweet peace which only comes when souls have been redeemed, fell upon my heart, and I was glad Jesus Himself did His own work for His own name's honor and glory. They sang hymns and prayed all night before the execution. They refused to eat, preferring to sing and pray till the last, and went to the scaffold singing and praising God, and were still singing when the drop fell, and they were gone from earth.

My heart cried out for the living that May morning, as another one went to the scaffold, "O God, save his soul! O God, forgive him all his sins. The same scaffold, the same sin, and the same Jesus to blot out all his transgressions." I believe God, where he says, Isa. 1:18, "Though your sins be as scarlet, they shall be as white as snow: though they be red like crimson they shall be as wool." If it were not for the promises of God in His blessed Word, I should give up in despair, sometimes, over those cases who have been so deceived by the devil. Yet God is able to snatch them as brands from the burning. Jude 22-23 says, "And of some have compassion, making a difference: and others save with fear, pulling them out of the fire; hating even the garment spotted by the flesh." Jesus said, "Whosoever will may come," I believe His promises are "Yea and amen to all that believe." When I see what saloons and other evils are doing to wreck lives and ruin souls, I wonder how God on His throne can ever forgive such premeditated, intentional sins. The keepers of these places sell themselves to Satan to be used by him to defeat God's plan of saving those who will come unto Him. O that all who claim to be Christians would unite to overthrow the means that Satan uses to lead down to eternal death so many precious souls!

The case to which I shall now refer was one in many respects especially touching. The condemned man had occupied *a prominent official position*. The dear, noble wife never turned away from her husband. Hers were the kind heart and hands that ministered to his needs and cheered the long, gloomy hours of his imprisonment. She stood by him in his trial and during those days of agony and suspense. Then came the verdict "Guilty," and the sentence of death! Yet, though her own heart was breaking as she thought of herself and her beautiful, helpless children, she still sought to cheer and comfort as best she could that poor condemned man whose heart was torn with anguish when he realized that because of his sin that faithful loving wife and those innocent children must be left disgraced and destitute. What is to become of the little ones who are powerless to help themselves and of the poor despised, rejected, forsaken mother, trying to earn with her own hands by toiling night and day enough to feed and clothe those helpless babes? O my God, will you not help me to provide a home for such as these? For the sake of these heart-broken mothers whose lives are doomed to be (only as helped by the grace of God) one great unending sorrow—for the sake of the poor children so cruelly robbed of their birthright—a father's good name and protection, these who are worse than orphans, yet for whom nobody seems to care, help me to do what I can—what thou dost require at my hands. This man was brought up in a Christian home and but for the power of evil associations with which he was brought in contact and the curse of the legalized saloon, would today in all probability have been a respected and honorable member of society.

I first found him one Fourth of July. While others were spending the holiday I went toiling through the heat to the prison and there I found my reward. My soul was borne upward by the Holy Spirit as I sang many songs of praise and tenderly led this poor man to the foot of the cross where he was saved. His wife was there a part of the time. I seem to see the parting even now of those dear ones! Well, God knows it all. Had I never known a wife's and a mother's love I could not have sympathized with them as I did. I thought—What if *my* boy had lived and come to such an end—and I wept with that faithful wife as she took leave. O, sisters, there is a power in even a look of love coming from a true heart.

I give two letters received from the condemned man and one written me by his wife. I omit the name of place and exact date and even the initials, as so few years have passed and I do not wish to do anything that might bring pain to the hearts of surviving friends. The family was of the most cultured and respected.

July, 1899.

Dear Sister Wheaton:

It was with the greatest pleasure that I read your card this morning. I was wondering where you were; but I knew that if your health permitted you, you were somewhere doing good to some poor unfortunate.

Yes, I am putting my entire trust in Jesus. He saves me from my sins and when the cares and woes of this life come to disturb my peace, I look unto the Savior and soon all is peace again. What would I do in a place like this and under such circumstances did not his gentle voice speak unto me and say, "Fear not, I will not leave nor forsake you." My wife was down to see me last Monday, and is coming today (Thursday). She wrote me that your songs and prayer were still ringing in her ears—so you see that your good work is not only felt by prisoners. I hope that you may be able to go on with the good work that so much delights you and that you may yet win many wandering souls and bring them into the fold of God and that when your work on earth is ended you may rest from your labors in the most beautiful palace in the city of heaven. You may think that strange that I said "palace," but I believe that heaven is a real and tangible city—the home of God, from where He sends the Holy Ghost to dwell in the hearts of all those who are willing to receive Him.

I will now say good-by, and if I never again meet you on this earth, I hope to meet you in heaven.

I am yours most sincerely in the hope of heaven.

—— ——.

August, 1899.

My Dear Mother, for such you seem to me, I will never while I am on this earth cease to think of you. I have remembered your voice since I first heard you sing and pray while in the cells of poor W—— and S——, the condemned men. I wished then that I could have seen you, and I told the boys that you were certainly born of God; and from that day I have desired to have your influence and prayers. I am still trusting in the love, mercy and power of the Savior to save my soul in the eternal world and to keep me from sin while I am in this. I have no other hope, no other desire than to serve my Master. I would want to attain to a state of perfection here, if such were possible, but you know that the cares of this life come in to rob us of the pleasure that we would enjoy in the anticipation of heaven. But some day the dark clouds that overshadow us and prevent us for a while from seeing the Savior's smiling face will be rolled away. I am glad to tell you that the sentence of R——, whose cell was next to mine, has been commuted to life imprisonment. He and the man P—— send their regards to you. P——'s sentence is respited until the 17th of November, and in the meantime he hopes for a new trial.

I will close, wishing you the choicest blessings of heaven, and I am yours very sincerely, trusting in the hope of eternal life,

Your brother in Christ,

—— ——.

The following from the *Star* of ——, ——, explains itself. The men are referred to in the above letter:

BOTH TWICE CONVICTED OF THE CRIME OF MURDER.

Everything is in readiness at the District jail for the double execution which is to take place tomorrow, when S—— and W—— will pay the penalty of their crimes. So far as outward appearances are concerned, the condemned men are in a better frame of mind than are most of the other prisoners in the big brown-stone prison. Their spiritual advisers are with them most of the time, and when they are absent the men pass the hours reading religious books and praying.

S—— and W—— have both been well-behaved prisoners and have given the jail officials no trouble whatever. The former has been particularly friendly with the guards and others, and today he thanked several of them for past kindnesses. He also desired to express his gratitude to his many friends for what they had done for him, and said he desired to do so through the *Star*. S—— has had many visitors during the entire time of his confinement in jail, but more especially during recent weeks. Most of them have been female relatives. They have been endeavoring to collect funds enough to defray the expenses of a decent burial. In the event of their being successful the body will be turned over to them after the execution by the undertaker employed by the government to prepare the bodies for burial.

Monday afternoon, just before the prison doors were locked for the day, the bell rang and the guard at the door admitted a woman who handed in her card on which was printed:

> "Elizabeth Rider Wheaton,
> "Prison Evangelist.
> "No Home but Heaven."

She had with her a number of tracts which she distributed to some of the prisoners. Her religious work is all done in prisons, and she makes a specialty of laboring with condemned men. She stated to the guards that she had traveled about 2,000 miles to see those in jail here before their execution. The warden admitted her to the cells. She had W—— and S—— join her in prayer and song in the latter's cell, and the men seemed greatly to appreciate her hour's visit. She next saw E—— S——, who is to die on the scaffold next week. He, too, appeared to enjoy her call.

—— ——

Star.

August, 1899.

Mrs. Wheaton.

My Dear Sister: I must write a few lines to you, in my husband's letter, as you have shown yourself so kind to him, poor fellow. I can see you now and hear you, in my fancy, singing those beautiful pieces. Oh, how sad I felt on that Fourth of July as I sat and listened, especially to the one called "Some Mother's Child," as I looked upon my dear husband and thought of his mother and how tenderly he had been reared by Christian parents, and was always a good and thoughtful son and husband until by reason of evil associations he fell into sin and kept going further and further from God until at last he was led to do the most dreadful of deeds. How I pity him!

O how happy I once was! Had a pretty home and everything to brighten it. But alas, they have vanished and now I feel alone, without anything. Did I say "alone?" No, not so, for the God that I have served and who has been with me these twenty years, is still with me; and I feel to say, "Though he slay me, yet will I trust him." I feel that he will open up a way for his children. Now, my dear sister, I would love to see you again in this life and talk with you, but if I never meet you here I trust I shall meet you above, where your voice will be heard with the angels of God. Please remember me to your lady helper. Would be glad to hear from you at any time. Good-bye.

Yours in love and the hope of heaven,

———— ————.

Two years later, while in the same city, a friend invited me to go to an open-air service and after I had sung and spoken to those who were gathered a dear lady clasped my hand and said: "I am so glad to see you, mother—don't you know me?" As I failed to recognize her she turned her careworn but lovely face so that the electric light shone full upon her and said, "Don't you remember me now?" When I still answered "No, I do not," the tears gathered in the dear eyes as she said, "My husband never forgot your singing and your prayers before he went away," and then it dawned upon me that she was the wife of the man the people hung to gratify the saloon men's greed. She said: "I do wish I could ask you home with me, but I have only a little hall room for myself and children. I am keeping boarders to make a living for myself and them." O how I wished for a home to which I could welcome them, but I, too, am a pilgrim and a stranger, and all I could do was to kiss the dear sister and commend her to the widow's God and her dear ones to the Father of the fatherless.

The letters following are from two brothers with whom I labored, and who showed much appreciation of my efforts with them and professed to be saved. I received a number of encouraging letters from them and from others in the same place before they were taken away. We can not always tell as to the sincerity of these poor men, or of their responsibility, some of them doubtless are so nearly unbalanced in mind, under such a strain, but we know the God of heaven before whom we must all stand will judge righteously.

October 18, 1903.

My Dear Mother Wheaton:

While my dear unfortunate brother, Mr. K., has given me space in his letter, I just wish to congratulate you for the wonderful good you did while here with us, as we have not forgotten your topic, "Salvation," and often speak of you and hope you will come again at your earliest convenience. Thank God there is some of us have the Spirit of God with us. Bless His holy name! And I for one can praise Him for the wonderful good He has done me, and through His wonderful love I have been granted a stay of execution, which was to take place the 21st of this month; for God in heaven knows I am innocent of this crime, as is also my brother. I am sorry to say I do not know much about the Bible, but intend to learn more about His wonderful love to man, and will serve Him to the end. Trusting that you will look upon us as your children, I will close, hoping to hear from you again,

Your unfortunate boy,

B. W.

Dear Mother Wheaton:

Received your letter and was glad to hear from you. It brought great joy to our bleeding hearts. We think of you and wish you could talk and sing for us every day. Your kind, loving words bring me near to God. When I leave this world I will go to my heavenly Father, where there is everlasting life, and if we never meet on earth, I will meet you in heaven. I shall never forget you and the prayer you made for me. We felt bad when you could not come back and tell us about our loving God. Pray for me that I may walk daily with God. I remain as ever,

Your dear boy,

A. W.

Columbus, Ohio.

THREE YOUNG MEN.

Some cases of special interest to me because of such recent occurrence, are the three young men mentioned elsewhere and from whom I received the following letters. I will first give a note very kindly written me by the son of the warden, in answer to an inquiry about the cases while they were awaiting some decision of the supreme court:

Colorado State Penitentiary.

Canon City, Colo., December 7, 1904.

Mother E. R. Wheaton. Tabor, Iowa.

Dear Mother: I have not answered your postal on account of my absence from the city, but I hope you will overlook the delay. The fate of the four prisoners under sentence of death is still undecided, as their case is in the hands of the Supreme Court. There is some doubt as to the legality of the law and it is a hard matter to tell what the outcome will be. No, my folks did not attend the Prison Congress this year on account of my sister's health. The boys at the prison often speak of you and some have started to forget the past and try to do better in the future on account of the good words you spoke to them. I hope you will come to see us before my father goes out of office, but if this is impossible, I pray that we may meet at some future time. I remain,

Yours respectfully,

Willard Cleghorn.

Canon City, Colo., May 3, 1904.

Dear Mother Wheaton:

I have received your kind letter and postal and I am very glad to know that you have not forgotten me. I have not forgotten you either, nor never will. For it was no other than you who put me on the right road to heaven, and I know that if I do all you told me that I will meet you there. I am praying both day and night, and I pray from my heart, and mean every word that I say, and I know that my sorrow is more than I can bear without God's help. I know that God has forgiven me all of my sins, and will save me too. I do not care who laughs at me for praying and asking God for help. There is nothing that can ever make me quit praying and believing in God, for He has done me good already.

With love and best wishes, and hoping to hear from you soon,

Yours sincerely,

F. A.

Canon City, Colo., May 3, 1904.

Dear Mrs. Wheaton.

It is with pleasure that I answer your most kind and welcome letter that brother A. and I received some time ago. We also received a postal card this morning. I have neglected my promise of writing, but hereafter will write more promptly. I have not been feeling well, but am better now. I hope you will forgive me this time.

It does my heart good to know that you are praying for us. I feel very grateful to you. Us boys pray and read the Holy Bible every day. I am trusting to our Heavenly Father, for He makes right the wrong. We are being treated most kindly by the warden and the officers of the prison.

I will close, as Brother A. wishes to say a few words.

Hoping to hear from you again, I ever remain

Your son in Christ,

C.

Canon City, Colo., May 17, 1904.

Mrs. E. R. Wheaton.

My Dear Mother: I received your kind letter and was very much pleased to hear from you, as all of us were. * * *

When I saw and read your letter and those little tracts, they certainly did take effect on me. As I read them and saw the terrible mistake I had made, it caused the tears to fall. I am trusting in God, but I can't come right out and tell you that I am really saved, for I don't believe in deceiving you. But I do believe that God has laid a hand on me, and I hope He will take a stronger hold on me. I know you will think more of me for telling you the candid facts. I have seen lots of people who would tell that they were really saved, when they knew they were not. But "God help my poor soul," is my regular prayer. I realize that I need His help in my present circumstances. I still ask you to pray for me that God will help me to look to Him. I try my best to do what is right, and never go to sleep a night without praying to Him to save my soul and spare me so that I may be of some benefit to His cause, and I do fully believe that He will answer my prayer, for when I pray I am sure I do it with all my heart and soul.

I am quite well at present, and hope that these few lines will find you the same. May God bless you and protect you, is my daily prayer. I hope to hear from you again soon.

From one of yours, and I hope, the Lord's sons.

Yours respectfully,

N. A.

Canon City, Colo., May 27, 1904.

Dear Mother Wheaton:

I take pleasure in answering your most kind and welcome letter received a few days ago. I am quite well at present. I am taking things as easy as I can and waiting most patiently to know how I will fare. I haven't forgot to pray and read the Bible, nor will I as long as I live. I am trusting in the Lord, for He makes all things right. I will close, hoping to hear from you again.

Very sincerely yours,

C. P.

Canon City, Colo., May 27, 1904.

Dear Mother Wheaton:

I take pleasure in answering your letter. You don't know how glad I was to hear from you. This leaves me well and in good faith and I am trusting in the Lord, for I know He will help me if I will only be good and do His will. I pray and read my Bible every night and day. Oh, if I ever do get my freedom I will make a man of myself and do God's will and make my poor wife and mother and father happy. I will never take a drop of whiskey or anything again. So good-bye. We have heard nothing of our case yet. The time seems so long.

From yours sincerely,

F. A.

The following are extracts from touching letters from the aged mother and young wife of this young man:

Kansas City, Mo., July 4, 1904.

Dear Mother Wheaton:

We received your card and were indeed glad to hear from you. Oh, I am praying to God all the time to spare my baby's life. How can I ever live if they take his life! Why do they want it? He did not kill any one, although the deed he did almost breaks my heart. F. never drank until he got with those people on Market Street. They got him to smoking hop and drinking whiskey. My dear and only child, will God and man have mercy on him? Oh, I thank you for going to see my poor baby boy! God bless him and save his life.

I hope you can see the Governor and see if he will do something for a mother to save her only child. I can hardly stand it. It has done F. so much good for you to see him. He always speaks of you when he writes home. Oh, I do hope the Governor will give you some hopes, for if I could get any hopes of F. being spared it would do me so much good! I pray day and night for my boy. He is on my mind all the time. Hoping to hear from you soon, I am

Sincerely yours,

Mrs. A.

Kansas City, Mo., July 4, 1904.

Mrs. E. R. Wheaton:

Kind Friend: I was truly glad to hear from you and that you are going to see my dear husband soon. I hope it will not be long till I see him, for it seems like years since I have seen poor F. I hope my loved one will come out better yet, for I can never stand it. I hope and pray that F. will have a show for his life. How short our young lives were together. F. was always kind to me and it almost took my life when I was robbed of my darling husband. I was an orphan girl. My dear mother died when I was five years old. I had a hard time all my life till I was eighteen, when I was married to F., last September. I was so happy with him. He was a good boy and never drank till he met with the Market Street gang and they got him to drinking and smoking that hop.

This is the Fourth of July and F.'s gray-haired mother and I are here grieving over the loved one in prison. If a wife ever loved a husband truly I love mine. I remain your friend,

MRS. F. A.

Canon City, Colo., Sept. 22, 1904.

Dear Mother Wheaton:

I was glad to hear from you, which I always am, for your letters are full of kind words and it is a pleasure to read them in my lonely cell and know there is one true friend who prays for me. Kind words are few for me now when I am in need and going through the most terrible and trying time of a lifetime. But I am living in hopes and trusting God for my future, come what may. I surely thank you for seeing the Governor in our behalf.

My mother and wife are well. Their letter to you must have been missent, for they wrote. This leaves me well.

Yours sincerely,

F. A.

Canon City, Colo., March 26, 1905.

Mrs. E. R. Wheaton:

Dear Mother: I was very glad to hear from you as I did not know what had become of you. Well, the law has been found good and the death watch is over us. Poor ———— was hung the 6th. Our time begins the 21st of May. Yes, I am trusting God and I know He has heard my prayers, and whatever comes will be for the best. P——— is getting better again they tell me. A——— is the same as ever. I wrote to my mother today and told her I heard from you.

Yours sincerely

F. A.

Canon City, Colo., April 12, 1905.

Mrs. E. R. Wheaton, Los Angeles, Cal.:

Dear Mother Wheaton: I was glad to hear from you. Your letters do me so much good, they always give me new hope. Of course you understand what I am going through, and at times hope seems hopeless for the time seems so long to me in this dreary cell, and to think if I had left that horrible liquor alone and stayed away from bad company where I could have been to-night—free and happy, at home with my wife and my poor old mother and father. But as it is I am sad and lonely and my loved ones are far away, heart-broken. But I believe my prayers will be answered yet, for I know God has heard them. But, the Lord's will be done. I know He will do what is best for me.

Well, dear mother, the boys are well and send their best regards.

Sincerely yours,

F. A.

Canon City, Colo., June 15, 1905.

Dear Mother Wheaton:

I received your kind and welcome letter and was glad to hear from you again. I will never have the pleasure of reading another letter from you in this world, for I have been put back in a horrible death cell again and the Board of Pardons and Governor have refused to save me from the terrible death I am doomed for, but I expect to meet you in heaven, dear mother, for I know God has forgiven me all of my sins. I want to thank you again for all you have done for me, for I know you have spent many a sleepless night on account of me. I felt a great deal better after seeing and praying with you the last time you were here than I had since I've been in this trouble. I am glad things are most at an end for I am very weary of these lonesome death cells. Of course I don't want to die nor am I glad of it, for I have lots to live for yet as you know, but the Lord's will be done. I know it will be for the best. Well, I will close for this time. I am to be hung in the next twenty-four hours, so good-bye, dear friend. Think of me sometime in the future.

From your son in Christ,

F. A.

Mother Wheaton:

Dear Mother: We just received your loving letter last night and was glad to hear from you. Oh, dear mother, my darling boy is gone; never can I see his loving face in this cruel world. Oh, it is terrible; it seems too hard for me to stand. Just think, my only darling child. But I know he is in heaven. He died on the 16th. We went to see him and he was so glad to see us. He kissed his papa and all of us and said he wanted us not to grieve any more than we could help.... His last words were "Good-bye, mamma," with a smile and wave of his hand just like I was coming back again. He said he would like to be buried close to home. Poor, darling boy; he loved to be close to home and mamma in life, but it is hard to think that he had to spend his last days away from us, all on account of whiskey.

Your friends as ever,

MRS. A. AND L.

(The above was from the aged mother and the young
wife.)

Think you, dear reader, that these experiences are passed by lightly when I must enter into the sorrows of these mothers and loved ones who must give up their dear ones in this way? Only the grace and love of God can sustain me and these dear bereaved ones in these trials. This was one of my saddest experiences, as I was personally acquainted with the parents and the dear young wife of one of these young men, having been entertained at their home some days at a time during their sorrow. This is only another example of what strong drink is doing in our land. God pity those who in the least favor this traffic.

I give below short extracts taken from *The Daily News* of Denver concerning these cases:

> "Not yet has the final word for F. A., C. P. and N. A., under sentence of death, been said.

> "It is likely that it will not be said for at least a week or ten days. The Board of Pardons adjourned late yesterday afternoon without deciding the fate of the three boys....

> "But, though the tragic element was lacking, there was present throughout the meeting an undercurrent of deep human woe. The mother of A. was there, clad in black, with a hopeless expression on her face pitiful to see. Beside her at all times was the wife of A., young, pretty in an indefinite sort of way, her blue eyes holding ever before them the wreck of her shattered girlish romance. Both women wept freely at times.

> "With the two women were a dozen of their women friends, whose coming had been actuated by a mixture of curiosity and sympathy.

> ### FRIEND OF ALL PRISONERS.

> "Mrs. Elizabeth R. Wheaton, friend of prisoners the world over, was there too. She sat next Mrs. A., the elder, and wept copiously in sympathy. 'Mother' Wheaton visited the boys at Canon City, and she told the board the impression of her visit, how, she was sure, they had repented of their deed and had their sins forgiven.

> "She also pleaded for their lives on the ground of opposition to capital punishment. She has been in state prison rescue work for twenty-one years, and her silver

- 231 -

hair, refined face and gentle manner have brought comfort to criminals everywhere."—News, May 6.

SESSION OF THE BOARD.

The Board of Pardons met in special session at 10 o'clock yesterday morning for the purpose of passing finally upon the applications of the three boys for commutation of sentence from death to imprisonment for life.

Interest in the proceedings of the morning centered around four women, two mothers, a sister and a wife of the condemned boys. They were Mrs. J. A., bowed with the weight of her seventy years, who had come all the way from Buffalo, N. Y., to be present at the meeting; her daughter, Miss A., of Denver; Mrs. J. A. and Mrs. F. A., mother and wife, respectively, of F. A. All four were present throughout the hearing and made personal pleas to the Board.

After the hearing was concluded they went together into the outer office of the executive chamber and sat huddled up in one corner of the big room, their eyes fixed on the door which led to the inner office where four men were deciding whether the boys they loved should live or die.

HEARD THE BAD NEWS.

When the news of the Board's action was conveyed by Secretary C. E. Hagar to the four women waiting in the outer office, their grief was pitiful in the extreme. Mrs. A. very nearly collapsed. She clung to the arm of her daughter and moaned in heart-breaking accents. The daughter, too, was almost overcome, but controlled herself for her mother's sake.

The mother and wife of F. A., while it was evident they were suffering keenly, maintained an outward composure except for the tears which welled from their eyes. They hurriedly left the capitol building together. The young wife will go to the penitentiary Friday to say a last good-bye to her husband.

PLEA OF ATTORNEY.

W. E., attorney for A., made a wonderfully eloquent plea for his client's life. It was logical, pathetic and at times scathing in its denunciation of the methods used by the police to extort confessions from the boys. He said these methods, in their horrible brutality, were without parallel anywhere.

"The only evidence upon which N. A. was convicted," he said, "was the alleged confession wrung out of him by police brutality. This confession was made after the prisoner had been 'sweated' and intimidated. One ear had been almost torn off, he had been cuffed, kicked and trampled upon, and then, under the influence of threats, he made his alleged confession."

NEWS THAT SON IS TO HANG BROKEN TO AGED WOMAN BY HER DAUGHTER AND CAUSES COLLAPSE.

Sitting and staring with a blank look into space, at intervals relieving the tension of her misery by low moans, and then again ejaculating pitifully, "Oh, my boy! My poor, poor boy! Can I live and know that you died upon the gallows?" Mrs. J. A. is now hovering on the borderland of life at the home of her daughter in Denver.

It was not until noon yesterday that Mrs. A. was told that the pardons board had refused to grant her son, N. A., a commutation of sentence from death to life imprisonment. Up to that moment when the terrible knowledge became hers she had a mother's hope that the pardons board must save her boy. From the moment she heard from her daughter's lips that the son and brother must die, Mrs. A. has been verging upon a semi-comatose condition, and under the constant care of a physician.

She was illy prepared to hear the news yesterday, for she had spent the night previous without closing her eyes in sleep. It was not until 5 o'clock that slumber came to her mercifully, and even then she merely slept in a fitful doze until 8 o'clock.

SUPPRESSED EMOTION.

The serious phase of Mrs. A.'s condition, her physician regards, is that with her it is all suppressed emotion. She does not cry out or rave, but endures her intense suffering in quiet. It is but seldom that tears come to her relief, and the only vent her emotion has is in her low moans for her "poor boy."

After the news was broken to her, Mrs. A. spent most of the day in bed. Late last night she was still in the same condition, and the gravest anxiety is felt by her relatives.

Mrs. A. is 70 years old. She lives in Buffalo, N. Y., and made the long trip of 1,500 miles to personally plead with the State Board of Pardons for the life of her son.

TO TEST GALLOWS.

Warden C. will today test the automatic scaffold upon which N. A. and F. A. will be executed next week. He will see that everything about the device is in perfect order and will make a final test just prior to taking the first of the two to his death. The execution house, where the men will be confined until the final summons, is 28x30 feet. It contains three condemned cells and across the hall from these are two large rooms. In the center of one is a large iron plate and on this the condemned is asked to stand after the noose and cap have been adjusted. The weight of the man causes the plate to drop about an inch. This closes the circuit of a current connecting with a bucket of water which stands on a shelf in a closet in an adjoining room. By a magnet arrangement a plug in the bottom of the bucket is pulled and the water begins to flow out. As soon as the vessel is empty an automatic connection releases a catch holding a bag of sand on the end of the noose.

The sand, being heavier than the man, falls, causing the body at the other extremity of the rope to be jerked off the floor to the height of three feet. The sandbag is in the room containing the closet where the bucket is and the rope from the noose reaches that room over a pulley and through a hole in the wall.

The condemned man does not see any of the details of the execution when he enters the death cell. The iron plate in the floor and the noose around his neck are the only parts he can see. He does not hear the dropping of the water nor the working of any of the mechanism.

The instant the man is jerked off his feet and suspended at the end of the rope his neck is broken. The time intervening between the pulling of the plug in the bucket and the falling of the sand is usually about a minute. The suspense to the prisoner, however, is not regarded as any more cruel than that experienced by a man in the electrical chair or on the scaffold while he awaits the fatal current or the springing of the trap.

The hanging apparatus was invented by a convict fifteen years ago.—*News*, May 20.

As shown by foregoing letters these cases were continued till June 16. Such is the suspense, sorrow of heart and grief through which many are constantly passing in this world, all on account of sin. What are we trying to do to lend a hand of relief?

Such, dear reader, are a few of the many, many cases of this class with which I have had to do in these more than twenty years of ministry to those that are bound. Some were hardened criminals, others innocent of the crime for which they were condemned and others no more guilty than thousands that the world honors. For all, Christ died; and many others beside these I have mentioned have given evidence of saving faith in the blood that is able to cleanse the deepest stain that sin has made.

One case is just as near and dear to my mother heart as another and yet how different in many respects are these condemned men—different in their natural inclinations and unlike because of their different circumstances in life. Among them are found the refined, the educated, the gifted, the beautiful as well as the low, the ignorant, the degraded. All must share the same fate. All are shown in the worst possible light to a gaping, sensation-loving, curious world. Let us, dear reader, take these cases home to our hearts as if they were our very own and so learn to have that charity that suffereth long and is kind. Even Moses and David took life, yet they were forgiven, and Moses who in haste slew the Egyptian, became the prophet so wonderfully used of God because of his meekness of spirit; and David in his thankfulness declared, "This poor man cried and the Lord heard him and delivered him out of all his troubles."

CHAPTER XV.

Work in Churches and Missions.

As stated in preface I have always as opportunity offered been ready to preach the gospel to all men. In this chapter I speak very briefly of some of the work done in churches and missions and give some letters from pastors and friends referring to this part of my labors.

STRANGELY LED.

I once had a young sister with me whom I had taken from Toronto, Canada. I had told her mother I would return her safely and had given her money to pay her fare home. As we returned through a field to the city from the poor farm where I had held a service, I said to the sister, "I am so hungry." She replied, "O wait till we get to heaven, then we shall have of the twelve manner of fruit, and drink of the water of life," and I was cheered and blest as I went along the way. The Lord showed me to trust Him. When I reached my lodging-house I was so weak and tired that I sat down to rest a few moments before ascending the stairs to my room. The landlady sat by her well-filled table after the boarders were all gone. She asked the servant for a plate, and I watched her while she cut off a nice piece of turkey and a piece of roast beef and then put some bread on the plate and handed it to me. I was, O, so glad, but feared she was going to ask pay for it, and I had only a dime. I asked, "How much is this?" and she replied, "Nothing." I was so overcome with gratitude to God for His goodness that I hastened to my room and thanked God for answering prayer, in giving me food I needed to give me strength for the meeting that afternoon on the street, and in the evening at the colored people's church. At the close of the meeting in the evening the preacher said: "The sister has given us a good sermon, and the gospel must be carried, so come up and give us a good collection." The people responded heartily and gave a very liberal collection, but after the meeting the preacher handed me 25 cents, keeping the rest. I felt very badly as I had prayed for money which I needed so much. I must go to another city, and no money for traveling expenses. I had been obliged to have some work done by the dentist which must be paid, and no money, but I kept believing, yet no open heart or door. I wondered why I was led to go to another place with no means provided. When I had gotten the amount needed I left, heart-sick, lonely and weary to go on alone in the work, and the sister to go home to Canada. A few days later I was walking along the streets of Lynchburg, Va. I met a man who said, "I am Rev. B—— from Chicago. I have met you several times in your work. Sister Wheaton, won't you come with me to church?" I said, "Where?" and he said, "To the First Baptist church."

When we entered the beautiful new church building the evangelist introduced me to the young pastor, who hurried by indifferently. He then presented me to some fine looking ladies who also passed by on the other side. When the evangelist had closed his sermon he said, "Now, friends, this is the lady I told you about who has done more good than we preachers. I know her, but she don't know me. Receive her as a sister. She is worthy." When the service closed, one after another came to speak to me and gave me their hand and invited me to their homes. A gentleman and wife came up and said, "We claim you as our guest." The husband said, "The carriage is at the door. I will walk and you may ride with my wife." I was at a loss to know just which invitation to accept, when the evangelist came up and said, "These are the people for you to go with." I did so and the Lord went with me. I was invited to preach that night and the Lord was there in mighty convicting power. At the close of the meeting the evangelist said, "Sister, how did it happen that I met you just as I did this morning?" I said, "Brother B., things don't happen with me. The Lord sent me to this place."

The next day a young lady called at the house and inquired for me. I went to the door and she handed me a small parcel saying, "Your friends from the First Baptist church sent you this." Thanking her I went inside and found it was fifteen dollars.

I was the guest of one of the F. F. V.'s, so was welcomed everywhere. Other churches and other preachers invited me to their pulpits. In a few days Mrs. Col. O. asked me if I would conduct a meeting for women only at the M. E. church if she would arrange for it. I was impressed that the thought was of God and agreed to do so. The meeting was appointed for Wednesday at 4 p. m. On the way to the church I was so burdened with the responsibility of the meeting that I told the sister (the kind friend who entertained me) that I could not talk, I must pray the rest of the way to church. To my surprise the place became crowded. I had expected perhaps a dozen women and no men; and here the place was full of elegantly dressed ladies, and the pastor of the church, Brother H., and a policeman were also present. I tried to proceed with the service, but seemed unable to do so. After prayer and singing, "How firm a foundation," I arose and said: "Is any one led of the Spirit to give me a text. I have no message." A sister arose and timidly said, "The 14th chapter of John." Well, the flood gates of Heaven were opened to my soul. God spoke and waves of salvation rolled over the church, and women, God bless them! arose and said, "I thought I was a Christian until today, but I find I have never begun to serve the Lord yet. I promise, by God's help, to begin anew today for Heaven." The dear

Lord touched proud hearts and melted them together until the place was filled with the glory of God. The pastor and people asked me to hold another meeting the following day for both men and women. I said I would do so in the fear of the Lord, and the Lord wonderfully blessed the services. Souls were brought in touch with God and saved. I said to them, "Friends, begin a revival at once. God is ready to work with you if you follow Him. My services are ended in this church. The prisoners, my special care, need me, and the poor and the colored people." I remained three weeks in that city, wonderfully blessed of God. When I left there were over fifty dollars in my hand, of free will offerings. I see why the Lord sent me to the city to arouse the sleeping church members and preachers, both white and colored, from their cold, lifeless spiritual condition.

Soon after leaving Lynchburg I received the following letter from the sister who planned the meeting, which greatly encouraged me:

Lynchburg, May 2, 1887.

My Dear Sister:

I received your letter several days since. I am truly rejoiced to know that you receive that peace and comfort which a child of God knows to be her portion.

My thoughts have followed you since your departure from our city and prayers from many hearts have ascended to the throne for your safety and success in the great work God has called you to do.

I have not known of a revival such as is now in progress at Dr. Hannon's church. Men and women are flocking to the meetings, old and young, to know what they must do to be saved. My son was happily converted last Friday night. He had long been cold and indifferent, but now all is joy and he works and speaks for God with willingness. He is in solemn earnest now in working, praying and speaking in the great congregation. Surely goodness and mercy have followed me all the days of my life and I will dwell at the feet of my Master forever.

Though God has sent tears to my eyes and grief to my heart, thanks to His dear name He has kept me from falling. I think you left a good influence among the fallen women here. I have been sent for to go to some since you left. I have sent this day a request to the official board of my church to give me the use of one room in the church where I can always meet them for the purpose of hearing of their desires to lead a new life. In this way my pastor can meet them and help me in this work. I await the result.

> Your friend with sincere love and prayers,
> Mrs. Lucy K. O.

I went on my way, and some time after was in San Francisco, California. Hearing one day, as I left the jail, of a holiness convention, I was impressed to attend. When I arrived a testimony meeting was in progress. I arose and began to sing, "Yes, I will stand up for Jesus," and the minister in charge came down the aisle to me and said: "Is this Sister Wheaton who held meetings in my church in L——, Va.?" I said, "My name is Elizabeth Wheaton, and I held meetings in that city. Are you Dr. H.?" and he said, "Yes." He returned to the platform and told the people of my work in his church and that about four hundred had been saved, and told the people to receive me as a child of God. So homes were opened. The work of God moved on. As I was a stranger in a strange city, I blessed God for the leadings of the Holy Spirit in all my pilgrim way. I have not seen Dr. H. since that time. He gave me a pressing invitation to his church in San Francisco but work on other lines prevented my acceptance.

LETTERS FROM OTHER FRIENDS.

> Wetumpka, Ala., Jan. 12, 1885.

My Dear Sister:

It would be impossible for me to express in words the Christian sympathy and love I have for you—one that has left all; yes, all—denying yourself and taking up the cross of Jesus, carrying the glad tidings of salvation to the despised, to the outcast, to the poor in spirit and to the oppressed. I pray daily that the good Lord may bless you.

Dear sister, those in the world whose minds are carnal, cannot understand your work, for your life is hidden in God, and cannot be discerned in any other way but by the Spirit. Our crosses will soon be over. Jesus will not let us suffer for Him long. He is coming for us soon. Then "Be not weary in well-doing, for in due season we shall reap, if we faint not." We are not the only friends you have in Wetumpka. Long will you live in our memory. I pray that the Lord may ever guide and lead you as He knows and sees best. I am your brother in Christ,

> A. J. ROGERS, Pastor.

Fort Wayne, Ind., Sept. 2, 1897.

Dear Mother Wheaton:

We were so glad to hear from you. Our meeting closed on Sunday evening, August 22, with twenty-eight persons asking the prayers of the church. We are beginning special services three evenings in the week.

We are planning to begin another revival meeting about the middle of October. Would be glad to have you with us. We are praying that the dear Lord may so order it if it is His will. The Lord is leading and we are expecting great things.

Remember us kindly to Mrs. H. I hope you will write again, so that we may be posted as to your movements. We are praying for you. Do not forget us. Mrs. Cooper and Merrill wish to be remembered to you. "The Lord bless and keep thee and cause His face to shine upon thee." Good-bye for a little while.

Fraternally,

M. C. COOPER, Pastor St. Paul's Church.

Fort Wayne, Ind., Sept. 29, 1897.

Mrs. E. R. Wheaton.

Dear Sister in Christ: Your letter received and I must say I hold it very sacred and dear.

I think of you often, and not only I, but a large number of others. We cannot tell the good you did while here, but God above knows and He will reward you. Many have been more willing to do their Christian duty. They seem to realize more fully what it means to be a Christian. O there is so much in it!

Dear sister, the Lord being willing, we are going to hold another revival campaign, commencing Sunday, October 17. I am so anxious I can hardly wait. I enjoy myself so much when I can be doing work for my dear Lord and Master, who did so much for me. I wish the Lord would see fit to send you this way during our revival, and my prayers shall be to that end. It is God's work and you are one of His workers. You have the constant prayer of St. Paul's church, and we are sure that we have yours. May God's choicest blessings rest upon and abide with you. "The Lord lift up His countenance upon thee and give thee peace."

LOUISE ROUX.

(From the Gazette, Fort Wayne, Ind.)

MRS. WHEATON, FAMOUS PRISON EVANGELIST, "LED BY THE LORD HERE"—HER FAITH IN THIS ABSOLUTE—OPENS INTERVIEW WITH PRAYER—LARGE AUDIENCES HEAR HER.

Mrs. Elizabeth Rider Wheaton is in town and last night and yesterday afternoon addressed a large audience at the revival services which Rev. Mr. Cooper, of St. Paul's M. E. church is conducting in a tent situated near his church, on Walton avenue. She reached this city Saturday evening over the Pennsylvania. Having missed a train at Warsaw en route to visit a sister who lives at Elkhart, she was directed, she said by the Lord, after prayer, to come to Fort Wayne to spend the Sabbath. On the way over her singing and praying on the train attracted attention to her and a member of the Wayne Street Methodist Church, on learning who she was, invited her and her sister, Mrs. Hoffman, to spend the night at his home. She had heard, she said, of the meetings that Mr. Cooper is conducting, and she said, with a manner of absolute confidence, that she had been directed to attend these meetings. Rev. Mr. Cooper said yesterday that the meeting was in progress as she and her companion entered and that he was impressed to speak to her. On learning her name he knew her instantly by fame as the widely traveled and much beloved prison evangelist. She was given a welcome and was at once asked to participate in the services. At the night meeting there were a thousand people, it is said, who listened enrapt to her prayers and moving appeals to the sinner to accept the salvation in which she so thoroughly believes.

The prisoners at the jail were her first concern Sunday morning. She told Mr. Cooper that after arising she turned to her Bible for guidance and her eyes fell upon certain

Scripture which contained the word prison three times. She took this as evidence that she should first visit the jail and thither she went. It is quickly apprehended by those who come in contact with her that she pauses not when directed, as she believes, to do a service in the cause of the Master, but goes at once. She has no questionings of faith.

A Gazette reporter found her last night at the home of Mr. Bower, No. 136 Walton avenue. Her physical appearance marks her as no ordinary person. Her face beams with a kindly smile, being plump and fresh with the vigor of apparent health, though gray hair indicates her past the prime of life. She dresses modestly in black and carries with her a satchel in which she keeps a Testament, her pass holder and some tracts. Her handshake is a model of firmness and heartiness, conveying the impress of intense earnestness. Before permitting the interviewer to proceed further than the salutations, Mrs. Wheaton kneeled and prayed for the Lord's blessing upon the interview. This unconventional prelude was novel in the experience of the reporter, but coming from such a woman seemed perfectly in place. There is reverence and piety proclaimed by her presence and no thought of incongruity obtruded. The prayer took the range of ready invocation and communion with the Lord, and as is probably the evangelist's wont, the prisoner and the fallen woman were not forgotten in her petition to the throne of grace.

Mrs. Wheaton was not inclined to talk about herself. "What has been done by me," she said, "was done of the Lord—His be the glory. I was called to this work thirteen years ago, and I walk by His guidance. I have never asked and could not accept a salary. I have never had a collection taken for me. It is a wonderful thing how He has led me. Here are some of the railroad passes that have been given me."

And here she unrolled a leathern holder full of passes from all the leading roads. Some were "Account of Missionary Work" and some "Account of Christian Work." It is evident that she has traveled this country over, and her ministrations have also extended to the old world.

Mrs. Wheaton again attended the services last night, and moved all by her stirring words. Many could not repress the tears. Her address was not anchored to a formal text, but was a strong appeal, nevertheless, to the sinner to repent. The audience was slow to pass out after the meeting, being anxious to meet the speaker.

The following from Bro. Snyder and his estimable wife who are my very dear friends and whose home is always open to me when I am in Baltimore, are very much prized. They explain themselves. Their work for God and souls is very exceptional:

During the winter of 1894, Mother Wheaton was conducting a service at the state prison, when one of our men expressed his desire that she should attend our services. This was my first introduction to this noble child of God, and since then she seldom comes East without visiting our church; we all love her, but she rarely stays over a day at one time, as her work calls her away.

In 1898, we induced her to remain with us a week. At this meeting hundreds of people attended and many souls were saved. One of the wealthiest ladies of the church received her pentecost and is now one of our best workers. During the day Mother Wheaton would visit the outcast of the city. I recall a case of an old colored woman that we found in a miserable hovel, dying without Christ; how, after preparing the room and then praying to Father for the body, she seemed to be brought back to life by the prayers of God's saint that she might be led to Christ, and after she gave her life to Him we administered the Lord's supper. Mother Wheaton has always been a blessing, whenever she has come to my church; good people are made better, bad people made good.

CHURCH OF THE REDEEMER, BALTIMORE, M. D.

The church was dedicated to God by "Mother Wheaton" before it was finished; while the building was in course of erection she paid us a short visit; with the moon shining through the open windows, mortar, bricks, etc., around us, she was prompted to take the church to God in prayer. I will never forget the scene. Thousands have been saved and many sanctified. The work is still spreading.

Baltimore, Md., January 19, 1901.

Dear Mother: Your kind letter to your children received today. Began special meetings Wednesday night, the 16th. The three nights have been blessed and owned of Father. Those in and out of the church saved. Thirty-three at the altar.

You were mentioned last night in the meeting. I told them they could look for you to come in at any time, as I believe Father is going to send you. Never in my ministry did I feel more in harmony with the divine Spirit. As I am writing I am thinking of our citizenship in heaven. What a time we will have!

How I longed for you to shout with me Wednesday night over the conversion of a man 60 years of age, who never knew Christ. I could not sleep, but praised the Father all that night. He had his wife and daughter with him in church last night.

Mrs. Snyder joins me in much love to you and Sister Taylor. As ever,

Your son in the Gospel,

J. K. SNYDER.

Baltimore, Md., October 20, 1902.

Dear Mother Wheaton:

Your kind letter came today. Mrs. Snyder and Eddie often speak of you; and once a day, at least, we pray for you.

Yesterday several of the boys in the Sunday School formed a committee, and without a word being spoken about you, came to me and asked of you and wanted to know when they would have you with us.

Last week had fifteen born again; four last night. So you see Father is still blessing your children.

God bless you and keep you, is the prayer of your son,

J. K. SNYDER.

1737 North Broadway, Baltimore Md., June 23, 1903.

Dear Mother Wheaton:

Your long expected letter received. Our dear heavenly Father continues to bless us at home and at the church, souls saved and believers sanctified. Glory! The Blood covers our sins.

Eddie was glad to know you had not forgotten him. He is a great help in the church; your prayers are not in vain. We remain

Your children,

J. K. SNYDER AND WIFE.

(From the Whosoever Will Rescue Mission.)

New Orleans, La., May 24, 1897.

Dear Mother Wheaton:

We are getting along nicely at the Mission. The Lord is blessing our work and many souls are being saved. We have started a branch mission further downtown. We call it "No. 2."

We will never forget you, dear mother; your visit did us so much good. The boys at the Mission often talk of you and Sister Kelley. We would like to have you visit us again soon, the Lord willing. Mother and all send kindest regards. Wife sends love to you both. Pray for us. I remain

Your brother in Jesus,

J. H. HAAG.

(From the Mission Worker, New Orleans.)

PRISON EVANGELIST.

"Mother Wheaton," the noted prison evangelist, arrived in the city on the evening of February 21, and spent several nights during her stay. This sister in Israel has visited nearly all if not quite every state prison in the United States and some in foreign countries, preaching to their inmates the glad tidings of great joy. She is a forcible speaker and very deeply in earnest. Her visit to this city was a pleasant one and resulted in much good to many.

During her stay here Mother Wheaton has been kept very busy about her Master's business. She has visited about all the prisons and eleemosynary institutions in the city, singing, praying and exhorting the inmates to a better life. She has been at the Mission every night, and we have had some wonderful meetings. Sister J. H. Haag has been her almost constant companion and the two have done splendid work. On her way from the Mission this Mother in Israel has several times stopped in at saloons, and talked to all present about their soul's welfare. She is intrepid— absolutely without fear—and well she may be for she leans upon the Everlasting Arm.

We do not know how long she will stay with us, but probably for some days, as she now has several invitations on hand. She will go when and where the Lord leads her. Our prayer is that she may be made the instrument of winning many souls to Christ that her crown in glory may be studded with precious jewels. She says of herself that she "has no home but heaven."

(From Pacific Garden Mission.)

Chicago, October 6, 1903.

My Dear Sister Wheaton, God's Chosen One:

How I praise my heavenly Father for your life and that I ever knew you, and for your unselfish mercy to the poor and neglected classes. May you long be spared to "gather them in from the fields of sin" is the prayer of

Your sister in Christ,

SARAH D. CLARK,
Pacific Garden Mission.

SUCCESSFUL MEETINGS.

During the early years of my mission work I arrived one day alone in a Southern city. Went to the postoffice and was reading my mail when a good old man stepped up and inquired who I was and where I stopped. I told him I had just arrived. He said, "Come home with me. My wife has a room and a home for good women like you." I was praying for an open door. Did not know where I was going to stay over night, but was sure God had sent me to that place. I found them kind, hospitable people. He was an old-fashioned Methodist preacher already superannuated, and he has long since gone to his reward. He sent for the pastor of their church and arranged for me to hold a meeting. I went at the request of the pastor to visit an old lady who was sick; thought best to have an open air meeting on the street and invite people to the church that night. During the service on the street I noticed a very well dressed, fine looking young man. When I closed he came to me and taking my hand asked me to call at his store a few doors away. I did so and he gave me a fountain pen and seemed unusually interested in what I had said.

The meeting that night was led by the Holy Spirit; souls were saved, Christians quickened into new spiritual life and power, and sinners awakened. Other services were held in several of the churches. God was honored and the Holy Spirit held right-of-way. Often I would have services in the white people's church till 9 p. m., then hurry to the colored people's church and preach and sing and pray till 11 o'clock. Then at 5 in the morning would meet again, at the Methodist church, such crowds of worshipers—devout, humble seekers after God. I left the city just as the meetings were at their height. In the next world when we all assemble together I expect to see many who were converted at that series of meetings.

CALLED TO THE MINISTRY.

The young man who seemed so interested in that first street service came to all the meetings. He was clearly converted and was called to the ministry. For some time he was a successful soul winner, manifesting a pure spirit and a godly life; but he afterwards became discouraged and went into business to support his family. In a letter from him in later years I received the following words:

> "At the time I got your postal I was in serious meditation on spiritual affairs and was fully considering re-entering the Gospel ministry. I know I was called of the Lord through His Holy Spirit to preach His everlasting gospel. Praise His holy name! He gave me the seal of His approval in the witness of His Spirit and the fruit of my labor in the salvation of souls. I know this of a truth from experience. You cannot imagine how I long, Oh, so intensely, to be again filled with His Spirit and to enter upon His work in the salvation of souls.
>
> Lovingly yours,
>
> I. H. N."

A COLORED WOMAN SAVED AND PREACHING.

In the year 1886 I was holding meetings in Houston, Texas. Was in a colored people's church one day, and was much perplexed as to how to reach the people's hearts. I wept before the Lord in prayer. I did not know it then, but God was working, using my zeal and grief to help save a soul. Finally a woman who came to scoff and ridicule was converted. She received a call to preach after vowing that women were never called to preach. Well, the years rolled by and one night in Oklahoma City I saw the Salvation Army gathering in a tent. I went in and was invited to read the Word and lead the meeting. I did so, and as the services were about to close a colored woman arose and said she wished to state that she was saved, and told how she was also called to preach by the Spirit of the Lord through what I said in that meeting in Houston, Texas, so long before. She labored for years as an evangelist and so far as I know is still preaching. In her evangelistic work she has labored successfully in many of the states.

At one time she wrote of her conversion as follows:

"When I was seeking life in the Lord, I did not want to eat for two weeks, and had no appetite, but I prayed on and the change came and I felt brand new. I loved everybody—white and colored. I seemed to have on a white garment, and that death had fallen beneath my feet and had no more dominion over me. It seemed that I had seen the Lord and He told me to go in peace and sin no more, and I was one more happy soul. I wanted to tell everybody what the Lord had done for my soul."

STRIKING EXPERIENCES.

Once while holding meetings in Wichita, Kansas, I was greatly troubled. I knew not why. I could neither preach nor sing. I did not know what was wrong. Suddenly a large man rose and rushed from the room taking his wife and children with him. He told me afterward that he came with the avowed purpose of killing another man who was there. And they both came there with the intention of killing each other.

At the same mission a man came running in and said that a young railroad man across the street in the jail was dying, having taken poison. I went to the jail where the young man was lying on the floor and kneeling beside him, took his hand and for two hours pleaded with God to spare his life and save his soul. And the Lord answered prayer. The doctors were amazed and perplexed, as they could not understand how the man could live, as all their efforts had seemed to be fruitless. It was simply one of God's miracles.

SAVED BY A HYMN.

Passing along the street one night in Louisville, Ky., I saw standing in a doorway a group of well-dressed young ladies, also a lady much older. I spoke to them and asked for a drink of water and some favor to further the conversation. When once in doors I saw a piano, and said, "Which one of you ladies will play a piece on the piano? I love music so much." A little boy four years old came in. They asked him to tell me what he intended to be when he grew up. He said, "A preacher. I am going to see my mamma in Heaven." He was their sister's boy. He sang for me while one of his aunts played the piano. In his sweet, lisping voice he sang, "I never will cease to love Him." I was impressed to ask him to come to the mission where I was going to preach that night, and sing that piece, and have the aunt play the organ. Both consented to go with me and when I asked him the little boy came on the platform and sang beautifully. His father had heard of my desire to have the child sing, and had straggled into the mission under the influence of strong drink. He was so convicted and heart-broken he wept, and that four-year-old boy walked from the platform down the aisle to that lonely, heart-sick father, who then and there gave himself up to God, and was saved before he left the hall, through the singing of a hymn!

God *will* forgive each penitent whate'er his sin may be,Whose heart is overflowing with *love* for bond and free.Oh, listen! brother, listen—'tis Jehovah's plan—And a *time is fixed* to right the wrongs of Man....

—Prison Poetry

ARTHUR C. HOFFMAN, NEPHEW OF E. R. W., SITTING ON FRONT OF ENGINE.

CHAPTER XVI.

Preaching the Gospel on Railway Trains.

The young man on the front of the engine in the foregoing illustration was my sister's son. I give here an extract from the account of his death June 7, 1890, as published at the time in the daily of Huntington, Ind., where it occurred:

KILLED BY CARS.

A. C. Hoffman, a switchman in the Chicago & Atlantic yards, was run over and killed this morning.

He was employed at night and about 5 o'clock this morning went to the coal dock to run down two cars that had been unloaded there. The track is very much inclined leading from the dock and it requires that brakes be set very tight. When the cars started down the track Hoffman ran from the rear end to the front of the head car to set the brake, but in doing so stubbed his toe and fell from the car to the middle of the track beneath. The car was running rapidly and no sooner did he strike the track than a brake beam of the car struck his right leg near the hip, fracturing the bones and bruising it otherwise. That threw him over and the flange of a wheel struck the lower part of his back, tearing the flesh all off clear to his backbone, exposing it to sight.

Hoffman was picked up and taken to the Arlington house, where he boarded, and Dr. L. Severance, the railroad surgeon summoned. He did all in his power to make the injured man easy and alleviate his pain, but it was out of the reach of medical skill to save his life and at about 10 o'clock he died in awful agony.

Hoffman's mother and brother live in Lincoln, Neb., where the latter is a physician. He also has a sister in Elkhart county, this state, all of whom have been telegraphed the sad news.

He was a good switchman and more than ordinarily intelligent.

It is a most distressing accident. The young man was here among strangers and died surrounded by the friends of so short an acquaintance but who did everything within human power to save him or make his end one of peace. His injuries were fatal though and nothing short of death would relieve him.

"ALL ABOARD!" So shout the railroad men, year in and year out, daily, hourly, their cry is to get on board the train. I often think if we preachers and mission workers were as faithful in *our* work to get people on board the old ship Zion, how many to-day would be en route for Heaven who are on the broad-gauge rapid transit to the bottomless pit of destruction. Will we not arise and shine for God as we have never done before?

Over fifty years ago when I was a small child, I stood at a flag-station waiting for the train. I was to go alone ON MY FIRST TRIP by this wonderful mode of travel. It was just the grandest thing to know I was really to ride on a railroad train—only four miles, yet I often think of it after these twenty years of constant travel. Have I ever had such a remarkable experience, going alone, too, and as there was no station or ticket office, I was obliged to pay my fare on the train. I had a silver 25-cent piece, and I sat down in the first empty seat I came to and waited to see what next! Along came a tall man in uniform and asked where I was going. I told him and handed him my money. I remember yet how kindly that conductor looked at me, hesitated a little and then handed me back my quarter, and let me ride those four miles free. I have never forgotten that act of kindness on the railroad, and during my pilgrimage I have been shown much kindness by the railroad officials.

My work among railroad men has been greatly owned and blessed of the Lord. Many of them saying, "You are the only preacher that ever speaks to us about our soul's salvation." They often say I remind them of their mothers who were good Christians.

The following by a railroad man will be of interest and profit to all, and will doubtless have more weight with his class than anything I could say here:

TO RAILROAD MEN.

BY ONE OF THEM.

Dear Boys: One time in my life these words came to me: "*Where will you spend eternity?*" Then and there I turned my back on sin and "set my face like a flint" toward God and heaven, and cried to God for Jesus' sake to forgive me; and near the hour of midnight while kneeling at my bedside I received the witness of the Spirit that I was saved. Then and there I was "born again" into newness of life. I was changed from a man of sin to a child of God, and since then such wonderful joy and peace fills my soul every minute of the time that I want to tell all of you about it.

Brother, isn't there in your breast at times an awful aching void? Aren't there times when after trying every pleasure and amusement the world affords, you just quietly sit down all alone before God, and realize that it is all in vain? These things don't satisfy; and there down deep in your heart is a longing that is never satisfied, a hungering for something that will give you complete joy and peace, and soul rest. Brother, there is only one thing that will give you this complete rest, and satisfy every longing of your heart, and that is salvation from sin. Jesus died on the cross that you might be free from sin and live through all the ages of eternity with Him in heaven. "If we forsake our sins he is faithful and just to forgive our sins and cleanse us from all unrighteousness." If we do the forsaking He will do the forgiving, and then through His atoning blood we become new creatures, and after we have received the clear witness that we are adopted into the family of God and can truly call Him Father, if we feel angry at times or have some desire for the world and the things of it, we can come to Him again and completely abandon ourselves to Him, our will, our life, our desires, our time, our talents to be used for His glory, then He will baptize us with the Holy Ghost and power so that it becomes a pleasure to do right and all evil becomes distasteful to us. By the power of the Holy Ghost He cleanses our hearts, and the Comforter which is the Holy Ghost takes up His abode in us, sanctifying us, causing us to live pure, holy lives. We railroad men whose lives are in danger at all times should be prepared to meet God, for one minute we are here and the next we may be standing at the judgment bar of God to answer for deeds done here on earth. Dear reader, are you prepared to do that? If not, make this the time that you will settle this forever by giving your heart to God, then if this little flame of life is snuffed out you will be borne on angel's wings onward and upward through the gates of pearl, over the golden paved streets of the New Jerusalem up to the great white throne where you will see Jesus in all His glory and majesty and hear Him say to you, "Well done, enter thou into the joy of the Lord."

Let me tell you, brother, when the Lord saved me and gave me such sweet joy and peace I told Him that I would never use beer or tobacco in any form, for I knew it was displeasing to Him, for He says, "What? know ye not that your body is the temple of the Holy Ghost which is in you?" (1 Cor. 6:19). "If any man defile the temple of God, him shall God destroy" (1 Cor. 3:17). "Cleanse ourselves from all filthiness of the flesh and spirit" (2 Cor. 7:1).

And, brother, perhaps you are a slave to tobacco. Many times you have felt that it was a dirty, useless, expensive habit, and you get thoroughly disgusted with it, and perhaps you quit it for a short time, and then how surprised and disgusted you feel because you find what an awful hold it has got on you. It is worse than a spell of sickness to try and quit it, and you soon take it up again, realizing as you do so that you are harboring something that is stronger than you are, appetite; and although you are a strong, robust man you have to admit that it is your master. And when you go home to meet your mother, wife, sister, you notice them shrink away from the breath made foul by the poisonous tobacco. And the times that it almost destroys the taste for anything else, and you use all the more of it till the disagreeable "heartburn" warns you that the deadly poisonous nicotine is eating away at the lining of your stomach, and you are more disgusted than ever, but you can't quit without torturing yourself.

Oh, how I loved my beer, plug of tobacco and pipe before I was saved, but I quit them all—drinking, chewing, smoking, swearing and all immoral habits, and I would have died before I would have indulged in any one of them in the least; but the *desire* was still there; at times I wanted them. And seven days after I was saved I was convicted for sanctification or a clean heart. There were some Holy Ghost Christian people who told me there was a place I could get in the higher or complete Christian life where God through Jesus' blood shed without the gate (Heb. 13:12) would cleanse my heart from everything that was displeasing to Him, and would so fill it with love and the power of the Holy Ghost that I would be *completely delivered from all desires that were wrong,* from anger, malice, pride, love of the world, lust, jealousy, etc., and take away the appetite for beer and tobacco. I found God's Word taught it, and believed He was "strong to deliver," and that it was God's will, even my sanctification (1 Thes. 4:3).

And I cried to God to give me "a clean heart, and a right spirit," and he answered my prayer. It was done instantly. I arose from my knees with a sweet sense of complete deliverance, and such joy and perfect peace filled my whole being that I couldn't praise Jesus enough for it. From that moment I have not had the least desire for those things any more than if I never had tasted them, and the very smell of beer or tobacco makes me sick. This is a wonderful, grand deliverance. Now I am as free as the very air—saved, sanctified, and sweetly kept by the power of God.

Brother, this is for you if you are willing to give up the foolishness of the world for Christ. The joy that we have in one hour in the service of the Lord is far greater than all the pleasure the world can give in a lifetime. This power of the Holy Ghost within us, this abiding Comforter fills us with glad sunshine all the time, and there is constantly a power like "a wall of fire round about us" warding off all evil.

Oh, it's glorious and grows better and brighter each day.

"Blessed assurance, Jesus is mine! Oh, what a foretaste of glory divine! Heir of salvation, purchased of God, Born of His spirit, washed in His blood."

Your fellow brakesman, in Jesus' name,

M. L. ODELL.

Cincinnati, Ohio.

TRANSPORTATION.

People sometimes ask me how I am able to get transportation on the railroads. Well, in a few words, it is because I pray to the Lord to have the way open to whatever place He wants me to go, and the railroad men know me and of my work for suffering humanity, and are glad to help me in it.

A KIND CONDUCTOR.

On July 17, 1903, I was on my way from Washington, D. C., on an important journey, and the conductor told me the train I was on did not stop at Sherwood, and I wanted to know where I should stop to get another train that would stop there. He told me at Defiance, and when we reached there I got off the train. Just then the conductor looked out and called for a porter to "put that lady back on the train." I was bewildered at this. He again called "put that lady back on the train." I said, "Isn't this Defiance?" "Yes, but I shall put you off at Sherwood." Who told that conductor to telegraph to headquarters to get a permit to stop the train for me? God did it! That conductor will never know how much his act strengthened my faith in God. Dear reader, do you ever think of the hardships and dangers through which these railroad men must pass? We put ourselves in their care without praying for them. I seldom enter a train without praying God to protect the railroad men and passengers, and give them His blessing. He does hear and answer prayer. How often the dear Lord has heard my cries for the safety of the trains!

Some of my

MOST INTERESTING GOSPEL SERVICES

have been held on railway trains. As I was once leaving Chicago over the C. & R. I. R. R. at night, a request was made that I should sing for the passengers. I was conversing with Mrs. Colonel Clark of the Pacific Garden Mission, Chicago. As she was to soon leave the train I said I would sing when she had gone. I sang some hymns, and then a gentleman requested that I should ask all in the car who were Christians to raise their hands. I did so and quite a number responded to this, and he then asked all who had raised their hands to give a word of testimony. He was the first one to speak and said, "I am a Christian. The last thing before I left my home for Chicago was to gather my wife and four little children around me and commit them to God's care and ask for my safe return. I have for years been a stock dealer and frequently come to Chicago. There is a young man in our neighborhood who is also a dealer in stock, but being unacquainted with the ways of the city, he did not like to go alone and as I was a Christian came with me. When there is an opportunity like this given, if I did not honor God and show my colors this young man could have no confidence in me. I speak for his special benefit." He closed with an exhortation to the unsaved to prepare to meet God and requested me to sing again. Then one after another arose and spoke. It reminded one of AN OLD-FASHIONED METHODIST CLASS MEETING. Prayer, testimonies and singing continued till after midnight. The young stock dealer and others were saved. Toward morning I fell into a sound sleep. I do not know how long I slept, but when I awoke the sun was high and our car was standing alone on the track. A lady passenger spoke to me saying, "How could you sleep during that wreck?" "What! has anything happened?" I said. "Yes, a wreck," she replied. The engine and other cars were gone and they were clearing up the wreck. I heard from that meeting years afterwards.

One night a meeting was held in the open air for the special benefit of railroad men. I asked all who wanted to be saved to raise their hands; then said, "Will you not give your hearts to God now?" One year from that time while in meeting a man arose and said that he was in the crowd that night, and raised his hand, and then at once looked to God and was saved then and there.

TRAIN SAVED FROM WRECK IN ANSWER TO PRAYER.

The Lord has often made known to me when the train was in danger. I could see the plots laid by wicked men to wreck the train, and when I have prayed, He, in answer to prayer, has delivered us from harm and death. He says: "The very hairs of your head are all numbered," and "I will never leave thee nor forsake thee."

At one time I had been in old Mexico and changing cars at El Paso, Texas, I found a heavy trainload of passengers on the way east. I was impressed all night of impending peril. I could not sleep, and walked the floor of the car in silent prayer. I went to the young sister with me and said, "The train is in great danger, and something will happen unless the Lord delivers us. The text comes to me so forcibly, 'What, could ye not watch with me one hour?' Watch and pray!" That night six train-robbers had determined to wreck and rob the train. They had stolen six horses and gone to a lonely place uninhabited for miles about. They bound and gagged the section foreman and his men, then took the switch-key and threw the switch to wreck the train. When they saw the train passing on they tried to hail it with their lanterns, but by some mysterious power of God their lights were put out, so that the engineer did not see them. Then they tried to board the train but were unable to succeed. It was a most remarkable occurrence. They either did not open the switch properly and the train set it back to its place, or the hand of God closed the switch. The newspapers published quite an account of this incident, from which source the above concerning the robbers was obtained, as they were caught and made confession.

A TRAIN IN DANGER.

In July, 1889, I was on my way from St. Joseph, Missouri, to St. Louis, having with me a man and his wife. About 1 o'clock in the morning I awoke with awful fear upon me of some impending danger. I told my friends that we must pray for God to save the train, and that no power but God's could avert the coming disaster, whatever it might be. Still the horror as of death was upon me, and later in the night the train suddenly stopped. The train men ran out with their lanterns and found that the engine had become uncoupled from the cars and just in front of the engine was a pile of iron. The iron rails of the track were set so that a wreck would have been the result if God had not interposed. God thwarted the well-laid plans that had been made to wreck and rob the train. This was in a lonely place where no help was near, and the robbers would have the best of chances to rob the train. On our return west a similar terror came upon me and I said, "Pray for this train, or something will happen to it before we reach St. Joe." I was terrified all day. Just as the train stopped at the depot our car was wrecked. The front wheels of the car were turned around crosswise of the track, tearing up the planks, rails and earth. Such a queer looking wreck, and apparently no reason for it! Yet we had been brought in safety to our journey's end and no one was injured.

IMPRESSED TO LEAVE THE TRAIN.

At another time after preaching at Canon City prison in Colorado, we had our baggage checked to Leadville in the same state. We held meetings on the train and some were moved to tears. When the engine whistled for Salida a dreadful feeling of fear and terror overtook me. Something seemed to say to me, "*Get off the train.*" I felt it was a command from the Lord. I told the friends who were with me what the words of the Lord were, and said that we must leave the train. We hurriedly left the train without waiting for another warning. I looked after the train as it moved away and said, "I wonder why I had to leave that train. Perhaps not till the judgment will I know." We went on the street and held an open air meeting, and some one invited us to hold a service that night in a church. We did so, and God poured out his Spirit on the people. After the meeting we went out and visited the saloons, and spoke to many about their souls. At about 11 o'clock at night we returned to the depot and I asked the agent what time the next train would leave for Leadville. He said, "I don't know. The train you got off from was terribly wrecked twelve miles up the road. The east-bound train crashed into it, and I have sent out two wrecking trains already." I told him of my presentiment of danger, and how God had impressed me to leave that train. He asked me to come into the office and explain my impressions and talk to him. We did so, and about 3 o'clock in the morning the wrecked train backed down to the depot where we were waiting and we again got aboard. I told the passengers as they looked at me as I came into the car, "The Lord warned me of the danger and impressed me to get off the train." I have taken the Lord as my guide all these years and He has never forsaken me.

A TELEGRAM RECEIVED.

Waiting for a train where I changed cars I was invited to sit in the ticket office, as the waiting room was uncomfortable. I was writing at the agent's desk when he handed me a telegram, saying, "I think this is intended for you, Mother." It was an announcement of the death of one of my brothers, and was being sent to another town, having to be transferred here, and the agent seeing my name handed it to me. I could see the hand of God in this.

HELPED TO CARE FOR WOUNDED MAN.

Once on my way from Burlington to Ft. Madison, Ia., I told the conductor I was impressed to go on that special train. When we were about a mile out of the city, the engine accidentally struck a man and hurt him badly. The man was put into the baggage car and as there were no seats, I stood behind him and held his head, and after we had gone twelve miles, warm water was secured and I washed the blood from his head and cared for him until we arrived at the station, when they took him to the jail, there being no other place for him, and there I helped the doctor dress his wounds. Then I knew why I was impressed to go on that train.

CONDUCTOR'S GOD BLESS YOU.

Once the conductor on a train said to me so kindly, as he assisted me from the train, "God bless you; let your good work go on. I gave the tracts you gave me to the trainmen—they needed them." How this cheered me, for I had tried to preach to them on the train, and I feared the scoffs or reproof of the railroad officials. How I do long to help and encourage the railroad men—they are so loyal and faithful, and have so much to contend with in their work. "Be not overcome of evil, but overcome evil with good."

A WOMAN'S FAITH ENCOURAGED.

On the way from Philadelphia to New York I was one day led to pass quietly through the car giving out tracts. After seating myself, a lady came and asked if she might speak with me about the work I was doing. She said, "If I only knew God could and would heal a person whose mind was shattered, I would give all that I possess. I am troubled about my daughter's grieving over the death of her husband." I told her God never fails to perform his miracles when we fully believe and accept God's way of healing the body and soul. She seemed much blessed and encouraged and kindly invited me to her home. "As ye go, preach." How glad she was to find some one who would tell her about salvation. She was a wealthy lady, as I afterward learned. We became fast friends and she learned of healing in answer to "the prayer of faith."

RIDING IN PARLOR CAR.

Leaving the Indian School in Indian Territory on one of the coldest mornings I ever experienced, myself and sisters were driven by two young Indian boys to a flag station. We were wrapped in warm blankets and hurried to the railroad. We were in danger of freezing, as the train was long delayed on account of the blizzard and snow drifts, and we sought the only place of shelter—a freight car in which the section foreman and his wife lived, where we shivered with the cold until the train came in sight.

We were compelled to stop in the parlor car (a luxury that I never indulge in) as platforms of the other cars were too icy to pass from one car to another while the train was in motion. We were much blessed, and I began singing, and praising the Lord. When the train came to a station, we arose to go into the other car, but a gentleman passenger called to the conductor and said: "How much is the fare for these ladies to remain in this car?" He and his companion paid the amount required and we were permitted to ride in the parlor car to Topeka, Kansas.

My soul was so blessed that I felt I must go into the other cars and hold services. We were invited to go to the diner with friends. When we arrived at the station where dinner was served, one after another of the passengers handed me some money. When we came in from dinner I knelt down in the car, and was praying in silence, thanking God for what He had given us, when I felt someone crush some paper in my hands. I looked to see what it was and found it was a ten dollar bill, given by the two gentlemen who had paid our fare in the parlor car. Of course I was greatly surprised, and as Sister Taylor was kneeling by my side, I said, "Sister, this must be in answer to your prayer. Did you pray for money?" She said "Yes, I prayed for hours last night." I said, "Why you should have been praying for souls." She answered, "I knew you needed money, and no one was giving it to you." Thus God hears and answers prayers and provides for the needs of his little ones.

I give below a letter received from one of the gentlemen who gave us the ten dollars who was a prominent business man in Pittsburg, Pennsylvania:

Pittsburg, Pa., March 25, 1899.

Mrs. E. R. Wheaton, Tabor, Iowa.

My Dear Madam: Your card of the 18th duly received and I was glad to hear from you and to have your good wishes, but was especially grateful for your prayers, for I believe in prayer. Do you realize how much a busy man needs the prayers of God's people?

Brother M., my companion whom you met last fall in Indian Territory, is well and I know will be glad to hear from you. I will see him next week, D. V.

If you pass through our city on your trip East, and I know of it, would gladly call upon you.

With best wishes for your welfare, and Mrs. Taylor's, too, I am,

Very truly your friend,

T. M. N.

The following brief extract is from a report of a service on the train as we were in company with a number of delegates on their way to the Convocation of Prayer at Baltimore, in January, 1903:

> We left Indianapolis at 3:05 p. m., Monday. After we started Mother Wheaton, who was with us, started up a song, then went to the front of the car, and standing in the aisle she began preaching to the people. She moved down the aisle still preaching, taking about ten minutes to come through the car. This she did several times, then went through the dining and palace cars. As she told of her prison work, how God could save criminals, we could see tears come into the eyes of the passengers. A U. S. marshal sitting near us became much affected, and made inquiry of Brother S. B. Shaw who the woman was, and said he knew what she said was true, and said he desired to be saved. A wealthy Mexican on the train, whose wife had recently died while he was on a trip to Europe, was also brought under conviction, and would have Sister Wheaton take dinner in the dining car; also had Sisters Wheaton and Shaw take a berth in the sleeper at his expense. I must not forget to tell you that Brother Shaw gave us an excellent talk standing in the aisle of the car.

FAVOR THE R. R. CO.

I sometimes have an opportunity to do a kindness for the R. R. Co., in return for the many favors they do for me. At one time I reached the railroad station at Fort Worth, Texas, before my train arrived. While we were waiting for a Santa Fe train, an old lady who was evidently not in her right mind and who had been sent by friends to go alone to other friends who lived at a distance, of her own accord tried to climb over one train to get to another and was injured. The injury was caused by her own mental condition and through no fault of the railroad men.

Before she left us, I wrote a little message of love and put it into her hand bag with my name and address on it. In a few days I received the following letter from her attorneys.

Fort Worth, Tex., November 21, 1898.

Mrs. E. R. Wheaton, Tabor, Iowa.

Dear Madam: We conclude from a kind and sympathetic letter you wrote to Mrs. Harper, the old lady who fell from the platform at the Gulf, Colorado & Santa Fe Railway depot at Fort Worth, Tex., on Friday night, the 11th day of November, that you likely saw the old lady fall. And perhaps you can tell us how she came to fall and who else saw her when she fell. Mrs. Harper has employed us to sue the railroad company for said injuries. She claims that she walked off of the platform where there were no railings and fell between two freight cars left standing on the track, left so far apart that she could see the railroad car she wanted to board between said opening so left. Will you please write us all you know about the matter, and who else saw it, if any one, and where such person or persons live if you know. By doing so you will greatly oblige,

Yours truly,

WYNNE, MCCART & BOWLIN.

In reply I assured them that it would be utterly unjust to bring suit against the railroad company—giving them the facts as far and as fully as I knew them. I learned later that this ended the contemplated suit.

CHAPTER XVII.

Street and Open Air Work.

THE MASTER'S QUESTIONS.

Have ye looked for my sheep in the desert, For those who have missed their way? Have ye been in the wild waste places, Where the lost and wandering stray? Have ye trodden the lonely highway, The foul and the darksome street? It may be ye'd see in the gloaming The print of My wounded feet.

Have ye wept with the broken-hearted In their agony of woe? Ye might hear Me whispering beside you "'Tis the pathway I often go!" My brethren, My friends, My disciples, Can ye dare to follow me? Then, wherever the Master dwelleth, There shall the servant be!

Many are the shocking sights and sad experiences I have witnessed in street and slum work. I have endured hardships and privations, suffered arrests and ridicule, and faced many dangers. But withal, the glorious victories have been many and precious souls have been saved:

I might give copies of many permits to hold open air services received in the earlier years of my labors, but perhaps these would not be of interest or profit, so I give only a few.

PERMIT TO PREACH ON BOSTON COMMON.

CITY OF BOSTON, EXECUTIVE DEPARTMENT.

Under Chapter 42, Section 11, of the Revised Ordinances, permission is hereby granted to Mrs. Elizabeth Wheaton, to conduct preaching service on the Common on Sunday, October 27, 1889, subject to the directions of the Superintendent of the Common, who will assign a location.

THOMAS NAST, Mayor.

October 22, 1889.

STATE OF LOUISIANA, MAYORALTY OF NEW ORLEANS.

City Hall, 11th day of December, 1886.

Permission granted to Elizabeth Wheaton and Agnes Hill to preach the gospel at such localities within the city of New Orleans as they may select; provided that in so doing they are careful not to interfere with the private rights of individuals or those of corporations granted them under municipal ordinances or the statutes of this state. By order of the Mayor.

E. L. BOWER, Chief Clerk.

MAYOR'S OFFICE.

Jacksonville, Fla., December 29, 1886.

Permission is hereby granted E. Wheaton and associates to preach the gospel within the city limits at such places as they may select; provided the streets and sidewalks are not obstructed and the rights of private property are not disturbed and there is no violation of City ordinances or statutes of the State.

P. MCQUAID, Mayor.

Galveston, Tex., Jan. 20, 1888.

To Whom It May Concern:

Permission is hereby granted to the bearer to hold religious services on the streets anywhere within the corporate limits of the city of Galveston, and the police authorities will lend such protection as is necessary to enforce order at such meetings.

R. L. FULTON, Mayor of Galveston.

Office of Chief of Police,
Denver, Colo., June 23, 1888.

To any Police Officer:

This woman has permission from the Mayor to hold services on the street.

M. HENNY, Chief of Police.

Sacramento, Cal., Aug. 24, 1888.

Permission is hereby granted E. Wheaton and associates to preach the gospel within the city limits at such places as they may select, provided the streets and sidewalks are not obstructed and rights of private property are not disturbed, and if not in conflict or violation of the city ordinances.

EUGENE J. GREGORY, Mayor.

FROM MISS JOSEPHINE COWGILL.

Some Years a Missionary in Jerusalem.

The following is contributed by a dear sister who has spent some years as a missionary in Jerusalem, Palestine, and may be known to many of our readers:

MISS JOSEPHINE COWGILL.

Many years ago, while engaged in missionary work in the city of New Orleans, La., I was one evening attracted by a large gathering of people. In the midst was a woman kneeling on the ground engaged in most earnest prayer. Many in the company were of the worst class of people, yet they were quietly listening and looking on with amazement. We were not accustomed to any one praying on the streets in that manner. This was the first time I had the privilege of meeting dear Sister E. R. Wheaton. I can never forget the impressions made upon myself and others by her prayers, exhortations and songs that evening. Standing near me in that company was a woman who had charge of one of the worst houses of prostitution in the city. Trembling and weeping she said to me "I never heard anything like that before. That woman makes me feel that I am an awful sinner, and yet she loves me." That poor woman went to her house, sent for a Bible and read it and spent the night in bitter repenting for her sins. She was gloriously converted and then called her household together and told them her experience and how the Lord had pardoned her sins and made her happy in His love. She then exhorted them to commence a new life; but if they would not, then they must leave her house.

While in New Orleans, Sister Wheaton and those in company with her were busily and successfully engaged in mission work among prisoners and others of the worst class. Some years afterward she again visited that city and the Lord greatly blessed her work. One night, on a store-box in front of a saloon, she preached to a large crowd. The saloonkeeper became very uneasy and called a policeman to "take her away." He came, but found it quite hard work to get her down and to another place. The people wanted to hear her. She sang a song, the chorus of which was, in part:

"If to Jesus you are true, There's a glory waits for you, In the beautiful, the glad forever."

Then with clasped hands she stood quietly gazing upward, with tears rolling down her cheeks. Then with much feeling she said: "I am homesick for heaven." I can never forget how those words impressed me and others at that time.

Some years after I again met Sister Wheaton in Los Angeles, California, where her work was like it had been in New Orleans. At one time, when she had kindly offered me the privilege of going with her to some other points, I made inquiry about how I should take my trunk. She replied: "Sister Josephine, pilgrims for God do not need a trunk. One valise is enough." Many times I have thought of that reply and the good it did me. I have never known of a more earnest and self-sacrificing Christian worker than Sister Wheaton. The results of her labors as she has gone forth "weeping and bearing precious seeds," cannot be fully known until with rejoicing she comes "bringing sheaves with her." In loving remembrance of her, I am,

Yours in His blessed service.

JOSEPHINE COWGILL.

Haifo, Palestine.

MY FIRST STREET MEETING.

My first street meeting was in Washington, D. C., near the old postoffice. I had spent the day in the jail, alms-house and hospitals. I was then a stranger in the city. Some one asked me to go to a hall where there was a little mission. We did so, and found they had gone to the open air meeting. When we arrived the meeting was in progress, one after another stepping out to testify or sing. No opportunity was offered me to take any part in the meeting, as no woman was allowed to testify. I looked to God in silent prayer to open some way for me to speak to the people. At the close of their service I spoke, saying, "The Lord has sent me with a message for you dear people, and now the friends have closed their meeting and we will not detain them, as they doubtless have other engagements." I began to sing and God filled my soul with glory. The needs of those poor hungry souls rose before me, as I sang and prayed, and the message of love came welling up in my soul. I spoke to them of righteousness, the coming Judgment and eternity. I had held meetings in many of the principal cities of America, some in Europe and other countries. But that night God anointed me for street preaching and for work in slums, dives and saloons.

Closing the meeting, I thought of being alone on the street at night with scarcely any money and not knowing my way back to my lodging place. I said, "Oh, Lord, you know all about it." Walking along I came to the mission and stepping in I took a seat near the door. While I sat praying, a brother rose and told the circumstances of the street meeting I had held, and that one of the worst men in the city had been converted through its instrumentality. The man had told the brother that God had saved him and he was going home to write eight letters to his people, some of them in this and some in the old country, to tell them what great things God had done for him. God knew I was there and sent the message to encourage me. After the service in the hall had closed a young lady who proved to be the daughter of the landlady where I had been staying, came to me and walked to her home with me. I could not have found my way alone, not having their number, but God cared for me.

Some extracts are given from reports of the work which were published at different points during the first few years of my labors:

CONVERTED TO CHRIST.

THE CASE OF THE UNFORTUNATE WOMAN—CARD FROM MR. M.

Editor Hawk-Eye: Last evening at about seven o'clock Mrs. Wheaton, the prison evangelist, and another lady of the evangelists and myself held a meeting on the levee. Mrs. Wheaton, who spoke on the future consequence of sin with unusual earnestness, had the effect of breaking down Mrs. A. into tears. Mrs. Wheaton went up to her and spoke to her. In a few moments the unfortunate woman broke into ecstasies of joy and commenced to leap around in a circle. For ten minutes she kept up praising God and leaping, when suddenly she leaped through the great crowd around, some now being horrified, who, like many poor, unfortunate people, never saw a sudden conversion. She ran up Jefferson street, where she was arrested and locked up.

Had the woman been rich or popular she would have been kindly treated, but being one of the unfortunate women of our city she was locked up in an unclean, old filthy cell, with a bunk for a bed. The police were informed that the woman was converted and a lady offered to take her home last night. But they kept her in that terrible cell with inmates in adjoining cells using obscene language. It is a sin and disgrace for the city fathers to continue to have women locked up with men in the same line of cells with such a horrifying stench and wooden bunks. The city police are guilty of an outrageous act in confining the woman in such a cell, when they ought to have given her better quarters, as they had the opportunity. This morning she was brought out before the police court; the woman still testified that she had salvation before that court and crowd of people. But good came out of it all as she witnessed a grand confession to the police court and people who never heard the gospel. She was, by the consent of Captain S., taken to Mrs. H.'s and is doing well and is converted. Last evening's *Gazette* stated that the woman went crazy by attending the street meetings and would be examined before the board of commissioners of insanity, which is every word of it untrue. The woman is sane and was not before any board.

A. H. MERTZ, in Burlington *Hawk-Eye*, Jan. 19, 1887.

A WONDERFUL CONVERSION.

In San Francisco a drunken girl came to my meeting on the street so desperate and dangerous that even the police at times seemed afraid of her. She seemed to be a veritable Magdalene. I was impressed with the words, "Down in the human heart, crushed by the tempter, feelings lie buried that grace can restore." How could it be done? I dealt faithfully with her and went away, returning to the city ten months later. She came again to my meetings, once very drunk as she usually was. I talked to her about her need of salvation and she was finally convicted. She waited at the close of the meeting to speak with me, but at first would not yield to God. Finally she sobered up and was wonderfully converted. I took her to my room and cared for her, and as she was a desperate character, and liable to do injury both to life and property, the Rescue Home at San Francisco refused to take her, so I took all the risks myself and took her to Helena, Montana, and left her at the Rescue Home at that place.

The following is an account of work in Seattle soon after this as reported by a paper of that city:

THE PRISON EVANGELIST.

MRS. ELIZABETH R. WHEATON CARRYING FORWARD HER MISSION IN SEATTLE.

About three o'clock yesterday afternoon two women, one quite elderly and the other about 25 years of age, whose dress and demeanor bespoke them to be missionaries, walked into the sheriff's office and asked Jailer Leckie if they might hold a short religious service in the county jail. The urbane jailor replied that he thought "a little prayin' wouldn't do them coves any harm," but they were eating and couldn't be interrupted for ten or fifteen minutes.

"Then we'll wait," said Mrs. Wheaton, laying her black shawl aside and taking a seat, in which she was followed by her sister evangelist.

"Perhaps you would like to know who we are," said the elder of the two women to a reporter who happened to be present. "Here is my card," and she handed over a small piece of pasteboard on which was printed with a rubber stamp, "Elizabeth R. Wheaton, Prison Evangelist. Jesus is Coming Soon; Prepare to Meet Thy God."

"That will tell who I am," continued the evangelist.... "Criminals and fallen women are the ones I try to reach. I would rather try to save a murderer or fallen woman than your smooth, respectable hypocrites, every time. Mary and I have just come through from san Francisco." * * *

At this moment Jailer Leckie announced that the prisoners were through eating, and the two women went below to pray with them. The younger woman held back, saying that she was afraid some of her old associates might be there, but she was urged on by her protector and a few minutes later the words of "Nearer My God to Thee," from two female voices, came floating through the prison bars. The prisoners gave them respectful hearing, and one or two seemed to be affected by the earnest words of counsel that fell from the lips of the evangelist. Later in the evening they held street services for the benefit of the workingmen near the Armory and relief tents.

BECAME A PREACHER.

One of the worst women I ever knew was converted in the spring of 1885 on the streets of Kansas City, Mo., where I was holding meetings. She came to the meeting to abuse and ridicule me. She heard my voice, she said, two blocks away, and became convicted. She came to where I was standing on a box preaching. I asked if there was any one there who would seek God and live a Christian life. I said if there was one such, let them come and kneel with me by the box and I would pray for them. She knelt there and cried mightily to God for mercy. But she went away unsaved and prayed and wept day and night. She could neither eat nor sleep. She saw herself a lost sinner. Her father had been a minister of the Gospel, but had died when she was very young. She had drifted to this wicked city in search of work, and you may know the rest. For it is but the story of many a poor orphan girl in her struggle for bread. She fell as thousands fall with none to pity or care. She was driven from one sin to another, until at last disgraced and filled with shame, she had tried twelve times to take her own life. Thus I found her a miserable woman. She came again to the meeting, this time alone, and was gloriously saved, and is still saved so far as I know. She became a successful preacher of righteousness, for she knew how to reach such as she had been. She became a terror to evil doers, brave in danger, and hopeful before discouraging obstacles. She has since told me she has saved many young girls' lives and characters by taking them in and giving them food and shelter when every other door except brothels and saloons was closed against them. Bless God for the homes open to shelter and protect the unfortunate girls.

THE BLIND ENCOURAGED.

One day while traveling in Montana, I went into a smoking car to hold a little Gospel meeting, singing and distributing tracts, when I found a blind lady there who seemed to be alone and neglected. I spoke to her kindly about her soul and invited her to go with me into the other car. I said, "I am always glad to do anything I can to help a blind person. My grandmother was blind several years before her death." She accepted it all gratefully and seemed very sorry to part from me when we changed cars. I exhorted her to a life of Christian service and to meet me in Heaven.

I never expected to meet her again, but some two years later I was holding an open air meeting in California and a lady said, "Would you allow me to testify?" and I said, "Certainly, if you are a Christian. Would be glad to have you." When she began to speak she said: "This lady don't know me, but I know her. We met once. Although I have never seen her, as I am deprived of sight, yet I know her. I met with her on the train one day," and she related the foregoing facts, stating that my kindness had won her heart and she had never forgotten my advice, and was now living a Christian life.

FORBIDDEN TO PREACH ON THE STREET.

One night when I attempted to hold a street meeting in F——, California—where I had been holding services for a few nights—the marshal said he had forbidden me to preach and sing on the streets. A gentleman looked up the law books and returned saying that it was not contrary to the laws of that city at that time to hold a gospel meeting on the street and that I could proceed, but the marshal came and forbade me, very unkindly and impolitely. At this crisis a gentleman came up and said that a saloon keeper down the street requested me to come and hold a meeting in front of his place. I said: "A gentleman has requested that we come and hold a meeting in front of his business place. We will go there, please," but the marshal in a very ungentlemanly way said I was not to hold a meeting on the street any place in that city.

I said we would go to a hall which had been opened for gospel services. It was several blocks away and only a few of the immense crowd would walk that distance. When I reached the place I sat down behind the door and cried and thought, what shall I do? I was sure the Lord wanted me to hold a meeting on the street. The blind lady mentioned in the previous incident was in the congregation and began to sing, "He is able to deliver thee," and I soon had the victory. The same sister had attempted to sing on the street, as this was her only means of supporting her old mother and sickly husband, and the marshal came along and without any warning pushed her off the street. A couple of strange gentlemen came and kindly led her to a place of safety. I heard soon after this that this man became suddenly insane and it took two men to hold him and take him to the jail and from there to the insane asylum.

THOUGHT THEY SAW A GHOST.

Once, in a city, another lady and myself were walking along a very lonesome street late at night. When passing a large dark building she remarked that it was a very dangerous gambling den. My heart burned within me. I was seized with an impulse to go in that place of iniquity and warn those men of their souls' danger. No sooner thought than done! I was soon in the room which proved to be vacant, but I could see light through the cracks of a closed door leading into the next room. I passed quietly across the room and opened the door and stood confronting a number of rough looking men who were seated at a long gambling table. Without a word I crossed the room with noiseless footsteps and dropping my Bible on the table and falling on my knees before them began to cry to God in their behalf. The men seemed to take an unexpected view of the situation, and rising simultaneously to their feet, they rushed wildly from the room upsetting their chairs in their haste, and I was left alone. The next day the report went out that a ghost had been seen there the night before, and some of the men vowed they would never touch a pack of cards again as long as they lived—that money could not hire them to do it. Truly "The wicked flee when no man pursueth."

HURT BY A SALOONKEEPER.

While I was at Springfield, Ill., I was led one Sabbath to go to the park to hold a gospel meeting, taking two sisters with me. We had a good meeting, and returning to the city I asked the street car conductor if there was another park where I could hold services. He directed me to a place in another suburb. We went there, and in a grove I saw some tables and men and women sitting at them, drinking. I began to sing a hymn, thinking we were in a public park, when a man rushed out of a house toward me, saying, "You shan't sing here." I said, "Please let me finish this verse." He replied, "No, I won't allow any one to sing here." I knelt in prayer. He did not say I should not pray. The sisters were looking at him, and said he hurried toward me in great anger. The sisters prayed to God to spare me. The man jerked me and pushed me over, when some of the men at the tables called out to him, "Let go of that woman. You don't know who she is. We know her." The men in the meantime running to us, laid hold on the saloonkeeper and took him away. I was very much hurt. I could not walk alone. The park proved to be a beer garden. We went to the nearest house and asked permission to rest till I should gain strength to return to the city. The people where we stopped were very indignant, and said the man had no license to sell liquor on Sunday, and was violating the city ordinance. There were no arrests. The whisky men must have their own way in this land of American liberty. They can ruin lives, break up homes, blight the prospects of the best people on earth and fill the prisons, almshouses, criminal insane asylums, brothels, graves of paupers, and doom souls by the multitude, and who cares? Who votes to put down the saloons? Who tries to save mothers' girls as well as mothers' boys, husbands and wives? Even the parents are overtaken by the demon of strong drink and sink into the most depraved conditions in order to satisfy their craving for alcohol. O, the awfulness of it all! Sisters, brothers, are you and I clear? Are we doing our best to stop this horrible traffic in whisky and girls, for one of these places can scarcely exist without the other. How many girls and boys are sacrificed yearly to fill the saloonkeepers' coffers and fill up hell? Think of these things.

WARNED TO LEAVE THE CITY.

Upon entering a town in Mississippi I inquired of a woman if she could direct me to a hotel, and she told me her sister and her husband kept one and I would be made comfortable with them.

We went to the hotel and left our luggage and went at once to hold an open air meeting. The singing attracted a considerable crowd, and at the close of the service many came to shake hands with me and thank me for the meeting, among whom were a number of colored people, who thanked the Lord in their characteristic way and asked me to preach again which I agreed to do that night.

As we turned our steps toward our hotel, we noticed a colored man walking a short distance ahead of us who, when we were out of hearing of the crowd, turned and said to us: "You women don't intend to hold another meeting on the street to-night?" and I said, "Certainly, I shall obey God." He said, "You have shaken hands with the colored people and the white people are angry, and they will mob you. I came along here for the purpose of warning you. If they saw me talking with you my life would be in danger." I told him I was not afraid, thanked him and told him I would do as the Lord led.

On reaching our hotel the landlord asked if I intended to hold another meeting on the street that night, and I told him I did. He said that the townspeople had forbidden me to hold another service and that I would have to leave his hotel at once, because I had shaken hands with the colored people. We told him we had made the appointment and we should keep our word. He went to his wife and told her to go and tell those women to leave the house and take the train, as we had associated with the colored people and the white people would not allow us to remain in town. She replied that we had paid our money and our money was as good as anybody's, and that we were respectable, honest women and she was going to treat us as such.

When we went down the street we heard a noise as of a mob, and we went praying the Lord to show us what to do, and He showed us our life was in danger and to step one side into the colored people's church where God's presence was revealed in mighty power and souls were convicted and converted.

In the morning two colored women called upon me, saying they had come to warn me and assist me to the train. One of them said that two nights before she had a terrible dream about a woman coming to preach on the streets and was so impressed that she sent her husband four miles to see if there was anything in it. This was the man that warned us that night. When he went home and told her what he had seen and heard, she dreamed again and the Lord told her to come and help us out of town, as the people would take my life. They carried our luggage and showed us to the train and got us safely on board, and with a "God bless you, Honey, we's prayin' for you," they were gone, and we went on our way with thankful hearts for our Lord's protecting care.

IN JAIL.

I have several times been arrested for holding services in the open air, but have been taken to prison but twice—once in Glasgow, Scotland, as related elsewhere, and once in Belleville, Illinois.

In 1889, Sister Anna Kinne wrote me from Belleville that they were holding meetings at that place, but had seen but little stir, that it seemed to be a hard field, and that she believed the Lord wanted me to come and help them in the meetings. I was, at the time, in Mississippi, but after praying over the matter I felt that I should go to Belleville in answer to her request.

The first Sabbath after reaching there I tried to hold services in the open air, but was stopped by policemen. I tried again with the same results. Then

I went to the mayor, but was refused permission to hold any such meetings. When I asked him if he would take the responsibility on the day of judgment, he said, "Yes." I then went to the jail and held services, and the sheriff kindly inquired about my work and showed considerable interest, and took down some notes. I then asked him for permission to hold meetings on the court house steps. This was readily granted, and I took Sister Kinne with me. The marshal of the town had bitterly opposed my work, and while we were singing he very rudely and unceremoniously came and took me by the arm and dragged me down from the steps.

I told him that the sheriff had given me permission to hold services, but he was very angry and refused to let me go on.

I said to those who had gathered, "We will have no open air meeting, but come to Buchanan Hall to-night, and we will have a meeting there."

I think it was the following night that I was impressed just before the opening of our services, to sing a hymn, standing in the mission door. I spoke to Sister Kinne of this and she said, "God bless you, Sister Wheaton, I will pray for you."

I went quietly down to the door and was standing there singing an old-time hymn, when out of the darkness there came two policemen. Without saying a word they took hold of me and dragged me along the street. I had no bonnet on, and my shawl was dragging along in the mud. I said, "Please let me get my shawl, and will you please let me ask one of the ladies at the mission to go with me?" But they refused and seemed glad to think that I was being disgraced. As I met two or three Christian people, one of them spoke kindly to me and I replied that I was suffering for Jesus' sake. "You seem to be well acquainted with the men," one of the policemen said. "No," I said, "only with a few Christians."

When we arrived at police headquarters they gave in the report that I was on the street holding a meeting and was having a row, etc., which was, of course, utterly false.

I was, of course, surprised at the treatment I was receiving. I opened my Bible, which I still held, and began reading in silence. The officer said, "Are you making all of this ado and trouble?" I replied, "I was standing in our mission door singing." He said, "Will you give bail for your good behavior?" I said, "I have no money for bail." Then he asked me if I had no friends. I told him I was a stranger in the city. "Then," he said, "I will have to send you to jail, or what will you do?" I said I did not know. He then told another policeman to take me to the jail across the square, and only a few blocks away. This policeman said to some boys who were standing outside, "You boys stay here, we do not want a mob." But the marshal said,

"Go along boys. She wants notoriety—give it to her." And so I went to the jail with a mob crying after me.

Arriving at the jail the kind jailor was shocked to see me in the officer's charge, and said, "You are not a prisoner?" I said, "Yes, I was singing in our mission door, but they arrested me." His wife came in and kindly said, "Come into the parlor, and I will make ready for you the spare bedroom." I was, of course, surprised and deeply touched. "No, indeed," I said, "I am a prisoner. Take me into the cell with the other women." Her little daughter came in and knelt down by my side and kissed my hand, saying how very sorry she was for me. It was on a Christmas eve, and the child was going to the Christmas tree.

Soon the sheriff came in in a hurry and said, "You are a free woman!" He, finding I had been arrested, had notified friends who had given bail and secured my release. Not understanding the sheriff, I said, "No, I am here in disgrace, and I want you to put me in the woman's cell." But he insisted that I was free. Then I said, "They have put me here in disgrace, and I want some one to come and take me to our mission, as it is dark." They then sent for someone to come for me, and such a shout as went up when I again entered the mission hall. One good old Christian friend said, "I told you that if she was a woman of God, and I knew she was, she would return to the hall before the meeting was over."

It seems that a reporter who was at the police station at the time of my arrest and heard the abuse of the officers had hurried to the sheriff's office, and he, as I have said, had secured my release.

We give here a verbatim copy of the paper signed by friends, the original of which I still have in my possession. Somehow the case was dismissed, and I was never brought to trial:

VERBATIM COPY OF A RECOGNIZANCE.

(12th, 24th, 1899.)

State of Illinois, St. Clair County, ss.

This day personaly appeared before the undersigned, William Bornmann, one of the Justices of the Peace in and for said County, Mrs. E. R. Wheaton, James West and Wm. Meyer, and jointly and severally acknowledged themselves to owe and be indebted unto the People of the State of Illinois, in the sum of Twenty-five Dollars, to be levied on their goods and chattels, lands and tenements, if default be made in the premises and conditions below, to-wit:

Whereas, The above bounden, Elizabeth R. Wheaton, was, on the 24th day of December, A. D. 1889, arrested for violation of the city ordinance, was adjudged and required by said Justice of the Peace to give bonds, as required by the statute in such cases, made and provided, for her appearance to answer to said charge. Now the conditions of this recognizance is such that if the above bounden, Elizabeth R. Wheaton, shall personally appear and be before me, in Belleville, on the 27th day of December, A. D. 1889, at 9 a. m., and from day to day, and from term to term, and from day to day of each term hereafter, until discharged by order of said Court, then and there to answer to the said People of the State of Illinois on said charge of violation of the city ordinance and then and there answer and abide the order and judgment of said Court, and thence not depart the same without lawful permission, then and in that case this recognizance is to become void; otherwise to be and remain in full force and virtue.

As witness our hands and seals, this 24th day of December, A. D. 1889.

Taken, entered into, acknowledged and approved before me, this 24th day of December, 1899.

WM. BORNMANN, J. P.

Wilhelm Meyer, [L. S.]
Jas. A. West, [L. S.]

This occurrence caused a great deal of excitement at the time. Some time after I met one of the editors of one of the principal papers of the town, and he stated that a serious calamity had overtaken all those who were active in the opposing and persecuting me, and mentioned some who had died and others upon whom God's judgments seemed to have fallen.

The following was taken from a paper published at Belleville:

Mrs. Elizabeth R. Wheaton, a well known prison evangelist who has labored in nearly all of the principal prisons of the United States, was arrested Tuesday evening by Policemen S. and S., while she was engaged in conducting a song service, standing in the door at the entrance to Buchanan Hall, where a series of meetings are being held by two other evangelists, Mr. and Mrs. S. D. Kinne. The officers, on arriving on the scene, ordered

Mrs. Wheaton to stop singing, but as she paid no attention to their command, she was at once arrested and hurried off to the police station, where she was questioned by the captain of police and the city marshal, and a little later she was removed to the county jail, but through the courtesy of the jailor she was not locked up in a cell. A complaint of disturbing the peace was made against her before Justice B., and a hearing was fixed for tomorrow before him, and a bond for her appearance was duly executed; but while these formal proceedings were being attended to Sheriff R., having heard of Mrs. Wheaton's incarceration in the county jail, repaired to the institution, immediately ordered her release, as there was no authority for holding her there, and when the officer from Justice B.'s court arrived with the bail bond for Mrs. Wheaton's signature, he was chagrined to find that the lady had been released by order of the sheriff. No further attempt was made to arrest her, and it is probable that the matter will be dropped. Mrs. Wheaton is an elderly lady and is deeply devoted to Christian work, especially among the unfortunates confined in jails and prisons, and she has a large number of testimonials as to her character and work from prison officials, railway managers and others in all parts of the country. Many prominent citizens expressed themselves yesterday as deeply regretting the action of the officers in arresting Mrs. Wheaton. The same lady, by written permission of Sheriff R., attempted to hold religious services from the court house steps on Sunday evening last, but she was forced to desist by the city marshal. Mrs. Wheaton applied to Mayor B. recently for permission to hold open-air religious meetings on the streets, but was denied the privilege on the ground that considerable disorder had been occasioned some months ago by the holding of such meetings by members of the Salvation Army, who held forth in Belleville for a time. The action of the mayor in refusing to allow the evangelist to hold open-air meetings, and the arrest of Mrs. Wheaton while engaged in conducting a song service in the door of Buchanan Hall, where the revival services are held, is causing a great deal of severe criticism, owing to the toleration of the parading of the principal streets by brass bands on Sundays, as well as other days, to draw audiences for minstrel shows, etc., the gathering of crowds on the public square by street fakirs, patent medicine peddlers, quack doctors and others, who deal out rough jokes, etc., in tones loud enough to be heard blocks away.

Belleville, Dec. 26, 1888.

CHAPTER XVIII.

Rescue Work.

A Mother's Plea for Her Fallen Daughter.

So tenderly reared in the pure country air,So innocent, gracious and true,A sweet loving daughter, so gentle and fair.Of the great wicked world naught she knew,She roamed on the hillside and plucked the sweet flowers,Nor far from my sight did she stray,Till a shy cunning charmer invaded her bowers,And stole my loved treasure away.

With words fair and lovely he won her young heart,Then wooed her far from the home nest,Then hastily pressed to the city's great mart,My darling he tore from my breast;So simple, confiding, ne'er dreaming of harm.She laid her young life at his feet,And the foul, venomed viper pierced her heart with a thorn,And left her to die in the street.

All wounded and bleeding and covered with shame,And knowing not wither to go,In the haunts of the vilest she cringed her away,To hide her disgrace and her woe;Could I know she had gone from this cold, cruel world,My grief would be easy to bear,But to satiate vile passions her life-blood is sold,And my broken heart pleads in my prayer.

Oh, bring back my darling, a poor bruised thing,The victim of Satan's deceit,O tell her I love her, though cursed by the fiendThat crushed her to hell 'neath his feet.O pity my daughter, my poor fallen one,Ye who have daughters so fair,And shield not the monster who spoiled my loved oneAnd drove my poor heart to despair.

—MARY WEEMS CHAPMAN.

Chicago, Ill.

For some years I have been quite intimately associated with friends who have, perhaps, the largest Rescue Home in the world. I am told that they have taken in more girls than any other Home of the kind. Over 1,250 girls have there been confined and never have they lost one of these young mothers by death. But, oh, it is a sad sight to see them, day after day carrying their load of sorrow in their hearts. Often when I am there, as I manifest toward them my love and sympathy, they tell me their story of woe sad as was the cry of Eve when banished from the presence of God. She yielded to Satan's devices because she believed the voice of Satan rather than the voice of God. She became an outcast—and so our sisters are still being deceived by the devil in human form and become outcasts from all that is good. Some of them have been won by a mess of pottage, a mere bauble or a gewgaw. Others have the promise of love—that which every human heart craves. These believe, trust, yield and are ruined and some of them are so young! so ignorant! Then there are some who have been basely betrayed or brutally forced and then left to bear alone their shame and disgrace—for, alas! the "traffic in girls" is not an imaginary thing, but an awful reality.

O that the good people of our fair land would awaken and see that justice is done in behalf of the helpless and innocent! Prevention is better than cure. Let us guard the children and put down every influence that would tend to demoralize either our boys or girls! But in the meantime, let us do all within our power to lift up the fallen and win back those who have gone astray and share the burden and sorrow of those who suffer through no fault of their own.

Those who have been daring in sin often make the most gifted, consecrated and valiant workers for God and souls when truly and fully saved. I bless the Lord for the privilege of seeking and finding some of these "diamonds in the rough." I have known many Christian workers who had once been criminals or fallen, but who had been rescued by some one who had a knowledge of human nature and a heart filled with the love of God who told them of the love of Christ and His wonderful power to save. O when we all meet in the great Hereafter what a time of rejoicing there will be among the rescuers and the rescued.

DRUNKEN WOMEN AND MEN.

I find hundreds of men and women, many young women, in drunkenness and crime, and the most open daring sins. In one of the largest drinking dens in the world I asked the proprietor if I might sing a hymn, and he gave his consent. I was obliged to go down stairs and through many rooms and hallways and then up a dark stairway to the platform where the orchestra was playing. When they ceased I sang a hymn which touched their hearts and they cheered the singing. I offered a prayer and they all seemed to appreciate it. There were hundreds of *men* only, drinking, miners and others. Then I went where there were both men and women drinking, and sang and prayed with them. At near midnight, while I was engaged in prayer, one of the poor, unfortunate girls clasped my hand and put a piece of silver in it, and stood holding my hand till I rose. She cried and spoke of her desire to be good. She was reminded of her old home and her mother. The proprietor then told me I must leave, as he found he would lose her from his den. He said he was once a Christian himself, and on coming west, saw the money to be made in that kind of business, and fell, and went deep in sin, leading others down with himself.

ASSAULTED IN A DIVE.

While in San Pedro, California, I went, one night, into a saloon to invite the men to a gospel meeting at the mission on the same block, and the keeper sprang up from his gambling table, where he was engaged with several others in a game of some kind, and rushing towards me, violently grabbed me by the arms, and then with both hands clutching me, rushed me to the door, using vile and insulting epithets to me as he went. At the door a lady said, "This is a public house; you dare not throw people out who have done you no harm." He finally released his Satanic grasp upon me. I had only spoken a few kindly words to two young men standing at the bar in the act of raising their glasses to their lips. I had just said, "Don't drink it, boys, please don't," when the assault was made. As the saloonist rushed at me, I said, "Don't touch me, please; I will go out." But he seemed fiendishly happy in injuring and insulting a helpless old woman, who only wished to do them all good, and see them saved in Heaven at last. The only excuse he ever made was that he thought I was Carrie Nation. Commenting on this occurrence, a Los Angeles paper contained the following item:

> San Pedro, March 29.—"Mother" Wheaton, a well known prison evangelist, was roughly assaulted by John Wilkins, a Front street saloonkeeper, shortly after seven o'clock last evening. Mrs. Wheaton was preaching to a large gathering in front of Wilkins' joint, and hearing loud cursing within, the aged reformer entered, intending to invite the blasphemers to Peniel Mission, where services are held every evening. She had scarcely passed inside the doors of the dive, when Wilkins rushed forward, seized her and thrust her backward. At the same time he applied vile epithets to her, shouting angrily: "Get out of here, woman, and be quick about it!"
>
> So badly was Mrs. Wheaton injured that she was unable to return to the mission without assistance. She is confined to her bed and is suffering severe pains from the shock.
>
> Wilkins explained today that he mistook Mrs. Wheaton for Carrie Nation, whom the former resembles. No arrests have been made.

In a city where I had been preaching the Gospel, a messenger came stating that a young girl had cut her throat. It was an extremely hot day and I had to walk a long distance across the city. Arriving at the house they told me that no one was allowed to go in. But I went right in and everybody stood back. Kneeling down by the poor girl I took her hand already growing cold in death. Poor child! Like thousands of others, she had been disappointed in life. The one who had plighted his troth had broken her heart, and rather than bear her shame she preferred death. Then and there I had the privilege of pointing this beautiful girl to Christ who said, "Neither do I condemn thee. Go and sin no more," and He who never turns anyone away heard and answered prayer.

One day I held a meeting in the Crittenden Home for Fallen Girls, in Washington. They all seemed so glad to hear me. (There were thirty girls.) They were deeply moved. After the meeting closed I took each by the hand and exhorted them to live pure and holy lives. And with tears in their eyes they promised to try and serve the Lord. One dear little girl in a short dress (fourteen years old), clung to me crying, and said Jesus had saved her just then, in the meeting, and she would be a good girl and live for Heaven. I clasped her to my heart and thought what Jesus said about him who offends "one of these little ones." Some heartless wretch had ruined the girl and left her to die alone. "Vengeance is *mine*, *I* will repay, saith the Lord."

A GIRL SAVED.

Trying to rescue a girl in a low dive in New York city in 1890, as I entered the den the keeper, a large, strong man, sprang up and struck me a blow. The girl caught his arm and cried out, "Don't strike her, she is a lady." But he thrust me out, and I said to her, "Fly for your life—out at the back door." I ran around the saloon and caught her away from an angry mob and with the help of the sisters with me, almost carried her six blocks to the Crittenden Home, and there she was reformed and converted.

A GIRL REJECTED AT RESCUE HOME.

In Ft. Worth, Texas, I once found in the jail a poor girl who was a very desperate character. She had been at the Rescue Home several times, and she was so very wicked that they refused to have her there again. They said it was of no use trying to reclaim her. I well remember the night that the Lord sent me to the jail to hold a meeting. The service was held after dark, as the prisoners were compelled to work during the day. I was intensely grieved and very much burdened over the case of this poor girl. So intelligent, yet so sinful! In my grief, I fell upon the floor weeping over her lost condition.

A sister who was with me, and on her way then to India, prayed for me as well as for the poor prisoners, and the lost girl. The meeting closed, and the next day we left the city, the sister going west, while I started north.

After we left Ft. Worth, my heart was still sad and greatly pained for the poor lost girl I had seen in the jail and I wrote to the superintendent of the Rescue Home and pleaded with her to try her just once more—not only for my sake, but for the sake of Jesus. She did so, and the result was that the girl was saved and began a life of virtue and usefulness.

A year or so later, I was again at Ft. Worth, and was holding services in the Girls' Rescue Home. As they assembled for the meeting I shook hands with each of them. I said of one of the girls to the matron, "This girl looks like a good Christian—who is she?" The girl herself replied, "Don't you know me, mother?" I said, "No." Then she answered, "I am the girl you rescued from the prison;" and the matron said that she was the best girl in the home. I went back after another year, and she was the matron's assistant. Still later the superintendent told me that she was a deaconess in New York, and was doing a great work. This same lady told me how she had shortly before come across my letter in which I begged her mother-in-law, who was the former superintendent, to help the girl and give her just one more chance! Oh, how wonderfully God had answered my prayers and the yearning of my heart that night when the burden of her soul rested so heavily upon me!

ROBBED BY HER OWN BROTHER.

A lovely girl was once drugged by her deceiver and left to bear her shame alone. She was led to a rescue home where she was cared for. Sometime after the birth of her child, which she dearly loved, her father died, and left her $1,000. She was induced by her brother to come to the city where he was living, and give him the money, which he and his wife used recklessly. They then moved, leaving the poor girl sitting on the steps without money enough even to buy milk for her babe. The poor girl was almost distracted with grief. I found her a temporary home with Christian people and a little later secured transportation for her to a rescue home in another city where she could be kindly provided for.

In that hour of despair, when I found her, she was almost ready to yield to the enemy of her soul, through temptation of the same wretch who had first effected her ruin. She could go hungry herself, she said, but she could not see her babe suffer for want of food.

Sisters, let us try by all possible means to befriend our own sex and help all who are thrown in our way, heavenward.

NEGLECTED BY THE CHURCHES.

I once went to a city where there are many churches and professors of religion, and yet there in the Home for Fallen Girls, where I held services I found the inmates neglected. I then went to the poorhouse where over a hundred poor and crippled destitute people were so glad to hear me sing hymns while they partook of their dinner. They seemed to wonder who and what I was, yet, how glad they were when they understood it was for the love of their souls Jesus had sent me to tell them of His great love. Thank God for the privilege of going to these places. God always finds a way when there seems to be no way.

So I must say in concluding that of all those who have my sympathy and my help, my prayers and my tears, prisoners, and all, the poor, abandoned, forsaken girl, who has no one to share her sorrow and her shame claims and receives my deepest sympathy and assistance. There is no one on whom Jesus had more compassion and yet the croakers are often the ones to send her to worse shame by their neglect and cruelty. Jesus said, "Neither do I condemn thee, go and sin no more."

"She is more to be pitied than censured, She is more to be loved than despised, She is only a poor girl who has ventured On life's rugged path ill-advised. Don't scorn her with words fierce and bitter, Don't laugh at her shame and downfall; Just pause for a moment, consider That a man was the cause of it all."

VISIT TO A HOSPITAL.

One Sunday, years ago, I visited a hospital in a certain city and found it in a most terrible condition. There were many sick, both men and women, and how glad they were to see me! The public were not permitted inside the grounds, but the superintendent being absent I was admitted. The patients were suffering with hunger, and were in a most filthy condition.

I found both colored men and women in the same room and all covered with body lice. One old colored woman was almost eaten alive with vermin, and starving. They would not give her even a drink of water. I gave her water and she drank a quart and begged for more. I asked her if she would like to have me bring her something to eat. She said, "Oh, yes, Honey." I said, "What can you eat?" She said, "A crust of bread—I's so hungry, been hungry so long."

My heart was sick at the sights and sounds of suffering and anguish. I told the Lord about it. All night I cried and prayed. I got up early, got a large, fat chicken, made soup, got provisions and a couple to help me carry the things, and went to that miserable place. I got access to the building with my food and all got a share. I never will forget the looks on the faces of those starving sufferers, and the tears coursing down their wan, pale cheeks, as I and dear Mary, my helper, fed them. One poor old white brother said he was ashamed to have us near him.

I took along clothing for the poor old colored woman, and had to take the scissors and cut the garment off from her, and put it in the stove. I found the mattress decaying under her.

I told the superintendent's wife I would be a witness against her in the day of judgment for treating the patients so cruelly. She said she did not have help. I said the state, county or city would send help, that that was no excuse for their starving and cruelly treating those sick helpless invalids. The old woman and the men told me they were compelled to live there in that one room altogether. It was terrible!

One man said he had killed vermin until he was so tired and weak he could do no more. They said that seldom ever any one left that death hole alive. The bodies were sold for dissection.

I went early the next morning to the judge's office to relate my experience and ask him if something could not be done to relieve the suffering of the patients that I found there in such a filthy condition and in such need of care and food and water. I told him I did not see the superintendent, Mr. V. Just at that moment a dudish young fellow in the room arose and said, "So you did not see V. when you went there yesterday; you see him now, don't you?" He was very angry and said I got inside by his absence, and that he would do so and so. The judge said angrily, "Woman, you talk too much." I said, "I have not begun to talk yet." The two men hissed and told me to leave the office. I had taken the precaution to take with me the sister who was traveling with me at that time, also the young man who had helped us to carry the clothes and provisions to the hospital the day before. They could have corroborated my testimony but the judge was evidently in league with the superintendent of the hospital and would not listen.

I went to a church in the place to a Woman's Missionary meeting and got permission to speak to the ladies in public about the awful conditions I found in their so-called hospital. They were surprised and greatly incensed, and told their husbands, and so there was awakened an interest that resulted in further investigation. Facts were found as I had stated, only, if anything, worse.

The outcome of these things being brought to light was that the old shanties which served as a so-called hospital were replaced by good buildings and kind caretakers took the place of the cruel superintendent— who died some months later after a long illness.

ANOTHER VISIT TO A HOSPITAL.

The following is a description of a visit to another hospital, as published in a paper at Chattanooga, Tenn. This was also early in my work.

A BAT CAVE.

A SANITARIUM FOR CATS AND HOTEL FOR DOGS—CALLED BY COURTESY THE CITY HOSPITAL OF CHATTANOOGA.

Mrs. E. R. Wheaton, the eloquent female evangelist, who has been in the city for the past week carrying on a series of prayer meetings in the jails and houses of ill fame, came into the *Commercial* office yesterday afternoon and gave a full and detailed report of the neglected condition of the city hospital. She says:

"As I approached the building I could not convince myself that I was really in sight of a hospital, for it reminded me more of a stable than anything else I could conceive of. I approached the gate and met a colored female mute who raised her hand in a deprecating manner as if to warn me of some unseen danger that I was about to come in contact with. I motioned the negro girl to lead the way and followed her into a dreary looking house that I had been told was really the only hospital of which Chattanooga could boast. Just as I opened the door six big hounds sprang from the different beds within the building and would have torn me to pieces had not I hastily slammed the door and shut them in. I applied to a poor cripple man who had the appearance of a half-fed mendicant where to find the keeper and I was informed that he was asleep, but if I would wait he (the cripple) would go and wake him up, and in a few moments he returned accompanied by a healthy looking man who seemed to care little whether I went in or remained out of doors in the rain.

"As I followed the keeper into the room six well fed hounds and one emaciated looking man occupied the beds that were in the rooms.

"I have wandered from one end of the land to the other, I have visited prison cells, opium joints, houses of ill-fame, almshouses, reformatories and every dreary den from New York to San Francisco, from Florida to Montreal, but with all the sights with which I have been confronted I have never seen a more cheerless abode and one so utterly void of comfort and cleanliness as the one occupied by the poor, hungry invalid that shared the beds of the well fed dogs.

"The sick man said he was suffering for the want of food and had been shamefully neglected since he was placed in charge of the manager of this cheerless institution. Two inmates have died within the past week and two are left to suffer.

"The other inmate was a colored man who evidently has little more of life's suffering to endure in this world.

"In this room six cats occupied seats of prominence, two purring on one bed and three others romping from place to place over the apartment, while the sixth was helping himself to the sick man's dinner.

"The buildings are without warmth in the winter and have no means of ventilation for summer. The confined air is contaminated with the odor that rises from unemptied and neglected vessels that are allowed to stand neglected from day to day. The keeper seems to be utterly indifferent with regard to the ease or comfort of the sick and it is very evident that while the city pays for food to support the sick and suffering, the countless and useless dogs and cats eat a large portion of the food which should be used exclusively for the unfortunate inmates."

Mrs. Wheaton has done much commendable work not only in Chattanooga but from one end of the land to the other. She has consecrated her time, wealth and character to the uplifting of fallen people, and by her devotion to Christianity and her liberality has won thousands of friends throughout the country.—Chattanooga Paper.

WORDS OF CHEER FROM OTHER RESCUE WORKERS.

The first of the following letters I carried with me on my second visit to Europe, mentioned elsewhere:

FLORENCE CRITTENTON HOME,
21 and 23 Bleecker Street, New York.

J. F. Shirey, 67 Farrington Road, East Coast, England.

Dear Brother: This will introduce to you Mrs. Elizabeth Wheaton, a prison evangelist. She is alone and unprotected in London. Please make the way for her as best you can where she can speak for God to the poor prisoners. She lives by faith and trusts Him for all.

God bless you.

MOTHER PRINDLE.

MOTHER PRINDLE.

New York, October 16, 1903.

My first acquaintance with Mrs. Elizabeth Wheaton was made in the Florence Crittenton Midnight Mission, New York City, in 1890. She impressed me then and has ever since as one whom God has called and endowed with special gifts for a grand and noble work. Her one strong hold is faith in God. When under the power of the Spirit she verily treads upon serpents and scorpions and all the powers of darkness seem to flee before her. As a singing evangelist for prison work, I do not know her equal. Her preaching is in the demonstration of the Spirit and with power. She gives the Lord's message with holy boldness, fraught with tender love to the sinner, and blessed are the results.

The midnight call given on train, when it was my privilege to be with her, was an hour never to be forgotten. Many will rise up and call her blessed in that great day who but for her favored and wonderful ministry would have gone into outer darkness. God bless her and her book.

MOTHER PRINDLE.

The following taken from "Beulah Home Record," Chicago, Ill., March 1, 1902, is explanatory in itself. Also the letter that follows:

We have had with us for a time, as our honored guest, Mother Wheaton, the Railroad Prison Evangelist. Like Jesus, the friend of poor sinners, she goes up and down the land in state prisons and homes where mothers' girls are sheltered, down into the coal mines, into the great lumber camps, and on crowded railroad trains, while speeding along, she preaches the everlasting gospel of our Lord and Savior, and gives out tracts. Thus she goes as God's flaming minister, sowing beside all waters, singing and praying poor sin-sick, tempest-tossed souls into the kingdom of God. Do you ask what is the secret of her success? It may be found in the Psalms, 126:6—"She goeth forth weeping," she has a burning love for souls. So you and I, dear reader, if we are to succeed in winning souls, our hearts must be full of love for them. We give Mother Wheaton a warm welcome to this great and wicked city of Chicago and a hearty welcome always to Beulah Home.

Berachah Home for Erring Girls,
2719 Lawton Ave., St. Louis, Mo.

We feel in Berachah Home that we shall not forget Mother Wheaton. She came into the "Home" and our lives just as God was leading us out in rescue work, and as she stood among us in our first "open meeting," we felt, "Here is a strong, brave soldier of the cross." We found hope and encouragement as she spoke to us of His service, and the Spirit witnessed "This is of God," as she sang one of her songs as only Mother Wheaton can sing them. We did not see her again until in the Baltimore Convocation of Prayer,

January, 1904, when God again used her to bring Mrs. Chapman and me to God's full thought for us there. She with others laid hands on us, with prayer, setting us apart for the "work whereunto we were called." May God bless her ministry to others, as He has to us in Berachah Home.

Mrs. J. P. Duncan, Mgr.
Mrs. B. G. Chapman, Treas.

THE PRODIGAL DAUGHTER.

"To the home of his father returning, The prodigal, weary and worn, Is greeted with joy and thanksgiving, As when on his first natal morn; A 'robe' and a 'ring' are his portion, The servants as suppliants bow; He is clad in fine linen and purple, In return for the penitent vow.

"But ah! for the Prodigal Daughter, Who has wandered away from her home; Her feet must still press the dark valley And through the wilderness roam; Alone on the bleak, barren mountains— The mountains so dreary and cold— No hand is outstretched in fond pity To welcome her back to the fold.

"But thanks to the Shepherd, whose mercy Still follows His sheep, tho' they stray; The weakest, and e'en the forsaken He bears in His bosom away; And in the bright mansions of glory Which the blood of His sacrifice won, There is room for the Prodigal Daughter, As well as the Prodigal Son!"

We've a Home for Prodigal Daughters, Our Saviour says gather them in; Will you help rescue these dear ones— Who have fallen in paths of sin? Your girl may be one of the "fallen," And you long to see her return; Oh, there's room for the Prodigal Daughter, As well as the Prodigal Son.

—Horace.

CHAPTER XIX.

Work in Canada and Mexico.

In my several visits to the prisons of Canada I have generally found the officers very courteous. There are sometimes there, as here, changes of administration, making the work of reaching the prisoners more difficult. In the large prison at Toronto the officers were especially kind and gave me the privilege of preaching the gospel to the prisoners as often as I could attend chapel services. Much interest was manifested and I trust good was accomplished.

MY SECOND EXPERIENCE IN STREET PREACHING

was in Hamilton, Canada. There for weeks, night after night, rain or shine, I sang and preached the gospel in the open air. I was especially helped of the Lord and met with blessed success.

In 1886, I took with me from Toronto, a dear young sister, who was called of God to join me in my work. She went with me to Florida and many other states. She afterward married an evangelist but died a few years later, being true to God, so far as I know, to the last.

SERVICE WITH Y. M. C. A.

During a visit to London, Canada, after visiting the prisons I went to the hospital to visit the sick. While singing, a message came over the telephone saying that the Secretary of the Y. M. C. A. requested me to lead their meeting on Sunday afternoon. Would I come? I said, "Better wait till I return to the city. I can't tell." The secretary had to know at once, so he could announce it through the papers. So I promised to go, as they had no speaker. I felt discouraged, as I could think of no message suitable for that large, mixed audience, and prayed for guidance. Sunday afternoon—still with no message in mind—I started to the hall. As I walked along the street, praying, I said, "Lord, give me at least a text to read." Just then I saw on the ground a scrap of paper, the torn leaf of a Bible. I picked it up, looked at it, and there my message, text and all, opened up to my mental vision. I went into the pulpit depending entirely on God, and the light broke in on my soul, and the power of God fell on the people. I told them how I was depending alone on the Lord for the words as He gave them to me. It was a victorious meeting. I leave results with the Lord.

A GIRL RESCUED.

In one of the Canadian cities I found in the jail a beautiful girl who was very dissipated and unruly. The officers could not control her—no one had any good influence over her. The Lord laid the burden of her soul on my heart. I treated her with love and respect, and tried in every way to win her for God. Finally, she realized that I loved her soul, though no one else cared for her. Then she sought the Lord. She was a Roman Catholic. I told her I would go to the House of the Good Shepherd and speak to the Mother Superior, and see if they would not take her in, as she had no home. She wept with joy at this, and told me of a plan some wicked men had made to be at the jail when she was discharged at 6 o'clock Saturday evening and take her to haunts of sin. I hurried out to the Sisters early in the morning and found them at mass, and waited, determined to save the poor girl from further downfall, and drunkenness. The Sisters, seeing my anxiety and sincerity, agreed to help me. Then I went to the officers of the jail and got them to release the girl at noon. She was taken to another city and thus saved. When the hour came for her release from the jail in the evening, sure enough several men made their appearance and watched and waited for her to come out. At last they began calling her name. Then the officers went out and told them the girl had been pardoned, and had left at noon for another city, with protectors. Another brand had been plucked from the burning for the Master's Kingdom.

SHUT OUT—OTHERS ADMITTED.

At one time amidst great inconveniences I reached Kingston Prison. I saw some of the officers Saturday night and they were kind and willingly consented that I should have opportunity to hold or assist in services the next day. The next morning I went to the prison through a drenching rain—without an umbrella, arrived early and waited for the chaplain. When he came, I told him my desire and what the other officers had said. But he refused to even let me go inside to listen to the service. When I asked his reason he said they would not allow women in the prison. Yet while I had been waiting I had seen several Catholic sisters enter. I have had similar experiences in our own land.

STONED.

One day as I was passing along the street in the quaint walled city of Quebec, some boys threw stones at me, while an old man urged them on, saying, "If it's Salvation Army ye are, ye should be killed." The Lord have mercy upon them and upon all who oppose His work or His workers. For ourselves we must not count these things strange. "It is enough for the disciple that he be as his Master, and the servant as his Lord."

AN INFIDEL DEFEATED.

While in Toronto, Canada, I often went to the parks on Sabbath days and held services—the mayor of the city, who was a devoted Christian, often himself helping in these open-air services. One stand in the park was usually occupied by the infidel element. They would hold the place all day so that others could not have the privilege of doing work for God—so as the place was public property upon which they had no rightful claim I went early and so secured the place before them. When their leader arrived the people were listening to the gospel in song and testimony from worthy witnesses. He was very angry—said it was his place to speak and he must have it, and ordered me to stop and leave the stand, but I kept on with the service as God directed and he went away a few steps and called for the people to follow him, and he would address them. No one seemed inclined to go and a bystander told him his followers were few and he had better desist from trying to disturb a religious service. So we had the victory and God was honored that day in the work which He sent his servants to do.

Among my papers I have found the following letters of introduction given me while in Canada by Hon. John Robson, Provincial Secretary:

Provincial Secretary's Department,
Victoria, B. C., Oct. 5.

Dear Brother:

The bearers of this are prison evangelists of a very high and deserving character, whom I asked to call upon you. If you could get up a meeting at Y. M. C. A. rooms for them, it might do good.

In haste yours,

JOHN ROBSON.

Provincial Secretary's Department,
Victoria, B. C., Oct. 5, 1888.

Dear Mr. McBride:

The ladies whom this will introduce to you are prison evangelists who are desirous of doing some work in the penitentiary, and I take the liberty of bespeaking for them a kind reception at your hands. They enjoy a high reputation and are well deserving of your kind attention.

Very sincerely yours,

A. H. McBride, Esq., Warden Penitentiary.

Victoria, B. C.

Mr. Robson bespeaks for Mrs. Wheaton and lady companion courteous attention at the hands of the warden of the Victoria gaol.

WORK IN MEXICO.

Not many years after engaging in special prison work I went into Mexico and have since gone there quite frequently. As a rule the people are ignorant and superstitious and consequently hard to reach with the gospel. But though I was compelled to speak through an interpreter it is surprising how soon they know if one is sincere and earnest. In the prisons they are very poorly cared for, often having to wait years for trial and sometimes dying of neglect. I am told that natives of our own land if thrown into prison there fare worse than others.

A BULL FIGHT.

Once while in Mexico I found there was to be a bull fight not far from the prison where I was to hold service. My heart was sad because of the intense anxiety of the Mexicans to see the exhibition. They came long distances and there were many very old people who seemed impatient for the hour to arrive when Mexicans, bulls and horses should be thrown helplessly together—that they might view the combat. This cruel sport—so long a favorite pastime both in Spain and Mexico—was at one time abolished but was afterward re-established out of policy—in order to please the Mexicans. For me to describe this kind of fiendish pastime would not glorify God, nor help the public, but would have a tendency to brutality, being neither elevating nor refining. But should we not, dear reader, try to do all in our power to lead people to a higher plane of morals and send missionaries to help people to know Jesus who satisfies every longing of the human soul, and gives peace and rest here, and a home in Heaven through eternity?

SIX UNDER DEATH SENTENCE.

At another time I visited a prison in Mexico where there were six men under death sentence. They could not understand me, but I knelt by those great, strong men and wept and prayed to God who could carry the message of love through my tears to their hard hearts and they were so affected that we all wept together. I am sure they were remembered that day by the God who sent me to show them *His* love for the lost and who gave me a love for the poor criminals that nothing can destroy.

DIFFICULTIES.

During my last trip into Mexico, 1902, I found the prisoners in one place in a most deplorable condition. They were almost starving and neglected in every way. I had considerable trouble in getting into the prison on that day, as I could find no one to interpret for me. So we went from one office to another trying to find some one to admit us to the prison. As I entered one public office a fierce dog came rushing at me from an adjoining room. I fled out of the door in dismay with the dog and an old Mexican woman at my heels. I tried to make her understand what we wanted and then hurried away. Finally we found a fellow decorated beyond description with tinsel and other adornings who furnished me an interpreter and admitted us to the prison. It was very difficult to make the poor prisoners understand how deeply I felt for them, but I could put my arms around the poor women who were there and I could take their little babes in my arms and thus show my sympathy, then telling the story of Jesus who said, "Father, forgive them, for they know not what they do."

MINISTERED TO A SUFFERER.

I found one poor wounded man who had just been brought into the prison sitting on the ground with bloody clothing and matted hair. He was weeping and tried so hard to explain something to me. The interpreter was evidently slow to tell me what the poor sufferer wanted. I was heart-sick to know what to do, as we had only a short time to stay and I could not bear to leave him without in some way ministering to him. But I thought of the fruit remaining in my handbag. I thrust an orange into his bony hands. He grabbed it and with both hands thrust it to his mouth eating peel and all. Poor man—he was evidently starving. Reader I wish I could make clear to you the pitiful sight! The sequel showed me why that was providentially left in my handbag. How thankful I was to minister to that poor fellow's need in even a small degree. How I longed to help them all.

CHAPTER XX.

Across the Sea.

I had greatly desired to preach the gospel in other lands and held myself ever ready to go at a moment's warning, anywhere the Lord should lead, and had been given letters of introduction to prominent people in Great Britain. In the year 1890 my mind was much exercised about the regions beyond—and without time for preparation, with but an hour's notice, the call came to go forward. I was in Philadelphia walking along the street praying—"O Lord, where next—what wilt Thou have me to do?" Looking up I saw the large posters of steamship lines and the thought came to me, "Go and inquire the price of a ticket to Europe." I obeyed the impulse and went in and talked with the steamship agent of rates and the time of departure of the first steamer. Then I left the office praying, O God, show me Thy will—make Thy way very plain to me. Then I went back to the office, feeling that I must get alone with the Lord. I asked the agent if I might go into a rear office which was unoccupied, to pray. He very courteously replied, "Certainly, madam." There I knelt before the Lord and inquired if He wanted me to go at once—that very night—on the first steamer, to Scotland. The answer came clearly: "Go, my child, nothing doubting." I arose, went into the front office and explained to the agent the nature of my mission work; and how for years I had obeyed the leadings of the Holy Spirit and that I had a sister traveling with me who was waiting at the depot for my return, to know where we would go next. Told him I would buy two steerage tickets for Glasgow, Scotland, if he would refund the money for the one in case the sister was unwilling to go with me. To this he consented, so I purchased the tickets and hurried to the railway station where I had left my friend. I knew we had only a few moments to catch the train for New York in order to reach the steamer Devonia for Glasgow. Hurriedly I said to her, "Do you want to go to Europe?" "Oh, yes," she replied. "When?" I asked. "Oh, some time," was the answer. Then I said, "I have two tickets. It is now or never. If you wish to go I will take you, if not, I will go alone and you can return the ticket and get the money for yourself." She said, "I will go." So we rushed to the gate, caught the train on the move, and reached New York in time to get aboard the Devonia.

ON THE OCEAN.

Leaving America's shores far behind us, we found ourselves doomed to a stormy voyage, but with plenty of missionary work to do. There was, in the steerage, much profanity, continual drunkenness of both men and women, and card playing at all times only when the passengers were sleeping or too sea-sick. While in mid-ocean we encountered a severe storm which greatly delayed us. There were only six Christians on board the steamer. I believe it was in answer to prayer that the ship was saved from wreck. After thirteen days on the ocean, we saw the shores of "Bonnie Scotland," and as we neared port there was great rejoicing among the passengers—almost all of whom were going home. But how different it was with me! I felt much as Paul did when he said to the elders of the church at Ephesus, "And now, behold, I go bound in the spirit unto Jerusalem, not knowing the things that shall befall me there: save that the Holy Ghost witnesseth in every city, saying that bonds and afflictions abide me." Like him I felt that suffering and persecution and perhaps imprisonment and death was before me in that strange land, but Paul was enabled to say, "But none of these things move me, neither count I my life dear unto myself, so that I might finish my course with joy, and the ministry which I have received of the Lord Jesus, to testify the gospel of the grace of God;" and with something of the same spirit I was enabled to say, as I wept before Him, "Lord, I will be true—only give me Thy grace sufficient for me."

IN A FOREIGN LAND.

I was a stranger in a strange land with only a few shillings and without any great degree of strength of body and, strange to say, for one reason and another I never saw one of those to whom I carried letters of introduction. How the Lord was teaching me not to lean on the arm of flesh! In answer to a letter of inquiry written to one to whom one letter was addressed, I received the following very kind reply from her husband:

11 Walker St.,
Edinburgh, Oct. 18, 1890.

Dear Friend:

Your letter of the 16th, with one from Miss Sisson, has just reached me, forwarded from Crieff. Since Miss Sisson's letter was written my dear wife has fallen asleep in Jesus and having left Crieff I am in lodgings for the present in Edinburgh with my sister and five children.

I have been praying over the subject of your letter, but I do not have any light on the matter nor am I likely, so far as I can see, to be in Glasgow for some time. Yet if the Lord sent you to Scotland He will certainly show you what He has for you to do. "Trust in the Lord with all thine heart and lean not to thine own understanding: in all thy ways acknowledge Him and He shall direct thy paths."

I enclose a one-pound note towards expenses.

Yours in Christ,

G. W. OLDHAM.

At the landing in Glasgow, I inquired of the policeman on duty and secured a room with his family. Then I went in search of a meeting. Found the carfare a penny a mile and other customs quite different from ours. The first meeting I found corresponded to our Y. M. C. A. meetings. But our special mission was to the lost.

That evening I received permission from the policeman to hold open-air meetings. Going along the street a woman who was drunk spied me and rushed after me beating me on the back. As I made no resistance other drunken women joined their companion in sin and I would have had a hard time of it had not the police protected me. These drunken women thought that I belonged to the Salvation Army, as the bonnet I then wore was quite similar to the one dear Mother Booth had worn and I was often told that I looked like her. I was in Scotland when she passed to her reward in the land where there are no slums, no sinners to rescue, to weep over and save. Had I been near enough how gladly would I have joined the great throng that gathered to show honor to her memory! Nearly every night while in Glasgow found us on the streets preaching, singing, and praying, with those who never went to church—many of them not even to the Salvation Army or missions. In many respects we found worse conditions than in our home-land. The public houses were always filled at night with men and often their whole families—drinking all kinds of intoxicants—women with infants in their arms as well as others drinking with men at the bar. And the most beautiful girls to be found were secured by the keepers of these houses to stand behind the bar and sell the drinks.

The prisons, my special burden, I found very difficult of access for missionary work. I found that women were not expected, there, to do that kind of work. Yet I fasted and prayed and wept before the Lord, pleading that the prison doors might be opened to me and at last I was successful in gaining admission to some of them. After some delay I was admitted to Duke Street jail, in Glasgow, and there held several services. It is a large prison, filled with the baser sort and those whom the public houses had been licensed to make drunkards—to cause to reel and stagger and abuse and kill when unconscious of what they were doing. The Lord's presence was revealed in our services there and souls got help from God, and I hope to meet many of them in heaven. We visited the poor in their homes, different penal institutions—all of the missions and Salvation Army Corps and many of the churches. While time lasts we will find much to do to help those around us.

MY LIFE IN DANGER.

Oftentimes my life was in danger when visiting the saloons, which are there called public houses—the keepers being called publicans. Often the keepers of brothels and other places of sin drew revolvers on me—threatening me with death if I did not leave, as they did not want to lose their customers and their money—which they were sure to do if souls were converted there, but the Lord always delivered me when death stared me in the face. One day I went into a public house where a woman kept a dive. She at once got very angry, demanded my business, and ordered me to leave her place. She clutched me with a fiendish grip, and pushed me out of the door, but purposely fastened one of my arms in the door as she slammed it shut. I prayed God to release me and with the help of the sister who was with me we got the door open enough to release my arm. I am sorry to have reason to say that, as a rule, I find the women who are in charge of brothels and saloons harder to deal with than the men. A woman of judgment and tact when fully saved can, in many cases, do more good than men from the fact that she can go where very few men could go without being looked upon with suspicion. What need, then, that we should be emptied of self and filled with the Holy Spirit, all given up to the Lord in order that we can work successfully for God and souls.

One Saturday night, while in Glasgow, I preached in a church. Great crowds had turned out in the city spending their week's wages. There was much drinking of both men and women. At the church was given a "Penny Tea," consisting of a cup of tea and a biscuit, thus drawing the crowds—and afterwards having some one preach to them.

A SONG STOPS A ROW.

When the services had closed, we were returning to our lodging and were attracted by a great crowd of people engaged in a row and a fight. I soon saw there was danger of bloodshed and stepping out in the street I began to sing an old time hymn. This drew the attention of many and they came running to hear. Then I talked to them of Jesus and His love, and we went on our way and held another service on another street. Then, coming to the quarters of a company of firemen, I asked if I might hold a service with them some time. One of them replied, "Yes, why not now?" It was then 10 o'clock and raining. I stepped into the street and began singing. Across the way there was a dance hall with dancing going on upon the three floors of the hall. As I sang, the windows of the hall were lowered with a crash, perhaps to keep out the rain—perhaps to keep out the sound of my voice.

As we proceeded with the service a policeman soon appeared and ordered me to stop. I told him I was not violating any ordinance of the city and only holding the service at the request of these firemen. He was angry and threatened to arrest us. He soon returned with two other officers, and while the sister who was with me was speaking, he took her by the arm and led her down the muddy street. I began singing, "He is able to deliver thee." The other two policemen took me by the arms and forced me through the deep mud in the street quite a long distance to the jail. Before being placed in the cell I was asked the cause of our arrest. I replied, "For holding open-air service on the street, and there is no law in Scotland to forbid us from doing so." We were placed in a room under guard to await the decision. We could hear the shrieks of men and women delirious from drink.

I was asked who we were, and replied, "We have come from America to preach the gospel." After cross-questioning and severely reprimanding me they asked if I would hold my peace if they would let me go. I answered, "I do not wish to disregard your request, but I must obey God, for that is why I am here. And according to your law it is no crime to hold open-air services; and it is a custom with the churches." "Then we will put you into the cell." Another said, "No, we cannot do that for this offense." Then he said I should be gone. I said, "Will you not send an officer to show us the way to our lodging, as you have arrested us without a cause and it is late at night?" But they refused to send a guide. I asked if they would give me the name of the policeman who arrested us, and told them the matter was not yet ended; that they did not know with whom they were dealing. At first they refused to give me the names asked for; but I said I should stay till they did so, and I prevailed. When we had started to try to find our way to our lodging place, we met a lady who kindly directed us to the street and number.

On Monday a sister who had been preaching among the policemen for some years, called to see me—having heard of my arrest and treatment. She was much surprised and said she could have those policemen all discharged for their conduct toward me. I said, "No, do not do that; I only want to see them and talk to them about their souls' salvation." "Then," she replied, "I will have them come and ask your forgiveness." As she started away, I handed her some recommendations and railroad passes I had had in America and letters of introduction to parties in that land. Glancing over them she exclaimed, "Is it possible? A lady with such a recommend! These letters are addressed to some of the best people in Great Britain. Will you trust me with these till I return?" "Certainly," I replied. She returned in due time, saying the policemen would come and make an apology. I was very glad, for I felt then that I could tell them it was the love of Christ for the lost ones of earth that constrained me to speak on the streets. Many ladies called during the day to give me their sympathy and show their interest. The policeman who caused the arrest came and asked me to forgive him. He bowed with us in prayer, and sobs shook his heavy frame while his tears fell like rain. He said, "It is like mother used to talk, and it is the same kind of religion she had in olden times." I believe that man found Christ his Savior that day. He told us of his wife sick at home and two "wee bairns," and as he could get no girl at home, he had overworked; and on that Saturday night had taken too much liquor in order to keep him awake.

He invited me to call upon his family. This I did the following day, and found it as he had said. The two other men that had a part in arresting us came the following day. One of them seemed very penitent when I talked to them, and both humbly begged my pardon for their conduct toward me.

While in Glasgow I was invited by General Evans, of the Gospel Army, to conduct special services for ten nights at their hall—commonly known as the Globe Theater. We copy the following from an editorial of the General's published in his paper while we were there:

> "Hearing of these evangelists we decided to invite them to Globe Theater, and truly we can say God has visited his people. They do not believe in forms and ceremonies like us formal Scotch Christians, but speak as they are moved by the Holy Ghost. They live by faith and do not ask for money or collections; however, they seem to get on very well, and I never yet heard them grumbling about having too little. They take whatever is given them as from the Lord, and give Him their sincere thanks accordingly. They have spent over a week speaking and singing every night in our meetings, and not a few have been impressed by the earnest words of our sisters. Some of the professors have had their short-comings pretty well threshed out, the writer coming in for his share. Our meetings have been well attended and I believe a really good work has been begun in our midst. The elder lady carries about with her a book full of newspaper clippings and numerous testimonials about her work in America. Her special field is in the prisons and among the unfortunates. She takes no stock in sensational worship, but there is always a great sensation wherever she puts in an appearance.... In closing I may say that our heaven-bound sisters have had some severe trials since leaving their native shores. Eternity alone will reveal the amount they have endured for the Master's sake. Before they had been many hours in Glasgow they were marched off to jail for preaching at a

street corner, and gathering a crowd. I trust this epistle will open up our cold, hard hearts and that we may receive our sisters as is our duty as a Christian community."

TUMULT IN A DIVE.

"Fear none of those things which thou shalt suffer: behold the devil shall cast some of you into prison that ye may be tried; * * * Be thou faithful unto death and I will give thee a crown of life."—Rev. 2:10.

One Sunday night, as I was on my way going from the meeting, being in company with General Evans and his wife and the sister who traveled with me, I saw a public house open and went in and began to speak to the men and women. I had only talked a few minutes when the proprietor came in and asked, "Are you a customer here?" I replied, "No, I am only speaking to these people about their souls." He said, "Now you leave, or I'll make you." He ran into a back room, and coming out he passed me quickly, running to the door and blowing a long blast on a police whistle. This aroused the people and brought to the scene several policemen and hundreds of people of all classes in general fright. A man rushed in and catching me by the arm cried, "Come out of this place, quick, or you'll be killed. You are in danger. You don't know where you are! This is the Gallow Gate; the worst place in Glasgow." I said to him, "Let me alone, I am obeying God." But as the policemen closed in around me there was a cry raised, "It is Jack the Ripper in disguise." The excitement in those days was intense all over Europe. Jack the Ripper was a fiend in human form that was killing women continually in the most horrifying manner and in cold blood. You might see on a bulletin board in the city that a murder would be committed on such a day and hour and these threats would be carried out. Yet he defied the detectives and police. Large rewards were offered for his capture. I saw that my life was in danger unless I could convince them of their mistake, of which I now saw the cause. I was dressed differently from them. I had on a long black cloak and had thrown my black shawl over my head concealing my bonnet, and carried a bag on my arm which contained my recommendations, railway passes, etc. I said: "You are mistaken, gentlemen, I am not Jack the Ripper" (removing my shawl), "I am a missionary from America; and preaching at the Globe Theater every night. Come and hear me there. There is no cause for this tumult." The General and his wife having come in, we passed out, the mob following us several blocks with shouts and screams giving me some blows as we went. But God delivered us from their cruel hands.

A MOB OF DRUNKEN WOMEN.

Another night when returning from the Globe Theater in company with General and Mrs. Evans we heard a great noise up the street and soon discovered that it was made by a mob of some kind. On their coming nearer, we found it was an immense crowd of drunken fallen girls. The General said: "Hide yourselves quick! There is no telling what they might do." The policemen had slunk away—not caring to try to make any arrests, as there were so many of them and they were so violent. Poor souls! They were some mothers' girls who perhaps had learned to love the taste of strong drink before they saw the light and were bound by both inherited and acquired appetite. I was told that on an average there were four drunken women in Glasgow for every drunken man. Such a statement seems beyond belief, but during our stay we saw much to indicate that it was true. What could the harvest be?

While in Scotland I received a very precious letter of encouragement and sympathy from Col. Geo. R. Clarke and wife of Pacific Garden Mission, Chicago. I give it here and the reader can easily realize how comforting it proved to me.

Chicago, October 29, 1890.

My Dear Sister Wheaton:

We received yours written from Glasgow last night. I am sorry they treat you so badly there. But that is the way nice appearing people treated our blessed Lord when on earth, and the way they would treat Him now should He come to earth in the flesh. But it is blessed to us, said Jesus, when men persecute us. We have a right then to rejoice as He told us.

The Lord will stand by you as He did by Paul. He "will never leave you nor forsake you." So you can boldly say: "The Lord is my helper and I will not fear what man shall do unto me."

The Lord's work is prospering at our Mission and we are much encouraged in it. We have large meetings and many precious souls for Christ every night.

We have started a noonday prayer-meeting for both sexes. The Lord is greatly blessing the meetings. We have souls converted there right along at every meeting.

We will pray for you and may the dear Lord greatly bless you in your work and labor of love which you do in His name.

We have only a little time left now to wait for Him. The signs are thickening and He will soon rush into view and then we shall hear Him say, "Well done, good and faithful servant, enter thou in to the joy of thy Lord." Praise His dear name. Glory to God! Hallelujah!!! What a meeting that will be! It will be our time to laugh then, but our persecutors will weep and wail. May God be merciful to them now and give them repentance before that awful day.

Don't be in a hurry to die and go to heaven. You are more needed by the Lord down here just now than in heaven. There are no sinners there to whom to preach His gospel and He tells us to "Go and preach" not "go to heaven." He will take us all home in His own good time. Let us patiently wait for Him and "occupy until He comes." With much Christian love we are yours in Christ.

COL. AND MRS. GEO. R. CLARKE.

IN PAISLEY.

I was summoned by telegram to go on to Paisley, Scotland, to hold services for the Gospel Army in that place. We went immediately. Found the city well informed of our coming by large striking posters which read: "Hear the American Prison Evangelists—Be sure to hear these ladies who have preached on the ruins of the Johnstown horror! Who have visited all the prisons of note in America—led murderers to the scaffold," etc. I was not accustomed to such sensational advertising and tore down the posters I came across and chided with the General for advertising us in such a way. He kindly explained that it was customary in their work in order to arrest the attention of the people and arouse interest in our meetings. Perhaps he was right but it was something of a trial to me to be brought before the people in that way.

We found much to do in Paisley, not only in the night services but on the streets, in the homes of refuge and in homes. Found twelve hundred girls employed in the Coats Thread Works and eight hundred girls in Clark's Thread Works. Found great poverty among the laboring classes, as there was much dissipation among both men and women.

Just before leaving Paisley I was called to go and hold services in the Refuge for Fallen Women. During the services there did not seem to be much feeling concerning their soul's salvation. It seemed I could not reach them. At last, near the close of the meeting, I said: "Girls, I am going away to my own land. I will never see you on earth again. Will you not try and live so you will meet me in heaven? If so, raise your hands." Not one hand was raised. Then I said, "Girls, won't you pray?" No sign yet. "Girls, shall I pray for you when far away? If so, raise your hands?" Not a hand went up.

I was almost discouraged. Could I leave that great crowd of lost women to go on in their awful career without at least one manifesting a desire for a better life? How could I meet them at the Judgment? At last I said: "Girls, I leave to-morrow for America. I am all alone. Only this young woman with me. How many of you will pray for *us* as we cross the ocean again to go to our own land? If any one will pray for us, won't you raise your hand?" *Every hand went up*, and God's Holy Spirit crept unawares into their hearts—so long unused to prayer, and the spell of evil was broken, and God reached them. O the melting, tender spirit which filled the room! And that company, I believe, gave God their hearts. In learning to pray for us, their sisters, they found God, and I trust to meet many, if not all, of those dear souls in heaven. Jesus said, "Neither do I condemn thee; go and sin no more." And then the confessions, the tears, the promises! Bless God, His word will not return void.

Shortly after my arrival in America I received the following letter, which explains itself, from the matron of this Home:

Female Refuge, Paisley, Scotland, March 23, 1891.

Mrs. Wheaton.

Dear Friend: Glad I was to know that you had in God's good Providence arrived safe at home among your dear ones, and rejoice also with you that the work is prospering in your hand.

I have been called upon to part here with dear ones since I saw you, but they are gone before me only a little while. My assistants are all with me yet, and with myself had much pleasure in your card. We often talk of you and your young friend that accompanied you. I do hope she is still with you. We have now a household of thirty inmates, many giving proof of a new life being theirs for time and eternity. With our united kind regards, I am

Yours truly in the Lord's work,

ANNIE J. BLUE.

I have already mentioned the fact that I found it difficult to gain admittance to the prisons of Scotland. I waited in Edinburgh for days, on expense, seeking opportunity to hold at least one service in the large prison there. While waiting I held services in the jail and missions and open air. Our meetings in the open air were largely attended, not only by the working classes, but also by others who would stop and listen, being attracted, at first, by the singing which usually drew large crowds. We were much blessed in these services and especially in the slums where large numbers of neglected children gathered around us, ragged and dirty, but with hearts glad to learn to sing with us.

RETURN TO AMERICA.

Various circumstances combined that seemed to require my return to America and after nearly two months of constant toil in Glasgow, Edinburgh, and Paisley, we hurried to Liverpool and November 15 took shipping for New York on the steamship Wisconsin. On this return voyage we encountered another fearful storm in which many ships went down.

The storm raged about four days. Men and women were in great fear; some weeping, some screaming, some praying, and some cursing. Among all that multitude there were only four Christians; only four souls ready to face eternity!

But our God is a very present help in time of trouble. There in that terrible hour, I was conscious of His presence and I knew that He was able to deliver us. When the storm had abated, with a heart full of gratitude and thanksgiving, I tried to sing, but could only utter softly the words of one old-time hymn:

"How firm a foundation ye saints of the Lord."

So wonderfully did God deliver us that in spite of that fearful storm we reached New York harbor after being only twelve days at sea.

On board these steamers a religious service is held every Lord's day, but it is usually led by the captain who is often an ungodly man. Many seemed to ease their guilty consciences by observing this form of religion. But my heart was often left more hungry and sad by a service which seemed to me mere form if not a farce and mockery.

During this return trip I supposed I was about out of money, and was somewhat tempted to doubt the promises, and I prayed much for guidance. When almost ready to land I took from my purse my small stock to have the steward get it changed for U. S. money, and to my glad surprise I found in another part of the purse a pound note. I could not tell how it came to be there. So I felt reproved for my lack of faith.

Among my old papers I find a touching letter written by a dear young sister to whom I became much attached while in Scotland. Had it not been that her family were largely dependent upon her she would have gone with me in my work. I give the following extract:

Glasgow, Nov. 17, 1890.

My Dear Sister in Jesus:

I received your card Saturday night; and was very much surprised to learn that you had gone so suddenly. But not our will but God's will be done. Dear sister, I hope you and Nellie will have a safe passage across the ocean and may the dear Savior be very present to both of you. You have His blessed promise, "Fear them not; for I am with thee."

Mrs. P—— and the husband were asking very kindly after you. Mr. L—— could scarcely credit that you had gone home so suddenly. Several others also in the hall wish you a special blessing in your effort to win souls for the Master, who will reward you in His own time.

Dear sister, you do not know and you will never know until you are within the Pearly Gates, how many precious souls have been brought to the knowledge of the truth through you.

May the dear Lord make us truly Holy Ghost workers and may we have a desire to point sinners to Jesus—the all-sufficient one—the author and finisher of our salvation. Glory to God! May we be more and more like Jesus, humble, meek and mild, loving one another as the Lord has also loved us. May we be clean, empty vessels for the Master's use. Dear Jesus, do strip us of everything that would hinder the blessing and would keep our joy from being full. Write soon; and if we do not meet again on earth, with God's help we will meet in heaven, Praise God!

Your loving sister in Jesus,
RACHEL SMITH.

SECOND VISIT TO EUROPE.

In the year 1896 the Lord made plain to me that it was His will that I should again go to Europe. While in Washington, D. C., I was led to return to Iowa, and there found that a band of missionaries who were ready to start for Africa had been praying that I might come and go with them as far as New York. When they saw me alight at their door, they shouted and praised the Lord. When I asked them the reason they said because God had answered prayer—that they had prayed God to send me to see them off for Africa.

While we were holding a few meetings in Philadelphia I felt directed to go on with them as far as London, so purchased my ticket with theirs, taking steerage passage across the ocean for the third time. Immediately after getting my ticket there came upon me a wonderful outpouring of the Spirit and an assurance that was unmistakable that I was in divine order. When I told those young missionaries I was going with them as far as London they told me they had been praying that I might be led to do that very thing. After a safe voyage we reached Southampton in seven days.

One Sabbath afternoon in London when we were holding an open-air meeting on the street, God opened the flood-gates of Heaven, and I with others sang and preached under the power of the Holy Spirit. A Christian came and said, "Sister Wheaton, there is a preacher here who wants to speak to you." I refused to go, as there were drunkards and toughs on their knees under conviction of sin. I thought he was a preacher who wanted to criticise my methods. They called me again, and I went to see what was wanted. I found a fine-looking, well-dressed man much past middle age under awful conviction of sin. He was a backslider, and had stopped in passing, being attracted by a hymn I was singing—one his mother used to sing. Yet he was unwilling to yield himself to God. Some of those in the company had talked with him and begged him to kneel. At last his stubborn will was broken, and he knelt there on that London street and confessed his sins to God. When he arose from his knees he said he had been on his way with a dagger then in his coat sleeve, to commit suicide, but was attracted by that song his mother used to sing, and could go no further. Thus by the power of the Holy Ghost that Presiding Elder was saved on the streets through faithful, honest trust in God, where the preacher and the drunkard knelt side by side in the dust. I hope to meet them in Heaven, and trust that all found peace with God. The word says, "Go out in the streets and lanes of the city, and in the hedges and highways." "Jesus came to seek and to save that which was lost," not the righteous but sinners. He came to save. How often people are waiting for Christians, who profess to have salvation, to speak to them, and how glad they are to receive the message if delivered in love.

I was located for a time at Woolwich, near the London Arsenal. There were stationed thousands of soldiers and they were often found in the public houses under the influence of drink. I would plead with them to quit sinning, turn to God, and seek salvation. Often tears were shed, and resolves made to serve the Lord. There are many incidents of souls being saved on the streets, in the slums and public houses, but space forbids my going into details, but suffice it to say that I have been given many proofs of God's love and mercy from among the thousands who have heard the gospel in those far-off lands, as well as in our home land. Then let us encourage our missionaries everywhere to press on until the Master says, "It is enough, come up higher."

I was much pained, while in England, to see so many young women there, as in Scotland, selling beer and other strong drink to customers in the public houses; beautiful girls selling their souls to the tempter to be lost forever unless in some way rescued before it is too late.

During this second visit to Europe I was often stopped on the street and asked to sing to the people, which I frequently did, regardless of remarks or criticisms, and the Lord blessed my singing to the good of many souls. While in London, night after night I would sing and preach the gospel to people who longed for salvation, but knew not how to get saved. How often we neglect an opportunity to do good. Years after some of our missionaries returning from Africa, passing through London, heard the people calling to them, "Where is that old lady who sang for us?" So we labor not in vain. In due season we shall reap if we faint not.

After spending several weeks in England (most of the time in London) I saw that precious band of young missionaries take the steamer for Africa. The next day I embarked for home at Southampton. Soon after starting we sighted the vessel on which they sailed and I could distinguish some of them waving their handkerchiefs in farewell. One of them died in Africa ten months later. By and by we shall meet again in the Kingdom of heaven, each one, I trust, bringing with us sheaves to lay at Jesus' feet.

During the return voyage the sea was stormy at times, yet the voyage was made safely, and on Sabbath morning, the day after my arrival in New York, I went to the Tombs prison to hold services. I was very tired, and after the services I was so faint I prayed for the Lord to open the way for me to have some refreshments, as I was to preach in the afternoon at a Rescue Mission. There were many elegantly dressed lady visitors at that meeting, but they all passed out and left me alone, when a young, humble-looking man came to me and said, "We are very poor, and are able to afford but one meal a day, and not a full meal at that, but it would be such a blessing to my wife and myself if you would come and share it with us." My heart was touched that this stranger should offer to share the little they had, when others never thought of my needs. I did not go with him, although I thanked him; it was so far to his home, but God will reward him. For Jesus said, "I was a stranger and ye took me in, hungry and ye fed me; I was in prison and ye came unto me, sick and ye visited me."

Behold a homeless wanderer, poor and thinly clad, To biting cold a victim, with hunger almost mad, Entering yonder mansion, dares to boldly steal What none should e'er deny a dog—the pittance of a meal! See the greedy sleuth-hounds of the outraged law Wage against this robber an unrelenting war; While *Christian* judge and jury, with ready wit, declare His crime an awful outrage, that merits prison fare! But he who rears his costly domes

O'er wreck and ruin of human homes, Plants in the breast a raging thirst And leaves his victims doubly cursed, Can roll in luxury, loll in pride And, with *the law*, his gain divide! Tho' every dime he pays the state A thousand cost in wakened hate!

—*Geo. W. H. Harrison.*

Learn that in many a loathsome cell A prisoned genius or a saint may dwell, Whose power, developed by an act of love, May lead a million to the Courts above. Shall it be yours to touch that vibrant chord And share the honor of the great reward? What heaven endorses that alone can stand; All else is stubble, built on shifting sand.

—*G. W. H. H.*

STATE PRISON, JOLIET, ILL.

CHAPTER XXI.

Travel and Toil.

TWO NIGHTS'S SERVICE.

At one time when suffering from nervous prostration I was lovingly cared for for some weeks in the home of dear brother H. L. Hastings, of Boston. One night while there I said to him: "I must go to the city tonight." He replied: "Sister Wheaton, have you prayed about it?" I said, "Yes." He answered, "Go and pray again." I did so and returned to his office, saying, "I must go to the city tonight." They were having watchnight service in the city. Again he replied: "The night is very cold and you are sick. Go and pray and find out the mind of God." Again I went to my room to inquire diligently of the Lord and was sure that the call of the Spirit was that I should go. Again I returned to his office and told him I must go to the city that night. Once more he replied: "Sister Wheaton, go and pray." As I wept before the Lord He showed me the city given up to idolatry and sin and again I went to Brother Hastings' office and said: "I must go to the city." He dropped his pen and hurriedly said: "Wife and I will go with you." It was one of the coldest nights Boston had known for years, but from one saloon to another the Lord led us and from one watchnight meeting to another until near midnight we entered a Mission hall. A fine-looking, well-dressed young man from the platform hurried down and said to me: "Mother, I am so glad to see you. Come on the platform and speak to the people." I looked at the man and he said: "Don't you know me, mother?" When I said "No," he answered: "Don't you know your boy?" I looked at him—so beautiful in the service of God—and then he said: "I was in prison and you came and prayed and sang for me. I was in the hospital, and got saved there, and God is still blessing your boy." Reader, did it pay? Yes, that night my heart rejoiced in my Savior for all He had done for me and for my "children" in prison walls. For seventeen years now this man has been a blessing in helping to save others.

Another watchnight I spent in St. Louis, Missouri. Feeling weary, I was about to retire for the night, when the Lord showed me to go on the street and do service for Him. So, doubting not, I pressed out for a cold night's work in the slums. The sister who entertained me went with me to the places of sin and also to six different watch-meetings, at which we witnessed for the Master, leaving the results with the Lord, who said: "And the books were opened, and another book was opened, which is the book of life; and the dead were judged out of those things which were written in the books, according to their works."

ONE WEEK'S WORK.

A few years since, on arriving in Omaha after returning from the East, I telephoned the jailer at the county jail: "Can I have a meeting?" "Yes," came the reply. There were a good many prisoners and we had a good service. Sister Kelley, of Tabor, Iowa, was with me. Our singing seemed much appreciated. Went from there to the city jail. Held services there, and in the evening in a Rescue Mission.

At midnight we boarded the train for Deer Lodge, Montana. En route our train stopped for a couple of hours at Ogden, Utah, and while there we visited the Florence Crittenton Rescue Home—where we were warmly welcomed by both the matron and the girls and had a blessed service. God bless them all!

PRISON AT DEER LODGE, MONT.

We arrived at the State prison at Deer Lodge on Saturday, and had the privilege of preaching to the many prisoners the following day. God blessed me in speaking, both to the men and women. We sang many old-time hymns and some new ones. Took each prisoner by the hand as they passed out, visited the sick prisoners and went to two churches that night, and visited the women prisoners on Monday morning, and had real victory in prayer for them. Then bidding goodbye to all we left for the prison at Boise City, Idaho, where we arrived Tuesday. Telephoned the warden asking permission to hold service at the prison. The privilege was granted and a team was sent for us. We found a large number of prisoners and the officials kind, and had a good service of an hour. Visited the poor, condemned men in their cells, prayed and wept with them, and commended them to the great loving God who said: "Though your sins be as scarlet, they shall be white as snow; though they be red like crimson, they shall be as wool." After seeing the sick we left the prison; but my heart was greatly drawn out for those men under death sentence. I felt that one of them (a foreigner) was innocent. I was almost overcome with sorrow. They were my "children" and I never would see them again in this world, and yet I was powerless to help them!

From Boise City we went to Salt Lake City. When we arrived at the penitentiary there and mentioned our desire to hold a service the warden's kind wife said: "The warden is in the city and they are under contract and must get their work done immediately—but you lie down and rest—you are worn out" (and I was). So I slept until I heard her tender voice, saying, "Mrs. Wheaton, lunch is ready and the warden says he will give you forty minutes after dinner in the chapel with the men." I was so glad and said: "This is all through your kindness and God will reward you." I found the men seated, waiting for me, in the chapel and thankfully I improved that opportunity, knowing that eternity would reveal the results of that service. I was permitted to see the two men under death sentence and sing and pray with them, and tell them of a Savior "mighty to save and strong to deliver;" then with sad heart I left them—never to meet them again till the trumpet should sound. Precious in God's sight were those poor, forsaken, criminals! And, reader, as I write these lines down in the slums of Chicago, I see opposite me the saloon open day and night luring men and women inside, fitting them also for the prison and perhaps for the scaffold!

Leaving the prison at Salt Lake, we hurried to the county jail, held services in two departments, and had a good time with the prisoners; then left for the city jail. Did what work we could there in the Lord's name and hurried to the depot, only stopping on the way to get a little lunch for the long journey before us. Weary and faint we reached the train just as it was leaving. Too weak to go further I got in the first car, which proved to be a dining car. I said: "The boys will allow me to sit here awhile," and I heard a voice saying: "Come in, mother, sit down. You are welcome in my car and you must have something to eat. You look tired and hungry"—and wasn't I? And when I told him of my friend in another car he had me bring her also and gave us both a good supper, and was I not thankful to God for that kind welcome from the dining car conductor, who knew me? Surely God will reward him. I hope to meet and know him in that land where we shall never get weary and hungry.

We arrived at Rawlins, Wyoming, at nine the next morning. We hurried to the prison. It was Decoration Day and most of the guards were off for a holiday—the men being locked in their cells. The warden kindly said to us: "I wish I could let you talk to the men, but my officers are gone and there is no one to guard them, and I am compelled to remain at the office to see after business." I was sure God had sent us, and said: "Will you permit us to see the men in their cells?" After much deliberation he said: "I'll tell you what I will do, I'll turn the men loose in the dining room if you think you can control them, and let you have an hour to talk to them." I said, "Surely I can manage those men—why, they are my children, sir," and so down the men came from their cells and O such a meeting! I was at home and my "boys" were on their honor and I talked to them as a mother and we sang together hymns that they knew, and bless God He was guarding the men, and I had nothing to do with the matter only to obey Him and tell them the old, old story of the redeeming love of a Savior who died to save us from our sins and give to us eternal life. As I grasped each one by the hand at parting, I found the men quiet and peaceable, humbly begging me to come again. Then I saw the heavy iron doors close between us and knew I would probably never see them together again as we were there, but looked forward to the great day in which, if he would, each man could have a part in crowning Jesus Lord of lords and King of kings.

After having dinner with the few officers present in their own dining room we hurried to the jail. There we were permitted to preach the gospel to the prisoners and they received us gladly. As I left the jailer expressed his appreciation of the visit, saying it was so good of us to come to help the prisoners—especially the girls.

Arriving at Lincoln, Nebraska, we attended the evening service of the National Campmeeting then in progress there and the next morning went to the prison. The warden kindly granted us the privilege of a gospel service with the prisoners. After holding this service and visiting the sick in the hospital we returned to the camp ground. Reached there during a testimony service just in time to be invited by the leader to sing a certain hymn. Instantly I was on my feet and soon on the platform saying, "Yes, I will sing, but first I must sing,

"The toils of the road will seem nothing When we get to the end of the way."

And shouts of praise went up to God all over that ground, for He especially anointed me to sing that hymn. I felt every word of it, for though weary and tired from the journey, I knew God had been with me and had given victory all along the way.

In this brief sketch I have failed to mention some services held in missions and also special services on all the trains on which we traveled—perhaps bringing to some their last warning.

One night during this week's journey a crowd of drunken men boarded the train. They were so abusive to me that I went outside the car door. When I went in the next car I found the same kind dining car conductor I have before mentioned. At his inquiry as to what was the matter I just knelt and prayed and then told him how the drunken men had acted. He said: "Come with me. This won't do. I will see that you and your sister have a sleeper." He went with me into the other car, and when the men saw the man in uniform with me they tried to be very polite. They were under the influence of drink and in a sense not responsible for their actions. Who is responsible? The saloon, the brewery, the devil who uses these things to make men and women oftentimes more like fiends than creatures made in the image and likeness of God, and all who fail to use their influence against the liquor traffic are responsible.

From Lincoln we went to Omaha where we parted feeling that the days had been spent for God and souls—the dear sister to return to her work in the missionary training home at Tabor, Iowa, I to hurry on to Chicago, taking with me one of the sisters I met for the first time in the slum mission work in Omaha a week previous.

So we turned over that week's work to the Lord of the harvest, who will see that the seed scattered along life's pathway shall bring forth fruit unto eternal life.

A PROFITABLE TRIP.

Walking along the street in Chicago on my way to the Cook County Jail to see the "car-barn bandits" and one or two others under death sentence, I was impressed that I must go to some State Prison for Easter, only two days off. I stopped and prayed, inquiring of the Lord where he would have me go.

I had been east and just arrived in the city, weary and worn, but I knew the voice of God was saying, "Go!" but where and by what route I knew not. I stood still until the Lord made it plain to go westward—to what place I need not know, but to go to the railroad office and get transportation. When I entered the office the kind official said, "What can I do for you, Mother?" At first I answered, "I hardly know what to ask for, as it is not yet plain to me just where to go;" but a little later I said to him, "I must go to Canon City, Colorado." "All right," he said, and gave me transportation. It was then too late, under ordinary circumstances, to visit the jail, but I felt that I must see those condemned boys before their execution, and I prayed that God would open my way and incline the heart of the jailer, Mr. Whitman, to grant me the desired opportunity. To my surprise I found Mr. Whitman on the street car. I told him that I must leave the city at once for western prisons and asked if he would kindly give me permission to see the condemned men who were in his charge, before I left, as I could not return before the day set for execution. He was very kind and answered, "Yes, I will send an officer with you to see the boys."

That hour will never be forgotten. Instead of tough, rough looking men I found "mother's boys" in the prime of their young manhood. Kindly, tenderly I talked to them, thinking to myself, what if it were my boy, now safe in Heaven? O sisters, it seemed to me my heart would break as I placed my hands on their heads, so soon to be cold in death and commended them to the God who sent His only begotten Son, who, when on the cross, said, "Father, forgive them, for they know not what they do!" I left the prison, praying that my message might not be in vain.

Upon leaving Chicago over the Santa Fe railroad on my way west, I prayed earnestly for direction as to what prison I should visit on Easter Sunday and was impressed to stop at Joliet. The warden, Mr. Murphy, and his estimable wife were kind and hospitable, as they always are, and the chaplain was willing that I should have a part in the services on the Sabbath. God was present in power in all the services. Many of the prisoners partook of the communion with their teachers and chaplain.

The Lord alone can reward the warden's wife for her special kindness to me at this time, for I was taken sick from overwork and detained over Monday. I then left at midnight for Topeka, Kansas, where the Lord sent me to the railroad shops to hold services at the noon hour while the men were resting after lunch. Our meeting with them was signally owned and blessed of God. At its close I shook hands with each of those hundreds of men and then went to the jail where the Lord again graciously met with us.

Reaching Pueblo on our way to Canon City we telephoned the jailer—also the matron of the Rescue Home—and obtained permission to hold services at each on our return.

At Canon City the warden and his wife gave us a most kind and courteous welcome and he granted the privilege of holding services for the prisoners in the chapel, also at the hospital and cell houses. I visited their night school. It was very interesting to see so many teaching other prisoners. The most important part of my work at Canon City, however, was seeing three young men who were under death sentence. While I prayed day after day for them, they came to see their true condition before God and, I believe, gave evidence of true repentance. I hope to meet them all in Heaven.

But oh, what a sad sight to see those young men in the prime of life, sentenced to die; and all on account of strong drink.

How pitifully they talked of home and mother and innocent childhood days! Their hearts were melted and broken. Poor boys! far away from home and friends, with few to care and many to cry out, "They deserve to die"—never seeing the cause, the rum traffic. Why not stop that which sends our young men by the thousands to a drunkard's or a criminal's grave? When I bade these young men farewell they were cheerful and confident that the Lord had forgiven them.

Arriving at Pueblo on the return trip, we went to the Rescue Home where we received a kind welcome; also held services in the prison there. I forgot to mention services held in jail and almshouse while in Canon City.

At Denver we found friends who received us kindly. We held services in their mission church. Also held service in the large jail in which I conducted the first meeting ever held after it was built.

Leaving Denver we went to Lincoln, Neb., to hold services in the State Prison on the Sabbath. Found there my friends, Warden Beemer and wife, who have always been so kind to me. Our meetings were crowned with success and victory. Also did personal work, which is important.

While I was there, two new prisoners were brought in.

Left Monday for Omaha and went at once to the County Jail and held meetings in the three different wards. God blessed His own word to the good of souls! There, as elsewhere, I met some who knew me. From Omaha I went to Chicago, where I spent some time in missions, etc.

SIX WEEKS' SERVICE.

About July 1, 1904, I spent some time in St. Louis, visiting the slums, dives and saloons, faithfully warning the multitudes I found in sin. Left there for Jefferson City, where I held services in the State Prison. We give here the following extract written by the sister who accompanied me on this trip:

MY TRIP TO JEFFERSON CITY.

I was glad to have the opportunity of visiting the prison in Jefferson City with Mother Wheaton, who is one of our oldest and most successful prison workers.

We were off early Saturday morning, July 2, and arrived there at 2:30 o'clock. We had dinner, then went to the prison. The guard first took us to see the women. They were all seated at machines, sewing very rapidly, and I was told I was not allowed to speak to them. My heart ached and I could not keep back the tears as I looked on the precious girls I had labored with in the jail at St. Louis, some seven or eight of them. At 6 o'clock we had a short meeting with a hundred and fifty shop girls. Many of them were moved to tears, and we believe good was accomplished. Sunday morning we had a good meeting in the jail, then at 2:30 went back to the prison and gave the gospel to twenty-two hundred convicts. It was a blessed time. I never saw such attention, and while Mother Wheaton spoke and we sang "He Pardoned a Rebel Like Me," I saw some of them wiping the tears from their eyes. These men are not all hard-hearted. As I looked at them and heard almost all of them join in with us and sing "We'll Never Say Good-Bye in Heaven," somehow I lost sight of the stripes and prison walls and bars, and thought how precious they are in God's sight, and I believe many will be gathered to praise Him, who was pierced for us all. After the meeting a young man asked permission to speak to us; his face shone with the glory of God as he told how he had been there five years, and had been saved two years and a half and called to preach the gospel. He proved his earnestness when Mother Wheaton asked if he would let her try to get him pardoned, and he answered: "No, I am guilty, and I not only feel it my duty to serve my time, but will make restitution as soon as I am out. Then I shall give myself to the Lord's work."

Returning to St. Louis I next went to Denver, Colo., to see Governor Peabody in behalf of the three young men who were awaiting execution. The governor was very kind and willing to do what was right. In Denver I had services in the jail, also spoke at two meetings and preached at night at a mission church. Next visited the State Reformatory for Young Men at Buena Vista, Colo. Most of the officers and all the boys attended the services. Leaving here in the evening arrived at Salt Lake City next day about noon. I hurried to the State Prison and was surprised to find a new warden, as the former warden had died. It being a working day had only a short service with the prisoners, but it was blessed of the Lord. Then visited the county and city jails, holding three services. Leaving here, traveling all night, arrived the next evening at Canon City, Colo. Hurrying to the State Prison we were kindly received and permitted to hold services in the cell houses till 9 o'clock. The warden informed me that one of the boys under death sentence had gone insane just the day before and could not be seen. One of the other boys under sentence of death said the last thing that this one had done was to write me a letter, of which I here insert an extract:

CANON CITY, COLO., July 12, 1904.

Dear Mother Wheaton:—

It is with pleasure that I answer your welcome letter, which was appreciated. We are waiting patiently to know the verdict. If it is God's will that I must be taken out of this world, I will go, but it is very hard, as I have done nothing worthy of death, but they look at it different, I suppose. Whatever got me into such a scrape I cannot tell. I have always worked hard for my living.

Dear Mother, I have done as you requested. I commenced to read the New Testament on the 28th of June and completed it on the 10th of July. I never forget to read the Holy Bible and to pray.

You wished to know if we boys had any work to do. It is beyond the warden's power to let us work under the circumstances, though he is very kind to us; also the other officials. We are allowed all the reading matter we can use and have exercise each day.

Dear Mother Wheaton, I hope that we will meet again on earth. If not, I pray we may in heaven. And may our Heavenly Father protect you in the work of His cause. I ever remain your son in Jesus.

C——. P——.

Leaving Canon City we hurry on, visiting next the State Prison at Lincoln, Neb. There we found another poor man under death sentence, who gladly listened while I taught him the way of life. Oh, the joy that filled my soul as I told him of the Savior who would pardon all his sins. After seeing the other prisoners who are always glad to see true friends, we hastened on to Omaha, Neb. Here I held four services in jails and Rescue Homes. When leaving Omaha as I was singing on the train I found some ladies crying; one of them, grasping my hand, said, "When you sang 'My Name in Mother's Prayer,' I thought how often my mother, who is in the baggage coach, has prayed for me, and I will never hear her pray again." I soon changed cars and bade farewell to the sorrowing friends, hoping to meet them with that mother where there is no death nor tears.

CRIMINAL INSANE HOSPITAL, CHESTER, ILL.

Resting for a short time at Tabor, Iowa, I then went to St. Louis and on to Chester, Ill., to hold services in the State Prison. We were here four days and held services in the State Prison, jail, and Criminal Insane Hospital, where there are more than one hundred inmates.

Once while holding services here one young man was saved and his mind restored. He has now been preaching the Gospel for several years. "Is there anything too hard for the Lord?"

We next visited Gatesville, Texas, where is located the Reform School for Boys. Obtained permission to see the boys and it fortunately being a holiday I was allowed to hold services in both the white and colored wards. The way the boys seemed to enjoy the meetings and to hear them sing was encouraging. Leaving for Huntsville, Tex., we went to different towns, holding services in jails and on the streets till Saturday, when we arrived at Rusk, Texas, and were met by the chaplain, Mr. Dawson, who treated us kindly and gave me the privilege of holding meetings on the Sabbath. Had a very impressive service in the afternoon in the prison yard where we gathered round a coffin to pay the last tribute of love to a departed prisoner, after which we held a meeting in the prison hospital.

We next visited the State Prison at Huntsville, Texas, where we were kindly given the entire time in chapel service, and also the privilege of holding services in the different wards of the hospital. Here all seemed encouraged and were much effected, the tears flowing freely upon many of the pale faces.

I received upon this visit the following kind tribute from the Assistant Superintendent and Prison Physician:

> I was present at the services conducted by Mother Wheaton at the Huntsville Penitentiary, on August 7, 1904, and noticed with much satisfaction that her remarks and singing were very much appreciated by the men, and

many of them seemed very much affected, and I think that the service will be conducive to much good hereafter.

T. H. BROWN,
Assistant Superintendent, in charge Huntsville
Penitentiary.

PRISON AT HUNTSVILLE, TEXAS.

Mother Wheaton visited the Huntsville Prison Hospital this morning and I think her words of cheer and advice given to the sick will be the means of doing great good.

W. E. FOWLER,
Prison Physician.

At the Woman's Prison, also located at Huntsville, we found over one hundred women prisoners all working on the farm except the few white women. We held meetings with these women in the afternoon and evening for three days, which were blessed of the Lord. While I wept with them I thought of the Scripture, "Weep with those that weep." Jesus loved me and saved me and has put a real love in my heart for those souls.

The kind chaplain took us with his invalid wife on Sabbath afternoon to visit the consumptives' prison a few miles from Huntsville. Here the prisoners sick with consumption are located on a farm. Had a blessed meeting with them. The weather being so warm my health would not permit me to visit the several stockades in this state, where are mines, sugar refineries or farms.

Returning to St. Louis, Mo., worn and weary, we were kindly entertained at the Berachah Home for Girls. Again we visited the slums, missions, and dives. The sin during these fairs and expositions is awful in the extreme. I have no time or desire to go to see the sights, but am after souls.

Next we went to Leavenworth, Kan.; was kindly given the hour for service Sabbath morning, at the State Prison at Lansing, also a service with the women prisoners. Also visited the Soldiers' Home, and by the kindness of the superintendent was permitted to speak to the aged soldiers.

We then found a welcome in the home of Sister Two-good, who accompanied us to the Old Ladies' Rest, where I held services in their lovely new home. In the evening till after 10 o'clock we were speaking to crowds on the streets who seldom attend church.

Returning then to Tabor, Iowa, weary with this six weeks' constant service, I was for some weeks unable to travel. One night when as I thought, near death, I cried mightily to God and he heard my cry, touched my body and healed me. After a few weeks' rest, yet scarcely able to travel, I started again on my mission seeking the lost.

RECENT WORK.

During these weeks of waiting the responsibility of finishing this book then in preparation, and getting it to its readers bore heavily upon me. Knowing that I could not attend to this and continue my work, I was in answer to prayer assured that I should be relieved of the burden of managing the publication, sale, and distribution of the book. After much prayer about the matter I was relieved of this burden in a very satisfactory manner, Bro. C. M. Kelley taking the management of the same for the Lord.

While yet weak in body, receiving indication from the Lord that I should be about His work, I went on my way, taking with me a young sister from the Training Home, who expects to devote her life's service as a missionary in Japan, the Holy Spirit assuring her also that she should accompany me on this trip. I leave it for her to write the account of the following few weeks' work.

I was blessed with an opportunity to travel a few weeks with "Mother Wheaton" in her work in prisons, etc. Leaving the Home at Tabor, Ia., September 28, 1904, we first visited the jail at Council Bluffs, where Mother Wheaton held a Gospel service. A number of the prisoners asked for prayer. We next went to Chicago, where on the Lord's day we visited the county jail, where were about 540 men and a few women. After their chapel service we were given access to the corridors where we could talk to all. We also took part in several services at the Beulah Rescue Homes, some missions, etc.

On October 15, we were at Ft. Madison, Iowa, and visited the several wards in the State Prison and sang and prayed with the sick. On Sabbath Mother Wheaton conducted services in the chapel, also at the county jail and the Santa Fe Railroad Hospital.

We next attended the National Prison Congress in session at Quincy, Ill. We here had opportunities to witness for God. Monday evening, by invitation, Mother Wheaton spoke at the Soldiers' Home, where God poured out His Spirit and melted the hearts of some who were steeped in sin. The following morning we visited the hospital and prayed and sang with the sick who seemed very glad to hear the good old-time hymns. We then went to the jail where one woman accused of murder was especially touched and broken up, seeing there was someone who loved and cared for her. It is the love of Jesus that brings sinners to repentance. The day following, October 18, we held service at the Chaddick Boys' School which is under Deaconess' management. Here Mother Wheaton spoke to ninety young boys.

Provision was made for those in attendance at the Prison Congress to take an excursion down the river, but instead of going with this company we went to the House of Correction, where the superintendent seemed glad to have Mother Wheaton speak to the prisoners, both men and women, even calling in the men from their work.

GROUP OF DELEGATES AT THE NATIONAL PRISON CONGRESS, QUINCY, ILL., OCTOBER, 1904.
Mrs. Wheaton in upper right hand corner.

October 19 we returned to Chicago. The next morning we took the train for Marquette, Mich., on the shore of Lake Superior, where is located a State Prison. Upon our arrival there we went to the chaplain, who kindly gave permission to conduct the next Sabbath morning services. We then visited the poor house, where we sang and prayed with those who were lonely and sad, and knew nothing about Jesus. On Saturday it was stormy, but Mother Wheaton held a service at the county jail, which God blessed. The Lord's day, October 23, was a day long to be remembered by many of the prisoners, who that day received a ray of hope. The Spirit of God so anointed Mother Wheaton to speak that the prisoners seemed to be held spellbound, with hearts open to receive every word and song. In the afternoon we were given the privilege of talking and singing in the corridors and speaking to the prisoners in their cells. It was told us that these were the worst men in the state, twenty-four of whom were serving life sentences. But God touched their hearts, many being moved to tears. We left some of them with new hopes, calling upon God for help and asking us to pray for them. Mother Wheaton said they were all her own dear boys.

Journeying eastward we held services in Indianapolis, Ind., also in the State Prison at Columbus, Ohio, and in the Woman's Prison at Allegheny, Pennsylvania. Sabbath morning, November 5, Mother Wheaton spoke in the corridors of the State Prison in Philadelphia, and in the afternoon at the House of Correction. Here the Lord wonderfully spoke to the hearts of many young girls. Many men were moved upon by the Spirit. The officers looked on with amazement to see how attentive they all seemed to be.

At Trenton, N. J., at the county jail God moved upon hearts and many asked for prayer.

At the State Prison at Trenton, N. J., we received a warm welcome and Mother Wheaton was given opportunity to preach on the following Lord's day in the chapel. We visited the woman's department and held a service with them, all stopping their work and giving attention. God melted the hearts of those women who have gone away from Him. Jesus' blood is able to cleanse from every stain.

After a few busy days of service in New York city we returned to Trenton, for the service in the prison on the Sabbath. We then returned westward by way of Baltimore and Washington, D. C. We next held a service in the prison at Canton, Ohio, and then went to Mansfield to the State Reformatory, where were nearly a thousand young men. Here God wonderfully answered prayer. The superintendent and chaplain were very kind, supplying us with such things as we had need of. We arrived in Chicago November 20. Leaving there we went by way of Marion and Anamosa, Iowa, where we held services. We arrived at Tabor on Thanksgiving day, November 24, which was truly a thanksgiving day with us, for the wonderful way in which God had answered prayer and brought us safely through so many dangers and given us such glorious victories in His blessed service.

ROSA MINTLE.

INDUSTRIAL REFORM SCHOOL, HUTCHINSON, KAN.

Leaving Tabor December 15, taking with me Sister Taylor, who for several years has accompanied me at intervals in my work, silently praying for me while I preach, sing or pray, I started for San Francisco, California, via Santa Fe, New Mexico. We stopped at Hutchison, Kansas, where is located the State Industrial Reform School for Young Men. We net the wife of the superintendent of that institution, who kindly took us to the school. I had held service here with prisoners who were working on the buildings when they were being erected.

The officers arranged for a service in the chapel though it was a week day and just before Christmas. The meeting was owned and blessed of the Lord. Also at Santa Fe we were kindly entertained by the wife of the superintendent of the prison, and the officers gave us a service in the chapel and the prisoners, both men and women, privilege to attend. About half the prisoners being Mexicans I had to speak to them by the aid of an interpreter. This service was also signally owned of the Lord. We also held special service with the women.

We then left for the coast and had several services en route with the passengers and railroad men; also with a hundred soldiers who were going to their winter quarters. I had warned the soldiers about drinking. It seemed so sad to see them drinking and gambling. Poor boys, there seems to be no way of restraining them from strong drink so long as they can get it. Some trouble arose between them and other parties and one of the soldiers was badly cut in the throat. In a town in California I held services in a number of saloons and dance halls. It was Christmas day and I never saw more drinking among the people and I never want to witness such again. Why will people indulge in strong drink, when God has said no drunkard shall inherit the kingdom of heaven?

We arrived in San Francisco and found many open doors to preach the Gospel. I visited the State Prison at San Quentin. The chaplain was very kind, giving me privileges of the chapel services and a special service with the women. This prison was first opened to me in 1898 in direct answer to prayer. I also held services in the city prisons.

We also visited the Federal Prison on Alcatraz Island, where we held three services with the manifest blessing of God upon our souls. The kindness of the officers and the appreciation shown by the prisoners there will not be forgotten. I am sure God will reward those who are kind to His children, and who assist His workers in any way.

During the first four months of 1905 we found much to do for the Lord in Los Angeles, San Pedro and other places in California, one of these of special importance was the Reformatory at Whittier.

INDUSTRIAL SCHOOL, WHITTIER, CAL.

Early in May, having received a letter from one of the boys in Colorado under sentence of death, I hastened to that state to see the new governor in their behalf. I was kindly received and heard by the governor, but as the Board of Pardons was to soon meet he declined to make any promises. Tarrying several days for the board to meet, I met with them and made a plea for the lives of the boys who had, under the influence of drink, accidentally, as they claimed, taken life.

They received a reprieve for four weeks, but the two who were adjudged sane were executed June 16. I give elsewhere an extract from a letter received from the mother of one of these boys shortly afterward. Also an extract from a paper concerning the mother of the other.

After returning to Iowa and remaining but a few days, accompanied by a young sister from the Home, I returned to Colorado, visiting, en route, the jail at Council Bluffs, Iowa, and the State Prison at Lincoln, Nebraska, where we held service on the Lord's day. We then proceeded to Canon City to visit the condemned boys, and held services in the corridors of the prison till late at night. We next went to Buena Vista, where we held service in the State Reform School for Boys, and in the jail. On our return east we stopped at a camp meeting at Newton, Kansas, where the Lord blessed in the jail and in the work on the street. Going next to Chicago we held service in the county jail with about four hundred men. We next visited the prison at Joliet, Illinois, but only had service in the prison hospital and proceeded to Sioux Falls, South Dakota, for services on the Lord's day; then returned to Tabor, stopping in Omaha and holding a service in the county jail.

Taking with me the young sister whom I have elsewhere mentioned as having first known as an orphan girl, now starting for India, I spent a day at Plattsmouth, Nebraska, where we talked and sang in a tent meeting, on the street, and in the jail. The time set for the missionary band to sail being near, we hurried westward, stopping at but a few places till we reached Sacramento, where we had work to do for souls in the prison and other places. We next visited the prison at Salem, Oregon, and also made a short stay at Portland. Upon reaching Tacoma we learned that the time of sailing had been put off a week, so we improved the time seeking out the lost in mission work, etc.

The company of nine missionaries, including one child, boarded the steamship "Minnesota," and by the kindness of the general superintendent of the company we were permitted to spend a night before sailing on board the vessel with them, which was a time very much enjoyed in the Lord. The parting was not one of sadness, but of sweet peace and calmness. As we looked into the faces of the dear ones as they were being borne away we rejoiced that God has a few whom He can trust to carry the precious Gospel to the heathen. As the vessel bearing its precious burden sailed from our view, the little company of anxious watchers kneeled down and committed the dear ones to Him who has said that His children are as dear to Him as the apple of His eye. We were afterward delighted to hear that they had a most delightful voyage, reaching Yokohama, Japan, in eighteen days, just in time to escape a very disastrous storm on the sea.

As a sister had accompanied some of the missionaries to the coast and was to return with me, assisting me in the work, we turned our attention to the needs of the lost ones about us. I will let this sister here give a brief sketch of our return trip, on which we trust much good was done for souls:

RETURN FROM PACIFIC COAST.

Mother Wheaton's companion to the coast, Sister Yarrett, having sailed for India, it was my privilege to accompany her from Seattle to Iowa. From the wharf, when we had committed the company of dear missionaries to the Lord, we went to the rooms of the Y. W. C. A. and held religious service while the young ladies had lunch. About two hundred young women lunch in these rooms daily. At night Mother Wheaton spoke at the Life Boat Mission with the anointing of the Holy Spirit, and many hearts seemed touched.

Early the next morning we left Seattle on board the S. S. Whatcom, en route to Victoria, British Columbia. This was a most enjoyable trip to me. At Victoria we had a very profitable service in the W. C. T. U. Rescue Home, and the Lord especially blessed the visit and service. Later we spent five days very profitably in Portland laboring in the Exposition Camp Meeting, visiting the jails, saloons and slums, preaching and singing the Gospel.

We next went to Boise, Idaho, where we held services in the Soldiers' Home and in the State Prison. Service with the women prisoners and prayer with the men under death sentence were special features of our visit to this place. We next spent a day in Rawlins, Wyoming, visiting the state and county prisons, holding short but profitable services in each. In the county jail here a raving maniac was quieted by Mother Wheaton's singing.

Another night and day's travel across the plains and beautiful country and we were in Omaha, Nebraska. Here we spent several days, being entertained in the Tinley Rescue Home. This indeed is a refuge for the fallen. Our time here was well occupied in the jails, missions and churches. Then we hurried on to Tabor. I to resume duties in the school room, and Mother Wheaton, after a few days' rest, to continue her pilgrimage seeking the wandering and the lost ones of earth till she shall be called from toil to her reward which shall surely be one worth gaining.

EMMA H. HERR.

ANOTHER TRIP.

After attending Prison Congress at Lincoln, Neb., Oct. 21 to 26, I left for western prisons and other institutions. Held services at Old Soldiers' Home, Grand Island, Nebraska, the 27th, then went to Rawlings,

Wyoming; held services on Sunday at the prison chapel with all the prisoners, then at the county jail. Had great liberty in both prisons. Left at night for Salt Lake City, Utah. Found open doors. Held services at state prison jail on Monday afternoon; also in the county jail, two services. Left that night for Ogden; held services in the county jail and at Crittendon Rescue Home. Left for Deer Lodge, Montana, where I was kindly received by the warden, Frank Conley, who has ever proved one of the best of friends to me in my work in prison— always arranging for services Sunday or week day and entertaining myself and any one I brought with me, and never letting me go away without something to help defray expenses along the way. Sunday afternoon at Butte City held two services at the county jail; took train at night for Walla Walla, Washington and arrived there at 3:30 a. m., and went to Chaplain Lacornu's home. After resting, prayer and breakfast, we went to the state prison, where I held services with the twelve women prisoners; then in the dining room, held services with the men— about eight hundred prisoners. The Lord was present in both services to own and bless and many were helped to a better life and higher aims. Left there for county jail where we had profitable service with men and women.

Left that night for Portland, Oregon. Was kindly entertained by one who has been preaching the gospel for nearly twenty years, who was convicted in prison while I was preaching in the prison in Bismark, N. D., one night after nine o'clock. He was converted and has done great good in the work, both in prison and outside ever since. Much of his success is due to his faithful Christian wife, who has ever been his true friend and helpmeet.

Called on Mrs. Smith, a prison missionary, who for years has done mission work in Salem and Walla Walla prisons. Then left for Salem, Oregon, where I held services with the prisoners in the jail on the Sabbath day, also with the women prisoners on Saturday afternoon. Was kindly received by the Superintendent of the prison and his family, also by the Bible school in charge of Brother and Sister Ryan, where I held services on Sunday night in the chapel with students and citizens. Left Monday morning for the South. Stopped in Sacramento, and went to the Rescue Home and held services for the girls while I waited for the train to Carson City, Nevada. Changed cars at Reno and waiting for neither rest or food hurried on to Carson City to see the Governor and the Attorney General about prison work. Found four men under sentence of death. I pleaded with the Governor for a commutation of sentence. Governor Sparks asked me if I could meet with the Board of Pardons and himself at 2 p. m., and gave me a letter to the warden to allow me to see the condemned men and hold services with them—also with all of the prisoners. The Governor also arranged for me to go to the prison with one of the officers. Found the poor men heart broken over their condition, and really sorry for their sin. They had all been drinking, and among the four of them they had killed a young man, and all were doomed to die.

When I entered their prison with the death-watch I was overcome with sorrow for the poor unfortunates who so soon would be in eternity, and as I came in the door one of the prisoners said, "O, it is Mother Wheaton." As I clasped his hand he said, "Mother, I knew you twenty years ago." I said, "Where?" and he said, "In San Francisco." Reader, you may try to sympathize or criticize at such a time, with them and me, but you never will know what the suffering is until you have passed through this ordeal of just standing alone with the good Lord and the condemned, so soon to die that horrible death. You cannot picture it, for death is awful to those not prepared to die—filled with remorse of conscience and sorrow for the deed done while under the influence of whiskey and possessed with the devil, which the strong drink causes—and then to have no hope in this world or the world to come, and alone with their conscience, the death-watch, myself and our God.

I knelt in prayer. First to ask wisdom of the blessed Christ who never turned anyone away, and then, taking each one by the hand through the iron bars, I was lost to this world and its opinions and criticisms. I entered into their heart-sorrow, and at once took hold on God for the salvation of their immortal souls. Quietly, but with strong faith in God and the atoning blood of Jesus our Saviour, I believed for their salvation. Human sympathy will not avail. It is the suffering and death of Christ which avails in the face of death. And I believe, if Jacob prevailed in prayer as a prince, it is our privilege to believe God hears and answers prayer and saves to the uttermost the vilest sinner who truly repents of his sins, and claims His promises. "Though your sins be as scarlet, they shall be as white as snow; though they be red like crimson, they shall be as wool." Isa. 1:18.

We wept and prayed together, and while I sang the good old hymns our mothers knew and loved and sung for us in childhood, we took hold on God by faith for their souls' salvation, and I believe God heard and answered our prayers, that fifteenth day of November, 1905, in that prison, and that those men that day were forgiven their sins. I know God's Word is sure, and I depend daily on the Bible and its holy teachings, and accept His promise, and receive the answer from God that His pardon is sure.

I told the men I had no hope for their lives to be spared—that the Governor had not given me any encouragement for them, but had invited me to meet with him and the Board of Pardons at 2 p. m., and see what they would do in the case. I pleaded with them to let go all hope of a life sentence, and prepare to die, for there was only one more day for them to live—that I had nothing to give them of hope, only in the precious blood of Jesus—that their days were numbered.

O, the human heart is susceptible to suffering, and my suffering was intense for them. I was weak and weary, having traveled two days and two nights without rest. Yet I could not rest when there was so much at stake for them. I abandoned myself to the Holy Ghost to guide me in the service, and then as I took each hand, so soon to be cold in death, I knew only God could save them. I shall not forget the parting with those poor, unfortunate men, all in the prime of life and strength of manhood. I will meet them again soon in the presence of God.

I was so weak in body that the officer kindly assisted me to the main prison, where I was to hold services with all of the prisoners. It was high noon, and the warden and officers urged me to take refreshments. I said, "No, I am soon going to the judgment, and I want to go with a clear conscience. How could I eat, when all these prisoners need the gospel so much?" And they kindly gave me the privilege of an hour's service. Then, after a hurried lunch, which was both breakfast and dinner, the state carriage was ready to take me to the Capitol to meet the Governor and Board of Pardons. But there was no hope, the Board refused to commute the sentence, and all four were executed November 17, for the death of one young man. Soon I must stand together at the judgment bar of God, with those whose lives were taken, one by the four under the influence of whiskey, which makes men and women crazy and worse than brutes; licensed by the laws of our land—the others by the men who, in their right minds, as executors of the law, put to death the helpless victims who had truly repented of their sins and promised to obey God and the rules, and live good law-abiding citizens.

I want it understood that I believe in law and its enforcement. I sympathize with both the murdered and the murderers. I believe in obeying God and His laws and enforcing discipline, and I assist the officers of the state to maintain law and order, but I say, give deliverance from the abominable saloon and all the evil that follows in its wake. Give us judges, jurymen and officers, who, in every sense try to banish and abolish the liquor traffic and the dens of sin, and there will be no need of our state officers having to take life which none can give.

Leaving the Capitol after the decision was made by the Board of Pardons and Governor, I went to the hotel to tell the two sisters of one of the condemned men that all hope of their brother's life was gone, and that they must prepare to face the awful sorrow of losing their brother. That scene was O, so pitiful! The brother and these two sisters were orphans. He was a good boy and supported the two sisters after the parents had died, but he had fallen into bad company who had led him astray. The sisters were heart broken. It seemed as if they could not give up that dear brother who had done so much for them. I helped them on the train, and went with them as far as Reno, Nevada, and we parted to meet again after all the sorrow and mistakes of our lives are forgotten and forgiven.

After leaving them I held services for the Salvation Army friends and on the street. Then left that night, though very weary, for the east. After taking the train, I could see in my mind those poor condemned men, waiting the few last hours until the law should have its way. Eternity alone will reveal all hearts and lives.

Arrived at Ogden, I went to the Crittendon Home, then on to the State Industrial School for Boys and Young Men, and had a service in all the cottages. Was with them two evenings. They all seemed cheered by the old good songs and the services. Saying "Good-bye" to all in their dining room at their daylight breakfast hour, I left them for the east.

I stopped at Columbus, Nebraska, a day, and at Omaha, where many railroad friends and others met and greeted me kindly. Then hurried on to Joliet, Illinois, State Prison, where dear Mrs. Murphy, wife of the warden, gave me a warm welcome to her lovely home in the state prison. Went with the chaplain to visit the hospital and spoke with the men at the Sabbath School hour, and then to the women's prison, where I was given the privilege of addressing all the female prisoners. Many were much affected, and shed tears as I spoke or sang to them "My Name in Mother's Prayer," "Is There Anyone Can Help Us" and "Old Time Religion." Shook hands with most of the women, prayed and sang for a sick girl in the prison hospital, and left for the jail. Spoke there, then on to Chicago. After some days in the city, busy for the Lord, I made a trip to Washington, D. C., and returned before the close of the year, and proceeded to the Pacific coast early in the new year.

O, how I praise the Lord for His grace and love, and the strength and endurance He gives me to keep going to carry His messages of love and good cheer to the lost ones in low and in high pursuits of life.

Dear Reader: We must here close the account of our travel and toil in the Master's vineyard, and we feel that it will all soon be over, and the victory be won. When I shall have finished my course I want to be able to say, like Paul of old, that "I have fought a good fight." I want, too, to know that the crown is laid up for me as one of those who have been faithful and that love the appearing of my Savior.

Though but sixty-one years of age, the excessive toil, the wearisome journeys, the heart-rending scenes and experiences for more than one-third of my life, have told upon my once strong body until I am now a physical wreck. Only in the strength of Jehovah and leaning upon His everlasting arm am I able to pursue the calling He has given me. "But the toils of the road will seem nothing when we get to the end of the way." You and I shall meet again, on that great Judgment morning, and must give an account to God. "Grace be with all them that love our Lord Jesus Christ in sincerity."

PRISONS AT JACKSON, MICH., DEER LODGE, MONT., AND FOLSOM, CAL.

CHAPTER XXII.

Letters from Prisoners.

The extracts from letters found in this chapter are gathered from my correspondence with those within prison walls who have been encouraged by the way and have received help; many of them having borne testimony to a clear conversion and a life of service for the Lord, even within prison walls. These will serve to show their appreciation of any effort made in their behalf. They have been a source of great encouragement to me in my work.

I should like to give more of similar character, and all more in detail, would space permit, but let these suffice as examples of the thousands of letters I have received during these twenty years from my "children." The names and that which might identify the individuals, I have omitted; for many of them are now good citizens and some are engaged in the work of the Lord. I have omitted many references to the instrumentality which God has seen fit to use in carrying His message of love to these souls, giving only what others thought were needed to show the writers' appreciation and gratitude. I have ever dealt with these, when present and by correspondence, as souls whom I must meet at the Judgment. The honor and praise for what good may have been accomplished belongs to Him whom I serve, and who has given me the commission, "Go and preach the Gospel."

Inman, Tenn.

Dear Sister in the Lord:

We write you a few lines praying that God will allow you to call again and preach for us, for we believe that the Spirit of God is with you. We need thy aid here. So, our dear sister in the Lord, we do wish to hear you once more, so will come much good in the name of the living God!

THE PRISONERS.

Boise City Penitentiary, July 29, 1890.

Elizabeth Wheaton, Portland, Oregon.

Dear Madam: I am instructed to thank you in behalf of all of us for your kind visit. We fully appreciate your labor, your courage, and integrity; your singleness of heart and purpose, your purity of motives; but above all do we appreciate your sincerity. Your indefatigable efforts, even in your old age, to reach the criminal, to lead him upward and onward to his true destiny under so many disadvantages, without money and without price, without the support of state or church, and, I may add, without the support of public sentiment which appears to be against you and us—all this, I say, inspires us with faith and confidence in you. And when I am paying you this tribute, I am at the same time aware that I am paying it to Him who came on earth to seek and save us, for without Him you would not love us as you do.

Come again, say we all.

PRISONERS.

Lancaster, Nebr., Oct. 25, 1903.

Mrs. E. R. Wheaton,

Dear Mother: We, the undersigned, as a token of our appreciation of your efforts in our behalf, respectfully request that you accept our assurance of appreciation of to-day's services, and especially the song service held in our cell-house, and best wishes for your future success.

Signed by 199 prisoners, each giving his number.

Bushy Mountain State Prison,
Petros, Tenn., May 4, 1896.

Dear Mother Wheaton: We, the undersigned, unfortunate children, assemble together to try to show you how grateful we are for the devout interest you are taking in the welfare of our souls. We hope and trust that the Lord will continue to be with you all along your journey, trusting that if we don't meet again on earth, that we may meet in Heaven.

Pray for us.

We enclose the following sums for each of us:

W. J.   25 cents

W. S.	10 cents
C. R. R.	10 cents

Walla Walla, July 11, 1889.

Mrs. Elizabeth R. Wheaton,

Dear Friend: Your postal received. You have the appreciation and kind thoughts of many here for your kind remembrance of us all in our secluded prison home. Aside from your own particular means and the many other ways adopted by religious people to draw the attention of the indifferent to the subject of their spiritual welfare, the evident disinterested motive which characterizes your extended labors, is of itself sufficient, to highly recommend your kind endeavors to all fair-minded people, and to give you a hearty welcome, from prisoners especially, wherever you may find them.

We would all, therefore, send you a kind word of encouragement and Godspeed in your good work and *labor of love*, believing that your gospel message is fully adapted to meet the spiritual wants of the whole human family under whatever condition found.

PRISONERS OF WALLA WALLA PENITENTIARY,
Per F. S.

Richmond, Va., August 23, 1885.

Dear Madam: I take much pleasure to introduce myself to you, and stating to you how I first found rest for my sinful soul. I am a stranger to you by name, but not by the love of Jesus Christ, and I was highly delighted to hear you speak to us. It lifted up my downhearted feeling and caused me to look around myself, and I do truly hope that those words that you have spoken may be as seed sowed in good ground, and take root and the future may tell. And for myself, when I first came to this place I was a vile sinner and thanks be to the good Lord that I have my soul awakened in Christ Jesus, and if it had not been for this place I think that I would have been a sinner until now, but now all my trust is in the Lord Jesus Christ and Him alone. Although I have many crosses and trials and temptations, my trust is in the Lord, and I truly pray and trust the Lord that after awhile we shall all meet in heaven where there will be no more parting.

I trust you will be successful in this work of the Lord. I desire your prayers.

I am your humble servant,

H. T.

Massachusetts State Prison, October 25, 1885.

Dear Madam: It is with much pleasure that I listened to your address to-day. Please accept my thanks for the interest which you take in the poor unfortunate prisoners. There are many skeptic ones among us because we see so much hypocrisy. May God bless you, and let me inform you that your motherly-like appearance sank deep into the hearts of many.

Our chaplain tries to do all the good he can, but no one knows what a prisoner's life is but a prisoner.

My poor mother used to pray like you. I will not forget your earnest advice. I wish there were more like you, for then there would be a true reform in prisons. These places ruin young men. O it is not understood by those men who govern us even. Some of the officers are not fit to be over young men. Every officer should be a religious man, but we have few in accordance with the text: "Love your neighbor as yourself." Many of them take God's name in vain.

I shall try to think much upon what you said, with God's help. Please pray for an unfortunate one. May God bless you.

J. J.

New York, Nov. 26, 1885.

My Dear Friend: Your postal reached me this morning and I can assure you it gave me pleasure to hear from you and see you had not forgotten Ludlow Street Jail. Today is

Thanksgiving Day, and to us poor unfortunates I can assure you it is a gloomy one, but we must give thanks to our Heavenly Father that we are not in a worse place than this. I for one do pray to Him and thank Him for His kindness and pray to Him to give us strength of mind to resist all temptations.

I cannot remember who you enquire about. I am the small man who introduced you to my wife and sister the first time you called.

We were treated today by our kind warden to a good Thanksgiving dinner and I pray before another Thanksgiving Day that I may have the pleasure of seeing you under more favorable circumstances. May God be with you in your good work is the prayer of,

Sincerely yours,

I. L.,
Ludlow Street Jail, New York City.

Cell No. 35—Tombs,
New York City, Sunday, Nov. 1, 1885.

Dear Sister Wheaton: Forgive me for calling you so as I cannot rightly call you otherwise. Your prayer today came from your very soul. I felt it deeply. It has entered into mine. I feel a new man. You were a Godsend to me. Your words have given new life, they have inspired me to live in the future a real Christian. I feel so light of heart since you were here, that I cannot find words adequate to properly express myself. I pray your good work may be crowned with success. I feel now that I am again a child of God. I shall pray and try to live as Jesus desires. I pray to Him that He will give me all encouragement to lead a Christian life and do His will only. O! how I have learned to love Jesus through your inspiring words of comfort and goodness.

I shall daily pray for your health and prosperity in Jesus. Do likewise for me, and may we meet in Heaven. To this end I shall ever pray and so sign myself,

A brother in Jesus,

J. M. S.

New York, November 10, 1885.

Dear Sister Wheaton: Many thanks for your kind visit today and for the memorandum book and envelopes you brought me.

I herewith reiterate every word and the combined meaning contained in my letter to you of last Sabbath. You were a Godsend to me from heaven. Formerly it was a hard task for me to stop to think as I do now. Now I can pray so easy, and it seems to do me so much good. Such a blessing I have never experienced heretofore. With pleasure I give this evidence of the goodness of our beloved and only Jesus. Him I shall worship daily, aye, at all times and in all places. I think of nothing more grand and noble than to believe in our Redeemer who offers His salvation for our souls. He is my God and no other will I have but Him. I love Him truly. In my prayers I have vowed to devote the rest of my life for His good cause. I sincerely hope that many, through you, may come out of darkness into light. God grant you good health to do His good work here. I will pray for you and ask you to do likewise for me, and others.

I pray to God daily that He may give me renewed strength to keep on in the good path which I have chosen, and may His spirit and love be alike with you and me, is the wish of Your brother in Christ Jesus.

J. M. S., Cell 35, Tombs, New York City.

Charleston, January 4, 1886.

My Dear and Much Esteemed Friend: As I sit here in the prison tonight I ponder upon the kind and good advice you gave me, and my heart of hearts goes out to you in gratitude.

My past life has been a blank, in fact, an utter failure. But since I saw you I have come to God in all simplicity and have asked Him to give me a new spirit and pardon my past sins; and since I have offered up this petition my heart seems lighter. How often have I cried out in my despair, O I am weary of the conflicts and strife of this life! weary with the constant struggle for a higher and better life! And when I see the lives of yourself and others—so Christlike, and hear you say mid darkest shadows: "Not my will, but thine be done," then I think of the rebellion in my heart and so oft find when I feel the path I am treading leaves the sunshine all behind.

As the way looks dark before me and the end I cannot see, Oft I long to drop the burdens and from sorrow be set free, But I know such thoughts are sinful; God knows best the way That will lead from earth's dark shadows to the brighter realms of day.

Words cannot express the comfort I have received since I saw you. I have prayed to God to help me every night and morning since and as I sit and ponder upon the past and think of the wasted hours that have drifted by, it puts me in mind of a song I learned when I was a child. I will only write you a couple of verses to let you see how true they are.

"Oh, the wasted hours of life that have drifted by; Oh, the good we might have done, lost without a sigh; Love that we might have sowed by a single word, Thoughts conceived but never penned, perished all unheard. Take the proverb to thy heart, take and hold it fast— The mill will never grind with the water that is past.

"Oh, love thy God and fellow men, thyself consider last, For come it will when thou must count dark errors of the past, And when the fight of life is o'er, and life recedes from view, And heaven in all its glory shines midst the pure and good and true, Then you will see more clearly the proverb deep and vast— The mill will never grind with water that is past."

May God bless you for what you have done for me. You have saved me from that downward road to ruin. May God bless you and permit you to return to us once more.

W., Charleston State Prison.

Nobesville, Neb., April 17, 1886.

Mrs. E. R. Wheaton,

Kind Lady: I will, according to promise, drop you a few lines. I am some better now than when you were here to see me. How glad I am that I met you last Sunday! I have felt better ever since, and I do believe that the good Father will answer your prayers. Don't fail to pray for me, that, if it is God's will, He will heal me, for God has got the same power that He had when He raised Christ from the tomb. And pray that He will give me the guidance of His loving Holy Spirit to lead me into all truth and at the last take me to Heaven.

There has not a day passed since you were here that I have not thought of you and prayed for you. You did more good here than you know.

My candle is going out.

Direct to JOHN W. C., Nobesville, Nebraska.

Charlestown, Mass., Jan. 10, 1886.

Mrs. E. R. Wheaton,

To My Dear Sister in Christ: "Whosoever believeth in Him shall not perish but have everlasting life." I believe and trust in God. My faith and my belief grow stronger every day of my life. I pray to God to keep me from evil, and to make me worthy of His kingdom, that I may meet you there, for I am a better man for knowing you. God bless you, my dear sister! My heart is full of love for my God, and for my fellowman. I cannot find words to express my feelings or to tell you how happy I am, and how precious Christ is to my soul. It passes my understanding. But I am satisfied, for I know that Christ has come into my heart to dwell. There are no doubts, no fears, everything is well with me. I thank God for it, and I want to see every one around me enjoying this great gift which comes from God. O how it would have rejoiced your soul to have been with us the last evening of the old year. We had a prayer meeting. I am told that there were one hundred and forty men in the chapel. Our warden was the first to testify. Many acknowledged Christ to be precious to their souls.

There are many here that are feeling uncomfortable. They will be at the feet of Jesus yet, crying for mercy. Pray for them. Pray for us all. Only think of it, one hundred and forty prisoners on their knees and their warden kneeling with them! O it was a blessed sight! I never heard Chaplain Barnes pray as he did that night. His whole soul went out to God. How he did plead with God for the salvation of our souls. God bless the chaplain. God bless everyone on the face of the earth, and may every one see as I see, and enjoy what I am enjoying. In His paths there is peace, and that in keeping of His commandments there is great reward.

There is a young man here by the name of Charles B. He has formed good resolutions with beginning of the new year. I tell him that he cannot keep them without he gets divine help. I am praying for him. Please make mention of him in your prayers, and with the help of God we will have him at the feet of Jesus crying for mercy. We had a prayer meeting last week and I am informed that we are to have them often. How good it is of the warden! God bless him. He is always looking for some way to benefit us. I praise the Lord for it.

I leave the prison this year. I hope that I may meet you again on earth. If not permitted, I will live a life that shall make me worthy of the kingdom and meet you there. I thank you for the letter read this day to us by the chaplain.

Your brother in Christ Jesus,

J. L. W.

Jeffersonville, Ind., May 22, 1887.

Mrs. E. R. Wheaton,

My Dear Kind Lady: In answer to your request I address this note to you trusting that this may be the commencement of life in a different sphere to that which I have heretofore moved in, so do not think that I am flattering if I tell you the truth. I have traveled from the Atlantic to the Pacific, from the British Possessions to the Gulf of Mexico. I have moved in all classes of society and have been a close observer. I have made myself acquainted with all kinds of religious sects from the Jewish synagogues to Mormonism, Protestantism in all its various forms, Catholicism, as well as Spiritualism, and I found so much hypocrisy and inconsistency existing that I felt inclined to believe Christianity a fraud, but I could see plainly that there were in every church some few that I could feel were true Christians. I could feel a secret convincing power almost irresistible when in their society, but it always seemed strange to me why more true converts were not made in proportion to the great work done.

It seems to me that the handling of God's cause should only be entrusted to those that are godly—then the fruit will bear witness to the quality and health of the tree. God will prosper His own, but it is not natural that the Lord can or will prosper one who is half God's and half Satan's. That is why I have remained in the world. I am earnest in everything I do. It is my nature, I cannot help it. Therefore, if I ever become a Christian, bold and true and faithful, too, I'll be.

I must refer to that now which I spoke of in the first of this note. All the convicts in this prison have been moved by your godly advice and teaching as this prison has never been moved before, either by man or woman. You won the hearts of the hardest criminals and a noticeable change for the better has taken place. We all pray God to bless and protect you wherever His wisdom may lead you, and even though this prayer comes from convicts, perhaps God will hear us. Some of us have been convicted by man, while God, being just, and our own consciences declare us innocent. Those of us who are innocent and can suffer with patience, what a virtue we possess. Such strength comes only of God.

I must close for want of room. Please answer if you have time. We hope to see you soon again.

Your humble servant,

H. McL., Box 340.

Tracy City, Tenn., Dec. 3, 1887.

Mrs. Elizabeth Wheaton,

Dear Friend: Your visit to this place was a great blessing. A great many of the men often speak of you and say that by the help of God they are going to live better the rest of their days.

I will thank you for every paper or good book you may send to us. The way that we do about papers and books is to place them among our fellow prisoners.

You have our prayers and best wishes and we hope you will come to our prison again, as your work will be remembered here for years to come. May God bless you all the way along.

There have been deaths here since you were here. Neither of those parties belonged to the church. Lots of the men spoke of the great warning you gave before you left, what you said about the last warning some of them would ever get, and sure enough it was true.

Yours in Christ,

W. A. M.

Carson City, Nev., Sept. 23, 1888.

Dear Kind Friend: Through the kindness of the Warden, we received your letter, with the song and accompanying texts, and I take the liberty of answering it and thanking you for your kindness in thus remembering us. I was seriously impressed by your kind words of sympathy and exhortation when you came to the prison and I should have liked to have spoken to you, but feared to trespass too much on your time. I am here under a life sentence for the crime of murder, committed during a fit of delirium resulting from drink. I have been here three years. Hitherto my life has been anything but a happy one. I was driven from home at the age of ten years, after the death of my mother. Since then I have associated with gamblers and men of that stamp, and the result of my ill-directed course is my present unhappy condition. What I have suffered, no one but myself will ever know. I would gladly end my life, if my death could blot out the crimes for which I suffer. I have one friend, who has taken an interest in me, and who has written me several kind letters and I thank God for letting me have one kind and faithful friend. She is weak in body, but strong in mind, and a faithful servant of God. She has advised me to give myself to God, and since you were here I have resolved to try to do so. Peace of mind is what I want, but fear I shall never attain it. I hope to hear from you again. Most of my fellow prisoners have read your letter and all entertain the greatest respect for you. Some to whom your kind words and motherly advice have brought tender memories, desire to be remembered to you.

You are passing through ... , where I have lived and where I spent the happiest of my boyhood days, but they are gone. I hope you may meet some of my old companions and that they may be benefited by your kind words.

Your humble, grateful servant,

M.

Stillwater, Nov. 2, 1888.

Dear Sister Wheaton: I was pleased beyond expression to receive your letter. It came like a benediction. I shall never forget you. The few words spoken have left an impress upon the tablets of memory that time can not efface. You can tell the boys wherever you see them in prison or out that Jesus is near—ever near. Tell them that I know that no locks ever were made that can lock the Saviour out. He came to me when I was, oh, so lonely, so broken-hearted and despairing! You know just how it was I was saved.

I am innocent in the presence of God, and still I am here; but never alone. Jesus is ever with me. Oh, how I wish every one in the wide, wide world could know our Saviour! How true is the fourteenth chapter of John, and especially the eighteenth verse: "I will not leave you comfortless. I will come unto you." Never in all my persecution and imprisonment has my Lord failed in that promise. I am very hopeful. My innocence is recognized and I hope soon to be at liberty. Had any one told me twelve months ago that this was all for my good I should have laughed them to scorn; but, thank God, I know it now. This life is but a few days at most compared to the home beyond, and I can and do say, "God's will be done." He can do no wrong, and right must prevail. God bless and prosper you until you go home.

Yours in His name,

H. R.

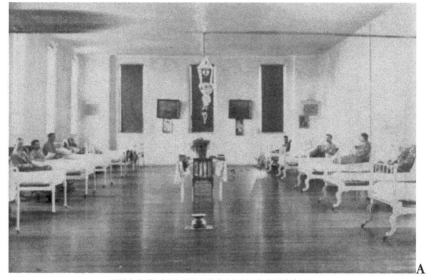

WARD IN PRISON HOSPITAL.

Stillwater, Nov. 14, 1888.

Dear Mother Wheaton: I received your letter and it came just right to comfort me, for I am in the hospital. In prison—not alone. In the hospital—not alone. Jesus is always with me. How I love Jesus who died for me! My heart always turns to Him, and when I heard I had to come to the hospital I just prayed to Jesus and left it all to Him, and I am cheerful and happy and hopeful even here. He is the Great Physician.

I can do anything for Jesus' sake but I am in such a queer position! Poor mother has been nearly killed and heart-broken about this, and she claims my presence for a time at least if I get out. Poor mother is nearly worn out but full of faith and hope. May God bless you and be with you forever.

Your son and brother in Christ,

H. R.

Little Rock, Ark., June 10, 1888.

Mrs. Elizabeth R. Wheaton.

Dear Sister: I will take the liberty and let you and Sister M. know who I am. My name is C. S. I guess you remember the coal mines and that evening when I was singing with Sister M. in her book. O I wish I had them songs!

I am so happy in Christ. I am going home to my mother above. I hope it will be very soon. That song

"A Ruler once came to Jesus by night To ask Him the way of salvation and light,"

made me a different man.

O the happy thoughts of a home which Christ our Redeemer has prepared for us and calls us to come to Him. "Come unto me all that are weary and heavy laden and I will give you rest." O, such a Saviour! Pray for me and I hope we may meet above. I hope to hear from you soon.

From your servant,

C. S.

Little Rock, January 13, 1889.

Mr. J. M. Ryder,

Indianapolis, Ind.

I received your most welcome letter and thank you for the information you have given me, but I haven't heard yet from your sister. The last letter I got she said that she was going to California. At that time she was at Salem, Oregon. Have you heard from her yet? There are some boys and men here would like to hear from her, for she came where some of us could not see the sun in a week, and about 150 feet under the surface of the earth. That was at a coal mine.

We all hope and pray to God, our dear Redeemer, for her to come back to us again.

Please answer this for I am a convict and glad to hear from such friends. In hope to hear soon, I remain,

Yours sincerely,

C. S.

Germantown, Ark., Nov. 29, 1889.

My Dear Sister: I am at Germantown at the present time working on Mr. W. H. Ward's farm or plantation, and the Warden of the camp and the guards are followers of Christ. There are several of the boys with me which were at Coal Hill at the time you were there.

O sister, God worked that all right, His name be praised. One of the Coal Hill wardens got five years in the penitentiary. That is God's work.

God be with you and bless you is my daily prayer, that you will keep strong and well to preach to the poor prisoners and pray for them that they will "flee from the wrath to come." O sister it is terrible to think and study over how the Book of Life tells us about that everlasting torment, and how sweet it is to think that there is a life eternal.

Sister, there are three ways, "a broad road," "a narrow way" and "a highway," that are thus brought to our attention in the Scriptures.

The broad road to destruction, the narrow way to life, the highway to holiness.

"And an highway shall be there, and a way, and it shall be called the way of holiness; the unclean shall not pass over it; but it shall be for those, the wayfaring man, though fools shall not err therein. No lion shall be there, nor any ravenous beast shall go up thereon; it shall not be found there, but the redeemed shall walk there." Isa. 35: 8, 9. Sister, am I right or wrong?

The first great judgment (trial and sentence) was at the beginning, in Eden, when the whole human race, as represented in its head, Adam, stood on trial before God.

The result of that trial was the verdict—guilty, disobedient, unworthy of life; and the penalty inflicted was *Death*. "Dying, thou shalt die," and so "In Adam all die." But, dear sister, the sweet and dear thought in "Christ we all shall live" is a great comfort to our poor souls. Ours is a rugged, steep and narrow way, and were it not that strength is furnished for each successive step of the journey, we never could reach the goal, but our Captain's word is encouraging: "Be of good courage, I have overcome"; "My grace is sufficient for thee, and my strength is made perfect in weakness." The difficulties of this way are to act as a separating principle to sanctify and refine "a peculiar people," to be "Heirs of God and joint-heirs with Jesus Christ." In view of these things, "let us come boldly to the throne of grace, that we may obtain mercy and find grace to help in time of need," "while we fight the good fight of faith and lay hold of the crown of life." Immortality, the divine nature.

Sister, I hope that we may meet together here in this world once more in life so we can talk about what Jesus has wrought, God will be with you. I know He is with me. Sister, I gave myself to Jesus and I feel more satisfied, and how sweet it is to have Jesus with you.

THE DAY IS AT HAND.

"Poor, fainting pilgrim, still hold on thy way, The dawn is near; True, thou art weary now, but yon bright ray Becomes more clear. Bear up a little longer; wait for rest; Yield not to slumber, though with toil oppressed. The night of life is mournful, but look on the judgment near. Soon will earth's shadowed scenes and forms be gone. Yield not to fear. The mountain's summit will, ere long, be gained And the bright world of joy and peace attained. Joyful through hope, thy motto still must be— The dawn is near. What glories will that dawn unfurl to thee! Be of good cheer. Gird up thy loins, bind sandals on thy feet, The way is dark and long, the end is sweet."

I hope to hear soon from you, dear sister. Meet me in heaven. Jesus is with me. Because He cometh to judge the earth, let the heavens be glad and the earth rejoice.

Your brother,

Germantown, Jan. 27, 1890.

Dear Sister: I received yours of the 28th. I am so glad that you have not forgotten me, and the words which I heard you say, although it is a long time since you said them at Coal Hill. "Believe on the Lord Jesus Christ and thou shalt be saved." Acts xvi., 31. Jails are dark, dull, damp, loathsome places even now; but they were worse in the apostolic times. I imagine tonight we are standing in the Philippian Dungeon. Do you not feel the chill? Do you not hear the groan of those incarcerated ones who for ten years have not seen the sunlight, and the deep sigh of women who remember their father's house, and mourn over their wasted estates? Listen again. It is enough. Oh, it is the cough of the consumptive, or the struggle of one in a nightmare of a great horror. You listen again, and hear a culprit, his chains rattling as he rolls over in his dreams, and you say: "God pity the prisoner." But there is another sound in that prison. It is a song of joy and gladness. What a place to sing in. The music comes winding through the corridors of the prison and in all dark wards the whisper is heard: "What's that? What's that?" It was the song of Silas and Paul in prison, and they cannot sleep. Jesus went to prison then, and as you say He will and does come nowadays also to visit the prisoners as they are shut up. God will be and is our helper. I will not fear, He leadeth me in pastures green.

Your brother in Christ,

C. S.

Germantown, May 16, 1890.

Dear Sister: Your letter of February 17th duly received, and glad to hear from you. But, sister, I am so glad to have some Christian friend to write to me in a place of temptation and trouble. I know that Jesus is my rock and my salvation and a shelter in a storm. Jesus is with me right now. He is waiting for us every day and hour. O, how many will there be that will call on Christ on that day, when the book of the Lord will be opened, with the seven seals, and who will be able to open the seals? No one is able to open it but the Lamb. Sister, this is my idea and opinion about that Day: There will be a great big scale, with a cross beam and Satan will be on one side of it and the people of all trades will be weighed, and if Christ the Son of God and our Redeemer is not there to balance them, what will become of them? Won't they be thrown down in hell?

Hoping and trusting faithfully that there be many of the poor prisoners among the hundred and forty and four thousand with the Lamb on Mount Zion, with the Father's name written in their foreheads and the harpers will be harping with their harps and singing the new song which no man could learn, but the hundred and forty and four thousand which were redeemed from the earth. O, what a day that will be! O that song is so true. O sinner give your heart to God and you shall have a new hiding place that day. O the rocks in the mountain shall all fade away and you shall have a new hiding place that day. "O sinner turn, why will ye die? God in mercy asks you why."

O, I am so happy tonight!

Your brother,

C. S.

Germantown, Ark., Dec. 18, 1890.

Dear Sister: Your kind words gladly received, and may God bless you and give you strength in your undertakings.

Sister, forgive those wicked men who put you in prison for preaching the gospel of our Lord Jesus Christ, for He, the Lord, said: "Father forgive them, for they know not what they do," and Silas and Paul in prison sang praises to the Lord our God and He delivered them from the prison in which they lay, and the jailor got saved.

Oh! my dear sister, I trust and pray to the Lord that we could safely say with Robert McChane, the ascended minister of Scotland, who, seated on the banks of Galilee's Lake, wrote, in his last sick days, and just before he crossed the Jordan (not the Jordan that empties into the

Lake of Gallilee, but the Jordan that empties into the "sea of glass mingled with fire"), these sweet words, fit to be played by human fingers on strings of earthly lute, or by angelic fingers on seraphic harps:

"It is not that the mild gazelle Comes down to drink thy tide, But He that was pierced to save from hell, Oft wandered by thy side. Graceful around thee the mountains meet Thou calm, reposing sea; But, ah! far more, the beautiful feet Of Jesus walked o'er thee. O Saviour! gone to God's right hand, Yet the same Saviour still, Graved on thy heart is this lovely strand And every fragrant hill."

O! is it not good to be with one's Lord and to think how sweet He says in his Book of Books: "I am the way," and in danger He speaks again: "Fear not, it is I."

The Lord is with me for I do not have to work in the ranks any more, and by His help I am assistant postmaster of this place.

Until we leave, and that time will be Christmas, address your next letter to Little Rock.

That you may save many souls from everlasting torture is my prayer every hour. My love to the poor sinful prisoners and to you, my dear sister in Christ.

A happy Christmas, and may God bless you to live and see many more.

I will sing now:

> "I was once far away from the Saviour"
> and

> "When Jesus shall gather the nations before Him at last to appear."

Oh! I am so happy! Goodnight,

Ever,

S.

Wichita, Kansas.

Dear Sister:

This is to acknowledge yours of the 15th inst., and was glad to hear that you have received my letter. Well, sister, we have our regular meeting every Sunday, and I will never cease praying to the Lord that He may help me to live my life, and that I can say, like our great Brother said, that no man can measure the glories which God has revealed to us. Glory to Thee, O God, glory to Thee! * * *

It is said that religionists make too much of the humanity of Christ. I respond that they make too little. If some doctor or surgeon of His day, standing under the cross, had caught one drop of the blood on his hands and analyzed it, it would have been found to have the same plasma, the same disk, the same fiber, the same albumen. It was unmistakably human blood. It is a man that hangs there. His bones are of the same material as ours. His nerves are as sensitive as ours. If it were an angel being despoiled, I would not feel it so much, for it belongs to a different being. But my Saviour is a man and my whole sympathy is aroused. Jesus our King is dying. Let couriers carry the swift dispatch. His pains are worse; He is breathing a last groan; through his body quivers the last anguish. The King is dying; the King is dead! His royal blood is shed.

I can imagine something of how the spikes felt; of how the temples burned; what deathly sickness seized His heart; of how mountain and city and mob swam away from His dying vision; something of that cry for help that makes the blood of all ages curdle with horror: "My God, my God, why hast Thou forsaken me?" * * *

O! Jerusalem, my happy home, When shall I come to thee; When shall my sorrows have an end? Thy joys, when shall I see? Jerusalem, my happy home, Would God that I were there! Would God my tears were at an end, Thy joys, that I might share.

I am so glad that I can write to you. I never will cease praying for you.

I remain, your brother.

C. H.

Washington County Jail.
Greenville, Miss., Jan. 29, 1889.

My Dear Sisters:

I cannot express my feelings when I read your kind letters. They make me feel as though you were still at my prison door. I know I am not the same boy that came to prison. I feel much better in every way. I read my Bible instead of novels, and find more pleasure in it.

I expect to get out of prison soon, and when I do I want to write you a long letter. Mr. McL. was to see me to-day, and read your letters. He said he would also write you to-day. There is a great change in him since you were here.

All the boys send love. Direct me as before, care Geo. S. If I get out I will work for him here. I am, as ever,

Your true friend and brother,

J. F. D.

Penitentiary at Yuma, Ariz., May 19, 1889.

Mrs. Elizabeth R. Wheaton.

Dear Friend: Your kind letter, written from Los Angeles, Cal., has been received, after much delay. We are all glad to hear from you, and thank you very much for your kind remembrance and the good advice given to us in your letter, and when you spoke to us here in the prison. Most all the boys hold you in kind remembrance and often express their wishes to see you and hear you talk again, and I sincerely hope it will be convenient for you to call and see us in the near future. The short visit you paid us awakened earnest thought in a number of the boys, and I am confident a few more such visits would result in much good to many of the inmates of this institution.

Asking your prayers, I remain,

Respectfully,

J. E. W.

KITCHEN AND DINING ROOM OF PRISON, DEER LODGE, MONT.

Deer Lodge, July 15, 1889.

Mrs. E. R. Wheaton.

Madam: I received your postal last Friday, and was very pleased to hear from you and to know that although far away you still hold us in kindly remembrance. There are so few who think of us after the prison door has closed. The boys who were so fortunate as to meet you, and even those who only heard of your good work, wish to be remembered to you. So far as we are personally concerned, there have been no changes, and we will very probably go through the same routine day in and out until our several times have expired.

I can safely say that you have made a greater impression upon us than any others we have been privileged to hear. In the intercessions you make with the Ruler of All, we ask to be remembered, and hope that you will receive all the returns of good which your work so richly merits. If you can find time in the future, you can give us no greater pleasure than writing us, even if only so much as may be placed upon a postal.

Yours very sincerely,

HERBERT A. M. (Librarian).

Cole City, Dade Co., Ga., July 5, 1890.

Mrs. Elizabeth R. Wheaton:

Yours of May 25th received yesterday in this camp and contents duly noted. How it thrills the hearts of the boys to hear the reading of a letter written by the hand of "Mother Wheaton," the friend of the unfortunate ones. Dear Christian Mother, you can't imagine the encouragement it gives to the boys here, especially those who are trying to do right. Your work has been implanted here so very deep that God cannot, according to His promise, obliterate it, for He approves of all good works. You shall have our prayers, and we desire to have your presence again when possible.

I intended to take your letter to Rattlesnake Camp No. 4 to read to the boys up there, as Capt. Brock promised me I might go, but for some reason, I know not what, I failed to get off, but I do hope and believe the way will be opened for us prison-bound boys who desire to do a work for Him to do it without fear.

I received also enclosed in your letter a most interesting pamphlet of "Capt. Ball's Experience," which is so grand. Also another of the "Widow and the Judge."

We have a very good Sunday school here now, and I am trying to make it as interesting as I possibly can, and any books and Sunday school papers and catechisms you can send us will be quite a favor. That would have been my business at No. 4 Camp to-day, if I could have gone, to organize a Sunday school.

I must close by asking an interest in your prayers. Write often.

Your friend and brother in Christ,

J. W. S., Camp No. 3.

Eastern Penitentiary, Philadelphia, Dec. 15, 1890.

Dear Madam:

Your invitation given any of the prisoners who may wish to write, I for one accept. I was greatly impressed with your words of truth and the earnest, determined manner in which they were spoken. I believe they proved an exception to the routine of professed Christianity we are used to, and have set more than one mind to thinking of their spiritual condition. I assure you they were not without effect, and that you are engaged in a noble work, of which I and others would be glad to hear more.

True it is that in the world around us are many persons struggling with poverty as great as ours, who are loaded with cares and anxieties which seem to hinder them in the service of God. There are many who cannot offer him a pure heart which has never been stained by sin, yet in the grief for misspent time and neglected grace would gladly atone for the past by fervent, grateful love, casting themselves upon the mercy of the Saviour.

I am an old soldier, have fought in the late war, but the greatest battle I have yet to fight is with myself—the battle of reformation.

Almighty God, in His wondrous wisdom, has chosen His saints from every rank of life—some poor and unknown to the world while they are in it; others great and powerful; no two have been exactly alike, even in their way of pleasing the Lord.

The "boys" here are satisfied your mission was for good, and left them knowing that for once they were not locked up within the hearing of false professors. To say that "locks" would not be necessary to hold a congregation within your hearing would be well founded. For a great many others this could not be said.

The boys from Block 9 send you their respects, and would be glad to hear from you again; would be glad to hear that you received this and that our appreciation of your service be accepted.

Respectfully yours,

A 2552.

Washington County Jail.

Greenville, Miss., Jan. 9, 1890.

Dear Sister:

Your postal of the 5th to hand. The boys are all glad to hear from you.

Mr. McL. was acquitted and was the proudest boy I ever saw. The St. Louis boy also got free and went home to his mother.

There has been a great change in the prisoners since you were here. They are always praying and singing, and you are remembered in every prayer. I don't think I am the same boy that came to jail; I know my poor old mother will be proud of me when I see her again. She lives in Mobile, Alabama, and it has been three years since she saw me, but I am praying to meet her soon and be a son to her, as I never was before. I feel like I could teach young men some good lessons if I get out of this place.

We received some reading matter from you a few days ago. Please let me hear from you whenever you can spare the time to write. All the boys join me in love and hope to hear from you again soon.

Your friend and brother,

J. D. (alias the Artist).

Penitentiary, Salt Lake City, Utah, April 14, 1901.

Mrs. Elizabeth R. Wheaton,

Dear Madam: Your welcome and interesting letter to hand and contents noted, being exceedingly pleased to hear from you. In response would state, your letter, though a great surprise, has been read by many of the inmates of this institution with great interest, you being the only one, so far, who has shown enough respect for us to address a few lines to us by mail. For this kindly remembrance and respect, please accept our united thanks, with the wish that as you are journeying along life's pathway you may escape many of the annoyances which you have been subjected to in the past, while dispensing the gospel tidings to a class of unfortunates. After your departure from here, am pleased to state, the "Boys" have taken a deeper interest in Jesus and His works than ever before, and I verily believe that were you to come again you would have no difficulty in bringing many of them to the foot of the Cross. Bibles that have lain for months in cells, covered with dust, have been taken up and read with avidity, selecting texts as you suggested for future guidance, and many are the prayers and kind words which ascend nightly to the Throne of Grace in your behalf—prayers for your future guidance and welfare, with health to sustain you in your glorious work of reclaiming the erring and fallen. God speed the good work along! We wish there were more like you, to bring a few kind and cheering words to sustain us, while undergoing this isolation. Your voice has lingered in our ears ever since you left, and many of the boys here would like to secure, if they possibly could, a copy of that wonderful song you sang for us, "Throw Out the Life-line." If you would kindly forward a copy, as it is not in our hymn-books, it would be very acceptable.

You may rest assured, no firmer, truer or better friends are to be found than those you possess in the Utah Penitentiary. Allow us to hope that when comparing this institution with some of the grander ones you may visit in the East, you will not speak disparagingly of your boys out West, but remember there are as many honest hearts beating beneath striped jackets here as you will find anywhere, with none more willing to do you a favor. In conclusion, accept our united and kindest regards. Hoping that after your life's labors are finished on this earth, you may find that "Haven of Rest," where it shall be said to you, "Well done, thou good and faithful servant; enter ye into the kingdom of Heaven," trusting these few lines may give you further encouragement, and hoping to hear from you again, with united thanks for past remembrance, I remain,

Yours most respectfully,

M. M.

Baton Rouge, La., October 11, 1891.

Mrs. Elizabeth R. Wheaton.

My Dear Sister: Yours addressed to the boys in prison here was received, and I shall take the responsibility of answering your letter, which is so full of the Word of God.

Your songs I shall never forget. I wish you could come and pray for us and sing those sweet songs to us every day.

I have got a life sentence in this prison. I do not know whether you remember me or not, but I remember you and always will, I hope, and I pray to meet you in Heaven. Since I listened to the songs you sang, I have felt that I was nearer Heaven than ever before. Your few minutes with us in this prison helped me more than all others that I ever heard preach the Word of God. Your service enlightened me more. I feel better and I think that every one in here will long remember your few minutes' talk with them on that blessed Sunday morning. I shall constantly pray and try to become as pure in heart as I think you are. Your home is surely in Heaven, and I will endeavor to reach that home and meet you there. Pray for me that I may become acceptable in the sight of our Lord.

I pray the grace of our Lord Jesus Christ and the love of God and the communion of the Holy Ghost be with you.

B. P.

Lancaster, Neb., Oct. 25, 1891.

Our Dear Sister in the Lord:

I received your kind note through our Brother Burge. I am thankful for your words to us and for the encouragement I received through you. I am trying to live a Christian life, to follow the teachings of the words of God in the book He has given. I am persuaded of myself I can do nothing, but by the help of God and our Saviour I am able to resist temptations and sin. The world looks down upon me from two standpoints—the one because of my color, and the other because I try to serve the living God through Christ our Lord. I feel that I am weak and need much help, both from the Lord and from the brethren and sisters. I need your prayers daily to help me in my surroundings and trials. We are hated and mocked, but this does not move us. My faith is strong and I will, through the grace of God, meet you in Heaven. In my imagination I still hear those words that you spoke to us, and I hope they will continue to ring in my ear.

I do not fail to mention you in my prayer to God the Father, in the name of our Lord and Master.

Our chaplain has just returned from the prison congress and he gave us a talk on prison reform.

From your brother that is colored, that had a talk with you in the warden's office.

J. H. No. 1579.

West Virginia Penitentiary, Jan. 31, 1892.

Dear Sister Wheaton:

Your letter to "Boys in the Penitentiary" was received, and it gave me pleasure to read it to them in the chapel, as also that enclosed for the female prisoners; and after reading the latter the officer in charge gave it to the sisters, and they can digest its helpful contents in the quietude of their own apartments.

At the very mention of a letter from you I could see many faces light up with interest, and I am sure your earnest and faithful appeals for recruits to the Master's cause on your visits to this place will never be forgotten; also that many hearts feel to thank you for the kindly and unabated interest that prompted your letter of cheer and encouragement. God bless you with power by His Spirit in your noble work. Twenty-six lifetime men are confined here, and I am one of the number; but I am glad to tell you that even here I have learned a freedom which is not compassed by iron bars, and I am looking forward with confidence when I will come into the full enjoyment of that inheritance which is "incorruptible, undefiled and fadeth not away." Have been here over thirteen years; converted twelve years and nine months ago, and have been trying to do something for my Master ever since, and I feel glad that He has wonderfully blessed and kept me in His love. Pray for us that God will save the fallen.

Yours in Christian love,

W. S. D.

Oregon State Penitentiary.

Salem, Ore., April 3, 1892.

Dear Mother Wheaton:

Your kind letter was handed to me by our Superintendent to-day, and we were more than pleased to hear from you. May our Father in Heaven protect and keep you for many years to come in the faithful work of rescuing the souls of men who are so far astray that each one saved seems like a miracle. Many a prayer has gone up from the solitudes of our prison cells for Mother Wheaton's health and success, and many of us in conversation have oft repeated, "God bless Mother Wheaton!" But we have not lost sight of Jesus, always our Friend. We have services every Sunday. Mother Smith (God bless her!) comes once a month, and each Sunday our pulpit is occupied by some minister from the city. Then some night during the week our choir has rehearsal; so you see, we have plenty of opportunity to worship and listen to the divine Word, and in consequence we are very grateful to our kind officials, who earnestly look out for our spiritual welfare, especially Mr. Downing, our good Christian Superintendent, who would not rest easy if he thought one of us was in want of anything that he could obtain for us that would be for our good. We often think of the difference between some other prisons and ours. "Oh, Father in Heaven, not as we will, but as Thou wilt, but spread a little divine love in those quarters where it is so much needed"—that is often our prayer.

God bless you and protect you in your noble work, and may the jewels in your crown be many, are the prayers of many of the inmates of this institution, and when you come again many an honest hand will unite with yours in our expression of love and faithfulness for Him who died on Calvary, not in the arms of a loving mother, but between two such men as many of us have been; yet one of them dwells with Him in Paradise, which proves to a certainty that He saves to the uttermost. God bless you again. Write us often, and when you reach those pearly gates there will be those to meet you who will say, "You showed me the way."

Yours in Christ.

Lancaster, Neb., Aug. 20, 1892.

Dear Sister in the Lord:

Yours of the 5th at hand. I always rejoice to hear from you, or to hear you speak, for your words are words of comfort, and are after the doctrine of our Lord and Master and according to the Scripture. It is a great comfort to me to hear or speak with those that live in Christ Jesus. No I have no thought of turning back to the poor and weak elements of this world. By the help of the Lord I will press on to the ends that I may claim all the promises, and I want to be found faithful in all good works, and in doing good to those that have need. The promise you spoke of can be found in Revelation, 14:12. You ask if I will seek to be such. Yes, with all my heart. God, that knows all our hearts, knows that my desire is to live and work for His sake and for His glory. As for me, I am not worthy to be called His child, but only a servant, because I have wasted my life in sin when I ought to have served my God and Lord. But four years ago the Lord drew me unto Him. I repented of my ways, gave my heart and soul to God the Father, and Jesus our Lord. I received forgiveness of my sins, and not many days after I received the promise of my Lord. That was the promise of the Comforter, which came to me—even me. And now shall I turn back? No, God helping me, I will endure all things; for He is able to keep me in the hour of temptation. And oh! His promises are so true to them that put their trust in Him. In Isaiah, 41st chapter and 10th verse, and again in 1st Kings, 19th chapter, 7th verse, we are told the journey is too great for us without God's help. But if we accept the help we shall be faithful to the end. And here is another promise that He will help in time of need: "Lo! I am with you always, even unto the end of the world." (Matt. 28:20.)

He has promised to reward us according to our works. (Rev. 22:12.) I have done nothing worthy of reward. But you have labored and have kept the faith, and God will reward you for all your trials and tribulations, and give you a crown that will never fade. Yes, God helping me, I will meet you in Heaven, where there is no more sorrow and no more weeping, but joy in our Saviour. May God bless you. May He give you health and strength to the end, is my prayer. Pray for me, for the prayer of the righteous availeth much.

Yours in Jesus,

P. B.

Ionia, Mich., October 21, 1894.

Mrs. Wheaton.

Dear Madam: I write to thank you for those pamphlets you sent me, and I think I can say they did me good. At any rate, I am trying to faithfully follow their suggestions. I practically devour any of that kind of reading, for, thank God, I do hunger and thirst after instruction in His word—I should like to have said righteousness, but I don't—there! I cannot finish what I was going to say, for a blessed thought has just come to me—that is, Abraham believed God, and it was counted to him for righteousness. I not only believe God, but Jesus Christ also. So I believe I may say I hunger and thirst after righteousness. Anyhow, I pray every day to get nearer to God. You will be glad to hear that I have decided to leave all and follow Him. I have consecrated my life to His service. When I get out, wherever I feel that He calls me, I shall go there, if it is to China. I am praying for sanctification. I want to get so close to God as to always be able to feel His presence. This is just two weeks since you were here, and I started to serve God. Praise the Lord, I think I am justified in saying that I am a new lad.

I have given up tobacco and don't feel the need of it any more than if I had never tasted it. I have given up profanity just as easily. Now I want to read the Bible every day. Since you were here I have read Corinthians I and II, Revelations, Proverbs, Ecclesiastes, Ruth, and am now reading the Acts of the Apostles. Before you came I had thought a little of being a Christian, but had not taken any steps towards it, but you decided me, and I thank you for it.

I must close now or my paper will give out. Pray for me that I may receive sanctification and have the indwelling of the Holy Ghost. God bless you.

I remain, yours sincerely and respectfully,

M. J. B.

Lancaster, Neb., Feb. 3, 1895.

Mrs. Elizabeth R. Wheaton.

My Dear Sister in Christ: Yours was received with welcome and thanksgiving to our Lord that comforts us through His Holy Spirit. Yes, God has given me grace to overcome many temptations. He is my whole trust and confidence, and I know He hears my prayers, and He will open a door for you here. There are some hungry souls here for the truth. I believe if you had been permitted to have service, some would have been saved. About the first of December there were some seeking quite sincerely. My desire is that I might be found faithful to the end, and I ask your prayers for me to Him who is able to save to the uttermost. I am so glad you had the Spirit of God in your service in Lincoln December 25. We had the follies of this world without the Spirit of God. But the world knows its own and they please not our Lord. And because we are not of the world, the world hates us, and that without a cause. I have been praying for you that God will give you the victory in all things. And now may the peace and grace of God our Lord be with all His saints and them that truly love Him.

From your brother in Jesus,

P. B. B.

Cole City, Ga., April 26, 1896.

Mrs. Wheaton.

Dear Mother: I take the pleasure of writing you a few lines.

I do hope that I can meet you and tell you the good you have done me. God is the one and the only one I look to.

I want to go to Heaven and believe I will. I believe some day, if we do not meet on earth again, that we will meet in Heaven.

Poor and needy though I be, God, my maker, cares for me; Gives me clothing, shelter, food; He will hear me when I pray. He is with me night and day, When I sleep and when I wake. Keeps me safe for Jesus' sake, He who reigns above the sky, Once became as poor as I.

He whose blood for me was shed, Had not where to lay His head. Though I labor here awhile, He will bless me with His smile. And when this short life is past, I shall rest with Him at last.

I hope and pray that you will have power and strength to obey the Master's will.

Good-bye,

P. McM.

Boise City, Idaho, May 11, 1896.

Mrs. Wheaton.

My Dear Mother in Christ: I hope you are well and enjoying the love of the Lord. It is a great thing to be in a position to work for the Lord Jesus. We are having good services now every Sunday, and we have a good Bible class of our own. The Lord has wonderfully blessed this place, and I hope to see many souls saved. Praise God! All the boys send love and wish to see you, and we all wish you success. God bless you in your good work.

W. B.

Waupun, Wis., Feb. 26, 1897.

Mrs. E. R. Wheaton and Mrs. Kelly,

Dear Friends: Enclosed please find P. O. order for $6.66, which is sent you with the best wishes of the inmates of this institution, as a slight token of the appreciation which we have of your efforts toward the uplifting of fallen beings like ourselves, and the upbuilding of Christ's Kingdom.

Although most of the contributions came from the C. E. members, yet they were not confined strictly to them.

It was a surprise to me, when in conversation with many of the boys, during our short time of liberty on Washington's Birthday, to find among them such a general feeling of friendliness and respect toward you, even from those who usually scoff at everything religious, and who are thoroughly hardened in sin and crime.

I am sure it will be gratifying to you to know that God so blesses your efforts that even the most hardened ones can feel the influence of His Holy Spirit in your ministrations.

Rest assured that we shall always hold you in kindly remembrance, and shall never cease to pray that God's richest blessing may crown your efforts.

While our contribution is very small, we know that you will receive it remembering only the motive which prompts its bestowal, which is the only method by which the value of a gift can be determined.

With renewed expression of our wishes and prayers for your success, we are,

Yours for Christ,

WAUPUN PRISON C. E. SOCIETY.
A. I. W., COR. SEC.

P. S.—The enclosed order is sent in the chaplain's name, W. G. Bancroft.

Eddyville, Ky., April 18, 1897.

Mrs. E. R. Wheaton.

My Dear Christian Friend: It is with pleasure that I write you these few lines to let you know that your visit to Eddyville was not in vain. Many of my brothers here express their appreciation of your visit. We have some earnest workers for the salvation of men in this prison. We are praying for you that God will strengthen you for His work. We hope to see you again soon, and receive a message from Jesus, for we receive you as His messenger.

All my brothers send their thanks to you, for they say you seem like a mother to them. Some of us have not seen our mothers for thirteen or fourteen years, and only live in hope of seeing them in heaven, when we can lay down these stripes and greet them there.

O my dear Christian friend, when I think of a wasted life and how easy a poor frail being like myself is led off, it almost crushes my heart, but thank God that the blood of Jesus Christ cleanseth from all sin, and that is my only hope. I want to meet you in heaven and, by the grace of God, I'll be there. We will not be in prison always. Jesus will come to claim his children soon. Those who oppress us now will all have to stand before that just Judge and give an account of what they have done to crush the hearts of their fellowmen. May God forgive them, is my prayer, for they know not what they do.

I hope to hear from you soon. May God bless you in His service.

Your friend in Christ,

L. P.

Laramie, Wyo., May 31, 1897.

Dear Mother Wheaton:

I got your letter some time ago and also the papers. Was real glad to get them and to hear from you. I also get the paper regularly, and when we are through reading it I send it to a little boy in Montana that I used to know. We still continue our Bible class and have several new members. We have changed the time from Thursday until Sunday, on account of some of the boys who work on the farm.

I got a good letter from a friend in Kansas not long ago. He tells me that my wife and little girls have joined the Christian Church. The happiest days of my life were spent with them, and if there is one of us four who has to be lost I hope it may be me. I want your prayers for our Bible class and that God will make me a better man; and especially for my wife and children I want your prayers. It will be four years to-morrow since I have seen them.

Some of the boys often speak of you, and I can assure you of a welcome by us if you ever come this way again. May God bless you and sustain you in this world for many years to come, is my prayer. The text of the sermon we heard to-day was John 3:16.

W. J. T.

Luke 15:15.

Waupun, Wis., July 4, 1897.

Mrs. E. R. Wheaton.

Madam: The privilege of writing is accorded me by the rules of this institution, and as I have no friends to whom I write, I will address this letter to you. I have not taken any great interest in your work, but have heard you speak before you visited this place last February, and under similar circumstances.

All are doing nicely here and are looking forward to the treat we shall get to-morrow by being allowed the liberty of the yard, as we celebrate the Fourth then.

The Christian Endeavor Society is getting along nicely, I guess, though I have not been present at their last two or three meetings, but some of the boys seem to take considerable interest in the work.

The front yard is very pretty. All the flowers are in bloom and nature seems to bless the convicts as well as those whose conduct permits them to remain out in a cruel world.

Flower Mission Day was observed here June 20th. Some ladies of the W. C. T. U. distributed some flowers and spoke in the chapel. Told us of the sufferings of Jennie Cassidy of Kentucky, the originator of Flower Mission Day, invoked a divine blessing on us, and sent us to our cells, feeling that our lot was not so bad as others have had to endure.

The prison is about the same, six hundred males and ten or twelve females; some changes in the discipline; the lock-step is dispensed with; we are allowed two books a week from the library, and other changes which lighten our burden.

Believing you will pardon this liberty I have taken, I am,

Most respectfully,

No. 6965.

Laramie, Wyoming, May, 1898.

Dear Mother:

Mr. —— requests me to answer your kind and most welcome letter. I was thinking of you this morning, and of your mission on earth, and how you had spent your life in the service of the Lord, and in trying to benefit others. We regard you as the Good Samaritan, and pray that the Lord will bless you in your work wherever you may go. The members of the Bible class unite in sending you their love and best regards, and will be delighted to have you visit us again. According to nature, your earthly mission will soon come to a close, but your acts of kindness and deeds of mercy will live on forever. Remember us in your prayers. It is written that the prayers of the righteous avail much. Our class has increased considerably since you were here. Some of the boys seem to be very much in earnest and sincerely repent of their past conduct. I hope to live the remainder of my life in the service of the Lord, and I hope to meet you in a brighter and a better world, where parting and sorrow are no more; where our tears are all wiped away, and the light of the Lord shines forever.

Sincerely yours,

F. P. 309.

Eddyville Prison, March 17, 1900.

Mrs. Elizabeth R. Wheaton, Prison Evangelist:

Though it has been one year the 5th of February past since I heard your kind, sweet, motherly voice, how glad and proud I am to see you once again and hear your kind voice, full of a mother's pity for her children. May God bless you, mother, in your journey from prison to prison to teach fallen men that there is a Jesus who loves them and will forgive their sins if they only believe on Him. Thank God for His Son He sent into the world to save sinners, for Jesus has pardoned all my sins, and I mean to serve God for the remainder of my life.

You are welcome—thrice welcome. If you did not love us you would not come to visit us each year so faithfully. May God bless and go with you wherever you may be or go.

Though I have only about three weeks to serve here yet, I thank God I will leave a saved boy through the blood of Jesus. Bless His holy name!

I highly appreciate your kind words and the advice you gave me. I will take your advice.

I will close by saying, "May God watch between me and thee." Amen. My motto through life is, "In God I trust."

I remain,

Your son in Jesus,

F. P. K., Jr.

Yuma, Arizona, May 25, 1903.

Dear Sister Wheaton:

Our kind Superintendent handed me your letter of the 22d inst., also the tracts you sent, which I distributed to those who I knew would read and appreciate them. I also showed your letter to several, and intended reading it, or having it read, during church yesterday morning, but our minister was late, so I thought best to wait till next Sunday. During the week I will pass it around to as many as I can. All to whom I showed the letter seemed glad to hear from you, and requested me to ask you to remember them in your prayers, and said to tell you they hoped you would be able to visit the prison again soon.

I am sorry I haven't a more favorable report of Christian progress in the prison; but Satan seems to hold the upper hand, and there has been no conversion for some time, and there has been quite a number of Christian boys sent out, and a great many new men came in of late, which may account for the small attendance at services.

I hope the Lord will open the way for some good revivalist to come to Yuma and stay for a while at least. This place needs a real stirring up.

I hope that the Lord will continue to bless you in your work for Him among fallen men and women, and that you may lead many to live better lives and be prepared for heaven.

Your brother in Christ,
R. C.

Frankfort, Ky., October 8, 1903.

Elizabeth R. Wheaton, Prison Evangelist.

Dear Mother Wheaton: It is a matter of the deepest regret that I am in prison, but I am very proud to have you call me one of your boys.

My dear mother was named Elizabeth. I was her pride and joy, but rejoice to think that my fall did not occur until after her death.

It would please my sweet wife if you could write her a letter of encouragement and good cheer.

I hope that your latter years may be many, and am certain they will be filled with the joy and blessedness which come to those who are serving the Master in such a noble work as yours.

Most respectfully yours,

H. E. Y.

DRUG DEPARTMENT IN PRISON HOSPITAL.

Frankfort, Kentucky, November 15, 1903.

Mrs. Elizabeth Wheaton, Tabor, Iowa.

My Dear Mother Wheaton: Your visit to those who were confined to their beds in our prison hospital October 6th was a great blessing to them. Your gospel hymns gave them visions of angels singing the praises of their Master, and your prayers carried them before the great white throne for mercy and pardon.

Prisoners need Christianity more than any other class of men, and when they get the love of God in their hearts they immediately become better prisoners, are more contented, and have more hope for this life and the life to come.

Surely your work is a noble one, and each song and prayer for prisoners makes your heavenly reward more glorious.

With many thanks for the kind words spoken to me, I remain,

Most respectfully,

H. E. Y.

Jefferson City, Mo., Sept. 2, 1904.

Mrs. E. R. Wheaton, Tabor, Iowa.

Dear Mother in Jesus: I thought I would address you in behalf of a Christian friend by the name of J., as he is sick. He requested me to write to you, and as I would like to hear from a Christian from the outside world, he said you would answer my letter. I am trying to live a Christian life. When I was almost ready to give up and go back to my sinful life, there was a bright light came in my pathway to refresh my soul and to point out the dark places wherein I stood. And this light was Brother J. When he talks to any one it is in a loving way, and to talk to him five minutes one can tell that he is one of God's true children. I enjoy greatly to hear him talk of Jesus' love, for it does my soul good. Have you any Christian papers and tracts that you would please send to me? I would enjoy reading them greatly.

I am your boy, saved in Christ Jesus.

Geo. W. R.

Huntsville, Texas, Feb. 17, 1905.

Dear Mother Wheaton:

Yours to our chaplain, Dr. M., has just been handed to me, and it affords me great pleasure to write you, for I often think of you, and the good lady that was here with you, and I knew it would be gratifying to you to know how sincerely the boys appreciate your words of kindness and Christian advice for their spiritual welfare. I have heard many of them speak of you, and it was always with heartfelt wishes for your success and happiness. I trust and pray that many lost souls will be brought to Christ through your noble work in the meeting you mention.

Through reading the Christian Herald I have been much impressed with the need of missionary work in India. And I pray that Miss Grace, who was with you here, will be abundantly blessed in her undertaking. I assure you that we will all be glad to see you at any time. God's richest blessings upon you. I beg to remain,

Yours in Christ,

W. H. S.

CHAPTER XXIII.

Kind Words from Friends.

We give here a few letters from dear friends who have been especially interested in the Master's work, some of whom have given me many words of encouragement, or otherwise been helpful to me in advancing the work of the gospel.

FROM H. L. HASTINGS AND WIFE.

47 Cornhill Place, Boston, Mass., January 27, 1886.

Blessed Sister:

Your card came duly. Glad to hear. Sorry you could not call. Mrs. Hastings wanted to see you. Come to our house when you will. If you go to New York, call on Miss Annie Delaney, Fruit and Bible Mission, 416 E. 26th St., New York, opposite the Bellevue Hospital—right in the middle of prisons and prisoners. Tell them I sent you. Miss D. is superintendent and has lived with us and can open doors there.

I was at State Prison one night. Heard many good testimonies from your friends there. Surely, your labors have been blessed. May the Lord direct your way in all these things, and guide your endeavors. How much you need the Heavenly Father's guidance. He will guide you with His eye. Pray that you may know and do His will, and pray for us that we may please Him in all things. Do you need some tracts or papers? Let us know.

Yours in the work,

H. L. HASTINGS.

Goshen, Mass., March 9, 1900.

My Dear Sister:

I am very glad indeed to hear from you, and to know that you are still alive and still at work.

It was a great shock to me when Mr. Hastings left us. But the Lord has been very good to me, and I feel that He means what He says: "E'en down to old age I will never leave thee." "I'll never, no, never, no, never forsake." This is a beautiful and a comforting thought to me at this time.

May God bless you, my sister, and keep you in health to do His work, is the prayer of

Your friend,

MRS. H. L. HASTINGS.
(Per E. B.)

E. E. BYRUM, AUTHOR AND EDITOR.

September 11, 1903.

During the past few years I have been acquainted with Mrs. Elizabeth R. Wheaton, and known of her earnestness and zeal in behalf of the unfortunate prisoners of our land. For many years her time has been almost wholly given to the work of relieving the distressed and discouraged in their cells, and in prison chapels.

Her songs and words of encouragement, mingled with tears, have caused the feelings of depression and sadness to flee away, and those bowed down with sorrow to grasp a ray of hope and look forward with renewed energy to a higher life, trusting in Him who is able to keep. Many years of continued evangelistic work in the penitentiaries and prisons of America have given her a wide range of experiences of prison life, a description of which cannot fail to be of intense interest to every reader. It was partially due to her untiring zeal that I was moved to write the book entitled "Behind the Prison Bars." Her written words will continue to warn and comfort after her departure from this world to her home beyond the cares of life.

E. E. BYRUM.

Moundsville, W. Va.

FROM MOTHER OF PRISONER.

Chicago, March 4, 1900.

Dear Friend:

I was greatly surprised and glad to hear from you, for my son has often spoken of you and has regretted that the quarantine has kept you away. I feel very grateful to you for taking an interest in my dear boy, for he is still very dear to me.

You cannot imagine my feelings all these years, knowing he was behind gloomy walls. My health has given way two or three times on account of it. Like so many others, he thought he knew best, and left a good home to go roving. The cause of his downfall is due to bad company, but then, his time is up in October. I hope to see him once more and keep him with me, for I am growing old—am nearly sixty-two.

I shall be very glad to welcome you to our home.

If you should see my dear boy before you come to Chicago, tell him I am waiting patiently until I see him.

This letter hardly expresses my feelings, but, sleeping or waking, my thoughts are nearly always with my absent boy. Once more accept thanks from a broken-hearted mother.

Mrs. M. E. F.

FROM A PRISONER'S DAUGHTER.

Denver, Colo., Jan. 7, 1903.

My Dear Mother Wheaton:

Praise God for salvation this afternoon! I am glad I found your address, for I have wanted to write to you for a long time and tell you the result of your visit to R. State Prison, where you talked with my precious father.

He wrote me soon after you left and said you left him under awful conviction. He confessed and forsook his sins and is now a man saved by the blood that was shed on the cross for him. He said that he was restless from the time you left until he found Jesus. He told how you and a young lady talked and prayed with him, and how, after he retired, he rolled and tossed in awful agony until about eleven o'clock, when he cried to God for mercy. God heard his cries and came to his release. O hallelujah! It just makes me shout to read his letters now. I can tell by them that he is really resting in Jesus. He before seldom wrote more than two pages, and now he writes from fifteen to twenty-four. And oh, such letters! I just can't help but cry for joy when I read them and realize that my precious papa is serving the only true and living God. I give God the glory and all of the honor for what has been done; and I praise God for using you as an instrument through whom He worked. Eternity alone can reveal the result.

My heart is full of praises to Jesus my King this evening. He has done so much for me lately. He blesses me in soul and body and supplies all my needs.

I may go to C. soon and try to do something for my father. Pray that God may lead me and that the devil may not hinder in any way, if God sees fit to release papa from prison. I am perfectly resigned to God's will.

Your sister for Jesus,

M. H.

(This daughter was a successful Christian worker.)

FROM AN EDITOR.

Ashburn, Ga., May 12, 1897.

Dear Sister:

Grace and peace be multiplied to you. I received your letter and communication for "Holiness Advocate," which will appear in the next issue. Always let me know where to find you. I would have written sooner, but have been away to Macon, where I saw Sister Perry. She has been here and visited the convict camps since you were here. I have been visiting those camps pretty regularly since you left here. You put it on me and I am trying to be faithful. You asked me in your letter if you knew me. Yes, I met you here. It was in front of my store. You held the street service here at Ashburn, while waiting for the train, and I was with you until the train left. Well, sister, I will never get done praising God for ever meeting you. It marked a new epoch in my experience. I want you to take my paper on your heart. Ask the Holy Spirit to run it for me and the Father to supply financial help. I am trusting Him for it. How glad the prisoners in the camp will be to hear from you in this way. I will send up to both the camps a bundle of the issue containing your letter. I want you all to pray for the

South, that a deeper work may be done in the hearts of the Holiness people; that the missionary spirit may get hold of us so that we will send out our sons and daughters to tell of Jesus' love to a perishing, dying world.

May the Lord bless you and use you in the future even more powerfully than in the past. Come and see us when you can.

Yours, bound for Heaven,

J. LAWRENCE,
Ed. Holiness Advocate.

Ashburn, Ga., August 25, 1898.

Dear Sister Wheaton:

Your letter came to us all right, and you have no idea what gladness it brings to us all to hear from you, and yet conviction. For it certainly convicts us for the little we are doing when we see how the Lord is enabling you to put in full time. Pray for me that I may be more zealous. Things are taking a deeper move in the South. A great number of the Holiness people are getting down for a real experience. We have been satisfied long enough with a profession. So you may expect something from the South in the near future. Men and women giving themselves for the foreign field and for the home field, working in the slums and in the prisons and wherever God may lead them. Love to all the saints at Tabor. I have never met any of them, but I do love them and the work they are doing. "Blessed be the tie that binds."

God bless you, and may you be preserved blameless unto His coming.

Yours in Jesus' love,

J. LAWRENCE.

FROM AN EX-PRISONER.

Sioux City, Ia., Jan. 31, 1901.

Mrs. Wheaton: I don't suppose you will remember me, but possibly you may, as I think I was one of the most wretched in or out of prison at that time. It was at Sioux

Falls, So. Dak., between three and four years ago, if I remember correctly. You visited the prison and spoke to us in chapel, and later in the day you and a lady with you, came around to the cells. I was in cell No. 13. You shook hands with me and asked, "Are you a Christian?" I replied, "No." Again you asked, "Have you ever been one?" "No." "Will you meet me in Heaven?" you asked again, and I answered, "I will try to." You spoke only a few words, saying, "Do not be discouraged." These few words and that warm hand-shake helped me very much. I was indeed much discouraged. Life seemed dark indeed. I was serving an eleven years' sentence. I was under deep conviction of sin. Not long after that the blessed Christ came into my heart. I believed on His name and He saved my soul. Two years ago last August I was pardoned from the prison. The 17th of last March I became Superintendent of a Rescue Mission in Dakota, and for ten months or nearly that I was there and the Lord blessed our efforts by saving souls. I am now married. My wife was converted in the mission last June. She is an accomplished musician and singer and, the Lord being willing, we expect to go out and preach the gospel among railroad men in the near future.

I have often thought of you and your labor of love among prisoners. May God bless and encourage you in the work, is my earnest prayer. I heard that you were in Sioux Falls at the prison a short time ago. I did not know it in time to see you. If the prisoners only knew what joy and peace there is in the service of Jesus, it seems to me they would yield their hearts to Him. Again I wish you godspeed in your work. May you have many precious jewels for the Master's crown. To Him belong the praise and glory.

Good-bye, and God bless you and the sister that was with you. Never be discouraged. Jesus loves and uses you.

Yours, in His service,

T. F. M.

Sioux Falls, S. Dak., Feb. 9, 1904.

Mrs. E. R. Wheaton.

Dear Sister: Your card of November was received. Hope you will pardon me for not writing before. I am glad that you are still trusting Jesus, and working in His vineyard. May God bless, comfort, strengthen and keep you.

Jesus is coming again, perhaps soon. It may be that we shall be alive when He comes. If so we shall be caught up together with the dead in Christ to meet Him in the air, so shall we ever be with Him. Blessed be His name. (I Thess. 4-17.) I want to exalt Him. I want my daily life to be a testimony of His power to save and to keep. Many years of my life were spent in sin. Finally I was tried, convicted and sentenced to state's prison for a long term of years. God says: "Whatsoever a man soweth that shall he also reap, for He that soweth to his flesh shall of the flesh reap corruption, but he that soweth to the Spirit shall of the Spirit reap life everlasting." (Galatians 6:7, 8.) God's word is true.

I found my mind giving away and my body a physical wreck. I read the Bible and God showed me that I was a lost man. I tried to destroy my life, but God in his love and mercy would not permit it. I was in great darkness. I said to a friend, there is no hope for me in this life or the life to come, but I did not know Jesus Christ nor His saving power. God sent His ministers each Sunday morning to preach the blessed gospel, and one Sunday morning He sent "Mother Wheaton" to us. In the afternoon, I believe it was, she visited us in our cells. I had quarreled with my cell-mate, and he had left me. Mrs. Wheaton came and shook hands with me, and asked if I was a Christian. I said, "No." Again she asked, "Have you ever been a Christian?" I replied, "No." She said, "Will you meet me in Heaven?" I said, "I will try." With a warm hand-shake and a few words of encouragement, she left me. God helped me to believe in Jesus Christ, and there came into my life joy and peace such as I had never known before, even in my best days on the outside.

After my conversion I asked God if it was His will that I might be pardoned out. He also heard and answered that prayer. God is love. He loves the vilest sinner. To-day I have a loving Christian wife and two lovely children. I have no desire for the old life of drinking, gambling, etc., but my desire is to love and serve God and help my fellowmen to find Jesus, who is mighty to save and to keep. To Jesus belongs all praise and glory. If it is his will, may He use this testimony to bring souls to Himself.

T. F. M.

4064 Washington Avenue, St. Louis, Mo.,
October 25, 1899.

My Dear Mrs. Wheaton:

I thank you so much for your letter. I was greatly pleased in reading it. I will be so glad to see you when you come. I realize, as you say, that I have never fully let go of myself in the Master's work, but I have given my life to Him, and if I know my own heart, I am willing to be and do anything He shall choose for me. I love to help lost ones, and if the Lord should use me as He does you, I believe I should be the happiest person in the world. Do pray for me, won't you, that the Lord may lead me into all His will? Time is flying, and soon all of our opportunities will be over and our Lord will take us to Himself. Pray that the Lord will keep me busy serving Him. I love you and pray for you. May you be kept rejoicing in hope even though you see nothing but sin and sorrow around you. (Psalm 125:5, 6.)

Lovingly yours,

TULA D. ELY.

Sapphire, N. C., August 15, 1901.

My Dear Sister:

I received your letter to-day. I have been thinking about you and praying for you often, and see by your letter that God has made all of your trials a blessing to you and know that God can make up for any loss He lets us have. What a hard time you did have, dear sister. I praise God for bringing you through it with such joy. Sometimes it seems true He does with us like He did with Job—just tells Satan he may do everything but take our lives, and when our self-justification and friends are gone, He joins us in with Himself and makes us powerful in His own power. He knows whether we want Him, and if we do we will be taken through death to self and put to hard tests. It seems sometimes as if He hides His face to let us suffer and say, "Though He slay me yet will I trust Him." I am glad you are with the people who hold you up in prayer. We need one another's prayers in these times when Satan has so many snares. Tula is well. She and Mildred send love.

Affectionately and in Jesus, love,

CLARA D. ELY.

S——, Colo., June 24, 1903.

Dear Mother in Christ:

May this find you well and happy in the Lord Jesus. We have not forgotten you and we never shall. Our gospel tent meeting at P. was a blessed time. Souls were saved and sanctified. We give all the glory to Jesus. We are holding meetings here in our tent. The Lord is blessing the preaching of His Word. The Lord willing, we will begin a meeting at Raton, New Mexico, the 2nd of August. We would like to have you with us if it were the Lord's will. The Lord is helping us while we are here to open a home for poor girls. We have rented a five-room house and He is giving us everything we need for the home. Glory to God for all things!

My brother H. is with us in the gospel work. God is blessing him in singing the gospel. Remember us all in prayer. May the Lord give you many souls in your work. We both send love to you.

Your children,

J. E. AND WIFE.

The above is of especial interest to me though the reader may have to read between the lines, as it were, to understand why it is so. The writers are faithful and efficient workers in the Master's cause.

A TESTIMONIAL.

Columbia, South Carolina.

To Christian Women:

Dear Sisters: We have long known the bearer, Mrs. E. R. Wheaton, and can testify as to her arduous labors for the most needy classes. It was our privilege to have her in our Home for one week and we certainly received the Lord's blessing during that time. We are working for Christ, but her labors are more abundant, her trials far greater. As she goes forth without commission or salary she must depend entirely upon God. He usually supplies her through His people. Few of us could work where and as she does, but we may lovingly minister to her necessity and the dear Lord will surely bless in so doing. Yours in Christ,

MARIA JONES,
ELLA F. BRAINARD

The writer of the following sketch was an orphan girl making her home, when I first met her, with some of my relatives in Iowa. She was raised by her aunt and was kept in school and in society till she was grown. Having been converted at the age of twelve years and engaging some in Christian work, soon after my first acquaintance with her she received a call from God to devote her life wholly to His service. Being an orphan the Lord gave me a mother's love and care for her. She went with me to the Missionary Training Home at Tabor, from whence she went as a missionary to India. While at the Home she was faithful in caring for orphan children, etc., and traveled with me some, staying at one time several months as a worker in a rescue home in Chicago, and later spending some time in evangelistic work. I have elsewhere mentioned her trip with me to the Pacific coast on her way to India.

It was my privilege in the fall of 1903 to travel with Mother Wheaton in Gospel work in prisons, jails, missions, churches, etc. God made her a blessing to many souls who needed a mother's love and sympathy. She always lifts up Jesus, that souls might be drawn unto Him and be saved. We first visited the Reformatory for Girls at Mitchelville, Iowa. We were kindly received by the Superintendent who had been a friend of Mother Wheaton's for several years. He gave her the privilege of holding services in the chapel with the several hundred girls. She also visited the girls in their cottages, singing, praying and talking with them.

We then visited the prisons at the following places: Moundsville, W. Va.; Baltimore, Md.; Allegheny, Pa.;

Columbus, Ohio; Waupun, Wis.; Stillwater, Minn.; Frankfort, Ky.; Nashville and Brushy Mountain, Tenn.

In the hospital of the prison at Waupun we visited Mr. Colgrove, a prisoner who was converted fifteen years previously when Mother Wheaton was holding a service in the prison. He was a life prisoner but he yielded to the conviction of the Holy Spirit and was saved. During these years he proved by his daily walk that he was a Christian. He often conducted the devotional exercises, and he had taught three Bible classes, two in German and one in English, until his health failed. As I bade him goodbye he said, "I will meet you in the better world if I never meet you here again." He was in poor health and a few months later died a triumphant death.

The prison physicians gave permission to visit the sick, for they know the words of comfort and songs of cheer by Mother Wheaton will give them encouragement and a desire to live for the better world.

In a Gospel Mission I heard an ex-convict testify to how God had saved him from a life of sin. He said that he knew "Mother Wheaton" but perhaps she did not know him dressed as he was; for when she had met him before he was behind prison bars. He praised God for such a person who was willing to work among that class of people. I am sure there is much good accomplished in the prisons for individuals as Mother Wheaton stands at the door after services and shakes hands with the hundreds of prisoners as they pass out. Her "God bless you" is not soon forgotten. When her work is ended and the rewards of the righteous are given, many will arise and call her blessed.

GRACE YARRETT.

MOTHER WHEATON.

CHAPTER XXIV.

Sketches from Press Reports.

My call being not only to the prison bound but to every creature, the newspaper men have received their part of the Gospel message and were often instrumental in heralding some truth to their readers whom I have been unable to reach in person. I have often been interviewed by reporters regarding my work for the Master and they frequently give accounts of meetings held in the prisons, on the streets, etc., very correctly, though sometimes in a humorous style and from that standpoint of the onlookers or the prisoners. In this chapter I give a few sketches from reports of my work clipped from the papers.

A LABOR OF LOVE.

A WOMAN WHO LEFT A LUXURIOUS HOME TO SERVE THE UNFORTUNATE.

MRS. WHEATON AMONG THE CRIMINALS AT THE PENITENTIARY.

SHE VISITS THE HOSPITALS, JAIL AND WORK-HOUSE— AFFECTING SCENES WHILE SHE PREACHED.

A white-haird lady, clad in deep mourning, carrying a volume bound in morocco, visited the penitentiary yesterday. This was Mrs. E. R. Wheaton. In a few minutes she was delivering a sermon to the convicts. She is a remarkable woman. Four years ago she left a luxurious home in Ohio to preach the gospel to convicts, and since then has exhorted in the penitentiaries of thirty-seven States. She visits hospitals and the abodes of fallen women, also, and has ministered to the wants of thousands of unfortunates. An *American* reporter asked her how she happened to be engaged in the work.

"No member of my family was ever in a prison or afflicted as are those to whom I speak," she exclaimed; "my evangelical work did not originate in any morbid sympathy because of personal bereavement. I simply felt called of God to preach his word to the people, and have entered upon it for the remainder of my life. My heart and soul are in it, and though I am far from my dear ones I am happy."

She had been speaking to the convicts but a few minutes when the effect of her words of exhortation was visible. At first the majority were listless, but as she warmed to her cause they responded with closer attention and in fifteen minutes every eye was fixed intently upon the gentle, earnest woman, who sought to save their souls and bring a divine light to their benighted lives. When she closed her discourse and asked if any desired her prayers twenty hardened men of crime, with tears in their eyes, raised their hands and three advanced to the mourners' seat. With these she prayed and every word was fraught with all the potent power with which the voice of woman in prayer is capable. The three unfortunates were moved as men seldom are and at the close of the meeting professed conversion.

Mrs. Wheaton then visited the hospital department of the penitentiary, after which she went to the jail, work-house and city hospital and at each place delivered a discourse. To-day she will see fallen women.—Nashville American, Nashville, Tenn., 1887.

A PRISON EVANGELIST.

ELIZABETH R. WHEATON TALKS AT THE COUNTY JAIL.

Elizabeth R. Wheaton, the celebrated prison evangelist, visited the Buchanan county jail yesterday, and conducted a religious service of forty minutes' length. The evangelist pointed out the errors of her hearers and advised them to make early amends. The evangelist assured the audience that all they needed to be saved was faith. Wife murderer Bulling was one of the evangelist's most attentive hearers, and the horse thieves, burglars and other criminals were among her closest listeners. Sheriff Spratt thinks much good will result from Evangelist Wheaton's visit to the bastile.—St. Joe, Mo., paper, Aug. 8, 1889.

PRISON EVANGELIST.

Mrs. Elizabeth Rider Wheaton, prison evangelist, held services in the county jail this afternoon, lecturing and singing to the eleven prisoners there. She told in few words and four songs the whole plan of salvation, and it didn't take her but twenty minutes to do it. She talked a little while and sang "I Will Tell the Wondrous Story," following with a few words of comment her rich contralto voice burst into "You Must Be Born Again," followed in the same way. Then "It Pays to Serve the Lord," and "Parting to Meet no More," closing with a short prayer. These songs coming in the order they do, tell the whole story and make a very pretty one.— Unidentified.

EVANGELISTIC SERVICE AT PRISON.

Elizabeth Wheaton, a noble Christian woman who has consecrated her life to work in prisons, jails, reformatories, houses of correction, houses of refuge and hospitals, visited our city Saturday, and after presenting her credentials was given hearty permission to hold services at the prison on

Sunday, Father Murphy, the Catholic chaplain, whose day it was to officiate, kindly consenting to this arrangement. Her manner would probably not be agreeable to an æsthetic Christian audience in a fashionable, upholstered church, but she knows how to reach the hearts of the men and boys who wear the stripes, one of the prisoners, a Catholic, who has been behind the bars for almost seventeen years, remarking that this was the best service they had had there during his long term of imprisonment. No one, be he Christian or pagan, could have listened to the service at the prison chapel last Sunday without being convinced that there was an opening for unselfish work among prisoners and that this lady was pre-eminently fitted for such work. There is no mawkish sentimentality about her, but an all absorbing zeal in the work of leading the criminals, the erring, the lowly, the sick and the afflicted to Christ and a better life. It is doubtful if there is an ordained minister in the land who can do as much good in this field as this plain, unpretentious, but thoroughly consecrated woman. She has now been nearly five years in this work, and has visited nearly every prison in the United States and Canada, a few in Mexico, and also the jails, reformatories, houses of refuge and hospitals in all the prominent cities through which she has passed. She has traveled almost 100,000 miles and has never met with an accident. Wherever she goes she is kindly received, non-Christians in fact treat her better than those whose sympathy and co-operation she has a right to expect. Thus does the world ever recognize and honor earnest, conscientious and capable laborers in the cause of God and humanity. She never allows a collection to be taken up in her behalf, though frequently invited to speak in churches, but accepts such offerings as may come without solicitation. Last Sunday, while she and the citizens in the audience were retiring from the chapel, a Swedish servant girl, whose name is unknown to the writer, took from her scanty purse a silver dollar and gave it to Mrs. Wheaton. If the lesson of the story of the widow's mite be true this humble girl's gift was greater than that of the millionaire who gives thousands of dollars toward the erection of a magnificent church edifice.—Stillwater, Minn., Messenger, Oct. 27, 1888.

MRS. WHEATON'S ELOQUENCE.

CAUSES A SUFFERING WIFE TO FORGET HER BRUISES AND FORGIVE HER CRUEL HUSBAND.

The case of Henry Cooper was brought up before 'Squire F. yesterday afternoon at 2 o'clock.

Catharine Cooper stated that her husband had beat her brutally on last Saturday afternoon and that this was not the first ill treatment she had received at his hands.

The court room was converted into a prayer meeting and Mrs. Wheaton's prayers presented an affecting scene; before the trial was ended Mrs. Cooper asked to withdraw her prosecution and was willing to forgive her cruel husband. 'Squire F. ordered the prisoner to be taken to the workhouse to work out the cost of the suit.—Chattanooga, Tenn., paper.

FROM A PRISONER IN THE PRATT MINES STOCKADE, ALABAMA.

To the Chronicle:

Supposing a line or two from our prison, its surroundings, happenings, etc., would be acceptable, prompts me to drop you this.

The monotony of prison life is such that hardly anything transpires, that would command the notice of a news reporter, or draw an article from a newspaper correspondent. But, Mr. Editor, we had something to take place here last night that beats anything we ever saw or heard of.

About the time all the convicts had finished eating the evening meal, Captain P. J. Rogers announced that all should remain seated awhile, to hear preaching. Now to hear preaching is no uncommon occurrence here, Brother Rush preaches regularly for us, and occasionally other ministers deliver discourses upon the importance of living the life of a Christian, so when Capt. R. announced that we were about to have preaching, no one experienced much motion of spirit. The minds of those who gave the matter any thought were picturing in expectation, a man, perhaps baldheaded, clad in a long priestly robe with Bible and Hymn-book in hand, and of a solemn, or sanctimonious countenance, others, perhaps, drew a different man in appearance, but none had drawn the picture correctly.

Imagine our surprise when instead of a man, a woman of mature age, clad in the usual mourning apparel worn by the ladies, armed with Bible and Hymn-book, mounted the rostrum, and announced that she was going to preach to us. This announcement at once produced the most profound and reverential silence imaginable—every eye was at once riveted upon the face of the fair preacher, whose countenance wore a pleasant smile and indicated an affectionate and amiable disposition, and complete surprise or amazement was vivid upon the countenance of her entire audience. The discourse was one worthy of the attention of all who heard it—the sufferings of Jesus in and around Jerusalem—His temptation and trial of toil and misery—His holy life—His triumphant death and resurrection—His grand ascension to the realms of the blessed, were eloquently delineated. The certainty of death—the shortness of life—the never ending of the life beyond the grave were theories eagerly pressed for reception upon the minds of her hearers. Taking all in all, the discourse was well delivered and spiced with enough enthusiasm to produce good effect. But, Mr. Editor, the idea of a woman canvassing the world in behalf of the church is simply an incident so unusual that quite a number of us here eagerly inquire, what has become of the men? * * * *

Elizabeth R. Wheaton, for such is the name of our distinguished visitor, related among other things, that she was called and led by the God of Glory to go all over the world and preach the gospel to the lost children of men, that the prisons, saloons, dens of sin and pollution were the places of her special care. The huts of the poor and outcast were by her to be visited and that she did not ask for money, that her Master had promised to provide all things for her and did so daily.

SAW MOTHER WHEATON.

THE NOTED PRISON EVANGELIST VISITED THE COUNTY JAIL PRISONERS TODAY.

A kindly faced, white-haired old lady walked into the county jail this morning and asked permission to address the prisoners. She was "Mother" Elizabeth Rider Wheaton, the prison evangelist, who is known from coast to coast. As soon as her identity was made known Turnkey Reynolds and his corps of assistants did their utmost to assist the generous old lady. She was shown through the building, and then allowed to enter each ward.

From 11 o'clock until long after the noon hour she remained with the unfortunates, visiting them separately and then preaching to all. Tears were in the eyes of many of these hardened criminals before she had finished.

"Mother" Wheaton was met at the jail entrance and asked to explain her system of working. "It is all done by faith," she said. "I have faith in God, and that is sufficient. He will provide me with all that is necessary to carry on this work."

"Under whose guidance do you work?" was asked.

"The Lord's, and His only," was the reply.

"But are you not employed by some religious sect?"

"No. I do this on my own responsibility, and for the glory of God. For the past fifteen years this has been my life's work. I go where I please and do as I please."

"How far have you traveled?"

"Thousands and thousands of miles. Last year I was in Europe and have been all over America."

For the past forty years "Mother" Wheaton has been a professed believer in Christianity. Fifteen years ago she started in the work of visiting prisons, and has been in every place of detention in any city of note. She is received with the utmost courtesy both by the officials and the prisoners. Many of the latter have met her at different places, and most all the officials are acquainted with her and her work.—A Detroit paper.

THE PRISON EVANGELIST.

MRS. E. R. WHEATON DELIVERS AN ADDRESS AT THE PENITENTIARY CHAPEL SUNDAY MORNING.

The service at the penitentiary chapel Sunday was made memorable by the presence and discourse of Mrs. E. R. Wheaton, the world-known prison evangelist. Chaplain Winget conducted the services and offered the invocation and in a few explanatory remarks introduced Mrs. Wheaton. Mrs. Wheaton's hair is white as silver, but she still retains her ever-youthful appearance and sprightly step. She sang in an indescribably sweet, but powerful, voice "Some Mother's Child." At the conclusion of the singing Mrs. Wheaton preached a wonderful discourse. "I was on my way to Jerusalem," said she, "and had gotten as far as London, England, when the Lord turned me back to my own country and to my suffering boys in prison; and I said God bless my children, my boys, for I am their mother.

"Oh! how sad and discouraged many of you are, but if you will believe in God and read your Bible you will be comforted. How can any man have the heart not to believe the Bible and rest his case upon the bosom of the good Lord who died for us? I thank God that the good old-time religion still lives. The devil, my children, causes you all your sufferings and sorrows. Exchange him for Jesus. He will keep you. Forgive your enemies and submit yourself to the officers of the prison. You must obey—it is the Lord's will. He has placed you here for his own purpose, maybe for your soul's good and salvation. Jesus says, 'Come to me all ye that are heavy laden and I will give you rest.' Have faith. I am so sorry when some of you do wrong for the innocent must suffer with the guilty and society becomes stern with you. God bless you all."—Columbus, Ohio, paper.

MRS. ELIZABETH RIDER WHEATON PREACHES TO UNFORTUNATES.

VISITS THE BRIDEWELL AND HEARS THE COMPLAINT OF ONE OF THE CITY'S CHARGES.

"What's the use? What have I to hope for? Who cares for me? Who'll help me? What can I do when my time expires? Everybody's hand will be against me! A hopeless drunkard is past redemption."

Tears came to the eyes of Mrs. Elizabeth Rider Wheaton yesterday afternoon as she heard these words fall from the lips of a dejected prisoner at the bridewell. The prison and train evangelist whose work for fifteen years among convicts had brought her many such questions, which she was unable to answer to the satisfaction of the prisoners, spoke to the wretched man in tender tones, and told him of the consolation offered by religion.

"But," she said, turning to a reporter, "what can I do in one conversation? It needs many. I'm going back to Chicago next week, and I intend to devote considerable time to every prison and house of refuge in the city. I haven't done any work in the city since the anarchist execution."

Mrs. Wheaton's methods of evangelizing are sometimes dramatic. For instance, Mrs. Wheaton arrived in Chicago from St. Louis on a Wabash train early yesterday morning. Night before last, while the train was speeding along in the darkness, the occupants of the reclining chair car were startled.

"Look out!" cried a voice in shrill tones. "We're coming to a high bridge. Before we reach it we pass over a curve. The rails may be all right, the bridge may be safe; but who knows?"

The passengers turned around in their seats. They looked frightened and appeared anxious to know whether there was really an impending danger. They saw only a woman whose face, softened by grief, bore lines of pain and care. She was Mrs. Wheaton.

"But the Christian is not afraid to die," she continued. "He welcomes death as a release from care and a blessing."

Then the evangelist preached a sermon, to which all listened with attention.

Although Mrs. Wheaton has visited every state in the Union many times during her fifteen years of missionary work, she has been in a sleeping car but once. Railroads give her passes. She has no property, and, of course, can collect no money from convicts, though occasionally she receives a contribution on trains.

"The trouble of it all," said she after her talk with the man in the bridewell, "is not in the prisons. It is after the convicts get out. For that, humanity is to blame. Prisoners have not much hope, and some of them accept religion in a tentative sort of way.

"When they are released they are hounded by the police, marked by all citizens as ostracized men, unable to get employment, and, in fact, the second termers tell me they are reduced almost to the necessity of choosing between starvation and stealing. Those whose conversion is real do neither, because no man need ever starve in this country, but the weak go under and are brought back to jail. What the world needs is more Christian charity. We should forgive, as our Saviour did, seventy times seven."

In addition to her charm as a speaker, Mrs. Wheaton is a singer of no mean ability. She is not a believer in men who accept religion for the sake of business and put on a sanctimonious air. The view that she takes of life meets with favor among the convicts, and she sings a song called "The Twin Ballots," which illustrates her opinion on the temperance question. The song is about two rum votes that sanctioned the license plan, "but one was cast by a cunning brewer and one by a Sunday-school man."

The evangelist left last night for Pittsburg, but will return next week. She said she wished to impress upon people the fact that converted prisoners are not hypocrites, although the guards often suspect insincerity and treat a converted man worse than any other, because they think he is seeking to curry favor.—A Chicago paper.

A DISGRACEFUL PROCEEDING.

Thursday afternoon, Mrs. Elizabeth R. Wheaton, the noted prison evangelist, accompanied by a sister, asked permission from a policeman, which was granted, to hold a street meeting for religious purposes.

After singing some hymns, which, from their superior rendition, attracted a large crowd, Mrs. Wheaton, an elderly lady who has devoted seven years of her time entirely to prison evangelical work, began an earnest exhortation to sinners. After preaching for a few minutes Officer C. came up and said that the mayor had ordered him to put a stop to the proceedings.

Mrs. Wheaton said she would do her duty without fear of man and continued for a moment longer. Then the party knelt on the snow and began to pray for the mayor and the policeman. While they were praying the officer came up closely followed by Mayor J., and roughly pushed Mrs. Wheaton over. The mayor with fire in his eye as well as his complexion, spoke in a very rude manner to the ladies, practically endorsing the rough treatment already accorded the party.

Mrs. Wheaton showed *The Dispatch* credentials from very high sources and a very bulky bundle of railroad passes which gave substantial evidence of the manner in which she and her work are regarded elsewhere.

She has traveled over the United States and Mexico, and parts of Europe, and it remained for a Leadville mayor to break the record and treat her with indignity. She was very much shocked and grieved and said she felt deeply sorry for Leadville, which she had often heard spoken of as a wicked city.

The Dispatch is free to say that Mayor J. acted without adequate provocation and displayed an unnecessary exercise of authority. If the services had been prolonged to any great extent he might have sent a request to have them discontinued, but there was no occasion for any such arbitrary exhibition of power as was made.

Far greater blockades with less meritorious objects have existed without protest in Leadville. A medicine faker who pays a few dollars license can yell and sing and make night hideous for hours and it is all right, but a humble evangelical missionary, whose sincerity and good intentions are not doubted, however persons may differ concerning the methods, is unceremoniously made to move on. If the authorities displayed as much zeal in suppressing vice as they do in shutting off missionaries, Leadville would be a model city.

The prison evangelists, after having been ordered off Harrison avenue, visited both city and county jails, where they were kindly received and permitted by the officers to hold services among the prisoners. It is said that this is the first religious service held in the Leadville jails.—Leadville, Colo., Dispatch, March, 1891.

DISGRACEFUL.

Last night, when the ladies who have been conducting religious services in the park, were preparing to close, some miscreant in human form threw a small torpedo at them and struck Mrs. Wheaton above the right eye. It did not produce any serious injury, but was very painful at the time, and may terminate worse than at first supposed. This act evidently issued from some low, depraved fiend whom the darkness of the hour shielded from justice. The ladies departed from the city this morning, and the exact result of the disgraceful episode cannot be learned. As soon as it was done some man in the crowd offered $100 reward for the identification of the party who did the dastardly trick, but of course no one knew who the miscreant was except he himself.—Jacksonville, Ill., paper, June 26, 1887.

THE PRISON EVANGELIST.

"Elizabeth Rider Wheaton, prison evangelist, Chicago, Ill. Meet me in heaven. No home but heaven." This is what is printed on the card of a remarkable woman who visited the penitentiary and talked to the convicts at 11 o'clock on Sunday. This woman has been engaged in this work for about nine years, and she has visited nearly every prison and jail in the United States, Canada and Mexico. She is the Moody of the convict world. She asks for no money. She gives her services free, and trusts to Providence for her support. "The Lord provides," she says. She has held services in a different state or territorial prison the past five Sundays, from Stillwater, Minn. (where Cole Younger is confined and assists in and sometimes leads religious services), to Salem, Oregon. Mrs. Wheaton also visits reform schools. She is one of the chief advocates of the reformatory system being adopted in some of the Eastern prisons whereby convicts of different classes are graded and kept separate, wear different uniforms, etc., and are also let out on furloughs on trial or probation. Mrs. Wheaton devotes her whole time to prison work. She certainly accomplishes some good from all this effort. She was a Methodist before taking up this life work, but now holds to no sect.—Salem, Oregon, paper, Nov. 16, 1891.

A NOBLE WORK.

Among the evangelistic workers who go out among the people seeking the low and degraded and trying to lift them up to be better men and women, Elizabeth R. Wheaton is one of the chosen few who is well adapted to this work. She asks no pay and receives none, but with noble purpose and with heart and mind fully in the work which has been given her, she travels from Maine to California and from British Columbia to the Gulf of Mexico.

Her work is chiefly among the state prisons, county jails and reform schools. Here she meets a class of people schooled in vice and who have been kept face to face with the different evils all their lives; these are the people whom she seeks to save.

Mrs. Wheaton has just returned from a successful trip through Mexico and the South and is now on her way to Walla Walla, Portland and British Columbia. She stopped off here to visit our penitentiary and jail. Through the kindness of the warden she held a song service last Sunday at the State penitentiary, and the amount of good which she did was shown by the eager attention of the convicts, and the tear-stained faces of some who, when the good old-fashioned hymns were sung, thought of their far-away homes and mothers. Sunday evening she held services at the jail and on the street, both of which were much appreciated.—Unidentified.

GOSPEL FOR THE PRISONERS.

THE INMATES OF ATLANTA'S PRISONS HEARD PREACHING YESTERDAY.

The prisoners at police headquarters, at the jail and at the city stockade listened to the gospel of Christ yesterday.

Mrs. Elizabeth Rider Wheaton, the famous prison evangelist, of Washington, held services at all these places. Her talks were of the most interesting character and evidently made deep impressions upon her hearers.

The service at the jail was held in the morning, the one at the stockade in the afternoon, and the one at the police station at night.

Mrs. Wheaton is perhaps the most famous evangelist of her kind in the country. She makes a specialty of this work and follows it closely week after week. She has preached to convicts and prisoners in every state in the Union, frequently traveling as far as 700 miles between Sundays in order to make an appointment. She has letters of introduction from the governors of many states, and free passes on railroads. She is here with the Christian Workers, but is not a delegate.—Atlanta, Ga., paper, Nov. 14, 1893.

PRISON EVANGELISTS.

THE INMATES OF THE COUNTY JAIL TREATED TO A SERMON.

Mrs. Elizabeth Rider Wheaton, the prison evangelist, who has been traveling over the United States for ten years past, and two sisters from Washington, D. C., and Kansas City, arrived in the city this morning and held religious service in the county jail. The twenty-four inmates of the bastile were much pleased with the service.

Mrs. Wheaton and her companions held services yesterday at the prison at Lansing, Kan., where 900 convicts are confined. Lately they have come from the convict camp of South Carolina and Mrs. Wheaton can tell many tales of the sufferings endured by the prisoners there.—Unidentified.

THE NEWS AT LEAVENWORTH.

MOTHER WHEATON, PRISON EVANGELIST, VISITS THE UNITED STATES PRISON.

Religious services at the federal penitentiary at Fort Leavenworth yesterday were somewhat out of the usual order. Mother Wheaton, the prison evangelist, late of Washington, D. C., now of Iowa, preached to the convicts at the morning hour. Her address was a most effective one and men all through the audience were moved to tears. At the close of the service she stood at the chapel door and shook the hand of each prisoner as he went out.

Her head is white with age, yet she has visited the prisons of the United States and many in Europe, bearing messages of hope and cheer to the condemned. She is not alone a woman of ready speech, but is a sweet singer as well. Her life is dedicated to her work, and many is the unfortunate who has cause to bless the visit of Mother Wheaton. Mrs. T., of this city, accompanied her to the prison.—Leavenworth, Kan., paper.

JAIL SERVICE.

The inmates of the county jail were honored yesterday by a visit from that well known prison evangelist, Elizabeth Rider Wheaton, who was accompanied by a Mrs. S., of Kansas. Mrs. Wheaton conducted religious services and her talk had a deep effect upon murderer Williamson, the old man being visibly moved.

Mrs. Wheaton has made the visiting of prisons, condemned men and fallen women her life work, and in the course of her travels during the past seven years has visited Europe, the British provinces, Mexico and the United States. As an example of her earnest efforts it may be mentioned that during the past thirteen Sundays she has visited and held services in fourteen different state penitentiaries. Mrs. Wheaton is a lady of striking appearance. She has a motherly countenance and a magnetism which attracts the closest attention to what she says. Her discourse yesterday was eloquent, yet at times plain and pointed to severity. Mrs. Wheaton left yesterday on the afternoon train for the Pacific coast.—Sedalia, Mo., paper, November, 1891.

PREACHED TO CONVICTS.

Mrs. Elizabeth Rider Wheaton, the noted evangelist, and Mrs. Perry, who are engaged in preaching and working among the prisons, visited the Virginia penitentiary yesterday and held services in each chapel. Their exhortations and singing were of a high order and produced a powerful effect among the prisoners. Many of them made a profession of faith. Mrs. Wheaton has preached in most of the penitentiaries of the United States. She has also traveled and preached in Canada and Mexico as well as in the Old World. The ladies are being entertained by Superintendent Lynn and will remain in the city several days.

POLICE STATION SERVICES.

MRS. ELIZABETH RIDER WHEATON TALKS TO THE MEMBERS OF THE FORCE.

Mrs. Elizabeth Rider Wheaton, the evangelist, was at the police station last night at roll call and held a short service for the benefit of the members of the police force. She delivered an interesting address to the officers and offered a prayer, after which she led them in a song. The officers expressed themselves as having been greatly benefited by the service, and the evangelist was invited to call again.—Unidentified.

SERVICES AT THE WORKHOUSE.

"Mother" Wheaton, the prison evangelist, who was mentioned last Monday as holding meetings in Island Park the day before, called at the police station this morning to ask permission to talk and sing to the prisoners confined in the workhouse. The permission was granted. The lady has traveled extensively in her evangelistic work, making flying trips all over the United States especially. Within the last thirty days she has talked to prisoners at Walla Walla, Tacoma and in other northwestern cities. While in this city she is the guest of her sister, Mrs. Huffman, of Kenwood.—Elkhart (Ind.) Paper.

A Strange Life of Devotion in Neglected Fields.

The prisoners in the Dade coal mines made the acquaintance yesterday of two women—two religious tramps, if you please, using the word literally—whose adventures in evangelizing are probably without parallel.

They are Mrs. Elizabeth Rider Wheaton, the famous prison evangelist, and her temporary assistant, Mrs. P.

Mrs. Wheaton has for ten years been preaching in prisons, convict camps, houses of ill-fame and the like, not only in the United States, but in Canada, Mexico and Europe. One, upon meeting her, would naturally be very uncertain as to where one might or might not meet next this spirit-led traveler—recognizing which uncertainty, perhaps, she has printed upon her cards, in lieu of an earthly address:

"Meet me in heaven."

The two women visited the jail Thursday, becoming very much interested in the case of P. S., it seems, on account of his relationship to Rev. S. J. Mrs. Wheaton spoke of P. as a "beautiful black-eyed young married man."

They took part in the Christian alliance meeting Friday afternoon at 51 James street, at which over thirty people were present.

They will hold special services at the coal mine convict camps to-day, returning to Atlanta within a few days. They carry this letter—an "open sesame" to every prison and camp in Georgia:

> "Atlanta, Ga., June 30.—To the captain in charge of convict camps in Georgia: I desire that each of you extend to these ladies, Mrs. Wheaton and Mrs. ——, any courtesies possible during their stay with you; that they may be given opportunities to talk to the men and women in your charge. I will particularly appreciate any kindness shown them. The governor also requests that they be shown courtesies."

It is signed by George H. Jones, the principal keeper. "Courtesies," by the way, is spelled "curtisys" in the letter, but it's official, and "it goes."

Return to Atlanta—that is to say they will return unless the spirit moves Mrs. Wheaton to go on from Chattanooga to St. Louis, or Montreal, or Berlin, or somewhere else.

Coming to Atlanta on the Richmond and Danville, Mrs. Wheaton was moved to hold services in the smoking car. Just as the train was rolling out of Calhoun, S. C., Mrs. Wheaton spied some convicts at work.

Convicts!

Instantly she decided to stop over. She and Mrs. P. bundled up their wraps and packages and got off after the train had started. They knew nobody there. They had no money—that is, "not enough to count." Somehow or other they got transportation to and from the station, and supper, and to other works, and arranged a meeting. It was a glorious meeting, they say.

Mrs. Wheaton's faith—and railroad passes, she adds laughingly—have kept her going for ten years.

She traveled 5,000 miles between one Sunday and the second Sunday afterwards, collecting only fifty cents on the way.

The Lord will provide, she knows.

The faith that removes mountains is here in reality.

Always on the go—never stopping but a day or two in one place—meeting men to be hanged the next day—praying with fallen women—interceding with governors for human life—blindly following, without regard to time or distance, the mysterious dictates of what she calls "the Spirit."

She is so well known now throughout the United States—having been engaged in this work for ten years—that she is rarely refused a railroad pass. She has letters of commendation from governors and prison authorities. * * *

Mrs. Wheaton's services in the jails and convict camps are unique, remarkable for their fervency and impromptu character. Singing plays an important part. * * *

Mrs. Wheaton has made many wonderful conversions in the slums and prisons, and has seen many famous criminals in their last hours.

She is the guest in Atlanta of Mrs. J. H. Murphy, at 267 East Cain street.— Atlanta (Ga.) Herald, July 2, 1893.

PREACHING ON THE STREETS.

Thursday evening the sound of an alto voice singing a familiar hymn on Sandy street, near Murphy's corner, soon gathered a crowd, when a lady, whose hair was beginning to silver with gray, mounted a box and preached to the mixed assemblage a sermon, after which the singing was resumed, the meeting concluding with a fervent and earnest prayer. A reporter called at the hotel and learned that the lady was Mrs. Elizabeth R. Wheaton, a prison evangelist. Heretofore she has had a "sister" to travel with her. She showed the reporter stacks of letters from the wardens of various state penitentiaries, commending her, and praising the work she has done in this specialty. She has preserved files of newspaper criticisms, many of which are complimentary of the work she has done, and some from the secular press making light of her work.

That she is in earnest no one who considers that she has given up home and friends and roamed all over the United States, Canada, Mexico and in part of Europe to preach to unappreciative street crowds, prison convicts, etc., can doubt. And whatever may be said of the method, as was illustrated on the streets here last night, there are many reached with a sermon that have not perhaps heard one for months.—Unidentified.

PRAYER SERVICE IN JAIL.

Through the efforts of Mrs. E. R. Wheaton, the prison evangelist, the county jail was turned into a house of prayer last evening, and for an hour or more the walls of the building resounded with the shouts of prayer and praise of this earnest woman.

During the afternoon Mrs. Wheaton called on Gregory, the horsethief and desperado, and was the first to bring to the surface in his case any signs of remorse or sentiment of any kind. When the gray-haired and motherly woman took the hand of the confessed thief and ex-convict in hers and prayed for him great tears flowed down his cheeks and he was affected as none of the other prisoners had been. Gregory said he had known Mrs. Wheaton for fourteen years. She does not remember him, but says it is not unlikely that he has seen her if he has been in the several prisons in which it is said he has served time, as she has been visiting them all off and on in her work for a great many years.—Council Bluffs, Iowa, Nonpareil, Jan. 19, 1900.

THEIR WORK IS IN PRISONS.

Party of Evangelists Pay a Visit to the County Jail.

Mrs. Elizabeth Rider Wheaton, the prison evangelist, was in Butte for a short time yesterday on her way west, and between trains conducted services in the corridor of the county jail.

In addition to being an earnest exhorter, Mrs. Wheaton, despite the fact that she is well advanced in years, is the possessor of a fine voice. When she sings in a prison the most hardened criminals never fail to listen to her with great respect. During the services in the jail yesterday clerks and court officers ceased from their duties and with the people who had business in the building, blocked the passage ways leading to the jail to listen to her.

The other members of the party also delivered exhortations and joined in the singing. The farewell hymn, given in a clear soprano voice by Mrs. Wheaton, "God be with you till we meet again," was especially sweet. Whether the services made any lasting impression on the men behind the bars cannot be known, but the fact remains that when they were over there was an unusual quiet in the jail and the air seemed more wholesome. From Butte she went to Deer Lodge to visit the penitentiary.—Butte, Montana, paper, 1897.

STREET SERVICES.

On Wednesday and Thursday our town was visited by two lady missionaries or preachers of the gospel. They were perfect strangers here and claimed that their mission was to try to open the eyes of sinful people and beg them to come to Christ. They sang, prayed and preached upon the streets, and at the colored church, having been refused the use of some of the white churches. We know not whom these persons are, or from where they came, but we do know that they were very lady-like in their conduct, and there was a terrible earnestness about their work. They preached pure gospel in the most Christ-like manner that it was ever our privilege to hear—down upon their knees in the streets, surrounded by a motley multitude, begging God in a most pleading and fervent manner to save the sinners of this place, and singing glorious praises to Him on this beautiful day of national thanksgiving, was a spectacle that we had never expected to witness. Whether or not this is proper in the eyes of the world we cannot say, but if their work is earnest as it seems, they will be rewarded in heaven.—Unidentified.

FOR PRISONERS.

TOUCHING SCENES IN BANGOR JAIL.—GOOD DEEDS THAT SHINE IN MORAL DARKNESS.

Never were gospel hymns—words of comfort set to hopeful music, sang more sweetly and earnestly, or with better effect than were the songs of a plainly dressed woman of tranquil face and gentle manner in the echoing corridors of Bangor jail Tuesday afternoon.

This woman was Mrs. Elizabeth Rider Wheaton whose home is everywhere in earth's saddest ways. She is a prison evangelist and her card bears the simple admonition: "Prepare to Meet Thy God."

She came lately to Maine, and arrived in Bangor Tuesday noon from Belfast. On the train Mrs. Wheaton talked of Christian things, and she sang hymns to the passengers—"Throw Out the Life Line" and other well-remembered songs—in a way that reached the hearts of all. When she got here she went for a few minutes to a low-priced hotel, and thence to the county jail. The officials received her kindly, and the prisoners, who, after their dinner of soup, had gone into the work shop, were brought in to hear some of the kindest words and most touching songs that they had listened to for many a day.

Those innocent and comfortable Christians who have only heard hymns sung in churches or chapels to well-dressed and presumably good people can have no idea of the sweetly weird effect of gospel melodies swelling in the vast and dismal spaces of a jail, while gathered around are the very lost sheep that the shepherds of churches are commanded to find. It is a reproachful picture from the realism of blasted lives—a startling, chilling glimpse of the depth of wretchedness, lighted up by a feeble ray from the goodness that yet survives amid it all.

Some old and hardened habitues of jails mock and sneer at the voices raised in their behalf and scoff at the hands held out to lift them up, but most men, in jail or out, treat women like this with silent respect. It was so in the jail Tuesday.

When the men had filed out to the broom shop again Mrs. Wheaton went to a cell occupied by two elderly women and talked and sang to them. The women, whose wickedness all lay in drink, seemed pleased and affected. They thought this evangelist the kindest they had ever met.

The evangelist may hold some meetings here before she leaves. She was much pleased with her reception in Bangor, and would like to remain a few days. She has letters of recommendation from the governors of several states and from the officials of numerous prisons. She belongs to no army or organization, but travels independently, doing what good she can.— Bangor, Me., paper.

ELIZABETH R. WHEATON.

THE NOTED PRISON EVANGELIST PAYS THE TRINIDAD JAILS A VISIT.

Elizabeth R. Wheaton, the well-known prison evangelist, arrived in the city Monday evening and yesterday visited the county and city jails, where she talked and prayed with the poor unfortunates confined therein. * * * More than one poor fellow has blessed the short hour when her motherly presence and sweetly spoken words of comfort have made his fate seem easier to bear, while repentant tears have filled the eyes of many a hardened criminal when listening to her pleadings. She approaches the most degraded with a familiar motherly air, which at once wins their most profound respect and reverence. * * *

Mrs. Wheaton expects to leave today for Pueblo where she will be joined by a sister in the work, when they will continue their journey together. She spoke very highly of the courteous treatment received from the officers and of the cleanly condition of the jails.—Daily Advertiser, Trinidad, Colo.

VISIT FROM MISSIONARIES.

Elizabeth Rider Wheaton, better known as "Mother Wheaton," the prison evangelist, and Mrs. Elizabeth Taylor, of Tabor, Iowa, called at the Institution Thursday afternoon on a missionary errand. Mother Wheaton has spent fifteen years in evangelical work among the inmates of the various prisons throughout the United States. Her friends among the convicts are numbered by the thousands. We so rarely meet with any one who really sympathizes with us in our misfortune that when these two good women come inside the walls for no other purpose but to encourage us to do better and give assurance of their love and good wishes, we are made to feel that we are still human and may hope for a better day. By reason of the chapel building undergoing repairs, it was impossible for them to meet many of the boys or hold services.—A Prison Paper.

A REMARKABLE SCENE.

A WORK OF LOVE BY AN ELDERLY LADY.—THE SCENERY OF OAK CLIFF.

Last night the moon shed its full luster slightly dimmed by thin clouds.

The crowd stood by a negro church at the point of the hill, just above the creek banks at their intersection. The view from the top of the hill was enchanting.

The lady passed the crowd and stopped in the moonshine in front of the church. Here she was joined by a party of three other ladies and two men, whom she had preceded a little. Two of the ladies held babies in their arms.

In a strong and beautiful alto voice a song burst forth from the lips of the elderly lady: "I Will Tell the Wondrous Story of the Christ Who Died for Me." Her companions joined her in the song and the refrain echoed far and near over the hillsides: "Of the Christ who died for me."

The inhabitants heard it.

But this is the part of Oak Cliff inhabited by negroes. In response they swarmed out as would have done the followers to the signal of Roderick Dhu.

Pretty soon the church was filled and a few white people were among the audience drawn thither by the song.

The services were begun with prayer by the elderly lady, whose hair, when she had removed her bonnet, shone silvery gray. It was nothing out of the usual order of prayers except that it was accompanied with unusual fervor and simplicity being adapted to the circumstances. If any had assembled through curiosity she prayed that their hearts would be turned.

Then came other singing and prayer by a good colored sister named Cynthia Maria, who wore a white bonnet, and chanted her words, making the scene a wierd one.

Then the elderly lady rendered in beautiful solo, "Oh Christ, I am lost forever. I am to confront an angry God," from which she began her discourse, pleading to her colored hearers to open their hearts that night. She said she had the old time religion. This announcement was greeted with religious laughter from the congregation. The women had not been allowed to preach and she thought that there were souls in perdition on this account. People said that she had no business there last night. She had business in glory and was going to help crown Christ the Lord of Lords. For seven years she had been a pilgrim and had traveled from ocean to ocean and from state to state without receiving a salary or taking up a cent. There was the same God with her who was with Daniel in the lions' den, and who led the Children of Israel through the Red Sea. She had seen sore trouble, but there were few who knew it. She had the old-time religion, and that was what her hearers needed. She forsook home and country to go and preach the gospel to convicts and fallen women and most of her friends had forsaken her for this. She used to be proud. She had given up pride and given up style. She was glad that God had called the meeting. She did not know that she was to preach there until yesterday afternoon when someone informed her that the colored people wanted her to preach. She had visited the county jail last Sunday and prayed and sang with the prisoners. Some of them had forgotten about the old-time religion and requested her to sing the song having that title.

Here the woman began that song joined by the congregation, a large number of whom got happy. It required the efforts of several of the colored portion of the congregation to hold down one sister who wore a straw hat and got shouting happy and paid no attention to her surroundings.

After a short talk by Rev. B., colored, the congregation was dismissed.

AT THE COLORED CHURCH.

MRS. ELIZABETH R. WHEATON LECTURES ON THE IMPORTANCE OF CONVERSION—SHE SAYS THE HARDEST PEOPLE TO CONVERT ARE PREACHERS.

As a News reporter and a News special artist, guided by a friendly star, wended their muddy way last night to the little negro church upon the hill at Oak Cliff, they overtook two solemn looking figures going up an incline. One of them proved to be the famous prison evangelist, Mrs. Elizabeth R. Wheaton. This lady turned her face to the News emissaries and inquired in a sweet silvery tone:

"Going to church, brothers?"

"Yes, ma'am."

"Oh, God bless you, brothers, come on."

A few minutes later the church was reached. The penitent sister with the white bonnet, who was inspired on the previous night and started to shouting, had already arrived, as also had the good sister who called on the baseball man to run from the devil. What influence drives those simple worshipers to shouting and to imitate flying, is a question for the psychologists. Certain it is that the little and the great are linked together in this life and perhaps the present is linked to the future. Quien sabe. The meeting last night was free from shouting, but fervid with emotion. On arriving in front of the church Mrs. Wheaton turned her face to the pale moon, which had sailed high in the heavens, and sang "Sweet are the tidings that greet the pilgrims' ear." As she sung she gesticulated and her gray hair shone like silver. She had not gone beyond the third line of the said stirring hymn before the penitents inside of the church started to sing a hymn and then the scene was as impressive as the music was discordant. The hymns over, Mrs. Wheaton knelt on the wet ground and prayed while Deacon Banks did likewise inside of the church. The interjections were so many that he was forced to use short sentences.

"Come one, come all, while it is day."

"O, yes, Lord, we come, we'se a'comin'."

"O Lord, put the move on and call us away."

"O, yes, good Lord, we come."

At this point Mrs. Wheaton entered and ascended the low pulpit from which, for a moment, she silently surveyed the assembled multitude of black faces. She was wreathed in smiles, looking like the sun of righteousness shining on a dark, murky cloud of suffering humanity.

"God grant," she observed, "that nobody goes down to the lake of fire." "God grant it, ma-a-a-m." "Oh-oh-bo-bo." "Nobody knows de trouble I see," and any number of exclamations each giving vent to an exclamation suited to the feelings of the penitent. The mention of fire seemed to cause a panic among the good colored people with a single exception. He was a dude who did not deign to sit down, but stood near the door seemingly watching the females. Only once did he drop on his knees and that was when he discovered the News artist in the act of tracing his outlines on the flyleaf of a prayer book.

Mrs. Wheaton then lectured upon the importance of conversion. As she proceeded, describing the fate of convicts and other sufferers, the iron of the ways of the world seemed to enter her soul and she wept. Nobody who hears her doubts her sincerity. She does not criticise the fallen; she weeps for them. The folks in heaven do the same. Only once last night did she criticise, and she said she did it for a benevolent purpose, and as she did it (as indeed throughout her entire remarks) the colored woman with the man's straw hat interlarded her remarks with her own opinions rendered in a whanging, chanting voice. This was how it ran: "The churches have got away from the old land marks [yes, ma'am; deed they has, ma'am]. It is hard, hard work to reach preachers [yes, ma'am; yes, ma'am]. The big white preachers and the colored preachers are nearly just as bad [O Lord, yes; good Lord ye-e-s, ma'am.] They put on plug hats, jewelry and the trickery of the devil. If preachers would do their duty I would not have to visit the penitentiaries. Oh, the hardest work I have is to preach to preachers. [Dat's so, ma'am; dat's so!] How many of you are living in lasciviousness, the sin that's hidden but that God sees? It is going on in the churches among some of the preachers. [Ah, yes, ma'am: good Lord! Deed'n 'tis, ma'am]. Ah! I have got to go to judgment and I will tell you the truth. There are other sins, but I do not want to mention them because I feel that you know all about them; but they won't be hidden and unless you have a pure spirit and a clean heart you can never see the face of God. Now say you will sin no more. [Several voices in alto: A-a-a-men.] These white churches," proceeded Mrs. Wheaton, "are a little worse than the colored churches, for there is a little Holy Ghost left in the colored churches. Oh, how many of those white church members are going down to hell! It grieves me to think of it. I'm going to meet some of you in glory. After I get there the first ones I want to see crowned are the poor convicts who have been murdered on the scaffold after they had turned their faces to God, and those poor convicts who have suffered, oh, you know not how much, how much, without human sympathy."

At this point a sad-looking man volunteered a hymn, during the singing of which much of Mrs. Wheaton's remarks were drowned. Mrs. Wheaton resumed: "It troubles my heart to see the people drifting down, down to hell. I feel like getting down to the foot of the cross and crying mercy. For the attractions of this world I have no use; I have no use for newspaper puffs. [They's no good, ma'am: yes, ma'am.]"

The way in which the penitents chimed in as Mrs. Wheaton proceeded rendered it impossible to report her fully. The best that could be done was to catch sentences on the fly. The stronger she appeared to her colored listeners to seek for mercy the longer they sought it. Their bodies were moved by their souls. Some swayed from side to side; others placed their faces on their hands and wept; others wrung their hands, and there was weeping and wailing.

This was the state of affairs at the conclusion of the address. Just then Deacon Banks started a hymn and a few others drifted off into different familiar hymns, so that the music was varied. It was a spontaneous outburst of songs of praise from away down in the bottom of afflicted hearts which pays no attention to the measures of music. The singing was awful. One female screeched and no two voices were in harmony.

At the conclusion of the hymn a deacon kneeling by a chair prayed, striking the chair with his fists while a hundred voices accompanied him. It was impossible to follow him throughout, but among other things he said: "I know that hell is broad and eternity too long. Oh King, King, Lord have mercy on us. Guide us by the still water's side and give us new pastures. Bless this congregation in the hollow of thy hand, amen."

Mrs. Wheaton informed the News reporter that she will not go to Galveston.—Dallas News.

PRISON WORKER VISITS TACOMA.

"MOTHER" WHEATON CALLS AT COUNTY JAIL AND FEDERAL PENITENTIARY.—KNOWN ALL OVER THE WORLD.— TWENTY-ONE YEARS OF HER LIFE DEVOTED TO LABOR AMONG UNFORTUNATES OF MANY NATIONS.

"I trust in God and the railroad men."

This is the explanation of her ability to carry on her work, expressed by "Mother" Wheaton, the prison evangelist, who has an international reputation for her work in the penitentiaries of the United States, Canada, Mexico and Europe. Mother Wheaton is in Tacoma carrying on her work among prisoners, work that has taken her into every penitentiary in the United States and Canada. For over twenty-one years she has carried the gospel to the men in stripes and to those who wear the broad arrow of England's displeasure, and it is Mother Wheaton's boast that during all that time she has never asked for a contribution or received a cent of salary.

Mother Wheaton came to Tacoma from her headquarters in Tabor, Ia., accompanying Miss Grace Yarrette, a young woman who is going as a missionary to India.

MANY YEARS IN PRISON WORK.

There is no woman in the world, and perhaps no man, who has had the prison experience of Mother Wheaton. The last twenty years of her life have virtually been spent inside prison walls, and there is not many in the country in which she is not a familiar figure. Long terms and lifers all over the land know her. Frequently she inquires for some prisoner whom death or the leniency of the law has released, whom she has not seen or heard of for years.

Dressed in a soft gray suit, with a gray bonnet, Mother Wheaton's appearance is distinctly motherly, and her smile the personification of kindness and tenderness further bears out the "Mother" by which she is known to thousands of unfortunates. She is the guest of Mrs. Ellen M. Bates, 1211 North Prospect street. She is at work from the time she arises in the morning until services are over in the evening. While her principal work is in the prisons and penitentiaries she takes part in evangelical and religious work and finds time to visit rescue homes where her advice is eagerly sought.

MANY EXPERIENCES.

"Experiences?" Mother Wheaton exclaimed, when asked if her life had not been productive of many events out of the ordinary run. "Experiences, why I have had so many and such varied experiences that they are all a jumble in my head. I have been in nearly every prison in the land. I have consoled men who were but a few feet from the gallows and I have held the hand of those unfortunates as they sank into their last sleep in a cheerless prison hospital.

"I have seen sights that made my blood run cold and then I have had the joy of seeing the word of God prevail and the most case-hardened sinners the human mind could conceive of have reformed before me. It has been a curious mixture of sunshine and shadows, but after twenty-one years I think I can say that the sunshine has predominated. I put my trust in God for my work and I trust the railroad men for transportation, and between the two I believe I have been fairly successful."

ONCE TAKEN FOR CARRIE NATION.

"I have spent nights in the toughest slums of New York, Chicago and St. Louis, places where men by force of habit always carry their hand near their hip pocket, and I have not always been welcomed. Sometimes I have been roughly handled, yes, indeed. Why, one time I was mistaken for Carrie Nation. Of course I don't look like Carrie Nation, and I would never think of adopting smashing methods. I was holding services in San Pedro, California, one night, and went into a saloon. There were two bright looking young men standing at the bar and I asked them to come with me. The owner of the saloon was sitting at a faro table in the back end of the saloon, and as soon as he caught sight of me he rushed at me and literally threw me out into the street.

"When he learned afterwards who I was he was very sorry and avowed that he would never have treated me in that manner had he not thought that I was Carrie Nation and that I had a hatchet to chop up his expensive bar fixtures."

OPPOSES CAPITAL PUNISHMENT.

"As sad an experience as I ever had in my life was my effort to save the life of a young man who was condemned to hang in Colorado. I heard of the case through the young man's mother, who was heart-broken. I interceded with Governor Peabody and secured a reprieve for a year, and when Governor McDonald took office he fixed the date for the death of the young man. I tried to save him the second time, but public sentiment demanded his death. I don't believe in capital punishment. I have seen how a man can be punished in prison and I don't believe in taking a life to avenge a life, for stripped of all the specious arguments which surround capital punishment, it simmers down to nothing more than revenge."

ESTABLISHES NEW RECORD.

"I think I established a prison visiting record upon one trip. I visited five penitentiaries in as many states in a week. I started at Deer Lodge, Montana; from there I went to Boise, Idaho; then to Rawlins, Wyo.; then to Salt Lake City, and from Salt Lake City to Lincoln, Nebraska, all of which I call pretty fast traveling. I hold meetings on the train, in depots, at water tanks, any place I can gather a little knot of people together, and I could tell of some queer conversions in out of the way places, the last places in the world where you would expect the seed to sprout and bear fruit.

"I was over to the federal prison on McNeil's Island Saturday, and this morning I went to the county hospital. This afternoon I called at the county jail. I will be here a day or so longer and then must start East, as I have work to do in New York City. You see I will have to stop at the prisons on the way back and I have to make allowances for delays."

Mother Wheaton has become interested in Grace Russell, the young woman in the county jail, who is addicted to the use of morphine. Mother Wheaton will try to secure a place for her in some home.—Tacoma, Washington, paper of July 31, 1905.

I give the following extract from a Baltimore paper published while I was there attending the Convocation of Prayer in that city, January, 1903:

SPIRITUAL ADVISER OF FAMOUS CRIMINALS.

WORK OF "MOTHER" WHEATON IN PRISONS ALL OVER THE LAND.

For twenty years Mrs. Wheaton has been traveling throughout the United States, Europe, Canada and Mexico, working among prisoners in hundreds of prisons and penitentiaries. On a number of occasions she has converted criminals under death sentence. She has preached in the Maryland Penitentiary.

Mrs. Wheaton came to Baltimore direct from Ohio, where she had been holding prayer in the cells of the state prison with eight men condemned to die. She was in San Francisco a number of years ago when Alexander Goldenson killed his sweetheart, Mamie Kelly, and after Goldenson had been tried, convicted and sentenced to death "Mother" Wheaton prayed with him for forty days. The day of the execution, September 14, 1888, he was converted through her instrumentality, and just before walking to the gallows she tied her silk handkerchief about the condemned man's neck.

IS NOT A STRANGER.

OLD-TIMERS AT COUNTY JAIL GREET MRS. WHEATON AS LONG-TIME FRIEND.

Mrs. Elizabeth R. Wheaton, of Tabor, Ia., famous in this and other countries as a worker among the inmates of jails and penitentiaries, yesterday morning went to the county jail and prayed and sang hymns with the prisoners in the tanks.

Although her time was very much circumscribed, Mrs. Wheaton shook hands with most of the prisoners, many of whom had heard of her, and some of whom had met her in other prisons. John King, awaiting his transportation to Walla Walla, and one of the most admittedly professional criminals in the jail, stated that he had met "Mother Wheaton" several times before, both at Salem and at Walla Walla.

Both he and J. H. Le Roy, another old-timer, had many anecdotes to tell of her kindnesses in past years.—Paper of August 9, 1905.

> The above sketch was accompanied by a cut from protograph taken by the reporter and a nicely finished photograph presented me. From this photograph the cut was made that is inserted at the beginning of this chapter.—E. R. W.

PRISONERS ON BENDED KNEE.

INMATES OF COUNTY JAIL BOW IN PRAYER WITH MOTHER WHEATON.

On bended knees and with low bowed heads nine prisoners at the county jail reverently followed a prayer addressed to the throne of grace in their behalf yesterday by Mother Wheaton, the noted prison evangelist. Under the remarkable influence of the woman who came among them as a messenger of soul-saving, every rough instinct of the men was quelled and every scoffing word hushed on their lips. No more devout prayer meeting was ever held in a sanctuary than that which took place in the jail corridor.

Mother Wheaton and a younger woman called upon the prisoners and sang a song such as the men might have heard their mothers or sisters sing in the long ago, when their feet had not strayed from youthful paths of innocence. If there was any inclination to ridicule or make light of the service at the start, it was entirely subdued inside of five minutes. Mother Wheaton talked to the men and told of the work she has been doing for twenty years among the inmates of jails and penitentiaries. She declared that she and her assistant wanted to help save them.

There was no hesitation whatever when Mother Wheaton asked the prisoners to get down on their knees. One and all, the nine assumed the attitude of humble submission to the deity and remained in that position until their patroness had finished her petition for the pardoning of their sins. Some of the men were seen to blink significantly and wipe their eyes with handkerchiefs. When the prayer was done and another hymn rendered, the men joining in, hands were shaken all around before the visitors departed.

Mother Wheaton has been coming to the Council Bluffs jail for several years. She was in the city on her way from Nevada to Wisconsin.—*Council Bluffs Paper.*

CHAPTER XXV.

Furnished unto Every Good Work.

Who will man the life-boat, who the storm will brave? Many souls are drifting helpless on the wave; See their hands uplifted; hear their bitter cry: "Save us ere we perish, save us ere we die!"

See! amid the breakers yonder vessel toss'd, Onward to the rescue, haste, or all is lost; Waves that dash around us cannot overwhelm, While our faithful Pilot standeth at the helm.

Darker yet, and darker grows the fearful night, Sound the trump of mercy, flash the signal light; Bear the joyful message o'er the raging wave, Christ, the heavenly Pilot, comes the lost to save.

Who will man the life-boat, who will launch away? Who will help to rescue dying souls to-day? Who will man the life-boat, who will breast the wave? All its dangers braving, precious souls to save?

—

Sel.

The dear Lord wants workers, both men and women, whom He can trust in every line of Christian work, and what do Christians most need in order to be successful soul-winners for God?

First of all, it is to be born of the Spirit; then to be filled with the Holy Spirit, whereby we are sealed unto God. Then the fruits of the Spirit will be manifest in our lives. Of course, we should not presume to go out as mission workers without a divine call from God.

The first thing, then, is to know God and then to know ourselves as utterly helpless without the cleansing power of the blood of Christ on our own souls. Then the especial anointing for service in the vineyard of the Lord. If to these be added a thorough knowledge of human nature and a sincere desire for the salvation of souls, then the glory of God will be revealed in us and we will be forgetful of self and alive to the needs of others. We must see men and women lost, going down to eternal death and must reach them at any cost and be willing to gladly suffer the loss of all things that we might gain Christ and win souls for Him.

We should acquire from the Lord the gift of adaptation to any and all kinds of work, people and places. We must see the people from their own standpoint and then from God's standpoint and then have implicit confidence in God and in the power of the blood of Jesus to cleanse from all sin. We must be humble and meek and yet strong, through faith in God and His promises. Is anything too hard for the Lord? And has He not told us, "Greater works than these shall ye do because I go unto my Father?" Is He not at the Father's right hand, interceding for us and for the souls to whom He sends us?

We must be all things to all men that we might win some. We must watch for opportunities for service and be quick to use them when they are given us. We must be ready to launch out into the deep at the Master's command. We must have grace, not only to serve, but if need be, to die, in order that souls might be saved—souls that are going to destruction for the want of a kind word or a helping hand at just the right time. I have often found them upon the verge of suicide. Men and women in despair, both in prison and outside, were goaded into desperation and the enemy of their souls was urging them to end it all—that nobody cared, and God had forgotten them.

How glad I have been to clasp their hand and tell them there was One who cared; that He loved them still and I have seen the long pent-up tears start from their eyes and hope has sprung up once more in their desolate hearts. I hope to hear God say in the Day of Judgment of some, "Here are the discouraged, the tempted and tried ones, who were almost lost, but who were won through your faithfulness." To God be all the glory.

We must not seek our own ease. Jesus, in the Garden of Gethsemane, would have died in agony, only that an angel came and ministered unto Him, yet he prayed, "Not My will, but Thine be done." Such must be our heartfelt cry and we must abandon ourselves to God's will in all things and forgetting ourselves and the opinions of the World, seek to please Him only. Then He will make even our enemies be at peace with us.

Multitudes all about us are going down to despair for want of true love such as Jesus had when He said, "Father, forgive them, for they know not what they do," and "Neither do I condemn thee; go and sin no more."

Having this spirit, God has promised to furnish us unto every good work. That is, every work to which He calls us. We each have our responsibility to meet, our especial capability, our gift or talent. Then let us adapt ourselves to the work which God has given us to do—not ignoring the work of others, nor lording it over God's heritage, but each abiding in the calling wherein we are called, having charity for all, whether saints or sinners. Surely, with the field so wide and the work so great, there is the greatest need for love and the unity of the Spirit among all Christians. Why there are so many divisions, I know not. I find true and earnest hearts among all classes, all denominations and all nationalities.

Jesus prayed, before He ascended on high, for his children, that they all might be one as He and the Father were one—one in purpose and one in heart. If we manifest this oneness, sinners will come flocking home to God and souls will be saved and God will get all the glory. The lack of oneness among God's people stands in the way of souls and the poor and ignorant are at a loss as to what to think or believe.

Surely, there was never greater need for Holy Ghost, Spirit-filled Christian workers than now, when false doctrine is proclaimed on every side and in every form. But let Christians unite, losing sight of everything but God and souls and it will not be long until God will fulfill his promise that a nation shall be born in a day. Oh, that there might be a rallying of all of God's true children of every class and nationality; that they might, with united forces, charge upon the enemy and soon the world, which now seems to be at variance, would be won for God and for our Christ.

THE MASSES ARE NOT REACHED through the ordinary channels of the churches. Look at the need of the Gospel being carried to the railroad and street-car men, the soldiers, sailors, policemen, firemen, and postmen. Are we seeking to reach the people? We must get the love of God in our hearts to that degree that we will not only be willing to suffer, but to die for them, and mean it—mean business, and fast and pray and call mightily on God for help and direction, and look to Him for results. Don't expect an easy time—don't let us expect to be above our Master. Jesus had no place to lay His head. He went among the despised, the poor, the fallen, the lowest of earth; and if He were to return now, how many of us would He find filling the places appointed us?

The Lord is ready to do exceeding abundantly above all we can think or ask, and will bless every unselfish effort on our part to help save a lost world. When the end comes for you and me, dear one, let us have our lamps trimmed and burning, ready to go in to the marriage supper of the Lamb, which is to soon take place.

God help us do our part, to be instant in season and out of season; to keep free in our souls; to be filled with the spirit of Jesus; to be ever ready with a kind word, a "God bless you," a silent prayer, a warm hand-clasp. Let us be quick to follow the leadings of the Holy Spirit, humbling ourselves under the mighty hand of God. Let us take a firmer hold on God and be ourselves in His hands. Let us see our own responsibility as God sees it, and by His grace measure up to it.

Then the hosts of hell shall not be able to prevail against us and God will use us to his glory, and with hearts filled with love and compassion, we will go forward and God will go with us and give us victory.

MY BOY IN INDIA.

Some years ago the Lord made plain to me that I should support a famine orphan in India, and since that time He has enabled me to give twenty dollars per year for the support of my adopted son, John Ryder Wheaton, named for my brother, who departed this life a few years ago, and for myself. I give his picture and a copy of his first letter to me, translated by one of the missionaries; also some letters from Brother and Sister Jarvis, in charge of the Orphanage in Lahore, India. We ask the prayers of our readers for this dear boy, and if God should lay it upon any of your hearts to provide for one of these famine orphans, any money sent to the Missionary Home in Tabor, Iowa, will be promptly forwarded to any orphanage or missionary you may designate. God has laid this boy upon my heart, and the tie is dearer, perhaps, because I am alone in the world, having laid my only child in the grave with my husband. My heart was touched when I received this letter from John's own hand, and sometimes I long to see and know him for myself. He is being trained for a missionary, and when my labors are ended, I hope to see him coming home from India, bringing his trophies with him— precious souls from his own native land, and that there we may praise the Lord through all eternity together.

Lahore, Frontier Faith Mission, April 12, 1904.—Dear Mama:—Salam, I am well by the grace of Lord Jesus Christ, and hope you are well. Matter is this that I live here very happy, few days ago that the fever and cough attacked me so I went to the hospital, now I am well and do my duty. I learned the work of Gardener. I pray every day. May God help me and make me His true Christian and grant me abundant grace. I also hope that you do pray for me. I pray for you. Here are all well. I am also with other boys well. My compliment to you,

Your son,

JOHN WHEATON,
Head Gardener.

Ruthena

JOHN RYDER WHEATON, INDIA FAMINE BOY.

Frontier Faith Mission and Orphanage, Lahore, N. India, Dec. 11, 1901.—Dear Sister Wheaton—We have chosen for you a bright little boy by the name of Ruthena, about ten years old. He is one of our brightest little boys, one that bids fair to be something for God. He is a shoemaker by trade and is doing well at it. We are endeavoring to teach the boys trades, wanting them to be like Paul where they can preach the Gospel while they make tents for a living. Ruthena is a bright boy in every way and will be named John Ryder as you wished. We do not have time to write often but our hearts are with you.

Yours for India's redemption,

LAURA E. JARVIS.

Lahore, N. India, Sept. 18, 1902.—My Dear Sister—Your dear boy is healthy and well. He is such a help, and seems to know just what to do at the right time. We feel that we can count on him at all times. He is a precious Christian boy, and God is using him.

God is blessing our precious children, and the work is going forward. We are so glad to be on our own land. Our homes are only temporary, but our faith is in God for the permanent ones. He says no good thing will He withhold from them that walk uprightly.

Your Sister seeking the lost,

L. E. J.

Lahore, North India, August 20, 1903.—Dear Sister Wheaton—Your kind offering of twenty dollars for the support of your boy, John, is very thankfully received. The Lord bless and repay you. Continue to pray for him, and for the rest of our great family. God is hearing prayer for us. There are some slight fever cases among the children. This is our sickly season. Unite in prayer that our workers may keep well. We are all burdened because of the lack of workers and much has to remain undone.

Though burdened, we will stand at our post until Jesus comes. (R. V.) Our faith is in God. So many young people at home seem to be wasting their lives and talents, when they might be doing so much for God in this land.

Your brother seeking the lost,

ROBERT JARVIS.

Lahore, N. India, March 16, 1904.

My Dear Sister Wheaton—Greetings in Jesus' name. "Lift up your eyes, and look on the fields, for they are white already to harvest."

I write to tell you today that your boy John is quite poorly. He has been having an attack of lung fever. I believe that in answer to prayer God will raise him up. I felt he would have better care in the hospital than we could give him, so we took him there, but we go to see him frequently, and I will keep you posted as to how he is doing. I know you are interested and are praying for him. We thank you much for your interest, and all you are doing for him. I hope you are keeping well and seeing souls saved.

John was a real help in the garden outside of school hours. He has always been a willing little worker. God bless you much, dear Sister Wheaton, and use you greatly, is our prayer.

Your sister,

L. E. JARVIS.

Lahore, N. India, April 12, 1904.

My Dear Sister Wheaton—Greeting in Jesus' name. I am glad to write you this time that John is all right again. I think his sickness has drawn him closer to God. He is writing you a few lines that I will translate for him and send it with this.

Yours to be faithful,

L. E. JARVIS.

PREACHING IN THE PEST-HOUSE.

Just why the dear Lord saw best to permit me to take the loathsome disease of smallpox into my system, I know not; but I do know the same God that made man and pronounced him very good, permitted Job and many others of His people to suffer many things. Of one thing I am certain, the Lord permitted me to preach the Gospel in the pest-house. No one was allowed there but the physician of the Board of Health and those in charge, and there were many lost ones there and no gospel services for years and not even the superintendent and his family were allowed to go to church. I had held meetings in almost every other place and I now had opportunity to go there, this being the only way to get to them. During the summer of 1901 I was taken very ill and the sixth doctor pronounced the disease smallpox. There was no alternative but to prepare for the hospital, which I did unaided. This was remarkable; for I had been very near death, the suffering both mentally and physically was so intense and the agony so great. Surely God heard the prayers of His believing ones and raised me up to once more go forth to glorify His name by preaching His gospel and singing His praises. Bless His holy name!

I was hedged in with God. He got the glory of my healing. I bless the Lord that in answer to prayer He never let one person take the disease from me that we knew of. When leaving the minister's home where I was taken sick, I was shouting and praising the Lord. I told the mission workers I was sure I could go to Heaven even from the pest-house, with the smallpox. I told the young sister with me to bring the tracts for service in the hospital. I had told her that morning that there would be several doctors call and hold a consultation and pronounce the disease smallpox and they would take me to the pest-house, and I expected I would die there. I had such victory in my soul that I just shouted and praised the Lord.

In the hospital I was given the privilege of all the wards to sing and pray and talk with the patients. Some were in a very dangerous condition, and others convalescent. Others were trembling with fear, having been exposed and quarantined here to protect the public from contagion. Those were weeks of suffering, although full of service and song. The hymns were listened to with the greatest delight even by foreigners who could not understand our language. I often wonder why professing Christians are not as careful about the spread of sin as people are about the transmitting of disease. The same day I left the hospital the Lord sent me out on a long journey to preach the gospel on the train. As I was talking with the conductor, there was a sudden stop and he ran to find the cause. Our engine had become disabled on a bridge, and as a train was coming behind us, the trainmen ran to flag the coming train before it should overtake us; but it was too late. I dropped on my knees on the platform of the rear car and asked God to spare our lives. I arose, took in the situation, went to my seat in the center of the car and again knelt in prayer. I turned to look just as the engine struck our car, raising it about five feet in the air, crushing timbers and glass, and causing a panic among the passengers. I was blest of God through it all, and went immediately to work holding meetings while we waited some hours for help to come. I see so plainly the hand of the Lord in all this. I might have left the train when on the rear platform, but I felt impressed to stay with those on board and call on God for help. Do you wonder that when all our lives were spared I felt that as the Lord gave all on the ship into Paul's hands, so in this case, as in many others, the wise Master gave me those who traveled with me? "As thy days so shall thy strength be." "A thousand shall fall at thy side and ten thousand at thy right hand, but it shall not come nigh thee."

HOW THE LORD PROVIDES.

One night in San Francisco while holding a meeting in the Old Adelphi Theater, I was impressed to give a dollar to a sister who often sang and exhorted in our service and who assisted me that night. At the close of the meeting I handed her a silver dollar. She seemed much surprised and said, "No, I should not take this from you." I told her God showed me to give her that dollar and I must obey Him; so she took the money.

The next day, while waiting for the street car on a public thoroughfare, I saw a man giving out ladies' fashion plates. I spoke kindly to him and suggested how much more good he could do by giving out tracts. He replied that that was the way he made his living—that the firm paid him for his services. I told him that God would care for him if he only trusted and served Him, but he evidently thought me somewhat of a fanatic. Just then a well-dressed old gentleman spoke to me and said, "Do you belong to the Salvation Army?" I said that I did not and he then asked, "What is your work?" I answered, "I am a missionary to the prisoners and lost girls." He handed me a dollar and hurried on. The man with whom I had been speaking looked on surprised and said, "Who was that man?" I said, "I do not know; I never saw him before and may never see him again." He was evidently thinking, for I had told him that God provided for me and would provide for him if he would but work for Him, and God was giving him an object lesson. I said, "I believe the Lord sent that man to convince you that what I said was true for I never ask any person for money, but trust all to Providence."

Going on my way later in the day, outside the city where I changed cars, I saw hurrying toward me the same man who had given me the dollar in the morning. He said, "I have been thinking all day about you and what you said and here is another dollar for you." I told him how I felt God had used him to convince the fashion plate man, that if we fully trust and serve the Lord He will provide for us. I have never seen either of these men again since that day, but God sent me the two dollars in place of the one dollar I had given that poor woman the night before, in the meeting.

The sequel was given me sometime after this when I again met that poor sister. She said to me, "Sister Wheaton, I want to tell you about the dollar you gave me that night in the meeting," and then she said: "I had nothing in my house for my children to eat (there was a large family of them), and husband was out of work. I had to wash next day and had neither soap nor starch, and I had to go across the city to pray for a sick woman, whose son had said that he would believe in God and serve him if his mother were healed in answer to prayer. I had to take that young man with me and pay his car fare and my own. The mother was healed and the young man, being convinced, yielded himself to God and was converted and became a Christian." And then she added, "All this your dollar did, for I had prayed God to send me a dollar that night and you obeyed God and see what was accomplished through obedience to the God who hears the ravens when they cry and notes the sparrow's fall."

Then I related to her my experience to show how the Lord used a stranger to return me double, or two dollars instead of one, and perhaps saved two men—for God was evidently dealing both with the stranger who gave me the money and with the one with whom I was speaking on the street.

MISCELLANEOUS INCIDENTS.

I was once called upon to minister to the needs of a woman who was burned almost to death. I assisted the doctor as best I could to dress the burns. I took the scissors and cut the loose flesh from her arm, and held her while the doctor filed the rings from her hands.

If I had not been previously convinced by the Scriptures of the folly of wearing rings I think this awful sight would have been sufficient to satisfy any doubts in my mind, as they cut so cruelly deep into the charred and swollen flesh. She finally passed away to that land where there shall be no more death, neither sorrow, nor crying, neither shall there be any more pain.

While being entertained at a certain place a few years ago, a caller was announced one evening, to see "Mother Wheaton." Entering the parlor a tall, handsome man, dressed in the uniform of a policeman, advanced to greet me. I bowed politely, but perhaps a little distantly, as I did not know him. He came forward and extended his hand cordially, saying, "Don't you know me, Mother?" I said, "No, I do not know you." He said "I sang in — — prison in the choir. I served a term there and heard you sing and preach there. This is my daughter," and he presented a nice looking young lady who was with him. He said he now held a responsible position and was getting along nicely, and invited me to come and visit his family.

While holding meetings in a little town in one of the southern states, I was entertained at the home of a wealthy man who was accused of crime. He had a beautiful wife and lovely children. I was greatly troubled about his condition. I held meetings there in the home. I was treated very kindly and cordially welcomed, but he would not yield to God. I warned him faithfully, and plead with him to repent of his sins and become a Christian. I told him that a terrible calamity awaited him if he did not yield himself to the Lord. I went away believing it was his last chance of salvation. Not long after that he laid in wait to kill a man against whom he had had a grudge for some time; but the other man seeing his intention, drew his revolver and fired in self-defence. The man fell dead. He had had his last call. He had rejected the Lord and was ushered into eternity without a moment's warning.

One day years ago, in M——, Mississippi, I went on the street to hold a meeting. A policeman came along and forbade me after I had begun to sing, saying it was against the law to hold religious services on the street. My spirit was grieved as I felt the Lord had a work for me to do among the poor and lowly who were too poorly clad to attend church services. A sister (a woman of God who entertained me) was with me. She then proposed taking me to see a sick child, an infant. When we reached the house we found the young parents weeping over their dying child. My heart was touched with sympathy, and kneeling down I asked Him who said, "Suffer little children to come unto me," to heal the child for His glory. I believed His word where it says, "The prayer of faith shall save the sick." My faith touched divinity, the child was healed and the young parents, seeing the power of God manifested, were converted, and gave their lives to God for His service.

Height   Out Arms   Trunk   Head Length   Head Width   Cheek Width
Ear   Foot   Length Finger   L. Fore-arm   Color of Eyes   Marks & Scars,
BERTILLON MEASUREMENTS

PRISON AT ANAMOSA, IOWA. 1. FEMALE DEPARTMENT. 2. CELL HOUSE. 3. MAIN ENTRANCE.

CHAPTER XXVI.

Selections from My Scrap Book.

Many of the selections given in this chapter were written by prisoners and given me by them. The others may not all be new to the reader, but I have thought them of sufficient value to thus preserve, as they may be reread with profit, and no doubt may be read here by many who have not seen them elsewhere. Such will surely feel the time it takes to read them well spent.

Many of the songs I have sung are not in print here, as they are familiar or may be found in popular books; others I thought might be copyrighted and I do not know the owner, etc. I have not meant to use any copyright selections without procuring the right to do so, but if through mistake any have been used I shall be glad to make due requital.

THE AUTHOR OF FLOWER MISSION DAY.

I once visited this sister, a saint, meekly lying upon her bed, and when I asked if she would like for Jesus to heal her, she said God could use her better in that condition.

E. R. W.

Jennie Cassady was born in Louisville, Kentucky, June 9, 1840. She came to earth through no royal line of ancestry. No booming cannon and flying flags proclaimed the birth of a princess. No jeweled hand beckoned her to a place of rank and title. Nothing in babyhood or girlhood distinguished her above what is visible in ten thousand homes to-day. But as she stepped over the threshold into womanhood, there fell upon her a great calamity—a cruel accident made her a cripple and an invalid for life. But in her afflictions she arose to a sublimity and sweetness of soul that has challenged the admiration of two continents. And out of the awful shadows that fell upon her she has gathered up the sunbeams of God's smiles and scattered them into the dark places of earth. Out of that one little darkened room in Kentucky there has gone forth an inspiration that has fired the heart of heroic Christian womanhood. And out of the darkness that smote her pathway leaped the lances of light that pierces the gloom of prison walls. A gleam from that radiant life touches the poet's fancy, and gives us these beautiful lines.

J. M. CROCKER,
Prison Chaplain.

FLOWER DAY AT THE PRISON.

Composed and read by F. L. Platt at the Iowa State Prison at Anamosa, June 9th, 1894.

In a cottage in Kentucky, In the years that have gone by, Was a woman, oh, so lonely, She'd been given up to die.

As she lay upon her sick bed, Ere the spark of life had flown, Neighbors called, and strangers also, Whom before she had not known.

They had heard of her misfortune, Day and night she lingered there; And to make her life more cheerful Seemed to be their every care.

Now they come, with noiseless footsteps, As the rose is kissed with dew, Each one bringing in some sunshine, In "these flowers I've brought for you."

As she looked into their faces, Realizing death had come, "Take these flowers," she said, "I'm dying," They will brighten other homes.

Take them, give them to the children Who in orphans' homes are found, Who have parents silent sleeping Underneath some grassy mound.

Take them, place them by the bedside Of some one whose life is drear; They will bring a ray of sunshine, They will drive away a tear.

Take them, bear them to the prison, Where the trembling convict stands; They'll encourage and they'll cheer him, And they'll help him be a man.

They will speak to him of Heaven, Of a home with God above; They'll dispel the gloom and heartache, They'll recall a mother's love.

They'll remind him of a sister, With youth's bloom upon her brow, With whom he used to gather flowers When life was bright as yours is now.

They'll recall some little sweetheart In the early spring of life, Who, when summer flowers were blooming, He had asked to be his wife.

Oh, that wife! may God's own blessing Rest upon her loyal head; Though he's caused her many a heartache, She would love him were he dead.

Then with all these sacred memories Welling in these hearts of ours, Who in all this land of sunshine Could forbid this gift of flowers?

Bring the flowers with sweetest perfume, This is flower mission day; Some forlorn, discouraged prisoner, "You may rescue, you may save."

Blest the home that knows no sorrow, Blest that wife, whose tears are joy, Blest that mother who in old age, Can lean upon her darling boy.

Men, look up, the clouds have gathered, Some of them are silver-lined; There's a day when all creation Will be marshalled into line.

When these prison walls are sundered; When the grave gives up its dead, All may march the streets of Heaven Who by Jesus Christ are led.

LINES BY A PRISONER TO HIS WIFE.

These lines were handed me by the author. I insert them here because of their clear testimony to the saving grace of God and the love they manifest for wife and children:

Dearest wife, you know I love thee,Deep as yonder sky;Know that love can never fade,Affection never die.

Though in prison I am cast,And cannot now return,Yet on thee my love reclines,For thee my heart will burn.

God has made us one indeed,In ways the world can never know.One, like drops of water foundWithin the pure white snow.

God has made us one indeed;Has joined us, hand and heart;What God has joined together, wife,Let no man put apart.

As well might men uproot the earthAs by their scoff or scornThink to accomplish parting usBecause our hearts now mourn.

Nay, dear wife, I feel for thee,As ne'er I felt before,Prizing thee with deeper strengthFor pining sad and sore.

While there you wait my glad release,The day that sets me free,Await my coming home to wife;Yes, wife and children three.

And I will come. Have patience, wife,The time will wear away,And day by day approaches nearThat glad releasing day.

With little baby in your arms,Two others at your knee;I know, dear wife, your heart is sadAnd longs to see me free.

To help you in your daily toil;To earn for them their bread;To clothe and help and comfort them,And find a shelter for each head.

But cheer up, wife, and so will I,As mankind surely may,Till darkness fade in morning lightThat ushers in the day.

And oh, what joy will visit us,What peace in that glad hour;Our home shall then renew its strengthIn all its silent power.

Here as I lay me down to sleep,In my narrow little cell,I think of the happy times we've spentIn the shady wooded dell.

How we plucked the flowers beside our path,And strolled along the stream,Neither feeling aught of sorrow,For life was like a pleasant dream.

But alas, my dear one, all is changed;And we are parted now for years;But well we know that God will comeAnd wipe away our falling tears.

Sin, dear wife, hast brought the change;Sin has caused our grief and pain;But now that I trust in JesusI will never fall again.

In my very darkest momentsWould you know what comforts me?'Tis my living faith in Jesus,In Him who died on Calvary.

He died on the cross for you, dear wife,His precious blood was shed for me;All our sins on Him were laidWhen they nailed Him to the tree.

And now that blessed Saviour,Who was born at Bethlehem,Looks down from the heights of heavenOn the sinful souls of men.

His thoughts are full of mercy,His heart is filled with love.He is pleading with the FatherThat we might come above.

So we will trust our Saviour,And follow where He leads;And say, in faith believing,He'll provide for all our needs.

So we'll walk close beside HimAnd let Him take our hand;As He points, with face all shining,To that bright and happy land.

And oft to others round usThe story we will tell,How Jesus Christ saves sinners,The heavenly hosts to swell.

You will tell them, wife, how He found me,Sinful and all cast down,And how through love He raised me upAnd promised me a crown.

And when we see still othersCaught in Satan's snare,We'll lead them on to Jesus,And leave them in His care.

And when He treats them gently,As He treats both you and me,Other sinners, looking on,To His bosom soon will flee.

For thus the world around usFor Christ could soon be won;He'll end in glorious triumphThe work He has begun.

All glory then to Jesus!Sing praises to His name!He saved lost sinners years gone by,And today He'll do the same.

In language very simpleI've told to you, dear wife,My love to you, your love to me,And the love of Jesus Christ.

So we'll just keep on trustingIn the Saviour God has given;And He will fill with peaceOur journey on to heaven.

And we'll not forget the Father,But give thanks for all He's done,In giving us our Saviour,In His own beloved Son.

WOMAN'S LOVE.

TO MRS. WHEATON.

These lines are most respectfully presented as a prisoner's tribute of sincere respect:

O, woman's love, past understanding! So near to God's, so wondrous deep: Deep as the depths of space; expanding Till it blooms beyond death's mystic sleep

Throughout the earth, the rich and lowly It reigns supreme within her breast. O, woman's love! through its beauty holy She will win eternal rest.

Born of woman, purest, dearest Lily of fair Bethlehem, Christ to her will be the nearest In his bright home—Jerusalem.

A fadeless flower in beauty blooming 'Midst heaven's host of immortelles. His peerless love her soul perfuming She'll reign a queen mid arch angels

J. W. L.

Cole City, Ga., Sunday night, Nov. 17, 1889.

TAKE THIS MESSAGE TO MY MOTHER.

(Written by a Prisoner in Jackson, Miss.)

Take this message to my mother, It will fill her heart with joy; Tell her that her prayer is answered, Christ has saved her wandering boy:

Tho' through sin from home I've wandered, And I almost broke her heart; Tell her to be glad and cheerful, Never from the Lord I'll part.

CHORUS.

Take this message to my mother, It will fill her heart with joy; Tell her that her prayer is answered, Christ has saved her wandering boy.

How she wept when last we parted, How her heart did ache with pain When she said: "Good-bye, God bless you, We may never meet again."

O my boy, just look to Jesus, What a friend He is to all! Only trust Him, He will save you— Can't you hear His sweet voice call?

In this world of sin are many Who have wandered far from God. Will your mother's prayers be answered? Listen, sinner, you, her boy.

You have ofttimes heard this warning, In your heart conviction's deep; God is calling to the wanderer Who asks mercy at his feet.

NOT LONELY NOW.

I am not lonely, mother, now, Though far from me you roam. One dried my tears and smoothed my brow, And stilled the sob and groan. I am not lonely, mother, dear, For Jesus dwells with me, e'en here.

All day I feel Him by my side; And when betimes would come The Evil One, I quickly hide Behind my Precious One. Think you I'm lonely, mother, dear, When Jesus thus is ever near?

And when at night I think of thee, As in my cell I sit, Bright vision of thy form I see By His own presence lit. Can I be lonely, mother, dear, When thy pure spirit is so near?

Farewell, my darling mother-friend, And if for aye, Oh! fare thee well! Whate'er betide, unto the end, Christ's love for me I'll gladly tell.

The following was written by a young brother who, with his wife, were with me for a time in my work. In thanking them for a kindness done me I used the words, "Jesus is looking on," implying that He would reward them. Only an hour or so afterward the young brother handed me these lines, suggested by my words:

Little did I think when I spoke the words that they would make so deep an impression upon his mind. How little we realize what a word may do.

JESUS IS LOOKING ON.

"The eyes of the Lord are upon the righteous and his ears are open unto their cry." Ps. 34.

[TUNE, "ARE YOU WITHIN THE FOLD TONIGHT?"]

1. While traveling as a pilgrim Across life's desert drear, My feet ofttimes are weary, Mine eyes oft drop a tear; But when I look to Jesus, All weariness is gone, My heart then joys within me To know He's looking on.

CHORUS.

Yes, He is ever looking on, With anxious ear our cry to hear. He hears each sigh, He sees each tear; He knows each heart "with sorrow riven," He hears each word of joy or moan, And whispers gently in our ear, I'm looking, looking on.

2. When troubles rage around me, And trials fiery come, My thoughts are then directed To my eternal home. Though walking on the mountain, Or on the verdant lawn, This is the thought that cheers me, He's always looking on.

3. When friends do turn against me, And frown and persecute, I'm then brought nearer Jesus, Than when my foes are mute. While Jesus walks beside me, His arm I'll lean upon, And ne'er forget the promise, He's always looking on.

4. Take courage, brother pilgrim, And let us journey on, For soon life's many trials Will all have passed and gone; Then sweeping up to glory We'll join the ransomed throng, And sing God's endless praises, While He is looking on.

HOW GOD CALLS MISSIONARIES OUT OF PRISON CELLS.

S. H. HADLEY.
Superintendent of the Old McAuley Mission.

Some of the best missionaries this world ever knew are men who have been sentenced to long terms in prison. Wholly shut away from the world and its dreadful temptations, God had a chance to speak to them. Jerry McAuley was a wonderful example of this, and that drunken loafer and thief was finally used so wonderfully by the Lord God that his name has gone all over this world and has been an inspiration to millions. He was sent to prison from the Fourth Ward of New York for fifteen years at the age of nineteen.

One Sunday morning in the chapel the speaker was old "Awful" Gardener, an old-time ruffian and prize-fighter in New York, but God had got hold of him and he had been wonderfully saved. With tears streaming down his face, he told of the love of Christ, and he said, "Boys, I ought to be wearing the stripes the same as you are, and I feel a deep sympathy for you."

He also quoted some verses from the Scriptures, and after the boys had gone back to their cells Jerry found a Bible in the ventilator of his cell, and, looking it over aimlessly, tried to find the text that "Awful" Gardener had quoted, but instead he found that Christ came to save sinners, and the Holy Spirit showed him his dreadful past life. As the day grew into night, Jerry got down on his knees and began to pray. He had never prayed before, but now he cried to God for help and mercy. How long he was there he does not know, but some time during the night a glorious light dispelled the deep darkness of his soul, and he cried out, "Oh, praise God, I found Jesus, and He gives peace to my soul." The unusual sound brought the keeper, who asked, "What is the matter with you?"

Jerry answered, "I found Jesus, that's what's the matter with me."

He found some opportunities to breathe out the new-found hopes of his soul and the love of Jesus to the prisoners about him. Soon a revival broke out in the prison such as never had been seen before or since, and Jerry was the center of it all. He was pardoned in 1864, but when he got home he had no friends, no money, and he soon fell into bad company, and got to be a worse scoundrel than he ever was before. It was after this he became known as the dangerous East River pirate. He was reclaimed in 1868, and although he fell five times after that during the first eight or nine months, he was finally anchored to Christ.

Do you know that every drunkard uses tobacco? Jerry was no exception. Some faithful friends said to him. "Jerry, give up your tobacco for Jesus' sake," and he gave it up, and then he never fell afterward.

He was afterward married to Maria, his faithful wife, who also was redeemed from a drunkard's life, and in 1872 opened the world-renowned McAuley Mission, at 316 Water Street, down on the East Side, nearly under the Brooklyn Bridge.

He stayed here ten years, and then opened the Cremorne Mission, Thirty-second Street and Sixth Avenue, where he died in 1884, and had the largest funeral of any private citizen who was ever buried in New York.

The writer succeeded Jerry McAuley down there, and the work is going on night and day. Drunkards and thieves come in by the thousand, and, thank God, many of them are saved unto life eternal. The writer is also a convert of Jerry McAuley Mission.—*The Life Boat.*

OUTSIDE THE PRISON WALLS.

Free, free at last he left the dreary jail, And stepped into the dewy April night; Once more he breathed, untainted, God's pure air, And saw the evening star's sweet trembling light. How strange! how strange! and yet how strangely dear The old familiar turf beneath his feet! How wonderful once more to be alone Unwatched, unguarded, 'neath the sky's broad sweep.

Free! free again—but O, so old and worn— So weary with his wasted, ruined life— Full twenty years the cell, his only home— Full twenty years with hopeless misery rife! His thoughts sped backward till they reached that day When he had entered that grim house, a boy— Naught but a boy in stature and in years, But with a heart all bare of hope and joy.

For in a dreadful moment, crazed with rum, His hand had laid a fellow creature low, And for that glass of brandy in his brain Full twenty years of wretchedness and woe. And now, a gray-haired man, he walked again The very path his boyish feet had pressed So many, many years ago; And now he wandered lonely, seeking rest.

Where should he go? Where now his footsteps turn? No living soul was there to welcome him! No friend of all his youthful days he knew Would greet again this wanderer in sin. Unconsciously, he sought his boyhood's home, The low, white cottage he had held so dear; 'Twas standing in its old accustomed place, But strangers had dwelt there for many a year.

Where next? The tears stood in his mournful eyes; His breath came thick and fast—he could not stir, But leaned upon the old familiar gate With thoughts of mother—O, could he find her? Where was she now—that mother, sweet and good, Who tried with tears and prayers to save her boy, Who knelt alone at midnight's solemn hour And mourned for him who should have been her joy.

His faltering steps at last he vaguely turned Unto the silent churchyard near the sea, And stood alone while pitying moonbeams spread Around his form a veil of charity. Alone with God in that still, solemn place, Alone with hundreds of the silent dead, The outcast stood with lowly, sin-sick heart, The cold night dew upon his drooping head.

At last he found her in a place apart, Where moonbeams sparkled through the willow boughs, And shone upon her simple headstone white That marked the limit of her narrow house. 'Twas but a snowy marble, simple, plain, That bore her name, her age, and just below— "Died of a broken heart"—alas! he knew The cause of all that life and death of woe.

He flung himself face down upon the grass, Alone between the living and the dead, And wept and prayed beside the lonely grave Until in sorrow's slumber sunk his head. They found him in the morning, stiff and cold, His hands clasped o'er his mother's lowly grave, His head upon its turf, as though he thought That turf the bosom his poor heart had craved.

Upon his pallid cheeks the trace of tears Showed in the glowing ray of morning's sun, But o'er that face there shone a wondrous peace, A smile of joy now all his life was done. Men marveled that he looked so young again Despite his crown of sorrow-silvered hair, And tender-hearted women sighed and weptAnd smiled to think that they had found him there. Ah! God is good! with loving tenderness He saw the sad, repentant soul alone Weep out his sin upon his mother's grave, And gently led the weary wanderer home. This we believe: That now in Heaven's street The mother and her son are reconciled, And all the pain and sin of earth below Are blotted out, and he is God's own child.

—*Hattie F. Crocker, in Union Signal.*

IF WE KNEW.

If we knew the heart's sad sighing In the secret hour; If we knew the bitter crying O'er the tempter's power, Slower would we be to censure, Kinder in reproof; From the erring, peradventure, We would not stand aloof.

If we knew the hard, stern struggle Of the one who fell, Toiling on 'mid grief and trouble That none but God can tell, Our thoughts, perhaps, would be kinder, Our help more pitiful— Be of God's love a reminder To the tempted soul.

If we knew the fierce temptation, Could we feel the pain Of the deep humiliation, The tears shed all in vain, We, perchance, would be more gentle, Our tones more tender be; O'er his fault we'd draw the mantle Of fervent charity.

If we knew how dark and cheerless Seem the coming years, We might then appear more fearless Of each other's cares. Could our eyes pierce through the smiling Of the face so calm, See the bitter self-reviling, We'd apply the balm.

Did we walk a little nearer To Jesus in the way, Hear His voice a little clearer We would know how to pray. He has words of comfort given That we to them should speak, Ere the hopeless soul is driven His faith with God to break.

We shall know each other better, The mists shall roll away; Nevermore we'll feel the fetter Of this toil-worn clay. Only let us love each other, 'Tis our Lord's command, To each fainting friend or brother Reach a helping hand.

> —*Anna L. Dreyer, of Missionary Training Home at Tabor, Iowa.*

LITTLE GRAVES.

You have your little grave; I have mine. You have your sad memories; I have mine. For,

"There is no flock, however tended, But one dead lamb is there; There is no fireside, howsoe'er defended, But hath its vacant chair.

"The air is full of farewells to the dying, And weepings for the dead; The heart of Rachel for her children crying Will not be comforted."

- 436 -

I have pleasant thoughts sometimes about these little graves. I think what a safe place the little grave is. Temptations never come there. Sins never pollute there. Tears, pains, disappointments, bereavements, trials, cares, and snares, are all unknown in that silent resting place. And then, Jesus has the keys, and he keeps our treasures safely, and guards them securely. No mother's heart is anxious about a child that is laid in the little grave. No prayers of anguish go up for it as for those tossed by the storms of passion, sunk in the whirlpool of vice, or lost in the wide wilderness of sorrow and of sin. There is now no need of chiding, reproving, watching, and restraining. The chief Shepherd bears the lamb on his own bosom, and it is forever safe.

The little grave is a sacred place. The Lord of glory has passed into the sepulchre, and from it he has opened up the path of life. Hope blooms there, and hearts-ease and amaranth blossom amid the shadows that linger over it, and Jesus watches his treasures and counts his jewels in the little graves.

The little grave shall be opened by and by. The night is dark, but there is a flush of morn upon the mountains, and a gleam of sunlight glows along the distant hills. He who bears the keys of hell and of death, shall come back to open the little graves, and call the sleepers forth. Then cherub forms shall burst the silent tombs, and these green hillocks shall bear their harvest for the garner of our God.—Sel.

THE MOTHER'S WARNING.

Touch it not—ye do not know, Unless you've borne a fate like mine, How deep a curse, how wild a woe, Is lurking in that ruby wine. Look on my cheek—'tis withered now; It once was round and smooth as thine; Look on my deeply furrowed brow— 'Tis all the work of treacherous wine. I had two sons, two princely boys, As noble men as God e'er gave; I saw them fall from honor's joys To fill a common drunkard's grave. I had a daughter, young and fair, As pure as ever woman bore. Where is she? Did you ask me where? Bend low, I'll tell the tale once more. I saw that fairy child of mine Linked to a kingly bridegroom's side; Her heart was proud and light as thine, Oh, would to God she then had died! Not many moons had filled their horn, While she upon his bosom slept; 'Twas on a dark November morn, She o'er a murdered husband wept; Her drunken father dealt the blow— Her brain grew wild, her heart grew weak; Was ever tale of deeper woe A mother's lips had lived to speak? She dwells in yonder darkened halls, No ray of reason there does shine; She on her murdered husband calls. 'Twas done by wine, by cursed wine!

—*Temperance Banner.*

HARRY'S REMORSE.

It's curious, isn't it, chaplain, what a twelve months may bring? Last year I was in Chicago, gambling and living in sin; Was raking in pools at the races, and feeing the waiters with ten, Was sipping mint juleps by twilight, while today I am in the pen.

What led me to do it? What always leads a man to destruction and crime? The prodigal son you have read of has altered somewhat in his time. He spends his money as freely as the Biblical fellow of old, And when it is gone he fancies the husks will turn into gold.

Champagne, a box at the opera, high steps while fortune is flush; The passionate kisses of women whose cheeks have forgotten to blush. The old, old story, chaplain, of pleasure that ends in tears, The froth that foams for an hour and the dregs that are tasted for years.

Last night as I sat here and pondered on the end of my evil ways, There rose like a phantom before me the vision of boyhood days; I thought of my old, old home, chaplain, of the schoolhouse that stood on the hill, Of the brook that ran through the meadow—I can hear its music still.

And again I thought of my mother, of the mother who taught me to pray, Whose love was a precious treasure that I heedlessly cast away; And again I saw in my vision the fresh-lipped, careless boy, To whom the future was boundless and the world but a mighty toy.

I saw all this as I sat there, of my ruined and wasted life, And the thoughts of my remorse were bitter, they pierced my heart like a knife. It takes some courage, chaplain, to laugh in the face of fate, When the yearning ambition of manhood is blasted at twenty-eight.

—Composed and written by Harry S——while taking a retrospection of the past.

TWENTY—THIRTY-FOUR.

The line of dingy-coated men stretched along the broad granite walk and like a great gray serpent wound in and out among the wagon shops and planing mills that filled the prison yard.

Down beyond the foundry the beginning of the line, the head of the serpent, was lost at the stairway leading to the second floor of a long, narrow building in which whisk brooms were manufactured.

An hour before, on the sounding of a brass gong at the front, the same line had wound round the same corners into the building whence now it crawled. There, the men had seated themselves on four-legged stools before benches that stretched across the room in rows. Before each man was set a tin plate of boiled meat; a heavy cup of black coffee, a knife, a fork, and a thick bowl of steaming, odorous soup.

During the meal other men, dressed like the hundreds who were sitting, in suits of dull gray, with little round-crowned, peaked-visored caps to match, moved in and out between the rows, distributing chunks of fresh white bread from heavy baskets. Now and then one of the men would shake his head and the waiter would pass him by, but usually a dozen hands were thrust into a basket at once to clutch the regulation "bit" of half a pound. The men ate ravenously, as if famished.

Yet a silence that appalled hovered over the long bare dining-hall where eight hundred men were being fed. There was no clatter of knives and forks; there were no jests; they moved about as noiselessly as ghosts.

There were faces stamped with indelible marks of depravity and vice, but now and then the "breadtossers" would see uplifted a pair of frank blue eyes, in which burned the light of hope. Men were there who dreamed of a day to come when all would be forgiven and forgotten; when a hand would again be held out in welcome, and a kiss again be pressed to quivering lips. Men there were of all kinds, of all countenances, young and old; the waving, sunlit hair of youth side by side with locks in which the snow was thickly sprinkled. All these men were paying the penalty society imposes on proved criminals.

And now, their dinner over, they were marching back to the shops and mills of the prison, where days and weeks were spent at labor. Those men employed in the wagon-works dropped out of the line when they came opposite the entrance to their building. Those behind pushed forward as their prison-mates disappeared, and never for more than ten seconds was there a gap in the long, gray line.

The whisk-broom factory occupied the second floor of the building at the far end of the prison yard. On the ground floor men worked at lathes, turning out the wooden handles to the brooms that were finished, sorted and tied up-stairs. At the corner the line divided, sixty-five of the men climbed the stairway to the second floor, the other thirty entered the lathe-room below.

A dozen men in blue uniforms marched beside the line on its way from the mess-hall, six on each side, at two yards' distance. Their caps bore "Guard" in gold letters, and each guard carried a short, heavy, crooked cane of polished white hickory. On entering the work-room of the second floor, the men assembled before a railed platform, upon which a red-faced, coatless man stood behind a big desk. In cold, metallic tones he called the numbers of the convicts who in turn replied "Here!" when their numbers were spoken.

"Twenty-thirty-four!" called the red-faced man. There was no response.

"Twenty-thirty-four?" The red-faced man leaned over the desk and glared down. Then a voice from somewhere on the left answered "Here!"

"What was the matter with you the first time?" snapped the foreman.

The man thus questioned removed his cap and took three steps toward the platform. In feature the word "hard" would describe him. His head was long, wide at the forehead, and yet narrow between the temples. His eyes were small and close together. His nose was flat, and mouth hardly more than a straight cut in the lower part of his face. The lower jaw was square and heavy, and the ears protruded abnormally. A trifle above medium height with a pair of drooping, twitching shoulders, the man looked criminal.

To the question he replied doggedly, "I answered the first time, sir, but I guess you didn't hear me."

The foreman gazed steadily at the man. Their eyes met. The foreman's did not waver, but "2034" lowered his and fumbled nervously at his cap.

"All right," said the foreman, quickly, "but I guess you'd better report to the warden as soon as you get through in here. Don't wait for any piece-work. Go to him as soon as you have finished your task. I'll tell him you're coming. He'll be waiting for you at the front office."

"Yes, sir." The convict did not raise his eyes. He stepped back into the line.

Then, at the clap of the foreman's hands, the men broke ranks, and each walked away to his own bench or machine. Five minutes later, the swish on the corn-wisps as they were separated and tied into rough brooms, and the occasional tap of a hammer, were the only sounds in that long room where sixty-five men toiled.

Now and then one of the men would go to the platform where the foreman sat bent over half a dozen little books, in which it was his duty to record the number of "tasks" completed by each of the workmen "on his contract"—a "task" in the prison vernacular being the work each man is compelled to accomplish within a certain space of time. On the approach of a workman the foreman would look up and a few whispered words would pass between the two. Then the broom-maker would dart into the stock room, adjoining the factory, where, upon receiving a written requisition from the foreman, the officer in charge would give him the material he needed in his work—a ball of twine, or a strip of plush with which the handles of the brooms were decorated.

At ten minutes past three, 2034 crossed to the platform.

"What do you want?" asked the foreman, as he eyed keenly the man in the gray suit.

"A paper of small tacks," was the reply, quickly spoken. The order was written, and as 2034 moved towards the door leading toward the stock-room, the man on the platform asked in an undertone, "Anything wrong, Bill?"

"That's what I don't know, George," the foreman replied. "That man Riley's been acting queer of late. I've got an idea there's something up his sleeve. There's not a harder nut on the contract than that fellow, and by the way he's been carrying on, sullen like and all that, I'm fearing something's going to happen. You remember, don't you? What, no? He's that Riley from Acorn. He came in two years ago on a burglary job in Clive, where he shot a drug clerk that offered objections to his carrying off all there was in the shop. They made it manslaughter and he's in for fifteen years. There's another warrant ready for him when he gets out, for a job done four years ago in Kentucky. He's a bad one. A fellow like that is no good around this shop."

The guard smiled cynically at the foreman's suggestion that a convict may be too bad even for prison surroundings.

"But I've got my eye on him," continued the foreman. "I'm sending him up to the warden this afternoon. Say, George, when you go back, will you tell the warden Riley's coming up to call on him?"

"Sure, Bill," was the smiling reply of the guard as he moved away. Twenty-thirty-four had returned with a paper of tacks and gone directly to his bench.

It was a quarter of four by the foreman's watch when the door at the head of the stairway opened and the warden entered, accompanied by two friends whom he was showing through the "plant," as he preferred to call the prison.

"This is where the whisk-brooms are made," said the warden. "On the floor below, which we just left, you will remember we saw the boys turning out broom-handles. Well, here the brooms are tied and sewed through by hand, over at those benches. In the room beyond, through that door, we keep the stuff handy that is called for from time to time. In a further room is stored the material used in the manufacture of the brooms, the tin tips, the tacks, the twine, and about ten or twelve tons of broom straw."

As the warden ceased speaking, the foreman leaned across the desk and tapped him on the shoulder. "Riley's coming up to see you this afternoon. He's been acting queer—don't answer the call and the like."

The warden only nodded, and continued his explanation to the visitors.

"Now," he said, moving towards the door of the stock-room, "if you will come over here I'll show you our store-room. You see we have to keep a lot of material on hand. Beyond this second room the stuff is stored up, and is taken into the stock-room as it is wanted. Between the rooms we have arranged these big sliding iron doors that, in case of a fire, could be dropped, and thus, for a few minutes at least, cut the flames off from any room but that in which they originated. You see," pulling an iron lever which let the heavy iron sheet slide to the floor, "that completes the wall."

The visitor nodded. "Now, come on through the second room, and into the third," there, ranged regularly on the floor were huge bales of broom straw, and piled against the walls were boxes upon boxes of tacks, velvet, ornamental bits of metal, and all the other separate parts of the commercial whisk broom.

The visitors examined the tacks and the tins and felt of the bales of straw.

"Very interesting," observed one of the men, as he drew his cigar case from his pocket, and biting the tip from one of the cigars it contained, struck a little wax match on the sole of his shoe. He held the match in his hand till it had burned down, then threw it on the floor, and followed the warden and the other visitor under the heavy iron screen into the workingroom of the factory.

The foreman was busy at his books and did not observe the little party as it passed through on the other side of the broom-bins and out at the big door.

Two minutes later, 2034 happened to look out through the window across his bench and he saw the warden with his friends crossing the prison yards to the foundry. A guard just then sauntered into the room and stopped at the first of the bins. He idly picked up one of the finished brooms and examined it. His attention a moment later was attracted by some one pulling at his coat from behind. He turned.

"Why, Tommy, my boy, what is it?"

The two soft brown eyes of a little boy were turned up to him. "I'm looking for papa," replied the little fellow. "The foreman down-stairs said he come up here. Uncle George is back in the house, and mamma sent me out to find papa."

The guard patted the little fellow's head. "And we'll find him, Tommy," he said. He went over to the foreman's desk. "Bill, did the warden come up here? Tommy is looking for him; his mother sent him out."

The foreman raised his eyes from his books. "Yes," he replied, "he went in there, with a couple of gentlemen."

The guard looked down at the little boy. "He's in the store-room," he said, "you'll find him in there, Tommy."

Then he turned and walked out of the shop. The child ran on into the room beyond. His father was not there. The stock-keeper did not observe the little boy as he tiptoed, in a childish way, past the desk. Tommy passed on into the farther room. He knew he would find his father in there, and he would crawl along between the tiers of straw bales and take him by surprise.

He had hardly passed when the stock-keeper, raising his head from the list of material he was preparing, held his face and sniffed the air. Quietly he rose from his revolving chair and went to the straw-room door. He merely peered inside. Turning suddenly, he pressed upon the lever near the door and the iron screen slid down into place, cutting off the farther room. Then, snatching a few books that lay on his desk, he slipped out into the shop, and at that door released the second screen. As it fell into place with a slight crunching noise, the foreman turned in his chair. The eyes of the two met. The stock-keeper raised his hand and touched his lip with the first finger. He crossed rapidly to the desk.

"Get the men out! Get the men out!" he gasped. "The store-room is on fire!"

The foreman rapped on the table twice. Every man in that room turned and faced the desk.

"Work is over for today," said the foreman. His manner was ominously calm, and the men looked at one another wonderingly.

"Fall in!"

At the order, the dingy gray suits formed in the same old serpent, and the line moved rapidly through the door at the end of the room and down the outside stairs.

There, in front of the building, they were halted, and a guard dispatched to find the warden. He was discovered in the foundry. "Fire in the broom-shop!" whispered the guard.

The warden's face paled. He dashed through the doorway, and one minute later came around the corner of the building, just in time to see the first signs of flames against the windows of the rear room up-stairs.

Within five seconds, a troop of fifteen guards had drawn the little hand-engine from its house and hitched the hose to the hydrant nearest the shop. From all the other buildings the men were being marched to their cells.

"These men!" hurriedly whispered the foreman to the warden. "What shall I do with them?"

"Get 'em inside as soon as you can! This won't last long, the front of the building is cut off. It'll all be over in ten minutes."

The foreman gave an order. At that instant a woman came running down the prison yard. Reaching the warden's side, she fell against him heavily.

"Why, Harriet," he exclaimed, "what is the matter?"

"Oh," she gasped, "Tommy! Tommy! Where is Tommy?"

A guard at the end of the engine rail turned ashy white. He raised a hand to his head, and with the other grasped the wheel to keep from falling. Then he cried, "Mr. Jeffries, I—I believe Tommy is up there in the stock-room. He went to look—"

The warden clutched the man's arm. "Up there? Up there?" he cried.

The sudden approach of the woman and the words that followed had wrought so much confusion that the men had paid no attention to the foreman's command, and he had even failed to notice their lack of attention, in the excitement of that moment.

"Great God!" cried the warden. "What can I do—what can I do? No one can live up there!"

There was a crash. One of the windows fell out. "Get a ladder!" some one cried. A guard ran back toward the prison-house. Then, in the midst of the hubbub, a man in a dingy gray suit stepped out a yard from the line of convicts. His prison number was 2034. He touched his little square cap.

"If you'll give me permission, I think I can get up there," was all he said.

"You! you!" exclaimed the warden. "No, no; I will tell no man to do it!"

There was a second crash. Another window had fallen out, and now the tongues of flame were lapping the outer walls above.

The convict made no reply. With a bound he was at the end of the line and dashing up the stairway.

The warden's wife was on her knees, clinging to the hand of her husband. In his eyes was a dead, cold look. A few men bit their lips, and a faint shadow of a smile played about the mouths of others. They all waited. A convict had broken a regulation—had run from the line! He would be punished! Even as he had clambered up the stairs a guard had cried, "shall I shoot?"

The silence was broken by a shriek from the woman kneeling at the warden's feet. "Look!" she cried, and pointed towards the last of the up-stairs windows.

There, surrounded by a halo of smoke, and hemmed in on all sides by flames, stood a man in a dingy gray suit. One sleeve was on fire, but he beat out the flames with his left hand. Those below heard him cry, "I've got him!" Then the figure disappeared. Instantly it returned, bearing something in its arms. It was the limp form of a child.

All saw the man wrap smoking straw round the little body and tie round that two strands of heavy twine. Then that precious burden was lowered out of the window. The father rushed forward and held up his hands to receive it.

Another foot—he hugged the limp body of his boy to his breast! On the ground a little way back lay a woman, as if dead.

"Here's the ladder!" yelled the foreman, and that moment the eyes that were still turned upon the window above where stood a man in a dingy gray suit, witnessed a spectacle that will reappear before them again and again in visions of the night.

The coat the man wore was ablaze. Flames shot on either side of him and above him. Just as the ladder was placed against the wall, a crackling was heard—not the crackling of the fire. Then like a thunderbolt, a crash occurred that caused even the men in their cells to start. The roof caved in.

In the prison yard that line of convicts saw 2034 reel and fall backwards, and heard, as he fell, his last cry, "I'm a-comin', warden!"

He was a convicted criminal, and died in prison gray. But it would seem not wonderful to the warden if, when that man's soul took flight, the recording angel did write his name on the eternal Book of Record, with a strange cabalistic sign, a ring around a cross—that stands for "good behavior."— *The Youth's Companion.*

HIS MOTHER'S SONG.

Beneath the hot midsummer sun The men had marched all day; And now beside a rippling stream Upon the grass they lay. Tiring of games and idle jest, As swept the hours along, They cried to one who mused apart, "Come, friend, give us a song."

"I fear I cannot please," he said; "The only songs I know Are those my mother used to sing For me, long years ago." "Sing one of those," a rough voice cried, "There's none but true men here; To every mother's son of us A mother's songs are dear."

Then sweetly rose the singer's voice Amid unwonted calm, "Am I a soldier of the Cross, A follower of the Lamb? And shall I fear to own His Cause?" The very stream was stilled, And hearts that never throbbed with fear With tender thoughts were filled.

Ended the song; the singer said, As to his feet he rose, "Thanks to you all, my friends, good-night, God grant us sweet repose." "Sing us one more," the captain begged, The soldier bent his head, Then glancing round, with smiling lips, "You'll join with me?" he said.

"We'll sing this old familiar air, Sweet as the bugle call, 'All hail the power of Jesus' name, Let angels prostrate fall;'" Ah! wondrous was the old tune's spell, As on the soldier sang, Man after man fell into line, And loud the voices rang.

The songs are done, the camp is still, Naught but the stream is heard; But ah! the depths of every soul By those old hymns are stirred, And up from many a bearded lip, In whispers soft and low, Rises the prayer that mother taught Her boy long years ago.

—Safeguard.

PERFECT PEACE.

[Lines written by a lady on the steamship "Mongolia," near Malta. She was en route from China, where she had been a missionary for seventeen years, to her home in England. She gave the verses to Bishop Bowman, who was on the steamer with her, and he sent them to his wife, not knowing she had died a few days before he wrote his letter.—*A. Lowry.*]

Lonely? No, not lonelyWhile Jesus stands by;His presence always cheers me,I know that He is nigh.

Friendless? No, not friendless,For Jesus is my friend;I change, but He remainethThe same unto the end.

Tired? No, not tired,While leaning on His breast;My soul hath full enjoyment,'Tis His eternal rest.

Saddened? No, not saddenedBy darkest scenes of woe;I should be, if I knew notThat Jesus loves me so.

Helpless? Yes, so helpless,But I am leaning hardOn the mighty arm of Jesus,And He is keeping guard.

Waiting? Oh, yes, waiting,He bade me watch and wait;I only wonder oftenWhat makes my Lord so late.

Joyful? Yes, so joyful,With joy too deep for words;A precious, sure possession,The joy that is my Lord's.

—Divine Life.

SWEET REVENGE.

A few years ago while Robert Stewart was Governor of Missouri, a steamboat man was brought in from the penitentiary for a pardon. He was a large, powerful fellow, and when the governor looked at him he seemed strangely affected. He scrutinized him long and closely. Finally he signed the document that restored to the prisoner his liberty. Before he handed it to him he said, "You will commit some other crime and be in the penitentiary again, I fear."

The man solemnly promised that he would not. The governor looked doubtful, mused a few minutes and said, "You will go back on the river and be a mate again, I suppose?"

The man replied that he would.

"Well, I want you to promise me one thing," resumed the governor. "I want you to pledge your word that when you are mate again, you will never take a billet of wood in your hand and drive a sick boy out of a bunk to help you load your boat on a stormy night."

The boatman said he would not, and inquired what he meant by asking him such a question.

The governor replied, "Because some day that boy may become a governor, and you may want him to pardon you for a crime. One dark stormy night many years ago you stopped your boat on the Mississippi River to take on a load of wood. There was a boy on board working his way from New Orleans to St. Louis, but he was very sick of fever and was lying in a bunk. You had plenty of men to do the work but you went to that boy with a stick of wood in your hand and drove him with blows and curses out into the wretched night and kept him toiling like a slave until the load was completed. I was that boy. Here is your pardon. Never again be guilty of such brutality."

The man, cowering and hiding his face, went out without a word.

What a noble revenge that was, and what a lesson for a bully.—*Success*.

NO TELEPHONE IN HEAVEN.

"Now, I can wait on baby," the smiling merchant said, As he stooped and softly toyed with the golden, curly head. "I want oo to tall up mamma," came the answer full and free, "Wif yo' telephone an' ast her when she's tummin' back to me.

"Tell her I so lonesome 'at I don't know what to do, An' papa cries so much I dess he must be lonesome, too; Tell her to tum to baby, 'tause at night I dit so 'fraid, Wif nobody here to tiss me, when the light bedins to fade.

"All froo de day I wants her, for my dolly dot so tored Fum the awful punchin' Buddy gave it wif his little sword; An' ain't nobody to fix it, since mamma went away, An' poor 'ittle lonesome dolly's dittin' thinner ever' day."

"My child," the merchant murmured, as he stroked the anxious brow, "There's no telephone connection where your mother lives at now." "Ain't no telephone in Heaven?" and tears sprang to her eyes. "I fought dat God had every'fing wif Him up in de skies."

—*Atlanta Constitution*.

PERFECT THROUGH FAITH.

God would not send you the darkness If He felt you could bear the light, But you would not cling to His guiding hand If the way were always bright; And you would not care to walk by faith Could you always walk by sight.

'Tis true He has many an anguish For your sorrowing heart to bear, And many a cruel thorn-crown For your tired head to wear; He knows how few would reach home at all If pain did not guide them there.

If He sends you in blinding darkness, And the furnace of seven-fold heat;
'Tis the only way, believe me, To keep you close to His feet; For 'tis always
so easy to wander When our lives are glad and sweet.

Then nestle your hand in our Father's And sing if you can as you go; Your
song may cheer some one behind you Whose courage is sinking low; And,
well if your lips do quiver, God will love you better so.

—Selected.

A TRUE HERO.

Two men were sinking a shaft. It was dangerous business, for it was
necessary to blast the rock. It was their custom to cut the fuse with a sharp
knife. One man then entered the bucket and made a signal to be hauled up.
When the bucket again descended, the other man entered it, and with one
hand on the signal rope and the other holding the fire, he touched the fuse,
made the signal, and was rapidly drawn up before the explosion took place.

One day they left the knife above, and rather than ascend to procure it, they
cut the fuse with a sharp stone. It took fire. "The fuse is on fire!" Both men
leaped into the bucket, and made the signal; but the windlass would haul up
but one man at a time; only one could escape. One of the men instantly
leaped out, and said to the other, "Up wi' ye; I'll be in heaven in a minute."
With lightning speed the bucket was drawn up, and the one man was saved.
The explosion took place. Men descended, expecting to find the mangled
body of the other miner; but the blast had loosened a mass of rock, and it
lay diagonally across him; and, with the exception of a few bruises and a
little scorching, he was unhurt. When asked why he urged his comrade to
escape, he gave a reason that sceptics would laugh at. If there is any being
on the face of the earth I pity, it is a sceptic. I would not be called "a
sceptic," today for all this world's wealth. They may call it superstition or
fanaticism, or whatever they choose. But what did this hero say when
asked, "Why did you insist on this other man's ascending?" In his quaint
dialect, he replied, "Because I knowed my soul was safe; for I've give it in
the hands of Him of whom it is said, that 'faithfulness is the girdle of his
reins,' and I knowed that what I gied Him He'd never gie up. But t'other
chap was an awful wicked lad, and I wanted to gie him another chance." All
the infidelity in the world cannot produce such a signal act of heroism as
that.—*Selected.*

THE "KID."

It was not a long procession or a pleasing one but it attracted much
attention.

There was a policeman in the lead. Beside him walked a stockey, bullnecked young fellow in a yellowish suit of loud plaid. His face was bloody and his right wrist encircled by the bracelet of the "twisters" which shackled him to his captor. The face of the policeman was also bloody and his clothes were torn. Behind these two walked three other patrolmen, each with a handcuffed prisoner.

The "kid" and his "gang" had been caught in the act of robbing a saloon, and the fight had been lively, although short. The prisoners had been taken to the detectives' office, and photographed and registered for the rogues' gallery. They were now on their way to court, and thence, in all probability, to jail.

At Broadway there was a jam of cars and heavy trucks, and the procession had to wait. Nobody has been able to tell just what happened, but they all agree as to the essential points. First the bystanders saw a streak of yellow, which was the kid; then a streak of blue which was the policeman. The prisoner had wrenched the twisters from his captors' hand, and made a dash across the tracks. The policeman, thinking, of course that he was trying to escape, had followed.

Then everybody saw a little child toddling along in the middle of the track. A cable-car, with clanging bell, was bearing down upon it with a speed which the gripman seemed powerless to check. The baby held up its hands, and laughed at the sound of the gong. On the other side of the street a woman was screaming and struggling in the arms of three or four men who were trying to keep her from sacrificing her own life to save that of her child.

Then the kid stood there with the child safe in his arms, the steel twisters hanging from his wrist. He set the baby down gently at his feet, loosened the clasp of the chubby hand on his big red fist, and quietly held out his wrist to the policeman to be handcuffed again. He had one chance in a million for his life when he made that desperate leap, but he had not hesitated the fraction of a second.

CHARGED WITH MURDER.

"Prisoner at the bar, have you anything to say why sentence of death should not be passed upon you?"

A solemn hush fell over the crowded court-room, and every person waited in almost breathless expectation for the answer to the judge's question.

"I have, your honor! I stand here convicted of the murder of my wife. Witnesses have testified that I was a loafer, a drunkard and a wretch; that I returned from one of my debauches and fired the shot that killed the wife I had sworn to love, cherish and protect. While I have no remembrance of committing the awful deed, I have no right to condemn the verdict of the jury, for their verdict is in accordance with the evidence.

"But, may it please the court, I wish to show that I am not alone responsible for the murder of my wife! The judge on this bench, the jury in the box, the lawyers within this bar and most of the witnesses, including the pastor of the church, are also guilty before God and will have to stand with me before His judgment throne, where we shall all be righteously judged.

"If it had not been for the saloons of my town, I never would have become a drunkard; my wife would not have been murdered; I would not be here now, soon to be hurled into eternity.

"For one year our town was without a saloon. For one year I was a sober man. For one year my wife and children were happy and our little home was a paradise.

"I was one of those who signed remonstrances against re-opening the saloons of our town. One-half of this jury, the prosecuting attorney on this case, and the judge who sits on this bench, all voted for the saloons. By their votes and influence the saloons were opened, and they have made me what I am.

"Think you that the Great Judge will hold me—the poor, weak, helpless victim—alone responsible for the murder of my wife? Nay; I, in my drunken, frenzied, irresponsible condition have murdered one; but you have deliberately voted for the saloons which have murdered thousands, and they are in full operation today with your consent. You legalized the saloons that made me a drunkard and a murderer, and you are guilty with me before God and man for the murder of my wife.

"I will close by solemnly asking God to open your blind eyes to your own individual responsibility, so that you will cease to give your support to this hell-born traffic."—*Sel.*

MOTHER'S FACE.

There's a feeling comes across me— Comes across me often now— And it deepest seems when trouble Lays her finger on my brow; O it is a deep, deep feeling, Neither happiness nor pain! 'Tis a mighty, soulful longing To see mother's face again!

'Tis, I think, a natural feeling; Worst of me, I can't control Myself no more! It seems to stir And thrill my very soul! Try to laugh it off—but useless! Oh! my tears will fall like rain When I get this soulful longing Just to see her face again!

You won't know how much you love her (Your old mother) till you roam 'Way off where her voice can't reach you, And with strangers make your home; Then you'll know how big your heart is, Think you never loved before, When you get this mighty longing Just to see her face once more.

Mother! tender, loving soul! Heaven bless her dear old face! I'd give half my years remaining Just to give her one embrace; Or to shower love-warm kisses On her lips, and cheeks, and brow, And appease this mighty longing That I get so often now!

—*Sel.*

ONLY SIXTEEN.

Only sixteen, so the papers say,Yet there on the cold, stony ground he lay;'Tis the same sad story we hear every day.He came to his death in the public highway.Full of promise, talent and pride,Yet the rum fiend conquered him—so he died.Did not the angels weep o'er the scene?For he died a drunkard and only sixteen.Only sixteen.

Oh! it were sad he must die all alone,That of all his friends, not even oneWas there to list to his last faint moan,Or point the suffering soul to the throneOf grace. If, perchance, God's only SonWould say, "Whosoever will may come."—But we hasten to draw a veil over the scene,With his God we leave him—only sixteen.Only sixteen.

Rumseller, come view the work you have wrought!Witness the suffering and pain you have broughtTo the poor boy's friends; they loved him well,And yet you dared the vile beverage to sellThat beclouded his brain, his reason dethroned,And left him to die out there all alone.What if 't were your son instead of another?What if your wife were that poor boy's mother?And he only sixteen.

Ye freeholders who signed the petition to grantThe license to sell, do you think you will wantThat record to meet in the last great dayWhen heaven and earth shall have passed away,When the elements melting with fervent heatShall proclaim the triumph of right complete?Will you wish to have his blood on your handsWhen before the great throne you each shall stand?And he only sixteen.

Christian men! rouse ye to stand for the right,To action and duty; into the light.Come with your banners inscribed: "Death to rum."Let your conscience speak, listen, then come;Strike killing blows; hew to the

line;Make it a felony even to signA petition to license; you would do it I
weenIf that were your son and he only sixteen,Only sixteen.

THE DRESS QUESTION.

One day, at Louisville, riding with Mrs. Wheaton to visit the sick prisoners,
she said, "Do you think it your duty to rebuke Christians who wear
jewelry?" I saw her question was a kindly reproof to me, and said, "If the
Lord wants me to give up the jewelry I have, He will show me." "Yes, He
will," she answered; "for I am praying for you." The next morning the
friend who was entertaining me told me her little eleven-year-old daughter,
Emma, just converted, said, "Mamma, I wish you would read to me in the
Bible where it says not to wear jewelry." The mother read the verses. Then
the child said, "Mamma, if the Lord does not want me to wear jewelry, I
don't want to;" and she brought her little pin and ring to her mother. I took
my Bible and read, "Whose adorning, let it not be that outward adorning of
plaiting the hair and of wearing of gold, or of putting on of apparel; but let
it be the hidden man of the heart, in that which is not corruptible, even the
ornament of a meek and quiet spirit, which is in the sight of God of great
price" (1 Peter ii, 3, 4); and, "In like manner also, that women adorn
themselves in modest apparel, with shamefacedness and sobriety, not with
braided hair or gold or pearls or costly array, but (which becometh women
professing godliness) with good works." (1 Tim. ii, 9, 10.) Then I thought:
"The child is right. The Bible means just what it says." Then I recalled that
Mrs. Wheaton had told me how she went one day to visit a poor, sick girl,
to whom she had talked of the love of Christ until she was almost won. She
went again with a wealthy woman, who was decked with diamonds. As they
entered the room, the girl pointed to the jewels, and said: "O mother,
mother! I have wanted them all my life!" The rich woman tried to hide her
diamonds, and Mrs. Wheaton tried to turn the girl's attention again to the
Savior, but in vain. Her last thought was of the diamonds, and her last
words, "I have wanted them all my life!"

Sitting there, with this incident fresh in my mind, I quietly slipped off ring,
watch, chain, cuff-buttons, and collar-stud; and gold, as an adornment, was
put away forever.—*Abbie C. Morrow, in Revival Advocate, March 7, 1901.*

SONGS USED IN MY WORK.

ROCK ME TO SLEEP, MOTHER.

"Backward, turn backward, oh time in your flight, Make me a child again
just for tonight. Mother, come back from that echoless shore, Take me
again to your arms as of yore; Kiss from my forehead the furrows of care,
Smooth the few silver threads out of my hair; Over my slumbers your
loving watch keep, Rock me to sleep, mother, rock me to sleep."

LIFE'S RAILWAY TO HEAVEN.

Life is like a mountain railroad, With an engineer that's brave; We must make the run successful, From the cradle to the grave; Watch the curves, the fills, the tunnels; Never falter, never quail; Keep your hand upon the throttle, And your eye upon the rail.

CHORUS:

Blessed Savior, Thou wilt guide us Till we reach that blissful shore; Where the angels wait to join us In Thy praise forevermore.

You will roll up grades of trials; You will cross the bridge of strife; On this lightning train of life; Always mindful of obstructions; Do your duty, never fail; Keep your hand upon the throttle, And your eye upon the rail.

You will often find obstructions; Look for storms of wind and rain; On a fill, or curve, or trestle, They will almost ditch your train; Put your trust alone in Jesus; Never falter, never fail; Keep your hand upon the throttle, And your eye upon the rail.

As you roll across the trestle, Spanning Jordan's swelling tide, You behold the Union Depot Into which your train will glide; There you'll meet the Superintendent, God the Father, God the Son With the hearty, joyous plaudit, Weary pilgrim, welcome home.

By permission of Charlie D Tillman, owner of copyright.

MEET ME THERE.

1. On the happy golden shore, Where the faithful part no more, When the storms of life are o'er, Meet me there. Where the night dissolves away, Into pure and perfect day, I am going home to stay, Meet me there.

CHORUS:

Meet me there, Meet me there, Where the tree of life is blooming Meet me there. When the storms of life are o'er, On the happy golden shore, Where the faithful part no more, Meet me there.

2. Here our fondest hopes are vain, Dearest links are rent in twain, But in heav'n no throbs of pain, Meet me there. By the river sparkling bright, In the city of delight Where our faith is lost in sight, Meet me there.

3. Where the harps of angels ring, And the blest forever sing, In the palace of the king, Meet me there. Where in sweet communion blend, Heart with heart and friend with friend; In a world that ne'er shall end, Meet me there.

Words and music copyrighted by W. J. Kirkpatrick, Philadelphia.

GOD BLESS MY BOY

1. When shining stars their vigils keep, And all the world is hushed in sleep, 'Tis then I breathe this pray'r so deep— God bless my boy tonight.

CHORUS:

God bless my boy, my wandering boy, And keep his honor bright; May he come home—no longer roam— God save my boy tonight.

2. I know not where his head may lie, Perchance beneath the open sky; But this I ween, God's watchful eye Can see my boy tonight.

3. As pass the days, the months and years, With all the change, the hopes and fears, God make each step of duty clear, And keep his honor bright.

4. And when at last his work is o'er, And earthly toil shall be no more, May angels guide him to the shore Where there shall be no night.

THE GREAT JUDGMENT MORNING.

Tune—"Kathleen Mavourneen."

One cold Winter eve when the snow was fast falling In a small, humble cottage a poor mother laid; Although racked with pain she lay there contented With Christ as her Friend and her peace with Him made.

CHORUS:

We shall all meet again on the great judgment morning, The books will be opened, the roll will be called; How sad it will be if forever we're parted, And shut out of heaven for not loving God!

That mother of yours has gone over death's river. You promised you'd meet her as you knelt by her bed, While the death sweat rolled from her and fell on the pillow; Her memory still speaketh, although she is dead.

You remember the kiss and the last words she uttered, The arms that embraced you are mouldering away; As you stood by her grave and dropped tears on her coffin, With a vow that you'd meet her, you walked slowly away.

My brother, my sister, get ready to meet her, The life that you now live is ebbing away, But the life that's to come lasts forever and ever, May we meet ne'er to part on that great judgment day!

MY NAME IN MOTHER'S PRAYER.

'Twas in the days of careless youth When life seemed fair and bright, When ne'er a tear, nor scarce a fear O'er cast my day or night. 'Twas in the quiet even tide, I passed her kneeling there, When just one word I tho't I heard My name, my name in mother's prayer.

CHORUS.

My name, my name in mother's prayer, My name in mother's prayer! There is just one word I tho't I heard My name, my name in mother's prayer.

I wandered on, but heeded not God's oft repeated call, To turn from sin and live for Him, And trust to Him my all in all. But when at last convinced of sin, I sank in deep despair, My soul awoke when memory spoke My name, my name in mother's prayer.

That kneeling form, those folded hands, Have vanished in the dust; But still for me for years shall be The memory of her trust. And when I cross dark Jordan's tide, I'll meet her over there; I'll praise the Lord, and bless the word, That word, my name in mother's prayer!

OVER THERE.

Come all ye scattered race, And the Savior's love embrace; You may see His smiling face Yet with care; He is on the giving hand, Will you come at His command, Will you with the angels stand Over there?

CHORUS.

Over there, over there, There's a land of pure delight Over there, We will lay our burdens down, And at Jesus' feet sit down, And we'll wear a starry crown, Over there.

Yes, He went to Calvary, And they nailed Him to the tree, That poor sinners such as we, He might spare; From the bitter pangs of death, He does with His dying breath, Seal an everlasting rest, Over there.

God has placed us on the field, To the foe we will not yield, On our tower we will stand, By His care. Wave the Christian's banner high, Hold it up until we die, And go home to live with God, Over there.

THIS WAY.

Our life is like a stormy sea, Swept by the gales of sin and grief, While on the windward and the lee, Hangs heavy clouds of unbelief; Out o'er the deep a call we hear, Like harbor bell's inviting voice; It tells the lost that hope is near, And bids the trembling soul rejoice.

CHORUS.

This way, this way, O heart oppressed, So long by storm and tempest driven, This way, this way, lo here is rest, Rings out the harbor bell of heaven.

O tempted one, look up, be strong; The promise of the Lord is sure, That they shall sing the victor's song, Who faithful to the end endure; God's Holy Spirit comes to thee, Of this abiding love to tell; To blissful port, o'er stormy sea, Calls heaven's inviting harbor bell.

MORE TO BE PITIED THAN CENSURED.

There's an old concert hall on the bowery Where were assembled together one night A crowd of young fellows carousing, To them life looked happy and bright. At the very next table was seated A girl that had fallen to shame; How the fellows they laughed at her downfall, When they heard an old woman exclaim:

CHORUS.

"She's more to be pitied than censured, She is more to be loved than despised; She is only a poor girl who ventured On life's rugged path ill-advised. Don't scorn her with words fierce and bitter, Don't laugh at her shame and downfall, Just pause for a moment—consider, That sin was the cause of it all."

There's an old-fashioned church 'round the corner, Where the neighbors all gathered one day, To listen to words from the parson, For a soul that had just passed away. 'Twas the same wayward girl from the bowery, Who a life of adventure had led; Did the parson then laugh at her downfall? No, he prayed and wept as he said:

SOME MOTHER'S CHILD.

At home or away, in the alley or street, Wherever I chance in this wide world to meet A girl that is thoughtless or a boy that is wild, My heart echoes softly: It is some mother's child.

CHORUS.

Some mother's child, Some mother's child, My heart echoes softly: It is some mother's child.

And when I see those o'er whom long years have rolled, Whose hearts have grown hardened, whose spirits are cold; Be it woman all fallen, or man all defiled, A voice whispers sadly: It is some mother's child.

No matter how far from right she hath strayed; No matter what inroad dishonor hath made; No matter what elements cankered the pearl; Though tarnished and sullied, she is some mother's girl.

No matter how deep he is sunken in sin; No matter how much he is shunned by his kin; No matter how low is his standard of joy; Though guilty and loathsome; he is some mother's boy.

That head hath been pillowed on tenderest breast; That form hath been wept o'er, those lips have been pressed; That soul hath been prayed for in tones sweet and mild; For her sake deal gently with some mother's child.

Used by permission of Charlie D. Tillman, owner of copyright.

JUST TELL MY MOTHER.

'Twas in a Gospel Mission, in a distant western town, The meeting there that night had just begun, When in came a poor lost sinner who by sin had been cast down, Thinking perhaps that he might have some fun; But as he heard of Jesus' love, of pardon full and free, He sought it and the wanderer ceased to roam. And going to his room that night, his heart all filled with joy, He wrote a letter to the folks at home.

CHORUS.

Just tell my dear old mother, my wandering days are o'er, Just tell her that my sins are all forgiven, Just tell her that if on earth we chance to meet no more, Her prayers are answered and we'll meet in Heaven.

His mother got the message as she lay at death's dark door, Which told her of her boy so far away, How his sins were all forgiven and wandering days were o'er, And that his feet were on the narrow way. Her heart was filled with gladness, as it had not been for years, Her dear old face was all lit up with joy, As on her dying pillow she said amid her tears, God bless and keep my precious darling boy.

Your mothers have prayed for you, my friends, for many and many a day, Perhaps these days of life will soon be o'er, Come, give your hearts to Jesus, get on the narrow way, And meet her on that happy golden shore. Oh, come just now while still there's room, and pardon free for all. The Savior pleads, oh, do not longer roam. And then with Jesus in your heart, you will send the message To your dear mother, praying still for you at home.

SOON THE DEATH-BELL WILL TOLL.

When the last Gospel message has been told in your ears, And the last solemn warning has been given you in tears; When hope shall escape from its place in your breast, Oh, where will your poor weary soul find its rest?

CHORUS.

Soon the death-bell will toll—look after your soul; O, sinner be ready, for the death-bell will toll.

When the darkness of death shall compass you round, When the friends you have loved are all standing around; Unable to save you now from the tomb, Unable to alter your terrible doom.

When before the white throne of His Judgment you stand, "What have you to answer?" the Judge will demand; Oh, terrible moment to be standing alone, When mercy forever and forever is gone.

THE END OF THE WAY.

The following beautiful lines were written by a girl in Nova Scotia, an invalid for many years:

My life is a wearisome journey; I'm sick of the dust and the heat; The rays of the sun beat upon me, The briars are wounding my feet. But the city to which I am journeying Will more than my trials repay; All the toils of the road will seem nothing When I get to the end of the way.

There are so many hills to climb upward, I often am longing for rest, But He who appoints me the pathway Knows what is needed and best. I know in His word He has promised That my strength shall be as my day; And the toils of the road will seem nothing When I get to the end of the way.

He loves me too well to forsake me, Or give me one trial too much; All His people have been dearly purchased, And Satan can never claim such. By and by I shall see Him and praise Him, In the city of unending day; And the toils of the road will seem nothing When I get to the end of the way.

When the last feeble steps have been taken, And the gates of the city appear, And the beautiful songs of the angels Float out on my listening ear; When all that now seems so mysterious Will be plain and clear as the day— Yes, the toils of the road will seem nothing When I get to the end of the way.

Though now I am footsore and weary, I shall rest when I'm safely at home; I know I'll receive a glad welcome, For the Savior Himself has said "Come." So, when I am weary in body, And sinking in spirit I say, All the toils of the road will seem nothing When I get to the end of the way.

Cooling fountains are there for the thirsty, There are cordials for those who are faint: There are robes that are whiter and purer Than any that fancy can paint. Then I'll try to press hopefully onward, Thinking often through each weary day, The toils of the road will seem nothing When I get to the end of the way.

Appendix.

The matter which I have here appended I thought of too much value to omit from this volume. The first article is explanatory in itself. The second is by a prisoner whom I have known for many years. The third (regarding Christ in Gethsemane) was written by a prisoner as a letter to myself. I hope the reader may profit by the reading of each page.

E. R. W.

THE PERSONNEL OF PRISON MANAGEMENT.

Address of C. E. Haddox, warden of the West Virginia penitentiary, to the National Prison Association, at its annual session, Louisville, Ky., Congress of 1903:

This is the age of industrial development. On every side we see colossal enterprises undertaken and prosecuted to a successful and profitable conclusion.

Great railroad systems span the continent, carrying millions of passengers and countless tons of freight, with safety, celerity and dispatch, to the doors of factory, workshop, store and consumer.

Immense industrial enterprises are constantly being projected, consolidated and carried on in a manner to excite the admiration, mayhap, the wonder and fear of mankind.

Colossal financial transactions amaze the minds of those uninitiated to the magnitude and the intricacies of such undertakings.

The unexplored recesses of the earth are exploited in a manner and on a scale heretofore undreamed of and unknown, and every department of enterprise is carried on to a degree that distinctly stamps this decade as the acme of industrial enterprise and achievements, the golden age of industrial prosperity, and the acquirement of material improvement and material gain.

If it be asked why such strides have been made along industrial lines, the answer is that it is due to ORGANIZATION AND SPECIALIZATION.

The PERSONNEL of the management have devoted their lives, their talent and their energies to the special work before them. They have been drilled and educated along special lines; they have been deaf and blind to outside matters not relevant to the work in hand, and by close and careful study, by unceasing and constant labor, care and effort, having evolved, projected and carried on these immense enterprises.

The National Prison Congress at its meeting this year is mindful of the material progress of the country.

This association is equally ambitious along the lines peculiar to itself to obtain from the various penal institutions of the country the highest and best results morally, educationally, reformatively, and as an incident, punitively and financially.

How shall we keep pace in penal improvements with the great material progress of the outside world?

The answer necessarily must be, that improvements in our department of work must come, as they do elsewhere, by the investigation, the study, the thought and the effort of those who are in actual control, of those who are in a position to see, to observe and to know.

In other words, the question as to whether prisons are to improve, whether their work shall continue to be of a higher and nobler character, whether we are finally and forever to break away from the customs of the galleys of France, the prisons of Hawes in England, of the Mamertine of Rome and of Rothenburg in Germany, will depend utterly, entirely and absolutely upon the personnel of the prison management of the country.

Prof. Henderson, in his admirable address delivered at the Philadelphia meeting in 1902, on "The Social Position of the Prison Warden," says: "Some institutions have no marked qualities; they have walls, cells, machinery, prisoners, punishments, but no distinct, consistent and rational policy."

Where this is true it means that the worst possible condition of affairs exists. Such an institution has the dry rot. It is managed (or rather mismanaged) by time servers, too careless to feel the high responsibility devolving upon them, and too listless to acquaint themselves with the many opportunities spread before them to improve and keep pace with the onward march of progress.

Such officers in their abuse, by inaction, of the opportunities afforded them, commit "Crimes against criminals" and through them against society.

On the contrary institutions which have distinct features and characteristics, have them as the result of the careful investigation, the patient research and thought of those who are in responsible and actual control, and these characteristics and features reflect the wisdom and intelligence of those who have given their energies and their lives to the special work before them.

THE BOARD OF DIRECTORS.

In the management of penal institutions a Board of Directors or of Control is, ordinarily, the nominal head.

By the laws of most states they are supposed to fix the administration policy, to restrict and define the powers and duties of the officers in actual and intimate control.

In some institutions they meet a day or so each month, in most institutions not so frequently. Their duties while at the institution may or may not be largely perfunctory, and as they are generally active business men at home in other channels, the day or two a month or quarter is apt to be regarded by the unthoughtful as a respite or surcease from other duties. The main duty of a Board of Directors or of Control may be said to be the determining of the general policy upon which the institution shall be conducted, and a cursory oversight of the conduct of its affairs.

THE WARDEN.

The warden or superintendent is the one official who can give tone, expression and color to the institution. He is distinctly and positively its actual managing head, and upon his intelligence, interest, zeal, tact and discretion will depend, almost entirely, its weal or its woe.

He must be a man of intelligence, and be willing and anxious to increase his fund of knowledge and information.

He should be a profound student not only of the ordinary subjects that attract the student, but of prison systems, of laws, business, government, society as it exists, and of human nature in all its many phases.

HE MUST BE AN ORGANIZER.

No difference how elaborate a system may be found in any institution of this kind, the warden will always be an intensely busy and greatly occupied officer.

If he would prevent chaos and confusion and obtain from every official the highest and best work of which he is capable, he must organize every department thoroughly. Every officer and every inmate must know his exact duties, so far as it is possible to know them, and be made responsible for those duties and the warden must be enabled to appreciate a high order of talent and the accomplishment of good work, and to locate the blame for omissions and short comings, and provide for their correction.

Thorough system in every detail will conserve the capacities of all his subordinates and leave him in a measure free to observe the actual conditions and to plan and to put into effect improvements along moral, industrial, physical and financial lines.

HE MUST BE A FINANCIER.

The financial question in every prison in the land is an extremely important one. Funds for prisons are doled out grudgingly, and the demand for absolutely necessary purposes is always far greater than the supply.

A warden performs no more important function than when he sees that the funds of the institution are so used as to effect the highest possible results, and that all the forces of the prison are so energized and conserved as to permit, under ordinary conditions, a satisfactory and proper earning and economizing power. With the many demands made upon him for means for increasing the usefulness of his institution, a high order of financial aptitude is an absolutely necessary characteristic in a successful warden.

DISCIPLINE.

Discipline in a prison is its first requisite. Nothing can be accomplished until officers and convicts are under its sway and control.

The warden who would have control of those under him must himself at all times, be under self control.

The maxim "No one knows how to command who has not first learned how to obey," is a trite and a true one. The population of a prison is made up of a heterogeneous collection of people whose first instincts have been and are, not to obey.

To bring such people into habits of obedience and control requires the highest type of skill, tact and discretion. Punishments and reward must be so blended and combined as to effect the needful results with the least possible friction, and in the most humane and rational manner possible.

No warden can afford to delegate the matter of enforcing discipline entirely or partly, if at all, to another. His first duty to himself, that he may know actual conditions as they exist, is to preside over or assist in, the trial of offenders and to order discipline.

Individual treatment is a necessity in our dealings with delinquents, and a study of the many phases of delinquency is a prime requisite in a successful warden's repertoire.

Brainard F. Smith says: "Many a prisoner has been reformed—or, if not reformed, made a better prisoner—by punishment."

Will the warden have any higher duty to perform than to face his delinquent delinquents and to order in merciful severity, rational punishments for their short-comings?

But a warden's disciplinary powers are apt to be taxed more severely in another direction. The great problem ordinarily, is not so much the discipline of convicts as that of subordinate officers. If subordinate officers will obey the spirit and the letter of the rules, the convict has the potential influence of a powerful example to aid him. "Like master like man."

In institutions where officers are appointed solely with reference to their fitness, comparatively little trouble should be had in the matter of proper official discipline. But where places are given to heelers, ward-workers and political strikers, the matter of efficient discipline is a question of grave concern to the warden. In the absence of better material, however, he must address himself to organizing what he has to the highest efficiency possible, and insist and require a rigid regimen and adhere to his demands and requirements with Spartan firmness.

THE PRISON SCHOOL.

The educational work of a prison is of the highest, I may say, of the first importance. The education of the hands to work comes naturally, partly as an incident of the necessary work carried on in prison.

Nearly all convicts are densely ignorant. The polished, scholarly, shrewd criminal of whom we hear so much, and to whom the papers and books give so much prominence, is the exception, not the rule, in prison.

If the prison is to have a reformatory feature, it must come very largely through the school. Many prison schools are such only in name. The work accomplished is very meager. The results are very unsatisfactory.

To no part of prison work should a warden address himself with more ardor and determination than so to organize the prison school as to make it the great positive factor in dispelling ignorance and its attendant viciousness, and in quickening and enlivening the moral sense in those whose moral judgment is exceedingly obtuse.

The course of study in a prison school is necessarily a very elementary one, and unless followed by a supplementary course of reading and study, will be of little permanent and practical benefit. Many prison libraries, largely the result of indiscriminate and heterogeneous donations of all kinds of literature, good, bad and indifferent, chiefly the latter, are not in a position to be a positive force.

Let the warden see that his library is so arranged, classified and used as to be a source of information, profit, help and pleasure to the inmates, and that a course of reading along rational lines is laid out, encouraged, and, if possible, adhered to, in order that the preliminary school course may not have been in vain.

COURAGE NEEDED.

The warden must be a man of courage. I do not refer to the kind of courage necessary to face a regiment of depraved and wicked men shorn of their power and their stimulus to do evil, but that high moral courage necessary to clean the Augean stables of abuses of customs, to reverse policies of long standing that are nevertheless wrong in principle and in practice, to fight against unjust, improper and unwise legislative propositions concerning his institution; the kind of courage that prompted the chaplain in Chas. Reade's "NEVER TOO LATE TO MEND," to fight and destroy the iniquitous prison system of Keeper Hawes and his minions; the courage that will keep to the fore-front a persistent opposition to prostituting penitentiaries into eleemosynary institutions and political cribs and feeding troughs for political strikers.

He must have the courage to weed out and eliminate useless barnacles in the shape of incompetent and worthless employes, and substitute in their stead men of capacity, character and intelligence, who are in love with their work and believe in its dignity and usefulness; the courage to face demagogues in their efforts to take from the prison its educative, moral, reformatory and economic force, the right of the unfortunate inmates to learn the gospel of labor under right and just conditions.

OPTIMISM NECESSARY.

The warden needs to be intensely optimistic. He must have a reserve fund of enthusiasm. He must believe profoundly in the high character of his office and educate others constantly to believe in it. The ignorance of the great mass of the people as to the real function of penitentiaries and the methods by which they are carried on is amazing and mortifying to prison officials.

A part of the warden's mission is to acquaint the outside world with conditions as they exist inside, and to inspire the interest and support of the general public in measures for bettering and improving prison conditions. Legislative bodies especially, need to be brought into closer relations and the law makers made to realize their duty to the public and the convict in the enactment of wise, proper and righteous legislation.

Longfellow, in his beautiful poem, "THE BUILDING OF THE SHIP," tells why the master builder achieved success. It was because

"His heart was in the work and the heart Giveth grace to every art."

The warden's heart must be in his work. His whole soul must be animated and permeated with an honest and sincere desire to bring penology up to a higher and nobler standard.

He must have a reserve force of enthusiasm that will not be daunted and destroyed by temporary failures or the lapses of some discharged or pardoned convicts, who, in spite of care and pains, will return to their evil ways. The enthusiasm that can bear the harsh and ignorant criticism and misrepresentations incident to his work; the enthusiasm that in its contagion will inoculate directors, subordinate officers, the press and the people with a desire for more light on penal problems and a purpose to be governed by that light; the enthusiasm that will beget great patience for the exacting, difficult and trying problems before him; that will make him believe that "a convict saved is a man made"; that will make him believe with the great English novelist "It is never too late to mend," and that as infinite care and pains finally brought Robinson, the twice convicted thief, up to the estate of honest manhood, so, infinite care and pains should be exerted with every man under his charge.

Pessimism has no rightful place in a penitentiary. In the language of Socrates, "Why should we who are never angry at an ill-conditioned body, always be angry with an ill-conditioned soul?"

The ignorant Hawes believed in the profitless crank, the black-hole, the deprivation of food, of bed, of clothing, the tortures of the waist jacket and the collar, and a sign over the door, "ABANDON HOPE ALL YE WHO ENTER HERE."

The twentieth century warden believes in the gospel of productive labor, of education of hand, head and heart, in the deprivation of privileges, largely as punishment, the segregation of the desperate and nearly hopeless, the enlightenment of an all-powerful, all potential, all influential example and the motto of Pope Clement, "It is of little advantage to restrain criminals by punishment unless you reform them with training and teaching."

THE CHAPLAIN.

The chaplain occupies an extremely important but delicate position in prison management. It is possible for him to be of vast influence and power for good.

The chaplain needs to be a man of large heart, aided by an abundance of sound common sense. He needs to bear in mind constantly, in the difficult and delicate work he is called upon to perform, that the discipline of the prison must be upheld and enforced.

Associate officers are frequently disturbed with the fear that the chaplain's influence will subvert the discipline of the prison; that the shrewd, unprincipled convicts by pouring into his ears their imaginary tales of woe, may succeed in working him.

The chaplain's first requirement, if he would succeed, is not to lose sight of the majesty of the law and of the prison rules.

The chaplain and the warden should go hand in hand, the one sustaining the other. They need to have a perfect understanding, neither mistrusting the other. Frequent conferences ought to enable them to proceed along proper lines. The chaplain's opportunities are limitless. I do not undertake to say what direction his duties shall take him. That will be discussed fully in the Chaplain's Association.

It is personal, individual work that counts in a prison. All the chaplain's work should be thought out beforehand, be methodical, premeditated, intentional, systematic and thorough. His chapel service should be rational, of the proper length, with exercises, song service and preaching service carefully chosen. There should be no room in a prison service for the spectacular, the highly emotional and the haphazard sermons and addresses of a chance visitor. A reasonably rigid censorship ought to be exercised over the contributions of outsiders to the chapel service.

The influence of sight seers and idle visitors to prisons, always bad, reaches the acme of its perniciousness in the chapel service, if unrestrained and unguided by prison officials of experience and firmness, who alone are in a position to know that sickly sentimentality is the worst possible pabulum to offer men already too eager to justify their evil deeds.

THE PHYSICIAN.

A physician's duties in a prison are necessarily onerous, important and difficult. Convicts are constantly claiming that they are unable physically to do the work assigned them. No one can determine the truthfulness of their statements except the physician, and to determine whether the convict is really ill or exercising his usual finesse to shirk his duties, requires keen judgment of human nature as well as an accurate knowledge of his profession.

The convict, housed and hemmed in, is peculiarly susceptible to hallucinations and to thinking that he is afflicted with imaginary ills.

A physician needs a large fund of good judgment, will-power and common sense to combat successfully with this class of people. How far he should use some of the subterfuges supposed to be employed by physicians in the outside world in dealing with people afflicted with hypochondria, I am unable to say, but a certain amount of cheerfulness coupled with firmness is undoubtedly of great value.

SUBORDINATE OFFICERS.

The subordinate officers of a prison are very important factors in the management of a prison. They come in actual, continual, personal contact with the men.

No difference how capable and zealous may be the warden and his deputy, unless they have men of character, zeal, intelligence and discretion to carry out their orders and wishes faithfully and well, all their plans will come to naught.

Guards, keepers and watchmen should be of good moral character. It is useless to talk about reforming convicts unless they have continually the benefit of good examples set before them. Precept amounts to nothing unless re-enforced by good examples.

They should be educated and intelligent.

Their duties are largely discretionary, and in their contact with convicts a high order of intelligence is necessary to know the right thing to do. Strict integrity and truthfulness are prime requisites. An officer's word should be beyond question and he should be absolutely impartial in his dealings with his men.

No special system will bring the highest results with any kind of men behind it. Any system with men of character, conscience and capacity will achieve great good. Any system with men of bad character, ignorant, careless and indifferent, will fall to the ground.

A common impression prevails that any one is good enough for a prison guard, and if he is too old, too feeble and decrepit or too lazy for other work, his political strikers will try to unload him on the penitentiary authorities.

Prison Directors, Wardens and all in authority should set their faces resolutely against this erroneous and terribly harmful idea. Partisan politics should not be a factor in the appointment or the retention of any prison officer. All subordinates should be appointed under civil service rules and be required to pass a civil service examination, and after entering upon his duties be required to take up a course of study on penological questions and problems and be otherwise carefully schooled and drilled along the lines of their work. If time demonstrates their unfitness for the position they should be summarily removed. If they manifest an aptitude and an interest in their work they should be encouraged, promoted and protected against removal for partisan reasons.

Whenever directors in banks are elected with reference to their political proclivities and not with reference to their business sagacity, it will be proper to select prison officials for the same reason.

Whenever great business firms discharge their managers because their political views do not coincide with those of the owners, then and not till then should prison officials step down and out for political reasons.

What would be thought of directors of a business enterprise or the regents of a university who selected their business manager, their teachers, with regard to their views on finance or on the tariff, or who would remove a faithful, efficient and capable servant after years of experience in his work, merely because he did not coincide with the political views of the majority of his directors in a matter in no way germane to his work?

As Boards of Directors spend but a small percentage of their time at the institutions they control, it necessarily takes them years to get a clear insight into all the details of its work, and to make a change just when, through the process of time, the director becomes fitted for his work, is the height of unwisdom and folly. Boards of Charity and Correction having charge of all the institutions in the State would certainly be much more desirable. Such officers could devote their entire time and attention to the work, and thus be able to give all the institutions of the State uniform treatment and attention. Boards of Directors or of Control should be appointed and reappointed as long as they are efficient and manifest an interest in the work.

And so with all other officers from the warden down, and each should feel and know that faithfulness and efficiency is the only standard, and that they would not be expected, required or permitted to weaken their influence or their energies by undue or active participations in political effort or political manipulations.

The surest sign of unfitness for prison work and lack of interest in the work is an undue activity in political caucuses and conventions. The official practically advertises that he cannot hope to hold his place on account of his efficiency, but expects to do so because of his services as a political henchman.

THE DEMANDS OF THE AGE.

As this age demands a high order of talent and effort in the industrial, so it should demand and require great ability and power in the penal world.

The third of a century of the life of the National Prison Congress has witnessed great progress in the domain over which it has advisory power.

Many problems pressing for solution demand the highest functions of those in control.

Do punishments deter men from crime?

Do the universal customs of the times foster and beget much of the crime committed?

Does war beget murder elsewhere?

Is social vengeance a failure, and are other means necessary to prevent crime?

Should not executives now clothed with power to terminate or shorten sentences of imprisonment also have power to lengthen terms of imprisonment or to change from a definite to an indefinite term whenever they become in possession of facts regarding the convict's previous life or present character, which were unknown to the sentencing judge?

Should not United States prisoners incarcerated in the various state prisons have the restrictions of the indeterminate sentence and the parole, thus securing a uniform system of treatment for all prisoners and greatly promoting the discipline?

Should we go back of the commission of crimes and ascertain if the State itself is not committing a crime in imposing and permitting conditions that beget crime?

Should not the pardoning power be exercised frequently before the convicted man ever reaches the prison at all? Could not many a man be saved by being put on probation from the start, who otherwise would be in great danger of being lost?

Does the discipline of prisons have anything to do with the commission of offenses by convicts when released? Does the enforced restraint exerted to the very last moment of his release and then wholly relaxed, cause the released convict to swing to the other extreme like Jean Valjean, who after nineteen years of imprisonment for stealing a loaf of bread and an attempt to escape, robbed his benefactor, the Bishop, of his plate, and upon being forgiven robbed little Gervais of his forty sou piece, but afterward got his bearings, attained his balance and lived an honorable life?

Should any prisoner ever be released at the prison door, or should he not for his own sake as well as society's be required to live a period on probation and under oversight, subject to return for violations; in other words, should not paroles be, under proper restrictions, the universal and only rule?

To the solution of these and countless other problems let the highest order of talent, the best combination of head, heart and brain be summoned: let every prison be a school for study and investigation, and be engineered and controlled by men of skill, drilled and educated along these lines, and who are animated by a desire to contribute their full share towards the upbuilding and uplifting of the race and the amelioration of the woes that beset mankind.

MEDITATIONS OF A PRISONER.

PREFACE.

To any one who may read these lines I will say: Do not criticise; I know you will find many mistakes, but I hope you will remember they are written by one who has not had the advantage of an education. My school days ended when I was nine years old. Knowing this, I hope you will excuse mistakes. Respectfully yours,

E. S. K.

I often wonder if the busy world ever gives a thought to the men incarcerated in places made for the punishment of crime and reformation of criminals, but often failing of reaching the desired result. Why is this failure? It must be from defect in the law or prison discipline. Some think perhaps the rigid enforcement of the law in its severest way is right, and that the prisoner should be shown no mercy. But this is wrong in every detail and should be just the reverse, so far as consistent with good order and discipline.

A judge in sentencing a prisoner should give a sentence consistent with justice and mercy, regardless of public sentiment, considering his own judgment, and not the possible consequences of his act on his future. Until this is more generally practiced, I am afraid there will be many too severe sentences passed on minor criminals and first offenders, as now, which will work to the injury of the convicted instead of his reformation. In my humble opinion, one year would give the lesson desired to many a novice in crime who is now serving from three to ten years. It should be remembered that short sentences give a novice in crime a wholesome dread of the law and fear of prison life, while custom and association with criminals tend to harden. The cases of old offenders, require more severity as regards time of confinement. Nor can we say to the jurors—or, rather, gentlemen of the jury—be very careful of what you do. Don't treat the trust you have in charge too lightly; give it all the consideration you are masters of. Remember you have the liberty, and, perhaps the life, of your fellowman at stake. Be very careful of what you do. Allow no personal motive to interfere with your duty, for, if we believe in the Bible, those who do so will answer in the hereafter for actions in this life. Beware, then, of how you mete out justice to your fellowman. Do unto others as you would have others do unto you. Weigh well the evidence given against the prisoner. If you find that there is a motive on the part of the witnesses to convict the prisoner being tried, you may rest assured they will trifle with the truth. In such cases a juror should try and put himself in the defendant's place and try to assume his feelings and condition, as much as possible, and see how he would act in a like case. If all jurors would do this, I think they would give a just and true verdict in nearly all cases. But I fear as things are now they let the press have too much weight with the rendering of a just verdict, and it may be of what their friends will say to them if they have a different opinion. Yet the man who does such a thing is a coward, a devil incarnate, and unfit to be at large. Such action may be the cause of making a criminal out of a so far really honest man. May God forgive them who recklessly tamper with the liberty of their fellowman. Some may think I am not for punishment of crime. If so, they are wrong. I believe in punishment of crime. But I believe in tempering justice with mercy. There should be no lingering doubt in a person's mind when he gives his verdict against the prisoner. It is a very easy thing to place a man in prison, but oh! so hard to get him out. A lie sworn to and believed is one of the hardest things in the world to get righted. And I know from personal experience what it is. Though it seems hard to say a lie is more readily believed against a person charged with a crime than the truth, yet it seems easier to a great many to believe bad rather than good of their neighbor. Yet, thank God, it is not so with all. We have many noble and true Christians yet in this vale of tears— gentlemen and ladies who practice what they say by many kindly acts to the poor, unhappy men who are unfortunate enough to get behind prison bars. God bless them for such acts. It does not hurt them, and gives to the unhappy prisoner a little happiness—a ray of sunshine through the clouds that surround him. Continue your noble work. You will be the gainer in the end, from the knowledge that you have done in the Lord's work, if in no other way. Oh, could you see the happiness beam from the eyes of some of those here, after the call of some who take friendly interest in them, you would know the good they are doing. Others seem to say: Oh, well, I am forgotten by all. Poor heart; what a sad lot. It would seem the sooner that death ended their misery the better. But while there is life there is hope. I must say that many ladies of C—— are very kind in giving up their own pleasures on Sundays that prisoners in this prison may have some little change in their life. The visiting chaplains always bring a choir with them, and to them we give our heartfelt thanks, with a God bless you. I love to read of the progress made in these penal institutions where reform is practiced. I am sure the prisoners must take an interest in it all, for it is all for their own good. The Stillwater prison and Elmira prison must be models of neatness and good order, with a perfect system of discipline. It would be well for all prisons to copy them. If prisons are supposed to be erected for the purpose of reformation, why not make them in reality what they are intended to be? Of course, there are many different kinds of crime committed by men of different temperaments, all of which are thoroughly understood, or as nearly as possible. For example, take the greatest crime committed in the eyes of the law—murder—which is often called murder when there is no ground for it. The public outcry when one man is unfortunate enough to take the life of another at a time when he may have every reason to believe his own life is in the greatest danger. The cry is raised by some one, possibly an eye-witness—Murder! It is taken up by the press and conveyed to every one, and possibly a slight coloring given to it. The people believe it all. The consequence is the public mind is prejudiced against the prisoner, and it takes a great amount of proof by the defendant to change that belief, and should he not be able to produce this evidence, in spite of all he can say he is convicted of the crime of murder, when in reality he is guilty of manslaughter, if anything. For, no matter how truthful a man he may be known to be, his word, unsustained by evidence, is not accepted; while, on the other side, no matter how untruthful a witness be known to be, he is given credit for the truth. What kind of a state of affairs is this? No wonder we often hear the cry go up from some poor wounded or crushed heart saying: O, God, is there no mercy left in man? Is humanity wholly dead? Must death overtake me here? Shunned I am by all whom I once called friends—wife, children, it may be a brother—but never by a mother, God bless her.

Let us take a look at this class of sufferers. What will we find them? Idle? No. They are as a rule men attending to their work and submitting to all the courtesies of life, only asking the same in return. Surely, such cannot be very bad men, who, hearing the cry of distress, respond at once to the appeal. I know some such to have a heart as tender as a woman. Yet you will shut them up, it may be forever. Don't understand me to say that murder is not committed. Of course it is, and the law should deal with it accordingly. All true men regret the taking of human life, even on the field of battle. How much more so under other circumstances? And the causes are many which make men do this; some of them hard to understand, may be. In many cases of this kind they deserve punishment and should be punished. But, for God's sake, let the punishment be consistent with justice and mercy. If ten years is not sufficient punishment to make man control himself in future, why not be merciful and kill him at once? For as we hope for mercy, so must we show it to others. All other crimes should be dealt with accordingly. Give a man a chance to reclaim himself. Should he return to a life of crime in preference to an honest one, the law has its remedy and can act accordingly. This is well worth a trial, and by all means should be given one. But I hear some one who never gave these things a thought say: How is this to be done? I will answer, Very easily, if it receive the support of our legislative body, by the recommendation of the state governor. Provide your prisons with workshops of different kinds—provide them with schools, and teach the prisoners how to make a living by some useful trade. Give them a chance to improve themselves by an education. Make the prison a place of reformation, one of improvement as well as punishment, and instead of increasing crime you will reduce it, which should be the aim of all having the good of their fellowman at heart, and society will be the gainer. I would give a prisoner who would show by his conduct a spirit of reform a parole after half of his time, with conditions attached, as is done in the Minnesota state prison, so that, should he fall back into his old way of living, he would be returned to prison to serve out the remainder of his sentence. By this means you to all intents and purposes hold a power over him, and he will be very careful as to what he is about. This habit in time will grow upon him and be the cause of making him a good citizen and trustworthy member of society. To men serving life sentences I would, on the recommendation of the prison warden, give a parole after manslaughter sentence has been served. This is a class of men that deserve some looking after by the kindly interest of humane persons. Give them hope and encouragement. Do not leave them to their own morbid thoughts; you cannot tell what drove them to an act they will regret, whether in or out of prison. If hasty once, it is no reason to suppose they will be so again. Why not, then, look after them? Let some of you Christian people talk with them, and if you find they ought to be assisted, help them. You know not what good you may do, and without such aid a poor and friendless man in prison is without hope. Will you, as Christians, let him die believing the word Christianity a mockery? God forbid. I know there are many good Christians that feel and mean what they say. But I am afraid that many of the less courageous are deterred from doing all they would like to do by the sneers of the hard, cruel world. But this should only spur you on. If you feel you are right, push on; do not stop half way.

In connection with the parole law we should have our prisoners graded as first, second and third class, giving to the second grade or class advantages above the third, and to the first above the second, giving them a motive to reform their ways while yet in prison, and their partial liberty from the first class by parole. By this means you instill into the prisoner a habit for good which in time will take root and prove a blessing, not only to the prisoner, but also a source of pleasure to those bringing it about. It must be expected that some will fall again; but why should the many suffer for the few? I have heard and read such sayings as this: The worst men are the best behaved while in prison if there is anything to be gained by it. I dispute this.

No man can control or hide his real nature for any great length of time. Nature is bound to come to the surface sooner or later. The officers and guards of a prison should be men strict in the enforcement of the prison rules, humane and just in all their actions, men who by their own actions and deportment will gain and hold the respect of those under their charge. They should reward the good as well as punish the evil in men. It would, in my humble opinion, be nothing but true justice to the prisoner to put the whole power of pardoning, commuting and paroling prisoners in the hands of the governor. I do not say a judge will not give justice where clemency is asked. But it may be the case that a judge on the board of pardons has sentenced the prisoner, and probably in some way became prejudiced against the applicant, and it might be the cause of influencing his vote; consequently, it would look like a piece of injustice to the prisoner to allow that judge to sit on his case. I think it would be well for a governor to make himself perfectly acquainted with all pertaining to the mode of life of the prisoners, as much as possible. It ought to be remembered that when the prison doors close on a man your duty is only half done to yourself, the prisoner and society at large. He needs looking after mentally, morally and physically. Do not leave him to his own morbid thoughts, but help him to forget his surroundings as much as possible. Give him hope, for without hope we are lost to ourselves and the world. It is possible some will say they ought to be; but it must be a very heartless person who makes this remark. Remember, while you are walking about to-day, feeling self-conscious of your own strength to resist any and everything in the line of temptation, the time may come when you will lose control of yourself; or, it may be, some one dear to you will fall. In such cases, how many excuses you can find for yourself or him. Can you find none for those now suffering for the same? I feel impelled by some power to speak of those very people in a few lines. Perhaps it may catch their eye. Why will you follow one to prison with hate, malice and persecution, one who would not harm a single hair of your head, one who never had or has a single bitter thought against you, one that nightly asks God's protection to you and yours? And yet you persecute him, or it may be them, with all the might you can. Is it not enough that he has lost home, friends, wife, children and happiness at one false move? Is it not enough that he is condemned to a living death, hearing every hour of the day the clang of the iron bars that shut him out from the world, that separate him from all he loves? I say to you, is this not enough to satisfy the most bitter feelings of any avowed enemy? It ought to be. Yes, this ought to satisfy you without trying to obliterate the memory of the father from the child's heart and without denying him the privilege of communicating with them; without denying him the pleasure of doing something for them and of one day seeing them, which is all he has left to live for. To all to whom these lines refer, who read them, I will say, change all this. Ask God's help to give you strength to do right. In time you will feel a restful peace come to you, and it will make you content, if not happy. Try this, and may God in his mercy show you the way. And to all prisoners who may be suffering from the persecution of injustice by others, I will say the same. Say with all your heart: God forgive them, they know not what they do. And you will always find a comfort in helping one another. For as we hope to be forgiven, so must we forgive. What use in saying the Lord's prayer—Forgive us our trespasses as we forgive those who trespass against us? We must consider well the meaning of those lines, and if we cannot or do not comply with all they mean it is better for us not to use them. I thank God from my heart, I can say I forgive all my enemies. I have nothing but a kindly feeling for all mankind. I do not mean to say that I am not ruffled at times, for I am; I would not be human if I were not.

There is one class of men who come to prison that should command the attention of our lawmakers—namely, married men. Not on their own account, for they should pay the penalty of the law as well as another, but on account of their families. It must be remembered that when you take away the father and supporter of a family you leave them without the means of support; and if the mother happens to be a sick and weakly person, what is to become of them?

To be sure, we have the orphans' home and the alms-house, but this is only taxing more heavily the already over-burdened taxpayers of the country. Then it would be a commendable act of the legislative bodies to enact laws to provide for the improvement of such married men and give the earnings of their labor to their families. This, to me, looks reasonable and just, and easy of accomplishment, and should be acted upon by all means. Let me draw you a picture from my imagination: We will visit a family who are in easy circumstances these cold nights. What do we see? Well-clad and well-fed children, a happy, contented look rests upon the wife's and husband's faces. Why should it not be so? They have plenty to eat and wear; a full bin of coal. Again, visit one where the husband may be languishing behind the prison bars, but of the same class. It is not so cheerful, but still no want is felt, and the father and husband, although chafing at confinement, feels that his family is not in want. This, of course, will be a consolation to him. Now let us visit another house, where they have always lived from hand to mouth. The father is gone. The mother and children, poor souls, ill-clad, ill-fed, and, my God, it may be, no fire. What a picture to contemplate. It makes me shudder to think of it. Now come with me behind the prison bars and see the head of this family. Knowing the want and needs of his family, and knowing how impossible it is for him to alleviate their suffering, it is enough to drive a man insane. But, on the other hand, if this man could earn something for his family's support, it would relieve his mind of a heavy burden. Think well of this, and in the name of God change the law that certainly works contrary to what it was intended for. As it now stands, you simply provide punishment for the criminals. In so doing you cause untold suffering and shame to innocent ones. In God's name, let it cease to be so. Now, then, for fear I may tire the reader, I will close.

Very respectfully,

E.

CHRIST IN GETHSEMANE.

—— State Prison.
January 18, 1886.

Mrs. Elizabeth R. Wheaton,

    Prison Evangelist.

My Dearest Sister:—

"What might a single mind may wield, With Truth for sword and Faith for shield, And Hope to lead the way: Thus all high triumphs are obtained, From evil good—as God ordained The night before the day!"

"And being in an agony, He prayed."—St. Luke 22:44.

When the last supper was over, and the last hymn had been sung, our Lord and His Apostles—with the one traitor fatally absent from their number—went out of the city gate, and down the steep valley of the Kidron to the green slope of Olivet beyond it. Solemn and sad was that last walk together; and a weight of mysterious awe sank like lead upon the hearts of those few poor Galileans as in almost unbroken silence,—through the deep hush of the Oriental night,—through the dark shadows of the ancient olive-trees,—through the broken gleams of the Paschal moonlight,—they followed Him, their Lord and Master, who, with bowed head and sorrowing heart, walked before them to His willing doom.

That night they did not return as usual to Bethany, but stopped at the little familiar garden of Gethsemane, or "the oilpress." Jesus knew that the hour of His uttermost humiliation was near,—that from this moment till the utterance of that great cry which broke His heart, nothing remained for Him on earth, save all that the human frame can tolerate of torturing pain, and all that the human soul can bear of poignant anguish—till in that torment of body and desolation of soul, even the high and radiant serenity of His divine spirit should suffer a short but terrible eclipse. One thing alone remained before that short hour began; a short space was left Him, and in that space He had to brace His body, to nerve His soul, to calm His spirit by prayer and solitude, until all that is evil in the power of evil should wreak its worst upon His innocent and holy head. And He had to face that hour,—to win that victory,—as all the darkest hours must be faced, as all the hardest victories must be won—alone. It was not that He was above the need of sympathy,—no noble soul is;—and perhaps the noblest need it most. Though His friends did but sleep, while the traitor toiled, yet it helped Him in His hour of darkness to feel at least that they were near and that those were nearest who loved Him most. "Stay here," He said to the little group, "while I go yonder and pray." Leaving them to sleep, each wrapped in his outer garment on the grass, He took Peter and James and John, the chosen of the chosen, and went about a stone's-throw off. But soon even *their* presence was more than He could endure. A grief beyond utterance, a struggle beyond endurance, a horror of great darkness, overmastered Him, as with the sinking swoon of an anticipated death. He must be yet more alone, and alone with God. Reluctantly He tore Himself away from their sustaining tenderness, and amid the dark-brown trunks of those gnarled trees withdrew from the moonlight into the deeper shade, where solitude might be for Him the audience-chamber of His Heavenly Father. And there, till slumber overpowered them, His three beloved Apostles were conscious how dreadful was the paroxysm through which He passed. They saw Him sometimes with head bowed upon His knees, sometimes lying on His face in prostrate suffering upon the ground. And though amazement and sore distress fell on them,—though the whole place seemed to be haunted by Presences of good and evil struggling in mighty but silent contest for the eternal victory,—yet, before they sank under the oppression of troubled slumber, they knew that they had been the dim witnesses of an unutterable agony, in which the drops of anguish which dropped from His brow in that deathful struggle looked to them like gouts of blood, and yet the burden of those broken murmurs in which He pleaded with His Heavenly Father had been ever this, "If it be possible,—yet not what I will, but what Thou wilt."

What is the meaning, my beloved sister, of this scene for us? What was the cause of this midnight hour? Do you think that it was the fear of death, and that that was sufficient to shake to its utmost center the pure and innocent soul of the Son of Man? Could not even a child see how inconsistent such a fear would be with all that followed;—with that heroic fortitude which fifteen consecutive hours of sleepless agony could not disturb;—with that majestic silence which overawed even the hard Roman into respect and fear;—with that sovereign ascendency of soul which flung open the golden gate of Paradise to the repentant malefactor, and breathed its compassionate forgiveness on the apostate priest? Could He have been afraid of death, in whose name, and in whose strength, and for whose sake alone, trembling old men, and feeble maidens, and timid boys have faced it in its worst form without a shudder or a sigh? My friend, the dread of the mere act of dying is a cowardice so abject that the meanest passions of the mind can master it, and many a coarse criminal has advanced to meet his end with unflinching confidence and steady step. And Jesus knew, if any have ever known, that it is as natural to die as to be born,—that it is the great birthright of all who love God;—that it is God who giveth His beloved sleep. The sting of death—and its only sting—is sin; the victory of the grave—and its only victory—is corruption. And Jesus knew no sin, saw no corruption. No, that which stained His forehead with crimson drops was something far deadlier than death. Though sinless He was suffering for sin. The burden and the mystery of man's strange and revolting wickedness lay heavy on His soul; and with holy lips He was draining the bitter cup into which sin had infused its deadliest poison. Could perfect innocence endure without a shudder all that is detestable in human ingratitude and human rage? Should there be no recoil of horror in the bosom of perfect love to see His own,—for whom he came,—absorbed in one insane repulsion against infinite purity and tenderness and peace? It was a willing agony, but it was agony; it was endured for our sakes; the Son of God suffered that He might through suffering become perfect in infinite sympathy as a Savior strong to save.

And on all the full mysterious meaning of that agony and bloody sweat it would be impossible now to dwell, but may we not for a short time dwell with profit—may not every one whose heart—being free from the fever of passion, and unfretted by the pettiness of pride—is calm and meek and reverent enough to listen to the messages of God, even be they spoken by the feeblest of human lips,—may we not all, I say, learn something from this fragment of that thrilling story that—"being in an agony, He prayed"?

"The chosen three, on mountain height, While Jesus bowed in prayer,
Beheld His vesture glow with light, His face shine wondrous fair."

To every one of us, I suppose, sooner or later the Gethsemane of life must come. It may be the Gethsemane of struggle, and poverty and care;—it may be the Gethsemane of long and weary sickness;—it may be the Gethsemane of farewells that wring the heart by the deathbeds of those we love;—it may be the Gethsemane of remorse, and of well-nigh despair, for sins that we will not—but which we say we cannot—overcome. Well, my dearest sister, in that Gethsemane—aye, even in that Gethsemane of sin— no angel merely,—but Christ Himself who bore the burden of our sins,— will, if we seek Him, come to comfort us. He will, if being in agony, we pray. He can be touched, He is touched, with the feeling of our infirmities. He, too, has trodden the winepress of agony alone; He, too, has lain face downwards in the night upon the ground; and the comfort which then came to Him He has bequeathed to us—even the comfort, the help, the peace, the recovery, the light, the hope, the faith, the sustaining arm, the healing anodyne of prayer. It is indeed a natural comfort—and one to which the Christian at least flies instinctively. When the water-floods drown us,—when all God's waves and storms seem to be beating over our souls,—when "Calamity comes like a deluge, and o'erfloods our crimes till sin is hidden in sorrow"—oh, then, if we have not wholly quenched all spiritual life within us, what can we do but fling ourselves at the foot of those great altar stairs that slope through darkness to God? Yes, being in an agony, we pray; and the talisman against every agony is there.

And herein lies the great mercy and love of God, that we may go to Him in our agony even if we have never gone before. Oh, if prayer were possible only for the always good and always true, possible only for those who have never forsaken or forgotten God,—if it were not possible for sinners and penitents and those who have gone astray,—then of how infinitely less significance would it be for sinful and fallen man! But our God is a God of Love, a God of Mercy. He is very good to us. The soul may come bitter and disappointed, with nothing left to offer Him but the dregs of a misspent life;—the soul may come, like that sad Prodigal, weary and broken, and shivering, and in rags; but if it only come—the merciful door is open still, and while yet we are a great way off our Father will meet and forgive and comfort us. And then what a change is there in our lives! They are weak no longer; they are discontented no longer; they are the slaves of sin no longer. You have seen the heavens gray with dull and leaden-colored clouds, you have seen the earth chilly and comfortless under its drifts of unmelting snow: but let the sun shine, and then how rapidly does the sky resume its radiant blue, and the fields laugh with green grass and vernal flower! So will it be with even a withered and a wasted life when we return to God and suffer Him to send His bright beams of light upon our heart. I do not mean that the pain or misery under which we are suffering will necessarily be removed,—even for Christ it was not so; but peace will come and strength will come and resignation will come and hope will come,—and we shall feel able to bear anything which God shall send, and though He slays us we still shall seek Him, and even if the blackest cloud of anguish seem to shroud His face from us, even on that cloud shall the rainbow shine.

You do not think, my sister, that because God never rejects the prayer of sinner or sufferer, that therefore we may go on sinning, trusting to repent when we suffer. That would be a shameful abuse of God's mercy and tenderness; it would be a frame of mind which would need this solemn warning, that agony by no means always leads to prayer; that it may come when prayer is possible no longer to the long-hardened and long-prayerless soul. I know no hope so senseless, so utterly frustrated by all experience, as the hope of what is called deathbed repentance. Those who are familiar with many deathbeds will tell you why. But prayer—God's blessed permission to us, to see Him and to know Him, and to trust in Him—*that* is granted us not for the hours of death or agony alone, but for all life, almost from the very cradle quite to the very grave. And it is a gift no less priceless for its alleviation of sorrow than for its intensification of all innocent joy. For him who would live a true life it is as necessary in prosperity as in adversity,—in peace as in trouble,—in youth as in old age. Here, too, Christ is our example. He lived, as we may live, in the light of His Father's face. It was not only as the Man of Sorrows, it was not only in the moonlit garden of His agony, or on the darkening hills of His incessant toil, that prayer had refreshed His soul; but often during those long unknown years in the little Galilean village,—daily, and from childhood upwards, in sweet hours of peace, kneeling amid the mountain lilies or on the cottage floor. Those prayers are to the soul what the dew of God is to the flowers of the field; the burning wind of the day may pass over them, and the stems droop and the colors fade, but when the dew steals down at evening, they will revive. Why should not that gracious dew fall even now and always for all of us upon the fields of life? A life which has been from the first a life of prayer,—a life which has thus from its earliest days looked up consciously to its Father and its God,—will always be a happy life. Time may fleet, and youth may fade,—as they will, and there may be storm as well as sunshine in the earthly career; yet it will inevitably be a happy career, and with a happiness that cannot die. Yes, this is the lesson which I would that we all might learn from the thought of Christ in the garden of Gethsemane;—the lesson that Prayer may recall the sunshine even to the dark and the frozen heart; but that there is no long winter, there is no unbroken night, to that soul on which the Sun of Righteousness has risen with healing in His wings.

And that because true prayer is always heard. We read in the glorious old Greek poet of prayers which, before they reached the portals of heaven were scattered by the winds; and indeed there are some prayers so deeply opposed to the will of God, so utterly alien to the true interests of men, that nothing could happen better for us than that God should refuse, nothing more terrible than that He should grant them in anger. So that if we pray for any earthly blessing we may pray for it solely "if it be God's will"; "if it be for our highest good," but, for all the best things we may pray without misgiving, without reservation, certain that if we ask God will grant them. Nay, even in asking for them we may know that we have them,—for what we desire to ask, and what we ask, we aim at, and what we aim at we shall attain. No man ever yet asked to be, as the days pass by, more noble, and sweet, and pure, and heavenly-minded,—no man ever yet prayed that the evil spirits of hatred, and pride, and passion, and worldliness, might be cast out of his soul,—without his petition being granted, and granted to the letter. And with all other gifts God then gives us His own self besides,—He makes us know Him, and love Him, and live in Him. "Thou hast written well of me," said the Vision to the great teacher of Aquinum, "what reward dost thou desire?" "Non aliam, nisi te Domine"—"no other than Thyself, O Lord," was the meek and rapt reply. And when all our restless, fretful, discontented longings are reduced to this alone, the desire to see God's face;—when we have none in Heaven but Him, and none upon earth whom we desire in comparison of Him;—then we are indeed happy beyond the reach of any evil thing, for then we have but one absorbing wish, and that wish cannot be refused. Least of all can it be refused when it has pleased God to afflict us.

"Ye now have sorrow," said Christ, "but I will see you again, and your heart shall rejoice, and your joy no man taketh from you." Yes, when God's children pass under the shadows of the Cross of Calvary they know that through that shadow lies their passage to the Great White Throne. For them Gethsemane is as Paradise. God fills it with sacred presences; its solemn silence is broken by the music of tender promises; its awful darkness softened and brightened by the sunlight of heavenly faces, and the music of angel wings.

"I am baptized into thy name, O Father, Son, and Holy Ghost! Among thy seed a place I claim, Among thy consecrated host; Buried with Christ and dead to sin, Thy Spirit now shall live within."

"And we have seen and do testify that the Father sent the Son to be the Savior of the world."

Milton Keynes UK
Ingram Content Group UK Ltd.
UKHW030621061024
449204UK00004B/423

9 789362 519412